Writing OS/2 2.1 Device Drivers in C

Second Edition

Greg - good luck with your OS/2 work. Let me know if I can help.

Steve Mastrian
4-13-94

VNR's OS/2 Series

- O/S 2 Presentation Manager GPI Graphics
  by Graham C.E. Winn

- Writing OS/2 2.0 Device Drivers In C
  by Steven Mastrianni

- Now That I Have OS/2 2.0 On My Computer — What Do I Do Next?
  by Steven Levenson

- The OS/2 2.0 Handbook
  by William H. Zack

- The Cobol Presentation Manager Programming Guide
  by David M. Dill

- Learning To Program OS/2 2.0 Presentation Manager By Example: Putting the Pieces Together
  by Stephen A. Knight

- Comprehensive Database Performance For OS/2 2.0's Extended Services
  by Bruce Tate, Tim Malkemus, and Terry Gray

- Client/Server Programming With OS/2 2.0
  by Robert Orfali and Daniel Harkey

- OS/2 2.X Notebook: *Best of IBM OS/2 Developer*
  edited by Dick Conklin, Editor

- The Shell Collection: OS/2 2.X Utilities
  by Steven Levenson

- Using Workplace OS/2: The Power User's Guide to IBM's OS/2 Version 2.1
  by Lori Brown and Jeff Howard

- Writing OS/2 2.1 Device Drivers in C, 2nd Edition
  by Steven Mastrianni

- The OS/2 2.1 Corporate Programmer's Handbook
  by Nora Scholin, Mark Sullivan, and Robin Scragg

- OS/2 2.1 REXX HANDBOOK: Basics, Applications and Tips
  by Hallett German

Writing OS/2 2.1 Device Drivers in C

Second Edition

Steven J. Mastrianni

VNR VAN NOSTRAND REINHOLD
New York

DISCLAIMER
This book and software are provided "as is." The implied warranties of merchantability and fitness for a particular purpose are expressly disclaimed. This book and software may contain programs that are furnished as examples. These examples have not been thoroughly tested under all conditions. Therefore, the reliability, serviceability, or function of any program or program code herein is not guaranteed.

The information presented in this book was valid at the time it was written and was conveyed as accurately as possible by the author. However, some information may be incorrect or may have changed prior to publication. The author makes no claims that the material contained in this book is entirely correct, and assumes no liability for use of the material contained herein.

TRADEMARKS AND COPYRIGHTS

IBM, AT, OS/2, Personal System/2, PS/2, and Micro Channel are registered trademarks of the International Business Machines Corporation.
C/2, XT, and Presentation Manager are trademarks of International Business Machines Corporation.
Intel is a registered trademark of the Intel Corporation.
Lotus 1-2-3 is a registered trademark of Lotus Development Corporation.
MS-DOS, CodeView and Microsoft are registered trademarks of Microsoft Corporation.
Microsoft and Microsoft Windows are registered trademarks of Microsoft Corporation.
UNIX is a registered trademark of AT&T Bell Laboratories.

Copyright © 1993 by Van Nostrand Reinhold

Library of Congress Catalog Card Number 93-2264
ISBN 0-442-01729-4

All rights reserved. No part of this work covered by the copyright hereon may be reproduced or used in any form or by any means—graphic, electronic, or mechanical, including photocopying, recording, taping, or information storage and retrieval systems—without written permission of the publisher.

Van Nostrand Reinhold is an International Thomson Publishing company. ITP logo is a trademark under license.

Printed in the United States of America

Van Nostrand Reinhold
115 Fifth Avenue
New York, NY 10003

International Thomson Publishing GmbH
Königswinteror Str. 518
5300 Bonn 3
Germany

International Thomson Publishing
Berkshire House, 168=173
High Holborn, London WC1V 7AA
England

International Thomson Publishing Asia
38 Kim Tian Road, #0105
Kim Tian Plaza
Singapore 0316

Thomas Nelson Australia
102 Dodds Street
South Melbourne 3205
Victoria, Australia

International Thomson Publishing Japan
Kyowa Building, 3F
2-2-1 Hirakawacho
Chiyada-Ku, Tokyo 102
Japan

Nelson Canada
1120 Birchmount Road
Scarborough, Ontario
M1K 5G4, Canada

16 15 14 13 12 11 10 9 8 7 6 5 4 3 2 1

Library of Congress Cataloging-in-Publication Data
Mastrianni, Steven J., 1951-
 Writing OS/2 2.1 Device Drivers in C / Steven J. Mastrianni.—
2nd ed.
  p. cm.- (VNR's OS/2 series)
  Includes index.
  ISBN 0-442-01729-4
  1. OS/2 device drivers (Computer programs) 2. OS/2 (Computer file) 3. C (Computer program language) I. Title. II. Series.
QA76.76.D49M37 1993
005.4'3—dc20   93-2264
                                                         CIP

Project Management: Ray Campbell • Art Director: Jo-Ann Radin-Campbell • Production: mle design, Milford, CT 06460

DEDICATION

This book is dedicated to my sons Steve and Jeffrey, my daughter Laura, and my wife Debra, who put up with my absence while this book was being prepared.

ACKNOWLEDGMENTS

I would like to thank Dennis Rowe, Stacey Barnes, Mark Fiechtner, Frank Schroeder, Dick Conklin, Carol Bray, and John Soyring of the IBM Corporation for helping to make this book possible. I'd also like to thank Allan Wynn of IBM for supplying the information on the IBM OEMHLP device driver.

I would like to thank Marcello Lopez, Michael Kupka, Michael Glieneke, and Rhonda Morrison for their contributions to this book.

A special thanks to Dwight Vandenberghe of PentaSoft, Inc., Seattle, Washington, for providing me with the training and inspiration to write my first OS/2 device driver.

FOREWORD

Building upon the success of OS/2 Version 2.0 with well over 2 million copies shipped, IBM has now released an exciting new upgrade of this increasingly popular PC operating system. OS/2 Version 2.1 includes many new functional enhancements such as 32-bit graphics processing, integrated multimedia support, the ability to run applications originally designed for Windows 3.1 and much more.

OS/2 2.1 not only has superior abilities for running DOS applications, Windows applications and new 32-bit OS/2 applications, but it allows users to exploit the untapped power of their 32-bit PC's and advanced I/O devices. However, the PC hardware industry is not standing still. In addition to the introduction of the Pentium processor, the PC industry has seen an explosive growth in faster, more intelligent peripheral devices, including Fax/Modems, CD-ROM's, high resolution printers and display devices, mass storage, and new technology such as PCMCIA. Support for these new devices requires device drivers. In the case of high resolution video devices, several drivers may be required. Keeping up with the demand of users for state-of-the-art support of these devices can be a daunting task.

Writing *OS/2 2.1 Device Drivers in C* is the second edition of the very popular *Writing OS/2 2.0 Device Drivers in C*, which has sold more than 15,000 copies in over 30 countries. I think you will find this second edition even more helpful and informative than the first. More sample source code has been added, and all of the source code for the examples in the book is included on a disk attached to the back cover. Several more chapters were added with even more information covering device driver development — including a question-and-answer section covering commonly asked driver development questions.

Steve's writing style is clear and concise. He tells you what you need to know — without extraneous information, excessive use of buzz words, and acronyms. Developers of device drivers who read Steve's first edition have consistently told me they found his book to be a valuable addition to their libraries. I think you will find this second edition even more worthwhile.

OS/2 2.1 is going to make a difference in the way PC's are used. It will both preserve user's current 16-bit investments, and enable them to exploit 32-bit hardware and I/O devices. Authors like Steve help provide the technical support you will need to join this new PC revolution and move into the 21st century of computing.

John Soyring
Director of Software Development Programs
IBM Corporation

CONTENTS

INTRODUCTION .... **xxi**

CHAPTER 1. THE EVOLUTION OF PC DEVICE DRIVERS **1**
    Storage Devices 3
    Interface Adapter Cards 4
    The First Operating System For Personal Computers 4
    The First Bus 6

CHAPTER 2. UNDERSTANDING DEVICE DRIVERS **7**
    Device Drivers Today 10
    Device Drivers - A Summary 11

CHAPTER 3. THE PC HARDWARE ARCHITECTURE **13**
    The System Bus 13
    The IBM PC - Beginnings 14
    IBM PC XT 15
    The Interrupt System 15
    IBM PC AT 16
    The AT Bus 17
    The IBM PS/2 and Micro Channel 18
    Enhanced Industry Standard Architecture (EISA) 20
    Bus Wars 20
    Real Mode 21

Protect Mode 22
Using Addresses and Pointers 24
The Ring Architecture 25

CHAPTER 4. AN OVERVIEW OF THE OS/2 OPERATING SYSTEM 27
Roots..28
Processes and Threads 30
OS/2 1.0 - OS/2 Arrives 32
OS/2 1.1 - Presentation Manager Arrives 32
OS/2 1.2 - A Better File System 33
OS/2 1.3 - IBM's First Solo Effort 34
OS/2 2.0 - What OS/2 Was Really Meant to Be 35
The OS/2 Application Programming Interface 37

CHAPTER 5. THE ANATOMY OF AN OS/2 DEVICE DRIVER 39
Application-to-Driver Interface 39
DOS Device Drivers and OS/2 Device Drivers..40
Designing an OS/2 Device Driver 41
Tools Necessary For Driver Development 41
The Basics of Driver Design..42
Request Packets...43
OS/2 Device Driver Architecture 43
Device Driver Modes 45
The Device Header 46
Capabilities Bit Strip 48
Providing a Low-Level Interface 48
The Strategy Section 55
Initialization 57
A Common Strategy 59
Interrupt Section 60
The Timer Handler 65

CHAPTER 6. DEVICE DRIVER STRATEGY COMMANDS 67
Summary of Device Driver Commands..70
0H / Init 72
1H / Media Check 75

```
            2H / Build BPB .................................................................................. 77
            4H, 8H, 9H / Read or Write ............................................................... 79
            5H / Nondestructive Read No Wait ..................................................... 80
            6H, AH / Input or Output Status ......................................................... 81
            7H, BH / Input Flush or Output Flush ................................................. 82
            DH, EH / Open or Close ..................................................................... 83
            FH / Removable Media ....................................................................... 84
            10H / Generic IOCTL .......................................................................... 84
            11H / Reset Media .............................................................................. 86
            12H, 13H / Get/Set Logical Drive ....................................................... 87
            14H / Deinstall ................................................................................... 88
            16H / Partitionable Fixed Disks ......................................................... 89
            17H / Get Fixed Disk/Logical Unit Map ............................................. 90
            1CH / Shutdown ................................................................................. 91
            1DH / Get Driver Capabilities ............................................................ 91
            1FH / InitComplete ............................................................................ 92
```

CHAPTER 7. A SIMPLE OS/2 PHYSICAL DEVICE DRIVER 93
    Device Driver Specifications 93
    Application Program Design 94
    Device Driver Operation 95

CHAPTER 8. THE MICRO CHANNEL BUS 107
    Micro Channel Adapter Cards 107
    Micro Channel Adapter ID 108
    Accessing the POS Register During Debug 115
    Micro Channel Interrupts 116

CHAPTER 9. OS/2 2.1 VIRTUAL DEVICE DRIVERS 119
    The Virtual DOS Machine 120
    VDD Architecture 122
    VDD Initialization 123
    DOS Settings 124
    DOS Settings Registration 125
    VDD to PDD Communications 125
    The Virtual COM Device Driver 126
    The Virtual Timer Device Driver 128

xii   Contents

    The Virtual Disk Device Driver 130
    The Virtual Keyboard Device Driver 132
    The Virtual Mouse Device Driver 133
    The Virtual Line Printer Device Driver 133
    The Virtual Video Device Driver 134
    Virtual DevHlp Services By Category 136
    DOS Session Interrupts 147
    Sample Virtual Device Driver 152
    Establishing a VDD-PDD Link 161

CHAPTER 10. MEMORY-MAPPED ADAPTERS AND IOPL 163
    High and Low Memory Maps 164
    Application Program Access to Adapter Memory 164
    Access to Adapter Memory in the Interrupt Handler 166
    Input/Output Privilege Level (IOPL) 167
    The IOPL Segment 168
    IOPL From 32-bit Applications 171

CHAPTER 11. DIRECT MEMORY ACCESS (DMA) 173
    The DMA Controller 173
    Using DMA 177
    DMA and Micro Channel 181

CHAPTER 12. EXTENDED DEVICE DRIVER INTERFACE 183
    Device Driver Capabilities 184
    Request Lists and Request Control 187
    Request Format 190
    Read/Write/Write Verify Request 194
    Read Prefetch Request 196
    Request Control Functions 196
    SetFSDInfo 197
    ChgPriority 198
    SetRestPos 198
    GetBoundary 198

CHAPTER 13. DEBUGGING OS/2 2.1 DEVICE DRIVERS 199
- KDB Keywords 201
- KDB Operators 202
- KDB Command Reference 205
- Breakpoints 208
- Internal Commands 208
- External Commands 226

CHAPTER 14. AN INTRODUCTION TO PRESENTATION DRIVERS 239
- Device Context 242
- Data Types 244
- Instance Data 244
- Program Stack 245
- Presentation Driver Design Considerations 246
- Presentation Driver Errors 246
- Presentation Driver Error Codes 247
- Additional Presentation Driver Functions 248

CHAPTER 15. WORKING WITH POINTERS 251
- C Set/2 251
- Virtual Addresses 254
- Pointers In A VDM 255

CHAPTER 16. PCMCIA DEVICE DRIVERS 257
- The PCMCIA Software Trilogy 258
- OS/2 2.1 PCMCIA Initialization 259
- Client Device Driver Architecture 260
- OS/2 2.1 Restrictions 262
- Card Services Functions 262
- Calling Card Services 266
- Callbacks 267

CHAPTER 17. TIPS AND TECHNIQUES 271

APPENDIX A - DEVICE HELPER REFERENCE 275
- Device Helper Functions 275
- DevHlp Services and Device Contexts 280

Device Helper Categories 286
DevHlp Routines 290

APPENDIX B - REFERENCE PUBLICATIONS.....................................401

APPENDIX C - LISTINGS..403

Device Header, One Device 403
Device Header, Two Devices 404
C Startup Routine, One Device...405
C Startup Routine, Four Devices..407
Standard OS/2 Device Driver Include File 409
Skeleton Strategy Section 424
Sample IOCtl Call, 16-Bit...425
Sample IOCtl Call, 32-Bit...425
Sample Interrupt Handler 426
Sample Timer Handler 428
Simple OS/2 Parallel Physical Device Driver..429
C Startup Routine for Parallel Device Driver..438
Parallel Device Driver Include File 439
Parallel Device Driver Make File 440
Parallel Device Driver DEF File...440
Sample OS/2 Serial Device Driver 440
Serial Device Driver Make File 458
Serial Device Driver DEF File..458
Sample C Callable DevHlp Interface..459
C Callable Debugger Breakpoint 460
Data Transfer Routine 461
Sample DMA Routines 463
Obtaining POS Register Contents...473
ABIOS Specific Include File 475
IOPL Routine For 16-Bit and 32-Bit Applications 477
IOPL Routine Make File 478
IOPL Routine DEF File 478
IOPL Test Program, 16-Bit 478
IOPL Test Program Make File, 16-Bit 479
IOPL Test Program DEF File, 16-Bit..479

IOPL Test Program, 32-Bit 480
IOPL Test Program Make File, 32-Bit 480
IOPL Test Program DEF File, 32-Bit 481
Device Driver For Memory-Mapped Adapters..481
Memory-Mapped Device Driver DEF File...493
Memory-Mapped Device Driver Make File...494
Memory-Mapped Device Driver Header File..494
Memory-Mapped Device Driver Test Program - 16-Bit............................496
Memory-Mapped Test Program Header File - 16-Bit...............................498
Memory-Mapped Test Program Def File - 16-Bit....................................498
Memory-Mapped Test Program Make File - 16-Bit.................................498
Memory-Mapped Test Program - 32-Bit, 16-Bit Pointers 499
Memory-Mapped Test Program DEF File - 32-Bit..................................501
Memory-Mapped Test Program Make File - 32-Bit................................501
Memory-Mapped Test Program - 32-Bit, 32-Bit Pointers 501
Memory-Mapped Test Program DEF File - 32-Bit..................................503
Memory-Mapped Test Program Make File - 32-Bit................................503
Macros 504

APPENDIX D - OEMHLP AND TESTCFG 505
OEMHLP 505
TESTCFG 533

INDEX 541

LIBRARY ORDER FORM 549

TABLES

Table 4-1. OS/2 Priority Structure 31
Table 5-1. Device Attribute Word 47
Table 5-2. Capabilities Bit Strip..48
Table 5-3. Device Driver Strategy Calls 57
Table 6-1 Device Driver Strategy Commands..71
Table 6-2. API Routines Available During Init 74
Table 6-3. Media Descriptor Bytes..76
Table 6-4. Boot Sector Format..78
Table 9-1. DOS Settings...124
Table 9-2. DOS Settings Information 125
Table 9-3. Virtualized 8250/16450 Registers..127
Table 9-4. Virtualized Timer Registers 129
Table 9-5. Supported Virtualized Timer Registers..129
Table 9-6. Virtualized INT 13 Functions..130
Table 9-7. Virtualized Floppy Disk Ports 131
Table 9-8. Virtualized DOS Interrupts..148
Table 9-9. Virtualized BIOS Interrupts 149
Table 9-10. Virtualized DOS Software Interrupts 151
Table 11-1. DMA Channel Assignments...174
Table 11-2. DMA Controller Port Assignments 175
Table 11-3. DMA Channel Addressing 177
Table 11-4. DMA Mask Register..178
Table 11-5 DMA Mode Register..179
Table 11-6. DMA Command Register 180
Table 12-1. Capabilities Bits...185
Table 12-2. Volume Descriptor Word 186
Table 12-3. LstRequestControl Word Bits 188
Table 12-4. LstStatus Byte, Lower Nibble..189
Table 12-5. LstStatus Byte, Upper Nibble..189
Table 12-6. RequestCtl Byte..191

Table 12-7. Request Priority 191
Table 12-8. Request Status, Lower Nibble (Completion Status) 192
Table 12-9. Request Status, Upper Nibble (Error Status) 192
Table 12-10. Request Unrecoverable Error Codes 193
Table 12-11. Request Recoverable Error Codes 194
Table 12-12. Request Control Functions 197
Table 13-1. KDB Keywords 201
Table 13-2. KDB Binary Operators 202
Table 13-3. KDB Unary Operators 203
Table 13-4. KDB Parameter Definitions 206
Table 13-5. Page Bit Definitions (bit set/clear) 212
Table 13-6. KDB Register Definitions 219
Table 13-7. KDB Flag Register Definitions 220
Table 13-8. KDB Machine Status Word 221
Table 13-9. KDB Recognized Structures 227
Table 14-1. Presentation driver flag bits 241
Table 14-2. Device Context Types 243
Table 14-3. Data Types for Queued Date 244
Table 14-4. Graphics Engine Exports 245
Table 14-5. Presentation Driver Errors 247
Table 14-6. Presentation Driver Error Codes 248
Table 14-7. Job Error Returns 249
Table 16-1. OS/2 PCMCIA Card Services 263
Table 16-2. Card Services Register Interface (input) 266
Table 16-3. Card Services Register Interface (output) 266
Table 16-4. OS/2 2.1 Callbacks 267
Table 16-5. Callback Register Interface (input) 269
Table 16-6. Callback Register Interface (output) 269
Table A-1. Device Helper Functions 275
Table A-2. Device Helper Contexts 281
Table A-4. Read Only System Variables 319
Table A-5. Device Driver Events 372
Table D-1. OEMHLP Supported IOCtl Calls 507
Table D-2. Video Chip Set Information 518
Table D-3. TESTCFG IOCtls, Category 0x80 533

FIGURES

Figure 1-1. The Altair 8800. 1
Figure 1-2. Floppy disk. 3
Figure 1-3. Role of the BIOS. 5
Figure 2-1. Polled printer output. 8
Figure 2-2. Interrupt printer output. 9
Figure 2-3. The role of the device driver. 10
Figure 3-1. The IBM PC. 14
Figure 3-2. The IBM PC AT. 15
Figure 3-3. Micro Channel adapter. 18
Figure 3-4. IBM PS/2 Model 80 19
Figure 3-5. Real mode address calculation. 21
Figure 3-6. 80286 protect mode addressing. 22
Figure 3-7. 80386-486 flat mode addressing. 23
Figure 3-8. The 80X86 ring architecture. 25
Figure 4-1. Process and threads. 31
Figure 4-2. OS/2 1.3 EE 34
Figure 4-3. OS/2 2.1 Tutorial 36
Figure 5-1. Application-to-device driver interface. 42
Figure 5-2. Request Packet. 43
Figure 5-3. OS/2 device driver header. 44
Figure 5-4. Device driver header, multiple devices. 46
Figure 5-5. Start-up routine, one device. 49
Figure 5-6. Start-up routine, four devices. 51
Figure 5-7. Start-up routine with timer and interrupt handler. 53
Figure 5-8. Skeleton strategy section. 55
Figure 5-9. Interrupt handler. 60
Figure 5-10. Timer handler. 66
Figure 5-11. TickCount timer handler. 66
Figure 6-1. Request Packet definition. 68
Figure 6-2. Standard OS/2 device driver errors. 68
Figure 7-1. Application call to open the driver. 94

Figure 7-2. INIT section. ...95
Figure 7-3. OPEN section. ...97
Figure 7-4. CLOSE section. ...98
Figure 7-5. IOCtl 0x01, write port. ...100
Figure 7-6. IOCtl 0x02. ...101
Figure 7-7. IOCtl 0x03. ...102
Figure 7-8. READ and WRITE section. ...104
Figure 7-9. Timer handler. ...105
Figure 8-1. ISA and Micro Channel INIT section. ...110
Figure 8-2. Micro Channel vs. ISA bus interrupt handler. ...116
Figure 9-1. OS/2 2.1 VDMs ...119
Figure 9-2. VDD initialization section. ...153
Figure 9-3. VDD data segment. ...154
Figure 9-4. VDD input handler. ...155
Figure 9-5. VDD data port output handler. ...156
Figure 9-6. VDD user routines. ...157
Figure 9-7. VDD include file. ...158
Figure 9-8. VDD Make And DEF Files ...160
Figure 9-9. Registering PDD for VDD-PDD communications. ...161
Figure 9-10. VDD-PDD communications structure. ...162
Figure 10-1. PhysToVirt call. ...165
Figure 10-2. Mapping a GDT selector during INIT. ...167
Figure 10-3. IOPL Segment. ...169
Figure 10-4. IOPL DEF file. ...170
Figure 11-1. DMA setup routine. ...181
Figure 12-1. Driver Capabilities structure. ...184
Figure 12-2. Volume Characteristics Structure. ...185
Figure 12-3. Request List Header structure. ...187
Figure 12-4. Request Header structure. ...190
Figure 12-5. Scatter Gather Descriptor structure. ...194
Figure 12-6. Read/Write Request structure. ...195
Figure 12-7. Read Prefetch Request structure. ...196
Figure 12-8. SetFSDInfo structure. ...197
Figure 14-1. OS/2 2.1 Workplace Shell ...239
Figure 15-1. VMGlobalToProcess and VMProcessToGlobal ...253
Figure 15-2. Using VMAlloc. ...254
Figure 15-3. Calling VMLock. ...255
Figure 16-1. PCMCIA software architecture. ...259
Figure 16-2. ClientData structure. ...270
Figure A-1. ADD Device Class Table. ...357
Figure A-2. Retrieving an ADD's entry point using GetDOSVar. ...358
Figure D-1. Locating An EISA Bus Adapter Using OEMHLP. ...506

INTRODUCTION

This is the second edition to *Writing OS/2 2.1 Device Drivers in C*. The first edition of this book has already sold 15,000 copies in over 30 countries. This is not a testament of the book's popularity; rather, it is a statement of the tremendous popularity of OS/2. The book began as a collection of my notes taken while developing device drivers for OS/2 1.0. The collection of notes kept getting larger and larger, so I decided to put them together into a more organized form. I finished the first edition of the book in January of 1992 and it was first published in April of that year.

Since that time, OS/2 has undergone enormous changes. The latest release, 2.1, is rock solid, and contains some of the things we've been waiting for, such as support for CD-ROM drives, super VGA video, and multimedia devices such as the Sound Blaster. The addition of the Windows 3.1 support has enhanced OS/2's popularity, allowing the latest Windows 3.1 applications to run seamlessly on the OS/2 desktop. This is the OS/2 we've all envisioned, and IBM has made our vision real.

However, OS/2 device drivers continue to be a limiting factor in the acceptance and use of OS/2. This is somewhat discouraging, since OS/2 device drivers are not difficult to write. Using the examples I give you in this book, you should be able to have a simple OS/2 physical device driver up and running in less than one hour. Of course, some types of device drivers are more difficult. If you follow the guidelines I give you, however, you'll find that writing an OS/2 device driver can be an easy and rewarding experience.

As an independent software developer and consultant, I don't have time to read volumes of reference materials to get up to speed quickly at a new assignment. Reference materials have never been good about telling you how to do something anyway, since they're only references. Sometimes, a few source code examples are all that I really need to get started, and I've kept that in mind when writing this book. To help you get going quickly, I've included enough code so that you can begin writing OS/2 2.1 device drivers immediately. By the time you finish this book, you will have enough background and sample source code to easily develop your own OS/2 device drivers. You are free to use the code described in the listings section or on the companion disk for your device drivers.

The code in this book relies upon a library of C-callable functions for the Device Helper, or DevHlp routines. The DevHlp routines are the driver writer's API, and perform such functions as hooking interrupts, timers and converting addresses. At the back of the book, you'll find an order form for the C-callable library, or you can write your own providing you have a good knowledge of assembler programming and the parameter passing mechanisms via the stack. The cost of the library is $79 without the library source, and $149 with the library source. This is not inexpensive, but its cheaper than writing more than 100 assembly language routines from scratch. If your time is worth more, or you need to get going immediately, I recommend you buy the library. I provide free support via Compuserve, and offer free updates to the library for one year.

This text does not contain a complete discussion or reference for OS/2 2.1, nor is it a complete reference for device driver function calls or prototypes; readers should have a general understanding of OS/2 2.1 and the OS/2 religion, along with some OS/2 2.1 programming experience. See the Reference Section for a list of recommended reading. A complete reference for OS/2 1.3 device drivers can be found in *I/O Subsystems and Device Support, Volume 1* and *Volume 2* from IBM, which is part of the OS/2 1.3 Programming Tools and Information package. Complete documentation for OS/2 2.1 Physical Device Drivers and Virtual Device Drivers can be found in the *IBM Operating System/2 Version 2.1 Physical Device Driver Reference*, the *IBM Operating System/2 Version 2.1 Virtual Device Driver Reference* and the *IBM Operating System/2 Version 2.1 Presentation Driver Reference* which are part of the *IBM OS/2 2.1 Technical Library*.

In this book, I will discuss the issues, both hardware and software, that will directly affect your OS/2 device driver development. Some type of hardware background is helpful, but not necessary.

Generally, you can write all of your OS/2 device drivers, including interrupt handlers, in C. A device driver written in C can be completed in approximately half the time it would take to write the same device driver in assembly language. Most device drivers will work fine when written in C. Programmers who have written device drivers for other multitasking operating systems, such as UNIX or VMS, should find OS/2 device driver design concepts similar. Programmers not familiar with multitasking device driver design will find OS/2 device driver development somewhat more difficult. Your first OS/2 device driver could take about two months to complete, and subsequent device drivers should take slightly less time. Block and Presentation Manager device drivers are significantly more complex, and may take upwards of six to nine months or more to complete. I have included a short chapter on Presentation Device Drivers, but the topic of PM drivers could easily span an entire book in itself. I didn't feel that I could do the topic justice in the limited space of this book. Please refer to the *IBM OS/2 2.1 Presentation Driver Reference* for more complete information on writing presentation drivers.

To use the examples in the text or on the companion disk, you will need a compiler, assembler, and compatible linker. For OS/2 character mode and block device drivers, the Microsoft C 5.1 or 6.0 compiler, the Microsoft 5.1 or 6.0 Assembler, and the Microsoft 5.13 or later linker will be sufficient. For OS/2 Virtual Device Drivers, you will need a 32-bit C compiler, such as the IBM C Set/2 compiler version 1.1 or greater, along with the corresponding 32-bit linker and symbol file generator.

Debugging OS/2 device drivers requires the use of a kernel-level debugger. I recommend the kernel debugger supplied with the IBM OS/2 2.1 Toolkit. Other third-party debuggers are available, but the IBM kernel debugger is the only debugger which has knowledge of the internal kernel symbols. You may also wish to look at ASDT32, a 32-bit kernel debugger supplied with the IBM DDK. ASDT32 provides debugging output on the main display, eliminating the need for a debugging terminal. ASDT32 is also available to members of the IBM Developer Assistance Program via DAPTOOLS on IBMLINK.

If you are developing or plan to develop an OS/2 product, I recommend that you join the IBM Developer Assistance Program. This program, offered to qualified software developers, provides up-to-date information on OS/2 2.1, updates to the operating system and tools, and substantial discounts on IBM hardware and software. Call the IBM Developer Assistance Program at area code (407) 982-6408 and ask how to become a member. You may also join the IBM Worldwide DAP program by entering GO OS2DAP from your Compuserve account.

Unfortunately, two chapters planned for this book did not make it in time for this publishing. The two chapters are titled "IFS Drivers" and "SCSI/ADD Device Drivers". These two chapters will appear in the next printing. I apologize for this omission, since both are important topics.

In Chapter 1, I describe how device drivers for personal computers evolved from simple polling loops to the complex interrupt-driven device drivers found in today's real-time PC operating systems. In Chapter 2, I describe what device drivers are and how they fit into the total system picture. In Chapter 3, I describe the relevant parts of the PC hardware architecture necessary for device driver writers to be aware of. If you are already an experienced device driver writer, you may wish to skip these three chapters and proceed directly to Chapter 4. Chapter 4 begins with a historical look at OS/2 and provides a brief outline of the OS/2 operating system. Programmers already familiar with OS/2 will probably wish to skip this chapter and proceed directly to Chapter 5. In Chapter 5, I discuss the anatomy of the OS/2 device driver by presenting sample code fragments, listings, and various tables. Topics include the strategy section, interrupt handlers, timer handlers, request packets and device headers. Chapter 6 continues the architecture topic by describing, in detail, the strategy commands that the device driver receives from OS/2 and how the device driver should respond to them. In Chapter 7, I use actual code to show you how to build an OS/2 8-bit parallel port device driver. I also describe, in detail, the operation of the device driver for each request it receives from the OS/2 kernel. Chapter 8 describes the special considerations necessary for writing OS/2 device drivers for Micro Channel bus machines, such as the IBM PS/2. Chapter 9 describes Virtual Device Drivers, or VDDs, and contains code for an actual VDD. In Chapter 10, I show you how to handle memory-mapped adapters, and how to perform direct port I/O without a device driver. Chapter 11 explains how to use Direct Memory Access, or DMA, and includes several code listings to illustrate how DMA is handled under OS/2. In Chapter 12, I describe the Extended Disk Driver Interface, also known as the Strategy 2 or scatter/gather entry point. Chapter 13 provides a handy reference for the OS/2 2.1 Kernel Debugger commands. Chapter 14 contains an introduction to Presentation device drivers. In Chapter 15, I describe various types of pointers and addressing modes you will need to understand when writing your device drivers. Chapter 16 introduces the PCMCIA architecture and how OS/2 2.1 supports PCMCIA device drivers. Finally, Chapter 17 contains some helpful hints and suggestions, as well as a compendium of tips and techniques I've used when writing my OS/2 device drivers.

In Appendix A, you'll find a detailed description of the OS/2 Device Helper routines with their C calling sequence as provided by the C Callable DevHlp library described in the diskette order form in this book. Appendix B includes a recommended list of further reading. Appendix C contains source code listings for the device drivers and support routines discussed in the book. All of this code, without the library, is included on the free companion disk attached to the back cover of this book. You are free to use the code for your own use but you may not sell it or distribute it for profit without written permission of the publisher. Finally, Appendix D contains documentation for the IBM OEMHLP device driver which can be used by your driver to obtain such information as adapter IDs for EISA bus machines.

CHAPTER 1

The Evolution of PC Device Drivers

In 1976, a small company in Albuquerque, New Mexico, called MITS, founded by Ed Roberts, introduced a computer in kit form that could be assembled by a novice electronic tinkerer. The computer, called the Altair 8800, delivered technology into the home which had previously been confined to laboratories of large companies and universities. Based on the Intel 8080 microprocessor, the Altair provided much of the functionality of larger machines, but at a much lower price. The user could enter a program through the front panel switches and execute it. Later, a high-level language program called Beginner's All-purpose Symbolic Instruction Code, or BASIC as it's more widely known, was introduced for the Altair to make writing programs easier. BASIC was written for MITS by Bill Gates and Paul Allen.

Figure 1-1. The Altair 8800.

The first personal computers were quite expensive by today's standards. A kit containing the computer, case and power supply, less any memory or storage, sold for $2000.00, not a trivial sum in 1976. Four thousand characters of memory was priced at over $1000.00. In addition, many circuits were based on an electronic technology that was prone to interference from certain types of radio frequencies and small variations in the AC input voltage. The collection of electronic circuits and other equipment that comprise a computer system are referred to as the computer hardware. The programs that run on the computer are referred to as software.

A short time after the Altair was introduced, MITS introduced an audio cassette interface, which allowed the use of a standard audio cassette player/recorder for the storage of information. Using the audio cassette proved cumbersome. Since the computer had no direct control over the cassette player, it could not determine, for example, that the play and record buttons were pressed while recording, or if the player was even attached to the computer. Recording information on audio tape was also unreliable. In order to store a program or data onto the tape, the *data* had to be converted into audio signals before writing it to the tape. In order to read the data from the tape, the audio signals from the tape had to be converted back into machine code. Since the computer had to be programmed to read and write using the cassette tape unit, the user had to manually enter a program to perform those operations using the front panel switches.

A special integrated circuit, called an *Erasable Programmable Read Only Memory*, or *EPROM*, was added to solve the problem of having to manually enter the initial boot program. The EPROM was programmed to contain the cassette loader, and retained its contents even if power was lost. The EPROM contained only 256 characters or *bytes* of storage, so the loader program could not be very complex. The user could select this EPROM using the computer's front panel switches and start the tape program by executing the code located in the EPROM.

Storage Devices

Shortly thereafter, a floppy disk drive storage system was introduced, which provided for the storage of 250,000 bytes on an 8 inch floppy disk, using the same format that had been used by IBM on their larger computer systems (see Figure 1-2). Again, the boot program, this time for floppy disk, was programmed into an EPROM, so the user did not have to enter it manually. The disk boot program turned out to be much more complicated, and would not fit into the 256-character storage of the EPROM. This problem was solved by placing a more complex loader onto the floppy disk. The small boot program in the EPROM loaded the more complex disk loader, which in turn loaded the selected program or data from the disk.

Figure 1-2. Floppy disk. (Courtesy of International Business Machines Corporation.)

Software for this new computer was poor to nonexistent. Programs had to be written by hand on paper and entered manually. The person writing the program had to be somewhat of a computer expert since the programs had to be entered in a language of numbers called machine code. Machine code is the only type of instruction that a *Central Processing Unit*, or *CPU*, can understand. Machine code is a representation in the computer's memory of an instruction or piece of data, and is expressed in a pattern of ones and zeroes, called binary notation. The CPU is capable of recognizing certain patterns of these ones and zeroes, which are called bits, as instructions. Programming in machine code proved to be time consuming and prone to error, and the slightest programming error could be disastrous.

Interface Adapter Cards

Each device was connected to the CPU through an electronic circuit board called an electrical interface card, commonly known today as an adapter. The interface card plugged into the computer bus, which was connected to the CPU. A program that had to access a device would instruct the CPU to read from or write to the interface card, which would in turn issue the correct electrical signals to the device to perform the requested operation. The interface acted as a converter of sorts, converting CPU instructions into electrical signals to control the particular device. A motor, for instance, could be turned on and off using a program that commanded an interface to turn the motor on and off. The motor was not aware of the computer's presence or programming, but merely acted upon the electrical signals generated by the interface card.

Because a very limited number of these adapters were available, programs would control them by directing the CPU to directly access the adapter hardware. Programs that used particular adapters were written specifically to access those adapters. If the adapter was changed, the program would have to be rewritten to accommodate the new adapter's requirements. This was unacceptable, since a software supplier could not afford to support multiple versions of a program for each different type of adapter configuration.

The First Operating System For Personal Computers

With the introduction of the floppy disk for microcomputers, the first disk-based personal computer operating system was born. Called the Control Program for Microcomputers, or CP/M, it resided on a floppy disk. When directed to, it would load itself into the computer's memory to manage the attached devices, including storage devices, keyboards, and terminals. Once loaded into the computer's memory, CP/M took responsibility for reading and writing to floppy disks, tape drives, printers, terminals, and any other devices attached to the computer. The CP/M operating system was a generic piece of software, i.e., it could be used on any configuration of computer with the same type of microprocessor. To allow this generic operating system to manage different configurations of devices, CP/M accessed all devices through a hardware-specific set of programs called the *Basic Input/Output System*, or *BIOS*. By changing a small section of the BIOS program, users could add different types of devices while the operating system program remained unchanged (see Figure 1-3).

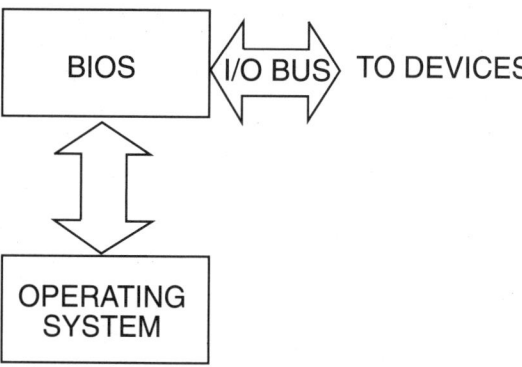

Figure 1-3. Role of the BIOS.

The CP/M BIOS code was an example of an early personal computer device driver. The BIOS code isolated the CP/M operating system from the device electronics and provided a consistent interface to the devices. Programs that wished to read from or write to a particular device did so by calling CP/M routines, which in turn called the BIOS. When reading a file from the disk, the programmer did not have to keep track of where the file resided on the disk, or command the disk unit to position itself where the file was located on the disk. The disk geometry parameters, which defined the size of the disk, number of tracks, number of heads, and the number of sectors per track, were handled by the BIOS code. The developers of the CP/M operating system were free to change the operating system without worrying about the many types of hardware configurations that existed. Today, the BIOS code is still responsible for defining the disk geometry.

Since that time, computer speed and storage have increased exponentially. The amount of computer processing power previously requiring the space of a normal living room can now fit on a small notebook-size computer. This increased performance has allowed the computer to perform more and more tasks for the user. In addition, the user's needs have become more sophisticated, and with them the software needed to provide a comparable level of functionality has become increasingly complex.

The functionality of the operating system and its environment have changed dramatically, yet the necessity for the device driver has only increased. The basic job of the device driver remains the same. That is, the device driver isolates an application program from having to deal with the specific hardware constraints of a particular device, and removes such responsibility from the programmer. Device drivers allow for the expansion and addition of hardware adapters, while allowing the operating system to remain intact. Thus device drivers remain the vital link between the computer system's electronics and the programs that execute on it.

For CP/M, the BIOS software solved the device independence issues, but did not solve all of the problems. The BIOS code resided on a floppy disk and was loaded along with the operating system at boot time. Users could change the BIOS code to reflect a new device configuration, but the BIOS code was in assembly language which was difficult for novice programmers to learn. If the BIOS code contained an error, the operating system might not load, or if it did load, it would sometimes not work or work erratically. The BIOS was difficult to debug, because the debugger used the BIOS code to perform its input and output! A few years later, the BIOS code was relocated into *Read Only Memory*, or *ROM*, and subsequently to *Electrically Erasable Programmable Read Only Memory*, or *EEPROM*.

Using a special technique, the contents of EEPROM can be modified by a special setup program. The contents of memory in EEPROM is retained even if power is lost, so the device-specific contents of the BIOS is always retained.

The First Bus

The Altair introduced the idea of a common set of circuits that allowed all of the devices in the system to communicate with the CPU. This common set of circuits was called the bus, and the Altair computer introduced the first open-architecture bus, called the S-100 bus. It was called the S-100 bus because it contained 100 different electronic paths. Connectors were attached to the bus, which allowed adapter cards to be plugged into them and connect to the bus. The S-100 bus was the forerunner of today's bus architectures.

Although prone to radio-frequency interference, the S-100 bus established itself as the standard bus configuration for 8080 and Z-80-based personal computers, and was the first attempt at standardizing personal computer hardware. The IEEE actually drafted and published a standard for the S-100 bus, called IEEE-696. Some S-100-bus computers are still in operation today.

CHAPTER 2

Understanding Device Drivers

The use of the BIOS code in CP/M to isolate the operating system from the specifics of devices was not a new idea. Large computer systems and mid-range computers, called minicomputers, had been using this technique for some time. But, this was the first time they were applied to personal computers.

The first operating systems were single tasking, i.e., they were capable of executing only one program at a time. Even though these early computers were comparatively slow in their operation, they were faster than the devices they needed to access. Most output information was printed on a line printer or written to a magnetic tape, and most input information was read from a punched card reader or keyboard. This meant that if a program was waiting for input data, the computer system would be idle while waiting for the data to be entered. This operation, called polling, was very inefficient. The computer was capable of executing thousands of instructions in between each keystroke. Even the fastest typist could not keep up with the computer's input ability to process each key.

If a program needed to print something on a printer, it would do so one character at a time, waiting for the device to acknowledge that the character was printed before sending the next character (see Figure 2-1). Since the computer processed the data faster than it could be printed, it would sit idle for much of the time waiting for the electromechanical printing device to do its job. As technology progressed, faster input and output devices became available, all well as faster computers. Still, the computer was at the mercy of the input and output devices it needed. The configuration of these

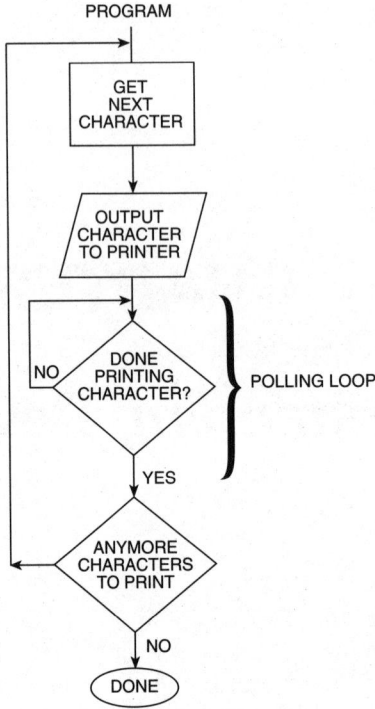

Figure 2-1. Polled printer output.

input and output (I/O) devices was also different. Some line printers printed on 8 1/2 by 11-inch paper and some on 8 1/2 by 14-inch paper. Magnetic tape storage devices used different size tapes and formats, and disk storage devices differed in the amount and method of storage.

The device driver solved the problems associated with the different types of devices and with the computer remaining idle while performing input and output operations. The device driver program was inserted between the program doing the I/O and the actual hardware device, such as a printer or magnetic tape drive. The device driver was programmed with the physical characteristics of the device. In the case of a line printer, the device driver was programmed with the number of characters per line it accepted or the size of the paper that the device could handle. For a magnetic tape device driver, the device driver was programmed with the physical characteristics of the tape mechanism, such as the format used to read from and write to the drive, and its storage capacity. The program performing the I/O did not require detailed knowledge of the hardware device. The device driver also allowed the programmer to direct a print operation with no knowledge of the type of printer that was attached. Thus, a new printer could be added, with its corresponding device driver, and the application program could run unmodified with the new printer.

The polling issue was also addressed. Since the device driver had intimate knowledge of how to talk to the I/O device, there was no reason why the application program had to wait around for each character to be printed (see Figure 2-2). It could send the device driver a block of, say, 256 characters and return to processing the application program. The device driver would take the characters one at a time and send them out to the printer. When the device driver had exhausted all of its work, it would notify the application program of that fact. The application program would then send the device driver more data to print, if necessary. The application program was now free to utilize the CPU to perform tasks that demanded more processing, thus reducing the idle time of the computer.

The device driver became even more important when operating systems appeared that could run more than one program at a time. It was now possible for more than one program to use the same I/O device, and often at the same time. The device driver was used to serialize access to the device, and protect the device from errant programs that might try to perform an incorrect operation or even cause a device failure.

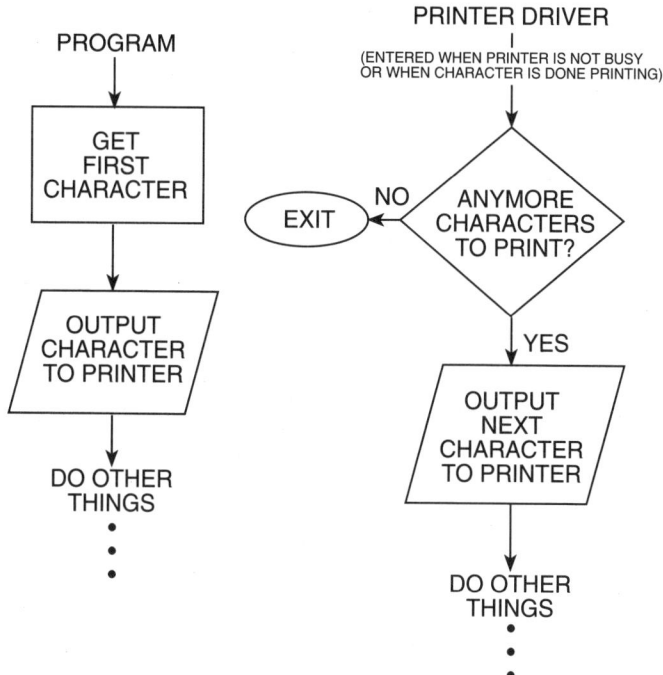

Figure 2-2. Interrupt printer output.

Device Drivers Today

Today, device drivers remain an irreplaceable and critical link between the operating system and the I/O device (see Figure 2-3). Many new I/O devices have appeared, including color graphics printers, cameras, plotters, scanners, music interfaces, and CD-ROM drives. The device driver remains a necessary component to complete the interface from the operating system to the physical device. Today's computers can run dozens and even hundreds of programs at one time. It is more important than ever for the device driver to free up the CPU to do more important work, while handling the relatively mundane tasks of reading and writing to the device.

Today, device drivers are more complex, as are the operating systems and devices they interface with. Device drivers can interact more with the CPU and operating system, and in some cases they can allow or block the execution of programs. They can usually turn the interrupt system on and off, which is an integral part of the performance of the system. Device drivers usually operate at the most trusted level of system integrity, so the device driver writer must test them thoroughly to assure bug-free operation. Failures at a device driver level can be fatal, and cause the system to crash or experience a complete loss of data.

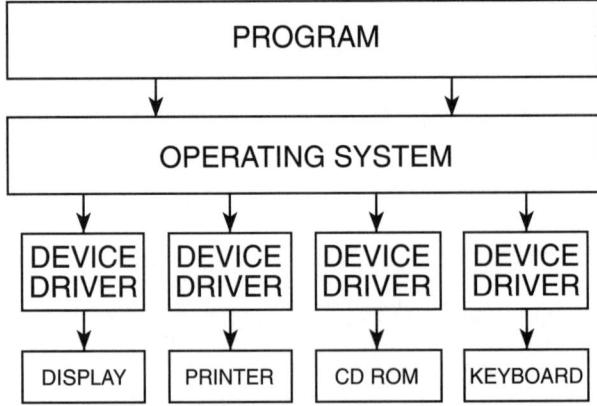

Figure 2-3. The role of the device driver.

The use of computers for graphics processing has become widespread. It would be impossible to support the many types of graphics devices without device drivers. Today's hardware offers dozens of different resolutions and sizes. For instance, color graphics terminals can be had in CGA, EGA, VGA, MCGA, SVGA, and XGA formats, each offering a different resolution and number of supported simultaneous displayable colors. Printers vary in dots per inch (DPI), Font selection, and interface type. Since all of these formats and configurations are still in use, the supplier of a graphics design package needs to support all of them to offer a marketable software package. The solution is for the graphical design program to read and write to these graphics devices using a standard set of programs, called APIs (Application Programming Interfaces), which in turn call the device driver specific to the hardware installed.

The device driver has an in-depth knowledge of the device, such as the physical size of the output area, the resolution (number of dots or pixels per screen), and the special control characters necessary for formatting. For instance, a graphics application program might direct the output device to print a line of text in Helvetica bold italic beginning at column 3, line 2. Each graphics output device, however, might use a different command to print the line at column 3, line 2. The device driver resolves these types of differences.

A user might wish to print a 256-color picture on a black and white printer in a lower or higher resolution. The device driver would resolve the differences and perform the proper translation, clipping and color-to-gray-scale mapping as required. While this method allows the graphics program to remain generic for any hardware configuration, it does require the software vendor to supply device drivers for the many types of input and output devices. Some word processors, for example, come with over 200 printer device drivers to support all makes and models of printers, from daisy wheel to high-speed laser and color printers.

Device Drivers - A Summary

In summary, the device driver:

- Contains the specific device characteristics and removes any responsibility of the application program for having knowledge of the particular device.

    In the case of a disk device driver, the device driver might contain the specific disk geometry, which is transparent to the program that calls the device driver. The device driver maps logical disk sectors to their physical equivalents. The application program need not be aware of the size of the disk, the number of cylinders, the number of heads, or the number of sectors per track. The device driver also controls the disk seek, which is the motion necessary to position the read/write head over the proper area of the disk. This simplifies the application code, by allowing it to issue only reads and writes, and leaving the details of how it is done to the device driver.

In the case of a video device driver, the driver might contain the size of the screen, the number of pixels per screen, and the number of simultaneous colors that can be displayed. Programs that need access to the display call the display device driver, which performs several functions. First, it maps the number of colors in the picture to those supported by the video adapter. This is especially true if a color picture is displayed on a black and white (monochrome) display. Second, if the resolution of the target display is smaller than the original, the device driver must adjust the size proportionally. Third, it might adjust the aspect ratio, the ratio of vertical pixels to horizontal pixels. A circle, for example, would appear egg-shaped without the correct aspect ratio.

In the case of a serial device, such as a modem, the device driver handles the specifics of the electronics that perform the actual sending and receiving of data, such as the transfer speed and data type.

- Allows for device independence by providing for a common program interface, allowing the application program to read from or write to generic devices. It also handles the necessary translation or conversion which may be required by the specific device.
- Serializes access to the device, preventing other programs from corrupting input or output data by attempting to access the device at the same time.
- Protects the operating system and the devices owned by the operating system from errant programs which may try to write to them, causing the system to crash.

CHAPTER 3

The PC Hardware Architecture

Writing device drivers requires you to have at least a limited understanding of the personal computer hardware architecture. Device drivers are special pieces of software because they "talk" directly to electronic circuits. Application programs, or those programs that use device drivers to access devices, can be written without a knowledge of the electronics. While you don't have to be an electrical engineer, you will need at least a basic knowledge of the hardware you will be interacting with.

The System Bus

The CPU is connected to the rest of the computer through electrical circuits called the bus. The bus contains the electrical paths common to different devices, allowing them to access each other using a very specialized protocol. The CPU is allowed read and write access to the computer's memory (and some devices) by means of the address bus. Data is moved to and from devices (and memory) via the data bus. The computer bus is the center of communications in the computer. To allow hardware interfaces or adapters to gain access to the CPU, the computer system is fitted with connectors to allow adapters to be plugged into the bus. The adapters must adhere to the electrical standards of the bus. Certain restrictions, such as bus timing and switching must be adhered to by the adapter manufacturers, or the entire system may experience erratic behavior or possibly not function at all.

The width of the bus, or the number of bits that can be transferred to or from memory or devices in parallel, directly affects system performance. Systems with "wider" busses will, in general, offer greater performance because of their ability to move more data in less time.

Today there are three primary bus architectures in the IBM-compatible marketplace. They are called Industry Standard Architecture (ISA), Enhanced Industry Standard Architecture (EISA) and Micro Channel Architecture (MCA). Of course, there are other types of busses used for non-IBM compatible computers, but they will not be covered in this book.

Figure 3-1. The IBM PC. (Courtesy of International Business Machines Corporation.)

The IBM PC - Beginnings

In 1981, IBM released the IBM PC (see Figure 3-1), a personal computer based on the Intel 8088 microprocessor. The 8088 was a 16-bit microprocessor, and was IBM's first entry into the personal computer market. IBM was known worldwide as a supplier of large data processing systems, but this was their first product for personal use. The IBM PC contained a new bus design called the PC bus. The PC bus was fitted with adapter card slots for expansion, and to make the bus popular, IBM released the specifications of the PC bus. This encouraged third-party suppliers to release many different types of adapters to be used in the IBM PC. This was a strategic move by IBM which led to the standardization of the PC bus architecture for all personal computers.

Storage was limited to a single floppy disk, capable of storing approximately 180,000 bytes of information.

The IBM PC was not a relatively fast machine, but users could, for the first time, have an IBM computer on their desks. Original sales projections for the IBM PC were a few hundred thousand units, but demand quickly exceeded availability. The personal computer revolution had begun.

Figure 3-2. The IBM PC AT. (Courtesy of International Business Machines Corporation.)

IBM PC XT

In 1982, IBM introduced the IBM XT computer. The IBM XT contained a built-in ten million byte (10MB) hard disk storage device, and the floppy disk storage was doubled to 360,000 bytes (360KB). The IBM XT was based on the IBM PC and retained the same basic design, except that users could now store ten million characters of data on the hard disk.

Computer hardware can process instructions relatively fast. The execution of a simple instruction may take less than one microsecond (.000001 seconds). The computer input and output devices, however, are relatively slow. For example, if the computer was receiving bytes of data from another computer over a phone line, the time to receive just one byte of data would be approximately 4 milliseconds (.004 seconds). If the computer was just waiting for more bytes to appear, it would be spending most of its time doing nothing but waiting. This would be extremely inefficient, as the computer could have executed thousands of instructions while waiting for another byte. This problem is solved by a hardware mechanism called the interrupt system. The interrupt system allows an external event, such as the reception of a character, to interrupt the program currently being executed. A special program, called an interrupt handler, interrupts the currently executing program, receives the character, processes it, and returns to the program that was executing when the interrupt was received. The program that was executing at the time of the interrupt resumes processing at the exact point at which it was interrupted.

The IBM PC and PC XT had an eight-level Programmable Interrupt Controller (PIC), which permitted up to eight interrupts on the PC bus. This represented somewhat of a problem, as several interrupt levels were already dedicated to the system. The system timer reserved an interrupt, as well as the hard disk, floppy drive, printer port and serial port. This left only two unused interrupts, which were reserved for a second printer and second serial communications port. If you happened to have these devices installed, you could not install any other adapter cards that utilized interrupts.

IBM PC AT

In 1984, IBM introduced the IBM PC AT personal computer. The IBM PC AT computer utilized the Intel 80286, a more powerful 16-bit microprocessor. The IBM PC AT utilized a newly designed bus, called the AT bus. The AT bus added eight additional address and data lines, to enable the CPU to transfer twice as much data in the same amount of time as the IBM PC. In another brilliant engineering innovation, IBM made the AT bus downward compatible with existing IBM PC adapter cards. The user did not have to give up a large investment in adapter hardware to upgrade to the IBM PC AT. The AT could use newly introduced 16-bit adapters as well as the existing eight bit adapters. The newer bus could still accommodate the older PC and XT bus adapter cards. Today, the AT bus remains the most popular IBM PC-compatible bus in existence, with over 100 million installed, and is commonly called the ISA bus.

The processor speed of the PC AT was increased 25 percent, and the combination of processor speed and greater bus width led to dramatic performance increases over PC XT. The PC AT was equipped with a 20MB hard disk, a 1.2MB floppy disk, and was fitted with a larger power supply to handle the increased speed and capacity. The color display was becoming more popular, but was limited in colors and resolution. IBM quickly introduced an upgraded model of the IBM PC AT, called the model 339. The newer version came with a 30MB hard disk and a 1.2MB floppy disk. To retain compatibility, the AT's floppy disk could also read and write to the smaller capacity 360K byte floppies for the IBM PC XT. Processor speed was again bumped up 33 percent.

The AT bus, however, had limitations. The electrical design of the bus was limited by the speed that data could be transferred on the bus. This was not a problem for the IBM PC AT, but as processors became faster and users demanded more power, the performance of the AT bus became a limiting factor.

The AT Bus

When the IBM PC AT was introduced in 1984, the bus requirements changed significantly. The IBM PC AT used the Intel 80286, which was also a 16-bit processor. The processor speed was increased by thirty percent. Since the memory address could be 16 bits wide, the processor could now issue only one address command to the memory circuits, cutting the time necessary to address memory in half. The data bus width was also increased to 16 bits, and 8 more interrupts were added.

The AT bus has 24 address lines, which limits the amount of directly addressable memory to 16MB, but recent IBM-compatibles have provided a separate CPU-to-memory bus, which is 32 bits wide. The peripheral address bus that the adapter cards plug into remains a 24 bit address bus.

The IBM PC AT was upgraded to run another thirty percent faster by raising the processor clock speed to 8 megahertz (Mhz). Performance increased dramatically, but a problem for future expansion now became apparent. The electrical design characteristics of the AT bus prohibited it from reliably running at speeds faster than 8 Mhz, with a maximum bus throughput of about 8MB per second. Users were demanding more power, and CPU makers such as Intel were producing faster and more powerful processors.

Adapter cards for the AT bus required the manual installation and/or removal of small electrical jumpers to define the characteristics of the card. There were jumper settings for the card address, interrupt level, adapter card port address, timing, and a host of other options. This sometimes made installation troublesome. An incorrectly placed jumper could cause the adapter not to work or the system to hang. Novice computer users had a tough time understanding all of the options and how to set them for various configurations. Boards were often returned to manufacturers for repair when all that was wrong was an incorrectly installed jumper.

The AT bus design allows for 15 interrupts, but adapters cannot share the same interrupt, or IRQ level. Once a device driver claims an interrupt level, the interrupt level cannot be used for another adapter.

The IBM PS/2 and Micro Channel

IBM's answer to the limitations of the AT bus was to create, from scratch, an entirely new bus architecture. This new architecture, called Micro Channel, was (and is) vastly superior to the AT bus architecture. Since IBM decided that the bus did not have to support existing adapter cards and memory, they were free to design the new bus without restrictions. The Micro Channel bus was a proprietary bus (which has since been made public) that was designed to solve all of the existing problems with the AT bus, and to provide for an architecture that would support multiple processors and bus-masters on the same bus using a bus arbitration scheme. In addition, the Micro Channel bus provided greater noise immunity from *Radio Frequency Interference (RFI)*, 32 address lines, 24 DMA address lines, and 16 data lines with increased speed (bandwidth). The first Micro Channel bus computer was twice as fast as the IBM PC AT, and had a maximum bus transfer rate of 20MB per second. Some Micro Channel adapters can manage as much as 160MB per second.

The Micro Channel bus supports multiple bus masters. Bus mastering allows an adapter to obtain control of the system bus to perform I/O at higher rates than if the CPU was used. The Micro Channel design supports up to 15 bus masters. The Micro Channel bus also has better grounding and more interrupt capability.

IBM introduced a brand new line of computers, called the *Personal System/2*, or *PS/2* (see Figure 3-4), which utilized the Micro Channel technology. The new computers offered several new features, such as built-in support for VGA color and larger-capacity *Enhanced Small Disk Interface*, or *ESDI*, hard disk drives. In the area of hardware, IBM made three major design changes. First, they designed the Micro Channel bus to be slot dependent. That is, each slot was addressable by the CPU. This differed from the IBM PC and PC AT bus machines, where adapter boards could be placed in any slot.

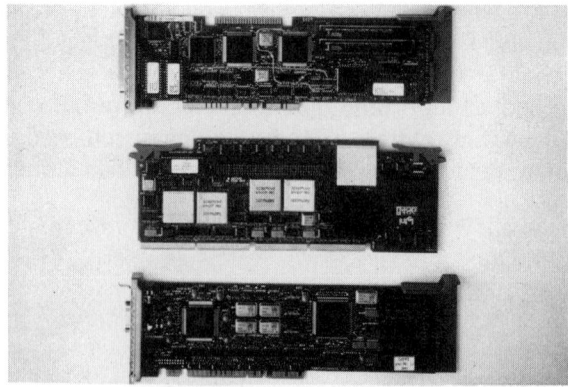

Figure 3-3. Micro Channel adapter. (Courtesy of International Business Machines Corporation.)

Second, they specified that each adapter (see Figure 3-3) that was plugged into the Micro Channel bus would need its own unique identifier assigned by IBM. The ID was stored in EEPROMs located on each adapter card. In addition, the EEPROMs would hold card configuration data, such as the memory-mapped address, interrupt level, and port address of the adapter. These special registers were called *Programmable Option Select* registers, or *POS* registers. These registers, addressable only in a special mode, eliminated the need for configuration jumpers required for AT bus adapters. The user would load a special configuration program, which would set the adapter configuration and program the EEPROMs and each adapter.

Third, they included 64 bytes of *Non-volatile Random Access Memory*, or *NVRAM*, which would hold the current configuration information for each slot. The contents of the NVRAM is retained by a low-voltage battery. When the computer was powered on, a *Read Only Memory*, or *ROM*, resident program would compare, slot by slot, the configuration of each adapter to the current configuration stored in NVRAM. If it found a difference, it would stop and force the user to run the setup program to reconfigure the system. This *Power On Self Test* or *POST*, also checks the size of memory and compares it to the amount configured in NVRAM.

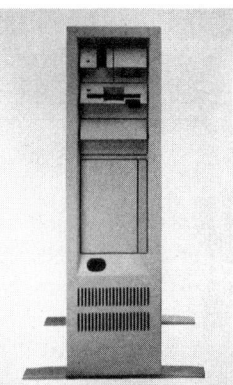

Figure 3-4. IBM PS/2 Model 80. (Courtesy of International Business Machines Corporation.)

Enhanced Industry Standard Architecture (EISA)

The third major innovation in bus technology was the introduction of the *Enhanced Industry Standard Architecture* bus, or *EISA* bus. The EISA bus was introduced in September of 1988 in response to IBM's introduction of the Micro Channel bus. Some of the motivation for the EISA bus was the same as for the Micro Channel. EISA was designed for high throughput and bus mastering, and is capable of 33MB per second throughput. The developers of the EISA bus maintained compatibility with existing ISA bus adapters by designing a connector that would accept either type of adapter card. It should be noted, however, that using an ISA bus adapter in an EISA bus system provides no increased performance.

The EISA bus, like the Micro Channel bus, supports multiple bus masters, but only six compared to Micro Channel's 15. This is still better than the ISA bus, which supports only one bus master. Throughput of the ISA bus machine is limited by the processor speed, as more work has to be done by the CPU. In a multiple bus master architecture like EISA or Micro Channel, the adapter card relieves the CPU of the responsibility of handling the high-speed data transfers, and thus is more efficient.

Bus Wars

Many benchmarks have been performed pitting the three buses against each other. With a few exceptions, the casual user will not notice much difference between them. However, increasing demands for higher transfer rates and increased CPU performance will soon make the traditional AT bus obsolete. The AT bus is handicapped by its 24-bit address bus and 16-bit data bus, which limits performance by permitting the system to transfer data only half as fast as EISA and Micro Channel bus systems. It is also limited by its interrupt support and bus-mastering capabilities. Without another alternative, this leaves EISA and Micro Channel as the natural successors to the ISA bus. IBM is gearing up for the challenge, and has recently specified a new mode of Micro Channel operation that will run on all IBM Micro Channel machines. The new specification, called Micro Channel II, allows for transfer rates of 40, 80, and 160MB per second, leaving the EISA machines in the dust. IBM is also beginning to price their Micro Channel systems at equal to or less than their ISA equivalents in an attempt to make the Micro Channel bus more popular. The EISA bus, however, maintains compatibility with the wide variety of inexpensive ISA adapters, and is not likely to be upstaged in the near future by the Micro Channel bus.

EISA promises to remain popular because of the large investment in ISA bus adapters and the reluctance of many users to embrace the Micro Channel bus.

Real Mode

The Intel processors are capable of operating in one of two modes. These are called real mode and protect mode. The most popular computer operating system, DOS, runs in real mode. In real mode, the processor is capable of addressing up to one megabyte of physical memory. This is due to the addressing structure, which allows for a 20-bit address in the form of a segment and offset (see Figure 3-5).

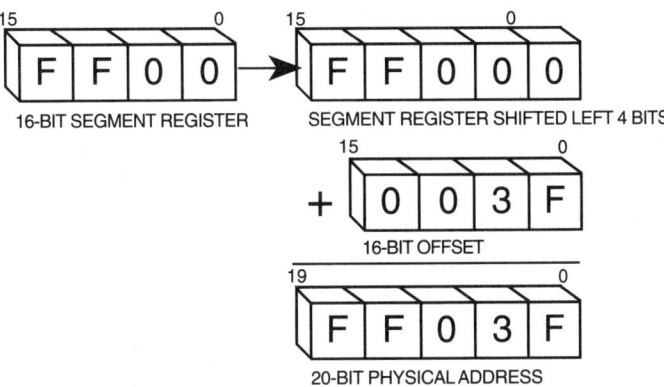

Figure 3-5. Real mode address calculation.

Real mode allows a program to access any location within the one megabyte address space. There are no protection mechanisms to prevent programs from accidentally (or purposely) writing into another program's memory area. There is also no protection from a program writing directly to a device, say the disk, and causing data loss or corruption. DOS applications that fail generally hang the system and call for a <ctrl-alt-del> reboot, or in some cases, a power-off and a power-on reboot (*POR*). The real mode environment is also ripe for viruses or other types of sabotage programs to run freely. Since no protection mechanisms are in place, these types of "Trojan horses" are free to infect programs and data with ease.

Protect Mode

The *protect mode* of the Intel 80286 processor permits direct addressing of memory up to 16MB, while the Intel 80386 and 80486 processors support the direct addressing of up to four gigabytes (4,000,000,000 bytes). The 80286 processor uses a 16-bit selector and 16-bit offset to address memory (see Figure 3-6). A selector is an index into a table that holds the actual address of the memory location. The offset portion is the same as the offset in real mode addressing. This mode of addressing is commonly referred to as the 16:16 addressing. Under OS/2 2.1, the 80386 and 80486 processors address memory using a selector:offset, but the value of the selector is always 0, and the offset is always 32 bits long (see Figure 3-7). This mode of addressing is referred to as the 0:32 or flat addressing. The protect mode provides hardware memory protection, prohibiting a program from accessing memory owned by another program. While a defective program in real mode can bring down the entire system (a problem frequently encountered by systems running DOS). A protect mode program that fails in a multitasking operating system merely reports the error and is terminated. Other programs running at the time continue to run uninterrupted.

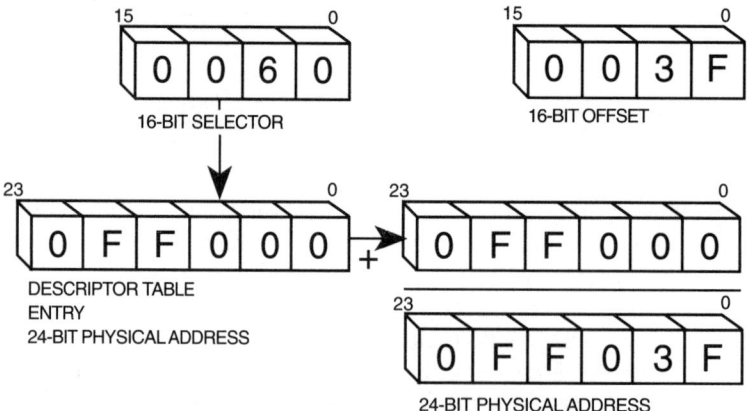

Figure 3-6. 80286 protect mode addressing.

To accomplish this memory protection, the processor keeps a list of memory belonging to a program in the program's *Local Descriptor Table*, or *LDT*. When a program attempts to access a memory address, the processor hardware verifies that the address of the memory is within the memory bounds defined by the program's LDT. If it is not, the processor generates an exception and the program is terminated.

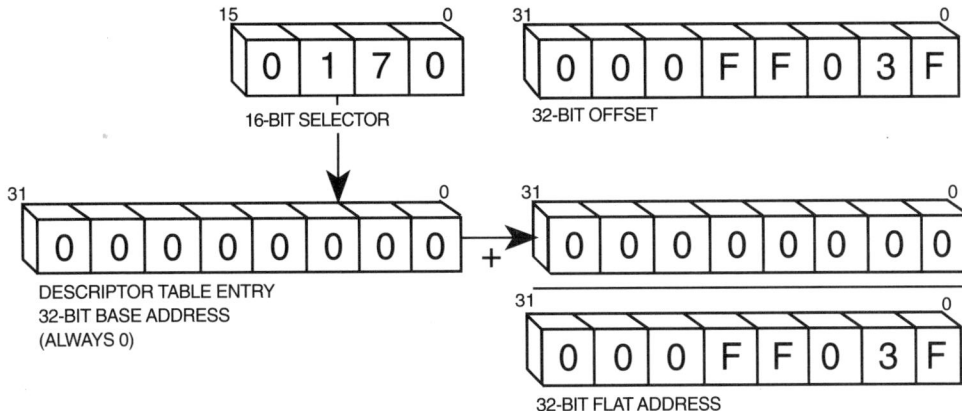

Figure 3-7. 80386-486 flat mode addressing.

The processor also keeps a second list of memory called the *Global Descriptor Table*, or *GDT*. The GDT usually contains a list of the memory owned by the operating system, and is only accessible by the operating system and device drivers. Application programs have no direct access to the GDT except through a device driver.

OS/2 1.x uses the protect mode of the Intel processor to run native OS/2 programs, and provides a single DOS "compatibility box" for running DOS applications. If a DOS session is selected while the system is running an OS/2 application, the processor stops running in protect mode and switches to the real mode to accommodate the DOS application. A poorly programmed DOS application can bring down the entire system.

OS/2 2.1 runs DOS programs in the protect mode, using the virtual 8086 mode of the 80386 and 80486 processors. This special mode allows each DOS application to run in its own protected one megabyte of memory space, without being aware of any other applications running on the system. Each virtual DOS partition, or *VDM*, thinks that it's the only application running. Errant DOS programs are free to destroy their own one megabyte environment, but cannot crash the rest of the system. If a DOS application fails in a VDM, a new copy of DOS can be booted into the VDM and restarted. For a more complete description of the Intel processors and their architecture, please refer to Appendix B for a list of recommended reading.

Using Addresses and Pointers

Writing an OS/2 2.1 device driver requires a thorough understanding of addresses, pointers, and the OS/2 2.1 memory management DevHlp routines. Since OS/2 2.1 is a hybrid operating system composed of 16-bit and 32-bit code, many of your device driver functions will involve pointer conversion and manipulation. Specifically, pointers might have to be converted from 16-bit to 32-bit, and from 32-bit back to 16-bit. Addresses might be expressed as virtual, physical or linear address. Several DevHlp functions require flat pointers to items in the driver's data segment, which is normally a 16:16 pointer. If you don't have a good understanding of 16-bit and 32-bit addresses or pointers, please go back and reread the previous sections. Refer to Chapter 15 for more information.

The Ring Architecture

In the protect mode, the processor operates in a Ring architecture. The ring architecture protects the operating system by allowing minimum access to the system and hardware.

Normal application programs run at Ring 3, which is the least trusted ring (see Figure 3-8). Programs that run in Ring 3 have no direct access to the operating system or hardware, and must adhere to very strict guidelines for accessing OS/2 or its supported devices.

Ring 2 is reserved for Input/Output Privilege Level (IOPL) programs (see Chapter 10) and 16-bit Dynamic Link Libraries, or DLLs. With OS/2 2.1, 32-bit DLLs run in Ring 3. Refer to Chapter 4 for a more detailed discussion of DLLs.

Ring 1 is currently reserved.

Ring 0 is the most trusted level of the processor, and is where physical and virtual device drivers run. Device drivers need, and are granted, full access to the processor and system hardware as well as the interrupt system and OS/2 internals.

Most application programs will run in Ring 3. Occasionally, for performance reasons, an application may need to write directly to adapter hardware and will do so through an IOPL routine at Ring 2, but will quickly return to Ring 3 to continue running. An example of such a program is the CodeView debugger. As an additional protection method, OS/2 can refuse input and output by a Ring 2 program if the user modifies the CONFIG.SYS file to contain the line IOPL=NO. Programs attempting to perform Ring 2 I/O will generate a General Protection, or GP fault if IOPL=NO appears in the CONFIG.SYS file. Users may also permit only selected programs to perform IOPL by entering the program names in CONFIG.SYS. See Chapter 10 for a discussion of IOPL.

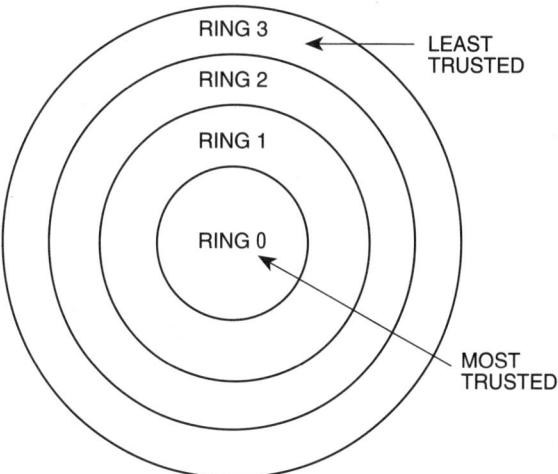

Figure 3-8. The 80X86 ring architecture.

CHAPTER 4

An Overview of the OS/2 Operating System

OS/2, introduced in late 1987, was billed as the successor to DOS. In fact, it was going to be called DOS before IBM got into the act. Over 500 programmers at IBM and Microsoft worked night and day to get OS/2 out the door on schedule. Both IBM and Microsoft trumpeted OS/2 as the replacement for DOS, and Bill Gates himself predicted that OS/2 would replace DOS on the desktop by 1989. This, of course, never happened. The reasons why OS/2 never caught on can be debated forever, but probably can be summarized in a few key statements.

First, when IBM announced OS/2, there were only a handful of applications ready to run on it. The few that were ready were just warmed-over DOS versions, which were recompiled and relinked under OS/2. They also ran considerably slower than their DOS counterparts.

Second, the graphical user interface for OS/2, called Presentation Manager, was missing. As a result, most application programs were written with dull, character-based user interfaces.

Third, the DOS compatibility box, or penalty box as it was sometimes referred to as, crashed frequently when DOS applications were run under it. It simply wasn't compatible with DOS. Some DOS applications would run, but most wouldn't. This was largely a result of the small amount of memory available to a DOS application, which was only approximately 500MB. Users were reluctant to replace DOS with an operating system that wouldn't run all of their favorite DOS applications.

Fourth, IBM made a big mistake by attempting to tie the OS/2 name to their recently introduced family of PS/2 computers. Users believed that OS/2 would run only on PS/2 machines. IBM also bungled the marketing of OS/2. IBM authorized dealers didn't know what OS/2 was, how to sell it or how to order it. No advertisements appeared for OS/2, and it wasn't actively shown at trade shows or in technical publications. OS/2 was virtually ignored until sometime in 1990, just following the introduction and huge success of Microsoft Windows 3.0.

Lastly, the timing was bad. OS/2 needed four megabytes or more of memory, and memory was selling for approximately $400 per megabyte. The high memory prices were due in part to high tariffs placed on the Japanese for dumping memory chips and to increased demand. Most systems had one megabyte of memory or less, so upgrading was very expensive. OS/2 was not cheap, about $350 for the Standard Edition, which, combined with the cost of extra memory, represented a substantial upgrade cost.

Spurred on by the huge success of Windows 3.0, Microsoft decided that it would abandon OS/2 and concentrate on the Windows platform, which is based on DOS. IBM, left without a multitasking solution for its PC-to-mainframe connection, had been counting on OS/2 to replace DOS. IBM finally woke up and realized that without some major changes in the way OS/2 was designed and marketed, that OS/2 would die an untimely death. The result of IBM's rude awakening was the introduction of OS/2 2.1 early in 1992.

Roots

OS/2 was originally called MS-DOS version 4.0. MS-DOS 4.0 was designed for preemptive multitasking, but was still crippled by the 640KB memory space restriction of real mode operation. A new product, called MS-DOS 5.0 was conceived, and IBM and Microsoft signed a Joint Development Agreement to develop it. MS-DOS 5.0 was later renamed OS/2. OS/2 was designed to break the 640KB memory barrier by utilizing the protect mode of the 80286 processor. The protect mode provided direct addressing of up to 16 megabytes of memory and a protected environment where badly written programs could not affect the integrity of other programs or the operating system.

When Gordon Letwin, Ed Iaccobuci, and the developers at IBM and Microsoft first designed OS/2 1.0, they had several goals in mind. First, OS/2 had to provide a graphical device interface that was hardware independent. The concept was that each device would be supplied with a device driver containing the specific characteristics of the device. Graphics applications could be written without regard to the type of graphics input or output device. This concept is referred to as *virtualization*. However, virtualization comes at a cost. When an application sends a request to the OS/2 kernel for access to a device, the kernel has to build a request and send it to the device driver. The device driver has to break it down, perform the operation, format the data, and transfer it back to the application.

Second, OS/2 had to allow direct hardware access to some peripherals for performance reasons. Peripherals such as video adapters require high-speed access to devices, and the normal device driver mechanism was just not fast enough. To solve this problem, OS/2 allows applications or Dynamic Link Libraries (DLLs) to perform direct I/O to adapter hardware. The video device driver, which resides in a Dynamic Link Library (DLL), can access the device directly without calling a device driver to perform the I/O. Dynamic Linking also allows programs to be linked with undefined external references, which are resolved at run time by the OS/2 system loader. The unresolved entry points exist in DLLs on the OS/2 system disk, and are loaded into memory and linked with the executable program at run time. The use of DLLs allows system services that exist in the DLLs to be modified by changing a DLL and not the entire system. A display adapter, for example, could be added simply by a adding a new DLL. Additional system functions and processes can be implemented as DLLs.

Third, OS/2 had to provide an efficient, preemptive multitasking kernel. The kernel had to run several programs at once, yet provide an environment where critical programs could get access to the CPU when necessary. OS/2 uses a priority-based preemptive scheduler. The preemptive nature of the OS/2 scheduler allows it to "take away" the CPU from a currently running application and assign it to another application. If two programs of equal priority are competing for the CPU, the scheduler will run each program in turn for a short period of time, called a time slice. This ensures that every program will have access to the CPU, and that no one program can monopolize the CPU.

Fourth, OS/2 had to provide a robust, protected environment. OS/2 uses the protect mode of the 80286 and above processors, which has a built-in memory protection scheme. Applications that attempt to read or to write from memory that is not in their specific address space are terminated without compromising the operating system integrity. OS/2 had to run applications that were larger than the physical installed memory. OS/2 accomplishes this with swapping. If a program asks for more memory than exists, a special fault is generated, which causes the existing contents of memory to be swapped out to a disk file, thereby freeing up the required memory. When the program accesses a function that has been swapped out to disk, a special fault is generated to cause the required functions to be swapped back into physical memory. Swapping allows large programs to be run with less memory than the application requires, but swapping can cause a considerable degradation in speed.

Fifth, OS/2 had to run on the 80286 processor. At the time that OS/2 was designed, the 80286 was the only CPU that could run a multitasking protect mode operating system. The 80386 machines were not available, so IBM and Microsoft committed to a version of OS/2 which would run on the 80286 platform. This was purely a marketing decision, based on the number of 80286 machines installed at the time. The implementation of OS/2 on the 80286 proved to be clumsy and slow. The operating system had to be designed for the 16-bit architecture of the 80286, but really required a 32-bit architecture to perform well. The 80286 could operate in the protect mode and real mode, but could not switch back and forth gracefully. It could switch from the real mode to the protect mode easily, but not back. The processor was designed to run in only one mode, not both. Because OS/2 had to support OS/2 applications and DOS applications all at one time, a way had to be found to change the processor mode on the fly. Gordon Letwin came up with the patented idea of how to do this with what has been referred to as "turning the car off and on at 60 MPH."

Lastly, OS/2 had to run existing "well-behaved" DOS applications. Well-behaved DOS programs were those programs that did not directly access the hardware or use shortcuts to improve performance. Unfortunately, most DOS programs used some type of shortcut to improve performance and make up for the relatively slow 8088 processor they were originally written for.

Processes and Threads

OS/2 introduced the notion of *threads*. A thread is defined as an instance of execution or path of execution through a piece of code. OS/2's multitasking is thread-based. A program always has at least one thread, called the main thread, and may have many more threads, each executing at the same time (see Figure 4-1). The additional threads are created by the main thread, and act as smaller "children" of the main thread. Threads inherit the environment of their creator, usually a *process*, and can be started or suspended by the main thread. A thread can only be destroyed by committing suicide.

To aid in multitasking, OS/2 offers four classes of priorities (see Table 4-1). They are *Real-Time-Critical, Normal, Fixed-High,* and *Idle-Time*. Real-Time-Critical is the highest priority, while Idle-Time is the lowest. Within each priority class, there are 32 separate and distinct priorities, numbered from 0 to 31. Most applications will run in the Normal mode, while time critical applications (such as a cardiac monitor) might run in the Real-Time-Critical class. The Fixed-High mode operates between Real-Time-Critical and Normal modes, and offers real time response but at priorities that can be dynamically modified by OS/2. The Idle-Time priority is reserved for slower background programs such as spoolers.

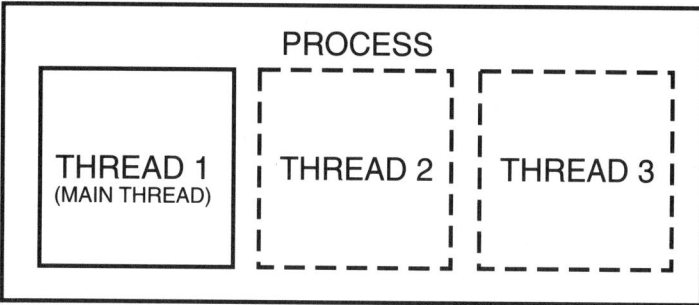

Figure 4-1. Process and threads.

One of OS/2's major advantages is its time-sliced, priority-based preemptive scheduler. This feature allows a critical or higher priority thread to preempt a currently running thread. This preemptive feature is what sets OS/2 apart from other multitasking systems such as UNIX. OS/2 runs the highest priority thread until it completes or gives up the CPU by blocking on an I/O request or system service. If a thread is currently executing and a higher priority thread needs to run, the lower priority thread will be preempted and the higher priority thread allowed to run. When the higher priority thread finishes or blocks waiting on a system service, the lower priority thread will get a chance to run again. If two threads with the same priority are competing for the CPU, each thread will alternate for one time slice worth of time.

Table 4-1. OS/2 Priority Structure

Priority	Use	Modified by OS/2
Idle	Spoolers, batch processors	Yes
Regular	Normal applications	Yes
Fixed-High (Foreground Server)	Special applications	Yes
Real-Time-Critical	Real time applications	No

Most UNIX systems do not use threads, so priorities in a UNIX system are *per process-based*, rather than *thread-based*. Since most UNIX kernels are not preemptive, a UNIX application will run until it blocks on I/O or system resource, or exhausts its time slice. Currently running processes cannot be preempted, thus a critical program needing CPU time has to wait until the CPU is free. The UNIX scheduler is a *round-robin* scheduler, that is, the system allocates equal time to every process in a round-robin fashion. If three processes are running, process A gets a time slice, process B gets a time slice, then process C gets a time slice, and then the whole operation begins again with process A.

OS/2 1.0 - OS/2 Arrives

OS/2 1.0 was introduced in the fourth quarter of 1987. The first release did not contain a graphical user interface, but instead contained two side-by-side list boxes with names of programs to execute. The *Application Programming Interface*, or *API*, was incomplete and unstable. Device support was virtually nonexistent, and OS/2 1.0 was only guaranteed to run on the IBM PC AT and IBM PS/2 line of computers. Many DOS applications did not run in the DOS compatibility box, and only a few thousand copies of OS/2 1.0 were sold.

OS/2 1.1 - Presentation Manager Arrives

The next major release of OS/2 contained the graphical user interface, dubbed *Presentation Manager*. OS/2 was beginning to take shape. It contained a better DOS compatibility box, which caused fewer DOS programs to crash, and had a consistent, more bug-free set of API routines. Documentation, in the form of manuals and books, was beginning to appear, and a few more DOS applications were recompiled and relinked under OS/2. None of these programs used the Presentation Manager, as they were not redesigned for OS/2. As a result, the applications were dull, character-based programs that didn't take advantage of any of OS/2's multitasking abilities or Presentation Manager. The lack of applications, together with the cost of a hardware upgrade, kept most users away from OS/2.

OS/2 1.2 - A Better File System

OS/2 had been using the file system known as *FAT*, named after the DOS File Allocation Table. The FAT was where DOS (and OS/2) kept a running "picture" of the hard disk, including the utilization and amount of free space. The DOS FAT file system was limited by design to filenames with a maximum length of 11 characters, and was inefficient in storing and retrieving files. The *High Performance File System*, or *HPFS*, was introduced in OS/2 1.2 to provide more efficient handling of large files and volumes, and to remove the 11-character filename restriction. HPFS can handle filenames with up to 254 characters, files as large as two gigabytes, and provides a very fast searching algorithm for storing and locating files. Unlike the FAT file system, HPFS is an installable file system, and a special device driver must be loaded before using it.

The DOS compatibility box was improved, but OS/2 still could not run many DOS applications. This was due, in part, to the fact that the compatibility box did not offer the full amount of memory usually available to DOS applications. The size of the DOS compatibility box memory was reduced when device drivers were loaded, and often would only offer 500K bytes or less for running DOS programs. OS/2 was used primarily by companies that had real-time multitasking requirements for their systems, but not for running DOS applications. For DOS applications which would not run in the OS/2 1.2 compatibility box, OS/2 had a built-in dual-boot facility which allowed the user to selectively boot up DOS or OS/2. While OS/2 was running, however, the compatibility box was virtually useless.

Printers did not work correctly. OS/2 did not work with the most popular laser printers, such as the Hewlett Packard Laserjets. The future of OS/2 was bleak.

When Microsoft announced that they would be abandoning OS/2 in favor of Windows 3.0, OS/2 faced an uncertain future. Microsoft had been stating that OS/2 was the PC operating system platform of the future, and now had reversed that statement. Many large companies had previously begun conversion of their flagship programs, such as Lotus 1-2-3, to run under OS/2, and were taken by surprise by Microsoft's change in direction. IBM was forced to take over the development of OS/2, and Microsoft could free up its programming resources to concentrate on Windows software. Microsoft and IBM did agree to cross-license each other's products, and together they agreed that IBM would assume complete responsibility for OS/2.

OS/2 1.3 – IBM's First Solo Effort

Figure 4-2. OS/2 1.3EE. (Courtesy of International Business Machines Corporation.)

Although OS/2 1.0, 1.1, and 1.2 were developed jointly by IBM and Microsoft, OS/2 Version 1.3 (dubbed OS/2 Lite) was the first version of OS/2 to be done entirely by IBM (see Figure 4-2). It took IBM a while to get up to speed with OS/2, but when OS/2 1.3 was released, many features that had never worked correctly had been fixed. Version 1.3 had better networking, communications, and graphics support and could finally print correctly. The OS/2 kernel was slimmed down and ran considerably faster than its predecessors. IBM produced detailed documentation and began to actively support developers through the IBM Developer's Assistance Program. However, OS/2 was used primarily by IBM installations for their PC-to-mainframe connection, and by OEMs for specialized applications.

IBM was still not actively marketing OS/2. Information was difficult to come by, and it was almost impossible to buy OS/2. Most IBM dealers didn't even know what OS/2 was, or how to order it. IBM failed to inform their resellers how to demonstrate and sell OS/2. OS/2 was going nowhere fast.

OS/2 2.0- What OS/2 Was Really Meant to Be

Before deciding to scrap its OS/2 development, Microsoft had been working on a new version of OS/2, called OS/2 2.0. Microsoft first displayed early running versions of OS/2 2.0 in the middle of 1990, and had released the infamous *System Developer's Kit*, or *SDK*, with a whopping $2600 price tag. The OS/2 2.0 SDK included early releases of the OS/2 kernel, 32-bit compiler, assembler, and linker. Many developers, however, balked at the price. The software contained several serious bugs, and for most developers, proved to be unusable.

IBM realized that, unless it made a radical change in the way OS/2 was designed and marketed, OS/2 would eventually become a proprietary internal operating system used only by IBM. IBM formed a team to assume the development responsibilities of OS/2 2.0. They mounted an enormous effort, and the commercial release of OS/2 2.0 was the culmination of that effort.

OS/2 2.1 represents a new direction for personal computer operating environments. Instead of having to deal with the 16-bit architecture of the 80286 processors, OS/2 2.1 was developed around the 32-bit architecture of the 80386 microprocessor. OS/2 2.1 will not run on an 80286 processor-based machine. This decision comes at a time when the 16-bit 80286 machines are obsolete, and the standard choice for personal computers is an 80486 machine with 8MB of RAM as a minimum configuration. With memory prices at $35 per megabyte of RAM, memory configurations of 8 and 16MB are becoming commonplace. Hard disk storage has decreased significantly in price, and most systems are sold with 100MB or more of disk storage as minimum.

OS/2 2.1 allows DOS programs to run in their own one megabyte of memory space without knowledge of other programs in the system. Even the most ill-behaved DOS applications, such as games, run flawlessly in their own protected area. In addition, users can boot any version of DOS they choose into a DOS session. The number of DOS sessions that can be started is unlimited in OS/2 2.1. DOS programs have access to 48MB of extended memory. OS/2 2.1 also supports DOS programs designed to use the *DOS Protect Mode Interface*, or *DPMI* Version 0.9. OS/2 2.1 runs Windows 3.0 and 3.1 applications in the real or standard mode. OS/2 2.1 allows *Dynamic Data Exchange*, or *DDE*, between DOS/Windows and OS/2 applications, providing up to 512MB of DPMI memory per DOS session.

OS/2 2.1 uses a desktop metaphor called the *Workplace Shell* for its user interface. The Workplace Shell represents an actual desktop using icons representing the actual items the user might find on his or her desk. It contains such items as a file folder, printer, network connection, and other icons that reflect the current configuration of the system. Printing a document, for example, is as simple as opening a folder, clicking on the document and dragging it over to the printer icon.

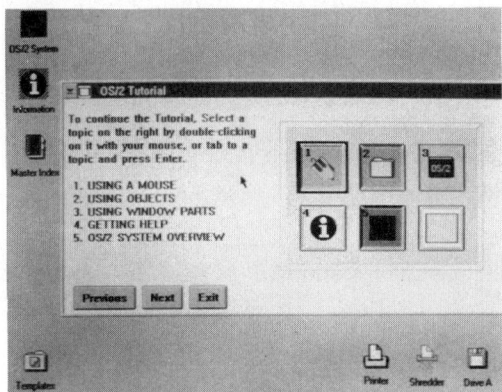

Figure 4-3. OS/2 2.1 tutorial. (Courtesy of International Business Machines Corporation.)

OS/2 2.1 represents a common platform for supporting many different types of applications. It runs DOS applications, Windows 3.0 and 3.1 applications and, of course, native OS/2 applications, all seamlessly. There is no longer a need to dual-boot DOS or to load three different operating environments; OS/2 2.1 runs them all.

The OS/2 Application Programming Interface

OS/2 2.1 offers a rich set of *Application Program Interfaces* (*APIs*) to allow programs to access system services. The OS/2 APIs are classified into eight major categories. They are:

1. **File System**
   File Systems (FAT, Super FAT, HPFS)
   Network Access (LAN Server, NetBIOS)
   Permissions
   DASD Media Management

2. **Graphics Interface**
   Graphics Programming Interface
   Video Input and Output

3. **Inter Process Communications**
   Shared Memory
   Semaphores
   Named Pipes
   Queues
   Dynamic Data Exchange (DDE)

4. **System Services**
   Device Monitors
   Timer Services

5. **Process Management**
   Threads
   Processes
   Child Processes
   Scheduler/Priorities

6. **Memory Management**

7. **Signals**

8. **Dynamic Linking**

CHAPTER 5

The Anatomy Of An OS/2 Device Driver

OS/2 device drivers, like other multitasking device drivers, shield the application code that performs I/O from device-specific hardware requirements. The application program need not concern itself with the physical constraints of a particular I/O device, such as timing or I/O port addressing, as these are handled entirely by the device driver. If an I/O card address is moved or a different interrupt selected, the device driver can be recompiled (notice I did not say reassembled) without modifying or recompiling the application code.

It should be noted that OS/2 device drivers can be configured during boot-up operation by placing adapter-specific parameters in the *DEVICE=* entry in CONFIG.SYS. The driver can retrieve the parameters and configure itself during the INIT section.

Conceptually, OS/2 device drivers are similar to device drivers in other multitasking systems, but they have the added responsibility of handling processor-specific anomalies such as the segmented architecture and operating modes of the Intel processors.

Application-to-Driver Interface

OS/2 device drivers are called by the kernel on behalf of the application needing I/O service. The application program makes an I/O request call to the kernel, specifying the type of operation needed. The kernel verifies the request, translates the request into a valid device driver *Request Packet* and calls the device driver for service. The device driver handles all of the hardware details, such as register setup, interrupt handling, and error checking. When the request is complete, the device driver massages the data into a format recognizable by the application. It sends the data or status to the application and notifies the kernel that the request is complete. If the request cannot be handled immediately, the device driver may either block the requesting thread or return a 'request not done' to the kernel. Either method causes the device driver to relinquish the CPU, allowing other threads to run. If an error is detected, the device driver returns this information to the kernel with a 'request complete' status. The OS/2 device driver may also "queue up" requests to be handled later in a work queue. The OS/2 Device Helper (DevHlp) library contains several DevHlps for manipulating the device driver's work queue.

DOS Device Drivers and OS/2 Device Drivers

DOS device drivers have no direct OS/2 counterpart. DOS device drivers are simple, single-task, polling device drivers. Even interrupt device drivers under DOS poll until interrupt processing is complete. DOS device drivers support only one request at a time, and simultaneous multiple requests from DOS will cause the system to crash.

While the DOS device driver is a single-threaded polled routine, the OS/2 device driver must handle overlapping requests from different processes and threads. Because of this, the OS/2 device driver must be reentrant. The OS/2 device driver must also handle interrupts from the device and optionally from a timer handler. It must handle these operations in an efficient manner, allowing other threads to gain access to the CPU. Most importantly, it must do all of these reliably. The OS/2 device driver, because it operates at Ring 0, is the only program that has direct access to critical system functions, such as the interrupt system and system timer. The device driver, therefore, must be absolutely bug-free, as any error in the device driver will cause a fatal system crash.

OS/2 2.1 device drivers no longer have to deal with the real-protect mode switching of OS/2 1.x, as all programs run in protect mode. OS/2 device drivers must have the capability to deinstall when requested, releasing any memory used by the device driver to the OS/2 kernel. OS/2 device drivers may also support device monitors, programs that wish to monitor data as it is passed to and from the device driver. OS/2 offers a wide range of device driver services to provide this functionality.

Designing an OS/2 Device Driver

Designing an OS/2 device driver requires a thorough understanding of the role of a device driver, as well as a solid working knowledge of the OS/2 operating system and design philosophy. Debugging OS/2 device drivers can be difficult, even with the proper tools. The OS/2 device driver operates at Ring 0 with full access to the system hardware. However, it has almost no access to OS/2 support services, except for a handful of DevHlp routines. Many device driver failures occur in a real time context, such as in the midst of interrupt handling. It may be difficult or impossible to find a device driver problem using normal debugging techniques. In such cases, it is necessary to visualize the operation of the device driver and OS/2 at the time of the error to help locate the problem.

Tools Necessary For Driver Development

One of the most important tools for device driver development is the *device driver debugger*. Generally, the best choice is the OS/2 2.1 *kernel debugger* or *KDB*. KDB uses a standard ASCII terminal attached to one of the serial COM ports via a null-modem cable. When OS/2 is started, KDB looks for a COM port to perform its I/O to the debugging terminal. For systems with only one COM port, KDB will use COM1. For systems with two COM ports, KDB will use COM2.

The KDB is not simply a debugger, but is a replacement kernel that replaces the OS/2 standard system kernel called OS2KRNL. KDB has knowledge of internal OS/2 data structures and provides a powerful command set for debugging OS/2 device drivers. Installing the debugging kernel is easy. The attributes of the hidden file OS2KRNL are changed to non-hidden and non-system, and the file is copied to OS2KRNL.OLD. The debug kernel is then copied to OS2KRNL, and OS/2 is rebooted. KDB will issue a sign-on message to the debugging terminal indicating that it is active. KDB can be entered by typing <cntl-c> on the debug terminal, or if KDB encounters an INT 3 instruction. These procedures are described in more detail in Chapter 13. The kernel debugger comes with the IBM OS/2 2.1 Toolkit, and is installed easily with the installation program supplied with the Toolkit.

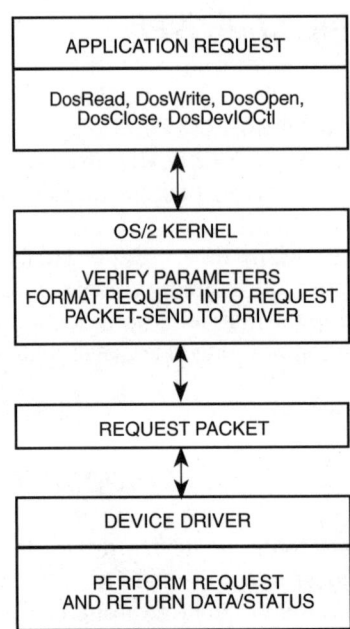

Figure 5-1. Application-to-device driver interface.

The Basics of Driver Design

The device driver receives two basic types of requests: requests that can be completed immediately and those that cannot (see Figure 5-1). It receives these requests via a standard data structure called a *Request Packet* (see Figure 5-2).

Requests that can be completed immediately are handled as they come in, and sent back to the requestor. Requests that cannot be handled immediately (such as disk seeks) are queued up for later dispatch by the device driver. The device driver manipulates Request Packets using the DevHlp routines. To minimize head movement, disk device drivers usually sort pending requests for disk seeks in sector order.

The OS/2 device driver plays an additional role in system performance and operation. When a device driver is called to perform a request that cannot be completed immediately, the device driver *Blocks* the requesting thread. This relinquishes the CPU and allows other threads to run. When the request is complete, usually as the result of an interrupt or error occurring, the thread is immediately *UnBlocked* and *Run*. The device driver then queries the request queue for any pending requests that may have come in while the thread was blocked. It is important to note that when an application calls a device driver, the application program's LDT is directly accessible by the device driver.

Request Packets

The first entry in the *Request Packet Header* (see Figure 5-2) is the Request Packet length, filled in by the kernel. The second parameter is the unit code. Applicable for block devices only, this field should be set by the device driver writer to zero for the first unit, one for the second, etc. The third field is the command code. The command code is filled in by the kernel. This is the code used by the switch routine in the Strategy section to decode the type of request from the kernel. The next field is the status word returned to the kernel. This field will contain the result of the device driver operation, along with the 'DONE' bit to notify the kernel that the request is complete (this is not always the case; the device driver may return without the 'done' bit set). To make things easier, a C language union should be used to access specific types of requests. The Request Packet structures are placed in an include file, which is included by the device driver mainline. Refer to the Standard OS/2 Device Driver Include File in Appendix C.

```
typedef struct ReqPacket {
   UCHAR    RPlength;             // Request Packet length
   UCHAR    RPunit;               // unit code for block DD only
   UCHAR    RPcommand;            // command code
   USHORT   RPstatus;             // status word
   UCHAR    RPreserved[4];        // reserved bytes
   ULONG    RPqlink;              // queue linkage
   UCHAR    avail[19];            // command specific data
} REQPACKET;
```

Figure 5-2. Request Packet Header.

OS/2 Device Driver Architecture

OS/2 device drivers come in two flavors, *block* and *character*. Block device drivers are used for mass storage devices such as disk and tape. Character device drivers are used for devices that handle data one character at a time, such as a modem. OS/2 device drivers are capable of supporting multiple devices, such as a serial communications adapter with four channels or a disk device driver which supports multiple drives.

OS/2 device drivers receive requests from the OS/2 kernel on behalf of an application program thread. When the device driver is originally opened with a DosOpen API call, the kernel returns a handle to the thread that requested access to the device driver. This handle is used for subsequent access to the device driver.

When an application makes a call to a device driver, the kernel intercepts the call and formats the device driver request into a standard Request Packet. The Request Packet contains data and pointers for use by the device driver to complete the request. In the case of a DosRead or DosWrite, for example, the Request Packet contains the verified and locked physical address of the caller's buffer. In the case of an IOCtl, the Request Packet contains the virtual address of a Data and Parameter Buffer. Depending on the type of request, the data in the Request Packet will change, but the Request Packet header length and format remain fixed. The kernel sends the Request Packet to the driver by passing it a 16:16 pointer to the Request Packet.

Device drivers are loaded by the OS/2 loader at boot time, and the kernel keeps a linked list of the installed device drivers by name, using the link pointer in the Device Header. Before a device driver is used, it must be "DosOpen"ed from the application. The DosOpen specifies an ASCII-Z string with the device name as a parameter, which is the eight character ASCII name located in the Device Header (see Figure 5-3). The kernel compares this name with its list of installed device drivers, and if it finds a match, it calls the OPEN section of the device driver Strategy routine to open the device. If the open was successful, the kernel returns to the application a handle to use for future device driver access. The device handles are usually assigned sequentially, starting with 3 (0, 1, and 2 are claimed by OS/2). However, the handle value should never be assumed.

```
typedef struct DeviceHdr {
   struct DeviceHdr far *DHnext;
                                  // ptr to next header, or FFFF
   USHORT DHattribute;            // device attribute word
   OFF    DHstrategy;             // offset of strategy routine
   OFF    DHidc;                  // offset of IDC routine
   UCHAR  DHname[8];              // dev name (char) or #units (blk)
   char   reserved[8];
   } DEVICEHDR;


DEVICEHDR devhdr = {
        (void far *) 0xFFFFFFFF,
        (DAW_CHR | DAW_OPN | DAW_LEVEL1),   // link
                                            // attribute
        (OFF) STRAT,                        // &strategy
        (OFF) 0,                            // &IDCroutine
        "DEVICE1 ",                         // device name
        };
```

Figure 5-3. OS/2 device driver header.

Device Driver Modes

OS/2 2.1 device drivers operate in three different modes. The first, *INIT mode*, is a special mode entered at system boot time and executed at Ring 3. When the OS/2 system loader encounters a "DEVICE=" statement in the CONFIG.SYS file on boot-up, it loads the device driver .SYS file and calls the INIT function of the device driver. What makes this mode special is that the boot procedure is running in Ring 3 which normally has no I/O privileges, yet OS/2 allows Ring 0-type operations. The device driver is free to do port I/O and even turn interrupts off, but must ensure they are back on before exiting the INIT routine. The INIT routine can be used to initialize a *Universal Asynchronous Receiver Transmitter (UART)* or anything else necessary to ready a device.

Ring 3 operation during INIT is necessary to protect the integrity of code that has already been loaded up to that point, and to make sure that the device driver itself does not corrupt the operating system during initialization. Ring 3 operation also allows the device driver initialization routine to call a limited number of system API routines to aid in the initialization process. For example, a device driver might use the API routines to read a disk file that contains data to initialize an adapter. The device driver also uses the API routines to display driver error and sign-on messages. The INIT code is only called once, during system boot. For this reason, the INIT code is usually located at the end of the code segment so it can be discarded after initialization.

The second mode, called *Kernel mode*, is in effect when the device driver is called by the kernel as a result of an I/O request.

The third mode, called *Interrupt mode*, is in effect when the device driver's interrupt handler is executing in response to an external interrupt, such as a character being received from a serial port.

In general, the OS/2 device driver consists of a *Strategy* section, an *INIT* section, and optional *interrupt* and *timer* sections. The Strategy section receives requests from the kernel, in the form of Request Packet. The Strategy section verifies the request, and if it can be completed immediately, completes the request and sends the result back to the kernel. If the request cannot be completed immediately, the device driver optionally queues up the request to be completed at a later time and starts the I/O operation, if necessary. The kernel calls the Strategy routine directly by finding its offset address in the Device Header.

The Device Header

A simple OS/2 device driver consists of at least one code segment and one data segment, although more memory can be allocated if necessary. The first item of data that appears in the data segment must be the device driver header. The device driver header is a fixed length, linked list structure that contains information for use by the kernel during INIT and normal operation.

The first entry in the header is a link pointer to the next device that the device driver supports. If no other devices are supported, the pointer is set to - 1L. A -1L terminates the list of devices supported by this device driver. If the device driver supports multiple devices, such as a four-port serial board or multiple disk controller, the link is a far pointer to the next device header. When OS/2 loads device drivers at INIT time, it forms a linked list of all device driver device headers. The last device driver header will have a link address of -1L. When a DEVICE= statement is found in CONFIG.SYS, the last loaded device driver's link pointer is set to point to the new device driver's device header, and the new device driver's link pointer now terminates the list.

The next entry in the device header is the *Device Attribute Word* (see Table 5-1). The Device Attribute Word is used to define the operational characteristics of the device driver.

The next entry is a *one word offset* to the device driver Strategy routine. Only the offset is necessary, because the device driver is written in the small model with a 64K code

```
DEVICEHDR devhdr[2] = {
        { (void far *) &devhdr[1],          // link to next dev
          (DAW_CHR | DAW_OPN | DAW_LEVEL1),  // attribute
          (OFF) STRAT1,                      // &strategy
          (OFF) 0,                           // &IDCroutine
          "DEVICE1 ",
        },

        {(void far *) 0xFFFFFFFF,           // link(no more devs)
          (DAW_CHR | DAW_OPN | DAW_LEVEL1),  // attribute
          (OFF) STRAT2,                      // &strategy
          (OFF) 0,                           // &IDCroutine
          "DEVICE2 ",
        }
};
```

Figure 5-4. Device driver header, multiple devices.

segment and a 64K data segment (this is not always true—in special cases, the device driver can allocate more code and data space if needed, and can even be written in the large model).

The next entry is an offset address to an IDC routine, if the device driver supports inter-device driver communications. (The DAW_IDC bit in the device attribute word must also be set, otherwise the AttachDD call from the other device driver will fail.) The last field is the *device name*, which must be eight characters in length. Names with less than eight characters must be space-padded. Remember, any mistake in coding the device driver header will cause an immediate crash and burn when booting.

Table 5-1. Device Attribute Word

Bit(s)	Description
15	set if character driver, 0 if block driver
14	set if driver supports inter-device communications (IDC)
13	for block drivers, set if non-IBM format, for character drivers, set if driver supports output-until-busy.
12	if set, device supports sharing
11	set, if block device, supports removable media, if character device, supports device open/close
10	reserved, must be 0
9-7	driver function level
	001 = OS/2 device driver
	010 = supports DosDevIOCtl2 and Shutdown
	011 = capabilities bit strip in device header
6	reserved, must be 0
5	reserved, must be 0
4	reserved, must be 0
3	set if this is the CLOCK device
2	set if this is a null device (character driver only)
1	set if this is the new stdout device
0	set if this is the new stdin device

Capabilities Bit Strip

The *Capabilities Bit Strip* word defines additional features supported on level 3 drivers only (see Table 5-2).

Note that if the device driver is an ADD device driver, and sets bit 7 and 8 in the device attribute word as well as bit 3 in the capabilities bit strip, the Init request packet sent by the kernel will be formatted differently than the standard PDD Init request packet. Refer to the appropriate ADD documentation for a description of the ADD Init request packet format.

Table 5-2. Capabilities Bit Strip

Bit(s)	Description
0	set if driver supports DosDevIOCtl2 packets and has Shutdown support.
1	for character drivers, set if driver supports 32-bit memory addressing, for block drivers, this bit must be 0
2	if set, the device driver supports parallel ports
3	if set, the device driver is an ADD device driver*
4	if set, the kernel will issue the InitComplete strategy command
5-31	reserved, must be 0

Providing a Low-Level Interface

The data segment, which contains the Device Header, must appear as the very first data item. No data items or code can be placed before the Device Header. An OS/2 device driver which does not adhere to this rule will not load. Since our OS/2 device drivers are written in C, a mechanism must be provided for putting the code and data segments in the proper order, as well as providing a low-level interface to handle device and timer interrupts. Since the Device Header must be the first item that appears in the data segment, the C compiler must be prevented from inserting the normal C start-up code before the Device Header. Additionally, a method of detecting which device is being requested needs to be provided for device drivers that support multiple devices.

These requirements are handled with a small assembly language stub that is linked in with the device driver (refer to Figure 5-5). The __acrtused entry point prevents the C start-up code from being inserted before the device driver data segment. The segment-ordering directives ensure that the data segment precedes the code segment.

```
;
;      C start-up routine, one device
;
            EXTRN   _main:near
            PUBLIC _STRAT
            PUBLIC __acrtused

_DATA       segment word public 'DATA'
_DATA       ends

CONST       segment word public 'CONST'
CONST       ends

_BSS        segment word public 'BSS'
_BSS        ends

DGROUP      group CONST,_BSS,_DATA

_TEXT       segment word public 'CODE'
            assume cs:_TEXT,ds:DGROUP,es:NOTHING,ss:NOTHING
            .286P
;
_STRAT      proc    far
__acrtused:                 ;no start-up code
;
      push  0
      jmp   start           ;signal device 0
;
start:
```

Figure 5-5. Start-up routine, one device. (Continued)

```
              push    es              ;send Request Packet address
              push    bx
              call    _main           ;call driver mainline
              pop     bx              ;restore es:bx
              pop     es
              add     sp,2            ;clean up stack
              mov     word ptr es:[bx+3],ax   ;send completion status
              ret
;
_STRAT        endp
;
_TEXT         ends
              end
```

Figure 5-5. Start-up routine, one device.

Note the _STRAT entry point. Remember that this is the address placed in the device driver's Device Header. The kernel, when making a request to the device driver, looks up this address in the Device Header and makes a far call to it. The assembly language routine then, in turn, calls the C mainline. Thus, the linkage from the kernel to the device driver is established.

Note the "push 0" in the beginning of the _STRAT routine. This is to notify the device driver which device is being requested. Each device supported by the device driver requires its own separate Device Header. Note also that each Device Header contains an offset address to its own Strategy routine. Using the assembly language interface, the device number is pushed on the stack and passed to the device driver Strategy section for service. The device driver retrieves the parameter and determines which device was requested. One of the parameters to main is the *int dev* (see Figure 5-8), the device number that was passed from the assembly language start-up routine. The assembly language start-up routine is modified to support multiple devices by adding entry points for each device's Strategy section. The modified source for this routine is shown in Figure 5-6.

The assembly language routine in Figure 5-7 provides the interrupt handler and timer handler entry points. The interrupt handler entry point provides a convenient place to put a breakpoint before entering the C code of the main interrupt handler. The timer handler entry point provides a place to save and restore the CPU registers. Note that the interrupt handler does not need to save the register contents, as this is done by the OS/2 kernel. The timer handler, however, must save and restore register contents.

```
;
;     C start-up routine, 4 devices
;
                EXTRN    _main:near
                PUBLIC   _STRAT1
                PUBLIC   _STRAT2
                PUBLIC   _STRAT3
                PUBLIC   _STRAT4
                PUBLIC   __acrtused

_DATA           segment word public 'DATA'
_DATA           ends

CONST           segment word public 'CONST'
CONST           ends

_BSS            segment word public 'BSS'
_BSS            ends

DGROUP          group CONST, _BSS, _DATA

_TEXT           segment word public 'CODE'

  assume        cs:_TEXT,ds:DGROUP,es:NOTHING,ss:NOTHING
                .286P
;
_STRAT1         proc far
__acrtused:                     ; satisfy EXTRN modules
;
   push         0
   jmp          start           ;signal device 0
;
_STRAT1         endp

_STRAT2         proc far
;
   push         1               ;signal second device
   jmp          start
;
```

Figure 5-6. Start-up routine, four devices. (Continued)

```
_STRAT2         endp

_STRAT3         proc far
;
    push        2               ;signal third device
    jmp         start
;
_STRAT3         endp

_STRAT4         proc far
;
    push        3               ;signal fourth device
    jmp         start
;
start:
    push        es              ;send address
    push        bx
    call        _main           ;call driver mainline
    pop         bx              ;restore es:bx
    pop         es
    add         sp,2            ;clean up stack
    mov         word ptr es:[bx+3],ax  ;send completion status
    ret
;
_STRAT4         endp
;
_TEXT           ends
                end
```

Figure 5-6. Start-up routine, four devices.

```
;
;       C start-up routine, one device, w/interrupt and timer
;
            PUBLIC      _STRAT
            PUBLIC      __acrtused
            PUBLIC      _INT_HNDLR
            PUBLIC      _TIM_HNDLR

            EXTRN       _interrupt_handler:near
            EXTRN       _timer_handler:near
            EXTRN       _main:near

_DATA       segment word public 'DATA'
_DATA       ends

CONST       segment word public 'CONST'
CONST       ends

_BSS        segment word public 'BSS'
_BSS        ends

DGROUP      group   CONST, _BSS, _DATA

_TEXT       segment word public 'CODE'

            assume  cs:_TEXT,ds:DGROUP,es:NOTHING, ss:NOTHING
            .286P
;
_STRAT      proc    far
__acrtused:         ; no start-up code
;
        push    0
        jmp     start   ; signal device 0
;
start:
        push    es      ;send Request Packet address
        push    bx
        call    _main   ;call driver mainline
        pop     bx      ;restore es:bx
```

Figure 5-7. Start-up routine with timer and interrupt handler. (Continued)

```
        pop     es
        add     sp,2        ;clean up stack
        mov     word ptr es:[bx+3],ax   ;send completion status
        ret
;
_STRAT          endp
;
_INT_HNDLR      proc    far
;
        call    _interrupt_handler  ;handle interrupts
        ret                 ;bail out
;
_INT_HNDLR      endp
;
_TIM_HNDLR      proc    far
;
        pusha
        push    es
        push    ds
        call    _timer_handler
        pop     ds
        pop     es
        popa
        ret
;
_TIM_HNDLR      endp
;
_TEXT           ends
                end
```

Figure 5-7. Start-up routine with timer and interrupt handler.

The Strategy Section

The Strategy section is nothing more than a big switch statement (see Figure 5-8). Common device driver requests, such as DosWrite and DosRead, have predefined function codes assigned to them. The device driver may elect to ignore any or all of these requests by returning a DONE status to the kernel. This tells the kernel that the request has been completed. The status returned to the kernel may optionally include error information that the kernel returns to the calling program.

```
int main(PREQPACKET rp, int dev)
{
    switch(rp->RPcommand)
    {
    case RPINIT:            // 0x00

        // init called by kernel in protected mode

        return Init(rp);

    case RPREAD:            // 0x04

        return (RPDONE);

    case RPWRITE:           // 0x08

        return (RPDONE);

    case RPINPUT_FLUSH:     // 0x07

        return (RPDONE);

    case RPOUTPUT_FLUSH:    // 0x0b

        return (RPDONE);

    case RPOPEN:            // 0x0d

        return (RPDONE);
```

Figure 5-8. Skeleton strategy section. (Continued)

```
        case RPCLOSE:          // 0x0e

            return (RPDONE);
        case RPIOCTL:           // 0x10

            switch (rp->s.IOCtl.function)
            {
            case 0x00:          // our function def #1

                return (RPDONE);

            case 0x01:          // our function def #2

                return (RPDONE);
            }

        // deinstall request

        case RPDEINSTALL:       // 0x14

            return(RPDONE | RPERR | ERROR_BAD_COMMAND);

        // all other commands are flagged

        default:
            return(RPDONE | RPERR | ERROR_BAD_COMMAND);

        }
}
```

Figure 5-8. Skeleton strategy section.

Note, however, that in the case of one of the standard device driver functions, the kernel will re-map the error value returned from the device driver to one of the standard device driver return codes.

If the device driver must return special error codes, it should use an IOCtl request. IOCtls are used for special types of operations, device driver-specific, which do not fit into the architecture of the standard device driver functions. An example might be such as port I/O or initialization of a UART. The IOCtl section of the device driver is called when the application issues a DosDevIOCtl call with the device driver's handle. Using IOCtls, the device driver can return specialized codes that might contain, for example, the contents of an I/O port or the status of the device. This flexibility allows the device driver writer to customize the device driver to fit any device.

Examine the skeleton Strategy section in Figure 5-8. Note the switch on the Request Packet command. A number of standard device driver functions have command codes predefined in OS/2 (see Table 5-3). It is up to the device driver writer to act upon or ignore any of the requests to the device driver.

The Strategy section is entered when the kernel calls the device driver to perform a particular operation. Refer to Table 5-3.

Table 5-3. Device Driver Strategy Calls

Event	Strategy section called
DosOpen call	RPOPEN
DosClose	RPCLOSE
boot	RPINIT
IOCtl	RPIOCTL
<cntl-c>	RPCLOSE
<cntl-break>	RPCLOSE
DosRead	RPREAD
DosWrite	RPWRITE

Initialization

The first thing that must be done in the initialization section is to save the DevHlp entry point address, passed in the Request Packet. This is the only time that the address is made available to the device driver, and it must be saved in the device driver's data segment. The INIT code generally performs two other functions. First, it issues the sign-on message to the screen that the device driver is attempting to load. Second, it finds the address of the last data and last code item, and sends them back to OS/2. OS/2 uses the code and data offset values to size memory. Only the first code and data segment of the device driver is re-sized by OS/2, so it may be desirable to place the INIT code and data into another segment which is discarded after the device driver is loaded. If a device driver fails installation, it must send back zero offsets for its code and data segments so OS/2 can use the memory space that the device driver had occupied during installation. Depending on the type of driver, you may wish to use this section to initialize your device, hook and interrupt or start a timer.

It should be noted that for Micro Channel and EISA bus systems which share interrupts, it is desirable to hook the interrupt in the OPEN section and release it in the CLOSE section. This allows other adapters which use the same interrupt to register for the interrupt without being refused. ISA bus interrupts should be hooked during INIT, since the driver should fail initialization if the interrupt cannot be given to the device driver.

If the device driver supports multiple devices, it will contain a Device Header with an entry for each device, with the previous Device Header pointing to the next Device Header. The last Device Header will contain a -1L, which terminates the list. For each device, the OS/2 kernel will call the Strategy entry point to initialize the device. If the driver supports, for example, four serial ports that use a single interrupt level, only the last valid initialized device should hook the interrupt. This will prevent previously installed devices from generating interrupts before the initialization has been completed. The code and data segment values returned to OS/2 to size memory should be exactly the same each time the INIT section is called.

During INIT, a limited number of API functions may be called by the device driver. This is possible because INIT runs as a single Ring 3 thread. Some of the APIs, especially those that perform file I/O, are especially helpful for initializing adapters using data that is resident in disk files. Refer to the INIT Strategy Command in Chapter 6 for a more detailed description of device driver initialization.

The driver should allocate necessary resources during initialization, such as memory and GDT selectors. If the driver supports a memory mapped adapter, the physical adapter address may be mapped to a GDT selector. However, because INIT is performed as a Ring 3 thread, the GDT selector cannot be accessed during initialization. Any function which creates or uses a GDT selector during INIT, such as AttachDD, will not allow you to use it during INIT. This is because INIT is run at Ring 3, and does not have access to the GDT.

With IBM PS/2s, the device driver should search the system for an adapter card with the correct ID and verify that it is configured correctly. The device driver may call special PS/2 Advance BIOS (ABIOS) routines (see Chapter 8) to verify the correct configuration of the adapter.

A Common Strategy

One of the most common techniques in OS/2 device driver design is for the Strategy section to request service from the device and wait for a device or timer interrupt to signal completion of the request. In this case, the Strategy section starts the I/O and issues a *Block* DevHlp call, which blocks the calling thread. When the device interrupt signals that the operation is done, the interrupt section *Runs* the blocked thread, completing the request. To protect against the request never being completed, such as with a down device, the Block call can contain a time-out parameter. If the timeout expires before the completion interrupt occurs, the Blocked thread is Run, allowing the Strategy section to send the proper error message back to the kernel.

Another method of timing-out a device is the use of the SetTimer DevHlp routine. A timer handler can be hooked into the OS/2 system clock, and ticks counted down until a time-out occurs. The Blocked thread can then be Run by the timer handler.

The number and type of commands supported by the Strategy section are up to the device driver writer. The device driver can process only the commands it needs to, and let the others simply pass through by sending a DONE status back to the kernel. Illegal function calls may optionally be trapped, and ERROR_BAD_COMMAND returned to the kernel.

Note that the OS/2 kernel periodically issues special requests to the device driver which are not generated by the application which opened the driver. An example of this would be the 5-48 Code Page IOCtl which the kernel sends to every OS/2 device driver immediately following the OPEN.

If the application that opened the device driver fails or is aborted with a <cntl-c> or <cntl-break>, the device driver is UnBlocked by the kernel with an unusual wake-up return code. The driver must return ERROR_CHAR_CALL_INTERRUPTED to the kernel, which will in turn call the CLOSE section of the driver.

In general, it's a good practice to trap all unsupported requests by returning the DONE and ERROR_BAD_COMMAND status to the kernel, but be aware you may have to make some exceptions for the unsolicited calls.

In the simplest of device drivers, the Strategy section may only contain an OPEN, CLOSE, and READ or WRITE section. In a complicated device driver, such as a disk device driver, the Strategy section may contain over two dozen standard device driver functions and dozens of additional IOCtl calls. IOCtl calls are actually Strategy functions, but are broken down one step further to provide more detailed or device-specific operations (see Chapter 6). For instance, a device driver might send a list of parameters to be used in initializing an I/O port, and return the status of that initialization operation. This type of function would not be able to be done with one of the standard set of device driver function calls because it is so device-specific. The IOCtl, however, is well suited to this type of functionality.

Interrupt Section

The interrupt section handles interrupts from the device. Interrupts may be caused by a character having been received, a character finished transmitting, or any number of external events. Interrupt processing should be quick and straightforward. The routine that handles the interrupt is appropriately called the *interrupt handler*. The interrupt handler is a subroutine that is entered upon the receipt of an interrupt for the IRQ level registered with the SetIRQ DevHlp call. All interrupts in OS/2 are handled by the kernel. With DOS, all a program had to do was to hook the interrupt vector that it wanted. OS/2, however, does not allow interrupt vectors to be changed, and if an attempt is made to change one, the application will immediately be kicked off the system.

To register for an OS/2 interrupt, the device driver must send the address of its interrupt handler and the requested interrupt (IRQ) level to OS/2 via a SetIRQ DevHlp call. If the SetIRQ is successful, OS/2 will call the interrupt handler upon receipt of an interrupt on that IRQ.

OS/2 will call the interrupt handler that registered for a particular IRQ until the interrupt handler claims the interrupt by clearing the *carry flag* (CLC).

The interrupt handler must be located in the first code segment of the device driver. A sample interrupt handler is shown in Figure 5-9.

```
void interrupt_handler ()
{
    int   rupt_dev;
    int   source;
    int   cmd_b;
    int   st_b;
    int   port;
    int   temp;
    int   rxlevel;

    port=UART_PORT_ADDRESS;
    outp((port+2),0x20);      // switch to bank 1
```

Figure 5-9. Interrupt handler. (Continued)

```
    source = getsrc ();                 // get vector
    switch (source)
    {

    // optional timer service routine

    case timer :

        st_b=inp (port+3);              // dec transmit cnt
        if ( ThisReadRP == 0)           // nobody waiting
            break;
        ThisReadRP->RPstatus=(RPDONE | RPERR | ERROR_NOT_READY);
        Run ((ULONG) ThisWriteRP);      // run thread
        ThisWriteRP=0;
        break;

    case txm    :
    case txf    :

        // spurious write interrupt

        if ( ThisWriteRP == 0)
        {
            temp=inp(port+2);
            break;
        }

        // keep transmitting until no data left

        if (!(QueueRead(&tx_queue,&outchar)))
        {
            outp((port), outchar);
            tickcount=MIN_TIMEOUT;
            break;
        }

        // done writing, run blocked thread

        tickcount=MIN_TIMEOUT;
        disable_write();
```

Figure 5-9. Interrupt handler. (Continued)

```
           ThisWriteRP->RPstatus = (RPDONE);
           Run ((ULONG)  ThisWriteRP);
           ThisWriteRP=0;
           break;

   case ccr    :

       // control character, treat as normal

       inchar=inp(port+5);

   case rxf    :

       // rx fifo service routine

       if ( ThisReadRP == 0)
          inchar=inp (port); // get character
       else
       {
       temp=inp(port+4);
       rxlevel=(temp & 0x70) / 0x10;

       // empty out chip FIFO

       while (rxlevel !=0)
       {

          inchar=inp (port); // get character
          rxlevel--;
          tickcount=MIN_TIMEOUT;

          // write input data to queue

          if(QueueWrite(&rx_queue,inchar))

            // error, queue must be full

           {
           ThisReadRP->RPstatus = (RPDONE|RPERR|ERROR_GEN_FAILURE);
```

Figure 5-9. Interrupt handler. (Continued)

```
            Run ((ULONG) ThisReadRP);
            ThisReadRP=0;
            break;
            }
         com_error_word |= inp(port+5);

         } // while rxlevel
      } // else
   } // switch (source)
  EOI (IRQnum); // send EOI
}
```

Figure 5-9. Interrupt handler.

If the device driver is running on an ISA bus machine, OS/2 calls the device driver's interrupt handler with interrupts disabled, since interrupts cannot be shared. On an EISA or Micro Channel machine, interrupts remain enabled when the interrupt handler is entered. Shared interrupts are one of the features of the IBM Micro Channel and EISA bus architectures, which allow more than one device to share a single interrupt level.

Device drivers which share interrupts must claim interrupts that belong to them by clearing the carry flag. Interrupt handlers on EISA and Micro Channel machines can refuse the interrupt by setting the carry flag before exiting the interrupt handler. The OS/2 kernel will continue to call all of the interrupt handlers registered for the particular IRQ until one of the handlers claims the interrupt. Only the interrupt handler that claims the interrupt should issue an EOI, which resets the interrupt so the interrupt handler can be entered again. If you don't issue the EOI, you'll never get another interrupt. Only the interrupt handler that owns the interrupt should issue the EOI.

Any extended time spent in the interrupt handler can cause performance problems. The interrupt handler must quickly perform its functions and exit. In the case of character devices, the OS/2 DevHlp library supports fast reads and writes to circular character queues.

For block devices, interrupt handling is fast because the interrupt is usually caused by a DMA completion or disk-seek complete. Data is usually transferred to the user buffer using DMA, eliminating the need to transfer data during interrupt processing. On a DMA transfer, the DMA controller is set-up, started, and the device driver exited to allow other threads to run. When the DMA completes, it will generate a DMA completion interrupt, causing the device driver's interrupt handler to be entered. The interrupt handler can then take the appropriate action, such as starting a new DMA transfer. Note that the interrupt handler is written in C. It could have written using assembly language, but it's much easier to write and debug when written in C.

Most UARTs and adapters contain some type of buffering, which allows a device driver a little slack when servicing higher data rates. The example in Figure 5-9 shows an interrupt handler for a serial I/O port utilizing the Intel 82050 UART. The UART has an internal 4-byte buffer and two internal timers. When an interrupt occurs, the UART is examined to determine the type of interrupt: transmit, receive, or clock.

The interrupt handler is not entered directly from OS/2, but is called from our small assembly language start-up routine (see Figure 5-7). When the SetIRQ call is made to register the interrupt handler, the address passed in the call is the address of the interrupt handler entry point in the device driver start-up code. The start-up code in turn calls the C language interrupt handler.

The interrupt handler routine is not difficult to write or understand. It can, however, be difficult to debug. Errors that occur in the interrupt handler frequently appear only in a real time context; that is, while the interrupt handler is being entered as a result of a hardware interrupt. The C library function printf, for example, cannot be called from within an interrupt handler. Application debuggers, such as CodeView, cannot be used in an interrupt handler. A debugger such as the OS/2 kernel debugger or similar must be used. A breakpoint placed in the interrupt routine will cause the program to stop, and further interrupts may pass undetected while the program is stopped. A problem may not appear when breakpoints are inserted, but will reappear when the program executes normally. It then becomes necessary for the device driver writer to "visualize" the operation of the interrupt handler and begin applying solutions until the problem is fixed.

The interrupt handler may receive unsolicited or spurious interrupts from the hardware, and they should be handled accordingly by the OS/2 device driver. In the sample interrupt handler, a check is made to see whether a valid read or write request is pending. If not, the device is reset and the interrupt handler is exited, effectively ignoring the interrupt. This is not a recommended practice.

Examine the case *rxf* section of the interrupt handler in Figure 5-9. This is where a received character is detected. When the UART receives a complete character, it sets the RX FIFO register bit which generates an interrupt. The interrupt handler examines the interrupt source register to determine if the interrupt was caused by a received character. If so, it checks to see whether a valid request is pending. If not, the character is thrown away and the interrupt handler exited. If a valid read request is pending, the UART is queried to see how many characters are in its four-character FIFO. (At high data rates, it is possible that a character had come in while we were handling an interrupt.) Each character is taken out of the FIFO one by one and written to a circular character queue. The OS/2 DevHlp library supports fast reads and writes to these circular queues. To prevent collision, queue reads and writes are protected by disabling interrupts around the queue accesses. The interrupt handler continues to receive characters and place them into the receive queue until the queue becomes full, the queue is emptied, or a specified time period has elapsed.

In the sample interrupt handler, data is passed back to the Strategy section of the device driver when the queue becomes full or when a specified time has passed without the reception of a new character. If the sample device driver was intended for use as a terminal device driver, the interrupt handler could have sent the data back to the Strategy section upon receipt of an end character, such as a carriage return. Optionally, the interrupt handler can return each character to the Strategy section as it is received. This method is more CPU intensive, however, and is generally not recommended. Data rates of 9600 *baud* and below can generally use the single-character method, but speeds in excess of 9600 baud may require external buffering, DMA, or a microprocessor-based adapter card. Overall system configuration should play a part in the design of your interrupt handler. A heavily loaded system may not be able to respond fast enough to multiple, high-speed interrupts on a character-by-character basis, especially if the driver is servicing several devices on the same interrupt level.

The Timer Handler

At 9600 baud, the time required to receive a character via a serial port is approximately one millisecond. If we received several characters, and no more characters were received within two or three hundred milliseconds, we could assume that there was an interruption of data. This could be caused by the lack of data, or because a terminal operator simply stopped typing. In any case, this would be a perfect opportunity to send the received data back to the application.

In OS/2, a device driver can "hook" the system timer interrupt with a call to the DevHlp library SetTimer function. The device driver passes OS/2 a pointer to a timer handler, and OS/2 calls the timer handler (see Figure 5-10) each time it receives a system clock interrupt. OS/2 also calls any other timer handlers that had been previously registered.

```
void timer_handler()
{
  if (ThisReadRP == 0)            // make sure we're waiting
        return;
  tickcount--;                    // decrement counter
  if(tickcount == 0)  {
    ThisReadRP->RPstatus=(RPDONE); // run blocked thread
    Run ((ULONG) ThisReadRP);
    ThisReadRP=0L;                // keep us out of here
    tickcount=MIN_TIMEOUT;        // reset tick-based cntr
    }
}
```

Figure 5-10. Timer handler.

The operation is simple. If no data appears within eight or ten 32-millisecond system time ticks, the assumption can be made that the flow of input data has stopped, or at least paused. The timer handler checks for a valid pending read request. This is necessary because the timer handler will continue to be called every 32 milliseconds, even if the device driver is idle. If a valid request is pending, the DevHlp Run function is called to Run the Blocked thread and send the data back to the requesting application. When the Strategy section becomes unblocked, it retrieves the data from the receiver queue and sends it to the application's data buffer.

The TickCount DevHlp could also be used to set up a timer handler that gets called every eight or ten ticks and checks if data has been read (see Figure 5-11). The TickCount method is more efficient, as the timer handler is not called until the count specified in the TickCount call is reached. The TickCount DevHlp routine can be also used to reset the tick count for a previously registered time handler.

```
void timer_handler()
{
  if (ThisReadRP == 0)            // make sure we're waiting
        return;

  ThisReadRP->RPstatus=(RPDONE)   // exceeded tick cnt,run thread
  Run ((ULONG) ThisReadRP);
  ThisReadRP=0L;                  // ensure no more entry here
}
```

Figure 5-11. TickCount timer handler.

CHAPTER 6

Device Driver Strategy Commands

Strategy commands are the commands that the driver receives from the OS/2 kernel, usually in response to a driver request from an application thread. The kernel uses the device driver Request Packet (see Figure 6-1) to communicate with the device driver. The kernel sends a request to the device driver by filling in the proper fields in the Request Packet, and sending the driver a pointer to the Request Packet.

OS/2 does not guarantee the order that the Request Packets arrive at the device driver are preserved in the same order that the API requests were issued from the application threads. It is possible that Request Packets may arrive out of order, and the OS/2 device driver is responsible for providing the synchronization mechanism between itself and application thread requests.

A Request Packet consists of two main parts: the Request Header and the command-specific data field.

RPlength contains the total length in bytes of the Request Packet (the length of the Request Header plus the length of the command-specific data).

```
typedef struct ReqPacket {
    UCHAR   RPlength;           // Request Packet length
    UCHAR   RPunit;             // unit code for block DD only
    UCHAR   RPcommand;          // command code
    USHORT  RPstatus;           // status word
    UCHAR   RPreserved[4];      // reserved bytes
    ULONG   RPqlink;            // queue linkage
    UCHAR   avail[19];          // command specific data
} REQPACKET;
```

Figure 6-1. Request Packet definition.

RPunit identifies the unit for which the request is intended. This field has no meaning for character devices.

RPcommand indicates the requested device driver function.

RPStatus is defined only for OPEN and CLOSE Request Packets on entry to the Strategy routine. For all other Request Packets, the status field is undefined on entry.

For an OPEN Request Packet, bit 3 (MON_OPEN_STATUS,08H) of the status field is set if the packet was generated from a DosMonOpen; otherwise it was a DosOpen.

```
#define RPERR                   0x8000 // error occurred
#define RPDEV                   0x4000 // error code
#define RPBUSY                  0x0200 // device is busy
#define RPDONE                  0x0100 // driver done bit

#define ERROR_WRITE_PROTECT     0x0000 // Write Prot
#define ERROR_BAD_UNIT          0x0001 // Unknown Unit
#define ERROR_NOT_READY         0x0002 // Device Not Ready
#define ERROR_BAD_COMMAND       0x0003 // Unknown Command
#define ERROR_CRC               0x0004 // CRC Error
#define ERROR_BAD_LENGTH        0x0005 // Bad Driver Req Len
#define ERROR_SEEK              0x0006 // Seek Error
#define ERROR_NOT_DOS_DISK      0x0007 // Unknown Media
#define ERROR_SECTOR_NOT_FOUND  0x0008 // Sector Not Found
#define ERROR_OUT_OF_PAPER      0x0009 // Out of Paper
```

Figure 6-2. Standard OS/2 device driver errors. (Continued)

```
#define ERROR_WRITE_FAULT            0x000A // Write Fault
#define ERROR_READ_FAULT             0x000B // Read Fault
#define ERROR_GEN_FAILURE            0x000C // General Failure
#define ERROR_DISK_CHANGE            0x000D // Change Disk
#define ERROR_UNCERTAIN_MEDIA        0x0010 // Uncertain Media
#define ERROR_CHAR_CALL_INTERRUPTED  0x0011 // Char Call Interrupt
#define ERROR_NO_MONITOR_SUPPORT     0x0012 // Mons Not supported
#define ERROR_INVALID_PARAMETER      0x0013 // Invalid Parameters
#define ERROR_DEVICE_IN_USE          0x0014 // Dev Already In Use
```

Figure 6-2. Standard OS/2 device driver errors.

For a CLOSE Request Packet, bit 3 (MON_CLOSE_STATUS,08H) of the status field is set if the packet was generated by a DosMonClose or a DosClose of a handle that was generated by a DosMonOpen. Otherwise, it was a DosClose on a non-monitor handle.

Upon exit from the Strategy routine, the status field describes the resulting state of the request (see Figure 6-2).

Bit 15 (RPERR) is the Error bit. If this bit is set, the low 8 bits of the status word (7-0) indicate the error code. The error code is processed by OS/2 in one of the following ways:

- If the IOCtl category is 'User Defined' (greater than 127), FF00 is INCLUSIVE OR'd with the byte-wide error code.
- If not 'User Defined' and Bit 14 (RPDEV - device driver defined error code) is set, FE00 is INCLUSIVE OR'd with the byte-wide error code.
- Otherwise, the error code must be one of those shown and is mapped by the kernel into one of the standard OS/2 API return codes before being returned to the application.

Bit 14 (RPDEV) is a device-driver defined error if set in conjunction with bit 15.

Bits 13 - 10 are reserved.

Bit 9 (RPBUSY) is the Busy bit.

Bit 8 (RPDONE) is the Done bit. If it is set, it means that the operation is complete. The driver normally sets the done when it exits.

Bits 7-0 are the low 8 bits of the status word. If bit 15 is set, bits 7-0 contain the error code.

ERROR_UNCERTAIN_MEDIA (10H) should be returned when the state of the media in the drive is uncertain. This response should NOT be returned to the INIT command. For fixed disks, the device driver must begin in a media uncertain state in order to have the media correctly labelled.

ERROR_CHAR_CALL_INTERRUPTED (11H) should be returned when the thread performing the I/O was interrupted out of a DevHlp Block before completing the requested operation.

ERROR_NO_MON_SUPPORT (12H) should be returned for monitor requests (DosMonOpen, DosMonClose, DosMonRegister), if device monitors are not supported by the device driver.

ERROR_INVALID_PARAMETER (13H) should be returned when one or more fields of the Request Packet contain invalid values.

RPqlink is provided to maintain a linked list of Request Packets. It is a pointer to the next packet in the chain, or -1L if this is the end of the chain. The device driver may use the Request Packet management DevHlp services PullReqPacket, PushReqPacket, FreeReqPacket, SortReqPacket, PullParticular, and AllocReqPacket to manipulate the linked list of Request Packets.

Summary of Device Driver Commands

Table 6-1 contains a summary of device driver Strategy commands. The commands are described in detail in the following subsections of this chapter.

Table 6-1. Device Driver Strategy Commands

Code	Meaning	Devices
0x00	Init	Character, Block
0x01	Media Check	Block Only
0x02	Build BIOS Parameter Block	Block Only
0x03	Reserved	N/A
0x04	Read	Character, Block
0x05	Nondest. Read, no wait	Character Only
0x06	Input Status	Character Only
0x07	Flush Input Buffer	Character Only
0x08	Write	Character, Block
0x09	Write w/Verify	Character, Block
0x0a	Output Status	Character Only
0x0b	Flush Output Buffer	Character Only
0x0c	Reserved	N/A
0x0d	Open Device	Character, Block
0x0e	Close Device	Character, Block
0x0f	Removable Media	Block Only
0x10	Generic IOCtl	Character, Block
0x11	Reset Media	Block Only
0x12	Get Logical Drive Map	Block Only
0x13	Set Logical Drive Map	Block Only
0x14	Deinstall	Character Only
0x15	Reserved	N/A
0x16	Partitionable Disk	Block Only
0x17	Get Fixed Disk Map	Block Only
0x18	Reserved	N/A
0x19	Reserved	N/A
0x1a	Reserved	N/A
0x1b	Reserved	N/A
0x1c	Shutdown	Character, Block
0x1d	Get Driver Capabilities	Block
0x1e	Reserved	
0x1f	CMDInitComplete	Character, Block

0h / Init

Initialize the device.

Format Of Request Packet

```
union
  {
    struct {                        // init packet(one entry,exit)
      UCHAR       units;            // number of units
      FPFUNCTION  DevHlp;           // &DevHlp
      char far    *args;            // &args
      UCHAR       drive;            // drive #
    }Init;
    struct {
      UCHAR       units;            // same as input
      OFF         finalCS;          // final code offset
      OFF         finalDS;          // final data offset
      FARPOINTER  BPBarray;         // &BPB
    } InitExit;
  }
```

Comments

The INIT function is called by the kernel during driver installation at boot time. The INIT section should initialize the adapter and device. For example, if the device was a serial port, the initialization section might set the baud rate, parity, stop bits, etc. on a serial port or check to see if the device is installed correctly. INIT is called in a special mode at Ring 3 with some Ring 0 capabilities. For example, the driver may turn off interrupts during INIT, but they must be turned back on before returning to the kernel. The INIT code may also perform direct port I/O without generating protection violations. Usually, the driver will allocate buffers and data storage during INIT, to ensure that the driver will work when installed. Because the memory allocations are done at Ring 3, the system can check to make sure the allocations are valid. If not, the driver can remove itself from memory, freeing up any previously allocated space for other system components. Since the INIT code is executed only once, and during system boot, its not necessary to optimize the INIT code. Do all of the work you can up front in the INIT section, as it may be time-prohibitive or even impossible to do some initialization during normal kernel-mode driver operation.

On entry, the INIT Request Packet contains the following fields as inputs to the device driver:

- A pointer to the DevHlp entry point. (in OS/2 1.x, this is a bimodal pointer)
- A pointer to the initialization arguments from the DEVICE= line in CONFIG.SYS.
- The drive number for the first block device unit.

The pointer to the initialization parameters allows a device driver to be configured at boot time, based on arguments placed on the DEVICE= line in CONFIG.SYS. See Chapter 8 for a discussion of how to do this, and a listing of the INIT section of an actual driver that performs this function.

Upon the completion of initialization, the device driver must set certain fields in the Request Packet as follows:

- The number of logical block devices or units the driver supports (block devices only).
- The WORD offset to the end of the code segment.
- The WORD offset to the end of the data segment.
- A pointer to the BIOS Parameter Block or BPB (block devices only).

A block device driver must also return the number of logical devices or units that are available. The kernel's file system layer will assign sequential drive letters to these units. A character device driver should set the number of devices to 0.

As a final step in initialization, both block and character device drivers must return the offsets to the end of the code and data segments. This allows the device driver to release code and data needed only by the device driver's initialization routine. To facilitate this, the initialization code and data should be located at the end of the appropriate segments. A device driver which fails initialization should return 0 for both offset values.

A block device driver must return an array of BPBs for each of the logical units that it supports. A character device driver should set the BPB pointer to 0.

If initialization is successful, the status field in the Request Header must be set to indicate no errors and the done status (RPDONE).

If the device driver determines that it cannot initialize the device, it should return with the error bit (RPERR) in the Request Header status field set. The device driver should return RPERR | RPDONE | ERROR_GEN_FAILURE. Whatever the reason for the failure, the status must always indicate that the request is done (RPDONE).

The system loader records the last non-zero code and data segment offsets returned for the devices which successfully completed initialization. These offset values are used to re-size the device driver's code and data segments.

If the device driver supports multiple devices or units, the kernel will call the initialization section for each of the devices or units. If your device driver has a single initialization section, the offset values returned to the kernel should be the same for each device initialization that is successful.

A limited number of OS/2 system API routines are available to the device driver during initialization. Those API routines are listed in Table 6-2.

Table 6-2. API Routines Available During Init (Continued)

Routine Name	Description
DosBeep	Generate a beep from the speaker
DosCaseMap	Perform case mapping
DosChgFilePtr	Move a read/write file pointer
DosClose	Close a file handle
DosDelete	Delete a file
DosDevConfig	Get a device's configuration
DosDevIOCtl	Do an IOCtl request
DosFindClose	Close a search directory handle
DosFindFirst	Find the first matching file
DosFindNext	Find next file
DosGetEnv	Get address of process environment

Table 6-2. API Routines Available During Init

Routine Name	Description
DosGetMessage	Get a system message
DosOpen	Open a file
DosPutMessage	Display message to handle
DosQCurDir	Query current directory
DosQCurDisk	Query current disk
DosQFileInfo	Query file information
DosQFileMode	Query file mode
DosRead	Read from file
DosSMRegisterDD	Register driver for SM events
DosWrite	Write to file

For more information about these functions, refer to the *IBM OS/2 2.1 Control Program Reference*.

1H/ Media Check

Determine the state of the media.

Format Of Request Packet

```
struct {                          // MEDIA_CHECK
    UCHAR      media;             // media descriptor
    UCHAR      return_code;       // see below
    FARPOINTER prev_volume;       // &previous volume ID
} MediaCheck;
```

Comments

On entry, the Request Packet will have the media descriptor field set for the drive identified in the Request Header (see Table 6-3).

The device driver must perform the following actions for the MEDIA CHECK request:

- Set the status word in the Request Header.
- Set the return code where:

    -1 = Media has been changed

    0 = Unsure if media has been changed

    1 = Media unchanged

To determine whether you are using a single-sided or a double-sided 8-inch diskette (FEh), attempt to read the second side. If an error occurs, you can assume the diskette is single-sided.

Table 6-3. Media Descriptor Bytes

Disk Type	#Sides	#Sectors/Track	Media Descriptor
Fixed Disk	—	—	0xF8
3.5 Inch	2	09	0xF9
3.5 Inch	2	18	0xF0
5.25 Inch	2	15	0xF9
5.25 Inch	1	09	0xFC
5.25 Inch	2	09	0xFD
5.25 Inch	1	08	0xFE
5.25 Inch	2	08	0xFF
8 Inch	1	26	0xFE
8 Inch	2	26	0xFD
8 Inch	2	08	0xFE

The Media Check function is called by the kernel prior to disk access, and is therefore valid only for block devices. The kernel sends to the driver the media ID byte for the type of disk that it expects to find in the selected drive.

2H / Build BPB

Build the BIOS Parameter Block (BPB). The driver receives this request when the media has changed or when the media type is uncertain.

Format Of Request Packet

```
struct {                           // BUILD_BPB
    UCHAR     media;               // media descriptor
    FARPOINTER buffer;             // 1-sector buffer FAT
    FARPOINTER BPBarray;           // &BPB array
    UCHAR     drive;               // drive #
    } BuildBPB;
```

Comments

On entry, the Request Packet will have the media descriptor set for the drive identified in the Request Header. The transfer address is a virtual address to a buffer containing the boot sector media, if the block device driver attribute field has bit 13 (DAW_IBM) set; otherwise, the buffer contains the first sector of the File Allocation Table (FAT).

The device driver must perform the following actions:

- Set the pointer to the BPB table.
- Update the media descriptor.
- Set the status word in the Request Header.

The device driver must determine the media type in the drive, in order to return the pointer to the BPB table. Previously, the FAT ID byte determined the structure and layout of the media. Because the FAT ID byte has only eight possible values (F8 through FF), it is clear that, as new media types are invented, the available values will soon be exhausted. With the varying media layouts, OS/2 needs to be aware of the location of the FATs and directories before it reads them.

The device driver should read the boot sector from the specified buffer. If the boot sector is for DOS 2.10, 2.10, 3.00, 3.10, 3.20, or OS/2, the device driver returns the BPB from the boot sector. If the boot sector is for DOS 1.00 or 1.10, the device driver reads the first sector of the FAT into the specified buffer. The FAT ID is examined and the corresponding BPB is returned.

The information relating to the BPB for a particular media is kept in the boot sector for the media (see Table 6-4).

Table 6-4. Boot Sector Format

Field	Length
Short Jump (0xEB) followed by NOP	2 bytes
OEM Name and Version	8 bytes
Bytes Per Sector	word
Sectors/Allocation Unit (base 2)	byte
Reserved Sectors (starting at 0)	word
Number of FATs	byte
Number of Root Dir Entries (max)	word
Number of Sectors Total	word
Media Descriptor	byte
Number of Sectors in a single FAT	word
Sectors Per Track	word
Number of Heads	word
Number of Hidden Sectors	word

The last three WORDs in Table 6-4 help the device driver understand the media. The number of heads is useful for supporting different multiple head drives that have the same storage capacity but a different number of surfaces. The number of hidden sectors is useful for supporting drive partitioning schemes.

For drivers that support volume identification and disk change, this call should cause a new volume identification to be read off the disk. This call indicates that the disk was properly changed.

4H, 8H, 9H / Read or Write

Read from or write to a device. Read (4H) / Write (8H) / Write with Verify (9H)

Format Of Request Packet

```
struct {                              // READ, WRITE, WRITE_VERIFY
    UCHAR      media;                 // media descriptor
    PHYSADDR   buffer;                // transfer address
    USHORT     count;                 // bytes/sectors
    ULONG      startsector;           // starting sector #
    USHORT     reserved;
} ReadWrite;
```

Comments

On entry, the Request Packet will have the media descriptor set for the drive identified in the Request Header. The transfer address is a 32-bit physical address of the buffer for the data. The byte/sector count is set to the number of bytes to transfer (for character device drivers) or the number of sectors to transfer (for block device drivers). The starting sector number is set for block device drivers. The System File Number is a unique number associated with an open request.

The device driver must perform the following actions:

- Perform the requested function.
- Set the actual number of sectors or bytes transferred.
- Set the status word in the Request Packet.

The DWORD transfer address in the Request Packet is a locked 32-bit physical address. The device driver can use it to call the DevHlp function PhysToVirt and obtain a segment swapping address for the current mode. The device driver does not need to unlock the address when the request is completed.

READ is a standard driver request. The application calls the READ Strategy entry point by issuing a DosRead with the handle obtained during the DosOpen. The READ routine may return one character at a time, but more often returns a buffer full of data. How the READ function works is up to the driver writer. The driver returns the count of characters read and stores the received data in the data segment of the application. READ returns one of the standard driver return codes.

Note: The functions IOCtl Read and IOCtl Write are not supported by the standard base OS/2 device drivers.

WRITE is a standard driver request, called by the application as a result of a DosWrite call. The application passes the address of data to write (usually in the applications data segment) to the driver and the count of the characters to write. The driver writes the data and returns the status to the application, along with the number of characters that were actually written. WRITE returns a standard driver return code.

5H / Nondestructive Read No Wait

Read a character from an input buffer without removing it.

Format Of Request Packet

```
struct {                              // NON_DESTRUCT READ/NO WAIT
    UCHAR      char_returned;         // returned character
    } ReadNoWait;
```

Comments

The device driver must perform the following actions:

- Return a byte from the device.
- Set the status word in the Request Header.

For input on character devices with a buffer, the device driver should return from this function with the busy bit (RPBUSY) clear, along with a copy of the first character in the buffer. The busy bit is set to indicate that there are no characters in the buffer. This function allows the operating system to look ahead one input character without blocking in the device driver.

6H, AH / Input or Output Status

Determine the input or output status of a character device.

Format Of Request Packet

```
No Parameters
```

Comments

The device driver must perform the following actions:

- Perform the requested function.
- Set the busy bit.
- Set the status word in the Request Header.

For output status on character devices, if the busy bit (RPBUSY) is returned set, an output request is currently pending. If the busy bit is returned set to 0, there is no current request pending.

For input status on character devices with a buffer, if the busy bit is returned set, there are no characters currently buffered in the device driver. If the busy bit is returned clear, there is at least one character in the device driver buffer. The effect of busy bit = 0 is that a read of one character will not need blocking. Devices that do not have an input buffer in the device driver should always return with the busy bit clear. This is a "peek" function, to determine the presence of data.

7H, BH / Input Flush or Output Flush

Flush or terminate all pending requests.

Format Of Request Packet

```
No Parameters
```

Comments

The device driver must perform the following actions:

- Perform the requested function.
- Set the status word in the Request Header.

This call tells the device driver to flush (terminate) all known pending requests. Its primary use is to flush the input or output queue on character devices. The Input Buffer Flush should flush any receiver queues or buffers, and return DONE to the kernel. The Output Buffer Flush should flush any transmitter queues or buffers.

DH,EH / Open or Close

Open or Close a Device.

Format Of Request Packet

```
struct {                        // OPEN/CLOSE
  USHORT sys_file_num ;         // system file number
} OpenClose;
```

Comments

The System File Number is a unique number associated with an open request.

The device driver must perform the following actions:

- Perform the requested function.
- Set the status word in the Request Header.

Character device drivers may use OPEN/CLOSE requests to correlate using their devices with application activity. For instance, the device driver may increase a reference count for every OPEN, and decrease the reference count for every CLOSE. When the count goes to 0, the device driver can flush its buffers. This can be thought of as a "last close causes flush."

The OPEN function is called as a result of the application issuing a DosOpen call. The kernel makes note of the DosOpen request, and if it is successful, the kernel sends back a handle to the application to use for subsequent driver service. The driver writer can use this section to initialize a device, flush any buffers, reset any buffer pointers, initialize character queues, or anything necessary for a clean starting operation.

The CLOSE is usually called as a result of the application doing a DosClose with the correct driver handle, but it is also called when the application that opened the driver terminates or is aborted with a <cntl-c> or <cntl-break>.

In most cases, its a good idea to make sure that the application closing the driver is the same one that opened it. To ensure this, the device driver should save the PID of the application that opened the driver, and make sure that the closing PID is the same. If not, the device driver should reject it as a bogus request. The driver can get the PID of the calling program using the GetDOSVar DevHlp routine.

All devices associated with the device driver should be made quiescent at CLOSE time.

FH / Removable Media

Check for removable media.

Format Of Request Packet

```
No Parameters
```

Comments

The device driver must perform the following actions:

- Set the busy bit to 1 if the media is non-removable.
- Set the busy bit to 0 if the media is removable.
- Set the status word in the Request Header.

The driver receives this request as a result of an application generating an IOCtl call to Category 8, Function 0x20. Instead of calling the IOCtl section of the device driver, the kernel issues this request. The driver must set the busy bit (RPBUSY) of the Request Packet status if the media is non-removable, and must clear it if the media is removable.

10H / Generic IOCTL

Send I/O control commands to a device.

Format Of Request Packet (DosDevIOCtl)

```
    struct {                        // IOCtl
      UCHAR     category;           // category code
      UCHAR     function;           // function code
      FARPOINTER parameters;        // &parameters
      FARPOINTER buffer;            // &buffer
      USHORT    sys_file_num;       // system file number
    } IOCtl;
```

Format Of Request Packet (DosDevIOCtl2)

```
struct {                            // IOCtl
  UCHAR      category;              // category code
  UCHAR      function;              // function code
  FARPOINTER parameters;            // &parameters
  FARPOINTER buffer;                // &buffer
  USHORT     sys_file_num;          // system file number
  USHORT     parm_buf_length;       // length of parameter buffer
  USHORT     data_buf_length        // length of data buffer
} IOCtl;
```

Comments

On entry, the request packet will have the IOCtl category code and function code set. The parameter buffer and the data buffer addresses are passed as virtual addresses. Note that some IOCtl functions do not require data and/or parameters to be passed. For these IOCtls, the parameter and data buffer addresses may contain NULL pointers. The System File Number is a unique number associated with an OPEN request.

If the device driver indicates (in the function level of the device attribute field of its Device Header) that it supports DosDevIOCtl2, the Generic IOCtl request packets passed to the device driver will have two additional words, containing the lengths of the Parameter Buffer and Data Buffer, respectively. If the device driver indicates through the function level that it supports DosDevIOCtl2, but the application issues DosDevIOCtl, the Parameter Buffer and Data Buffer length fields will be set to zero.

The device driver must perform the following actions:

- Perform the requested function.
- Set the status word in the Request Header.

The device driver is responsible for locking the parameter and data buffer segments, and converting the pointers to 32-bit physical addresses, if necessary.

Refer to the *OS/2 Version 2.1 Programming Reference* and the *OS/2 Version 2.1 Application Programming Guide* for more detailed information on the generic IOCtl interface for applications.

The third and fourth command-specific parameters of an IOCtl are the address of the application program's data buffer and parameter buffer, respectively. The format of the two buffers is entirely up to the driver writer. The parameter buffer might contain a list of USHORTs, UCHARs, or pointers. However, pointers are not recommended because, depending on the type of application sending them (16:16 or 0:32), the pointers might require further translation, affecting portability.

The data buffer parameter might be the address of a data buffer in the application program where the driver would store data from the device. It should also be noted that the IOCtl need not pass or receive any data.

Another feature of an IOCtl is its ability to send back device-specific information to the application. A standard driver request, such as DosRead or DosWrite, returns a value to the application which is used to determine whether or not the operation was successful. For something like a terminal driver, a simple pass/fail indication might be sufficient. Suppose, however, that the driver needed to tell the application that the data was in ASCII or binary format, or that a parity error was detected while receiving it. Here an IOCtl would be a better choice because the kernel 'massages' return codes from standard function calls to fit within the standard error definitions. The IOCtl, however, will pass back special error codes to the application exactly as they were set in the driver.

11H / Reset Media

Reset the Uncertain Media error condition and allow OS/2 to identify the media.

Format Of Request Packet

```
No Parameters
```

Comments

On entry, the unit code identifies the drive number to be reset.

The device driver must perform the following actions:

- Set the status word in the Request Header.
- Reset the error condition for the drive.

Before this command, the driver had returned ERROR_UNCERTAIN_MEDIA for the drive. This action informs the device driver that it no longer needs to return the error for the drive.

12H, 13H / Get/Set Logical Drive

Get/Set Logical Drive Mapping

Format Of Request Packet

```
No Parameters
```

Comments

On entry, the unit code contains the unit number of the drive on which this operation is to be performed.

The device driver must perform the following actions:

- For GET, it must return the logical drive that is mapped onto the physical drive indicated by the unit number in the Request Header.

- For SET, it must map the logical drive represented by the unit number onto the physical drive that has the mapping of logical drives.

- The logical drive is returned in the unit code field. This field is set to 0 if there is only one logical drive mapped onto the physical drive.

- Set the status word in the Request Header.

14H / Deinstall

Request deinstall of driver.

Format Of Request Packet

```
No Parameters
```

Comments

When a device driver is loaded, the attribute field and name in its header are used to determine if the new device driver is attempting to replace a driver (device) already installed. If so, the previously installed device driver is requested by the operating system to DEINSTALL. If the installed device driver refuses the DEINSTALL command, the new device driver is not allowed to be loaded. If the installed device driver performs the DEINSTALL, the new device driver is loaded.

If a character device driver honors the DEINSTALL request, it must perform the following actions:

- Release any allocated physical memory.
- UnSet any hardware interrupt vectors that it had claimed.
- Remove any timers.
- Clear the error bit in the status word to indicate a successful DEINSTALL.

If the character device driver determines that it cannot or will not deinstall, it should set the error bit (RPERR) in the status field and set the error code to ERROR_BAD_COMMAND (03H).

Deinstall Considerations

An ABIOS device driver maps its device name to a unit within a *Logical ID* (*LID*). It receives a DEINSTALL request for its device name, which implies a single unit of a LID. To honor the DEINSTALL request, it must relinquish the LID by calling DevHlp FreeLIDEntry at DEINSTALL time.

In honoring a DEINSTALL command, a device driver must remove its claim on the interrupt level by issuing an UnSetIRQ DevHlp call.

If the device driver's device is ill-behaved (that is, it cannot be told to stop generating interrupts), the device driver must not remove its interrupt handler, and must refuse the DEINSTALL request.

16H / Partitionable Fixed Disks

This call is used by the system to ask the device driver how many physical partitionable fixed disks the device driver supports.

Format Of Request Packet

```
struct {                        // PARTITIONABLE fixed disks
    UCHAR       count;          // number of disks supported
    ULONG       reserved;
} Partitionable;
```

Comments

This is done to allow the Category 9 Generic IOCtls to be routed appropriately to the correct device driver. This call is not tied to a particular unit that the device driver owns, but is directed to the device driver as a general query of its device support.

The device driver must perform the following actions:

- Set the count (1- based).
- Set the status word in the Request Header.

17H / Get Fixed Disk/Logical Unit Map

Get Fixed Disk/LU Map.

Format Of Request Packet

```
struct {                    // Get Fixed Disk/Log Unit Map
   ULONG    units;          // units supported
   ULONG    reserved;
} GetFixedMap;
```

Comments

This call is used by the system to determine which logical units supported by the device driver exist on the physical partitionable fixed disk.

On entry, the request packet header unit field identifies a physical disk number (0-based) instead of a logical unit number. The device driver returns a bitmap of which logical units exist on the physical drive. The physical drive relates to the partitionable fixed disks reported to the system by way of the PARTITIONABLE FIXED DISKS command. It is possible that no logical units exist on a given physical disk because it has not yet been initialized.

The device driver must perform the following actions:

- Set the 4-byte bit mask to indicate which logical units it owns. The logical units must exist on the physical partitionable fixed disk for which the information is being requested.

- Set the status word in the Request Packet header.

The bit mask is set up as follows: A 0 means that the logical unit does not exist, and a 1 means it does. The first logical unit that the device driver supports is the low-order bit of the first byte. The bits are used from right to left, starting at the low-order bit of each following byte. It is possible that all of the bits will be 0.

1CH / Shutdown

Begin shutdown procedure.

Format Of Request Packet

```
struct {                        // Shutdown
  UCHAR      func;              // shutdown function code
  ULONG      reserved;
} Shutdown;
```

Comments

This call is used by the system to notify a device driver to flush any data to the device and prepare to shutdown.

The driver is called twice, once for a Start Shutdown and then again for an End Shutdown. The function code is 0 for the Start Shutdown call and 1 for the End Shutdown call.

Level 2 device drivers are called with the Shutdown request. Level 3 drivers are only called if the shutdown flag of the Capabilities field is set in the Device Header.

1DH/ Get Driver Capabilities

Get a disk device driver's capabilities.

Format Of Request Packet

```
struct {                              // Get Driver Capabilities
  UCHAR      res[3];                  // reserved, must be 0
  FARPOINTER CapStruct;               // 16:16 pointer to DCS
  FARPOINTER VolCharStruct;           // 16:16 pointer to VCS
} GetDriverCaps;
```

Comments

This command returns the functional capabilities of the driver for device drivers supporting the Extended Device Driver Interface.

This command is issued by the system to see whether the driver supports the scatter/gather protocol. The driver must initialize this structure. The first pointer is a 16:16 pointer to the Driver Capabilities Structure, and the second pointer is 1 16:16 pointer to the Volume Characteristics Structure. Refer to Chapter 12 for more detailed information on this command and its associated data structures.

1FH / CMDInitComplete

Notify device driver that all PDDs and IFS drivers have been loaded.

Format of Request Packet

```
No Parameters
```

Comments

This command notifies the device driver that all drivers have been loaded, allowing the device driver to initiate any driver-to-driver communications or initialization. This command removes any problems associated with the order in which device drivers appear in the CONFIG.SYS file.

This command is issued by the system only if the device driver is a level 3 driver and has set bit 4 in the Capabilities Bit Strip word in the device header.

CHAPTER 7

A Simple OS/2 Physical Device Driver

This chapter outlines the operation of an actual OS/2 *Physical Device Driver* *(PDD)*. PDDs are the only type of drivers that can interface directly with adapter or system hardware. Chapter 5 discussed the various parts and design of an OS/2 PDD. This chapter will bring the parts together to form a PDD that can be loaded and tested under OS/2.

Device Driver Specifications

The requirement for this device driver is to perform I/O to an 8-bit parallel port, a common requirement. Although this device driver is designed for the 8255 parallel chip, it can easily be modified for any other type of 8-bit parallel adapter. This driver performs the I/O using the standard DosRead and DosWrite, and also shows how to perform the I/O using IOCtls. It is a good example of handling the differences between standard device driver request and IOCtls.

Parallel adapters are frequently used for reading switches or other pieces of hardware which cause single bits to be set or clear. I've added an additional function to this device driver to show how an OS/2 device driver can be written to wait for a single bit to be set or clear without using interrupts or compromising system performance. Writing a similar device driver under DOS would be simple. Since DOS runs only one program at a time, the program could wait around forever for the particular bit to be set. OS/2, however, runs many programs at the same time, and cannot afford to wait around for a bit to be set while keeping all other programs dormant. To accomplish this without polling, the OS/2 device driver hooks a timer interrupt, and polls the port at every tick of the OS/2 system clock (31.25 milliseconds). Between each clock tick, the driver is either idle or blocked by an application request, so other threads continue to run.

It is important to note that the amount of memory available for the stack in a device driver is extremely small, approximately 4K bytes, so it is important to keep the amount of local variables at a minimum.

The complete listing of this device driver can be found in the Appendix C.

Application Program Design

When the application is first started, it opens the device driver with a DosOpen API call described in Figure 7-1.

```
.
.
if ((RetCode=DosOpen("DIGIO$",
    &digio_handle,
    &ActionTaken,
    FileSize,
    FileAttribute,
    FILE_OPEN,
    OPEN_SHARE_DENYNONE | OPEN_FLAGS_FAIL_ON_ERROR
    | OPEN_ACCESS_READWRITE,Reserved)) !=0)
       printf("\nopen error = %d",RetCode);
.
.
```

Figure 7-1. Application call to open the driver.

If successful, the DosOpen call returns a handle to the application which it can use for subsequent access to the device driver. A handle is nothing more than a special cookie that OS/2 uses to allow access to a particular driver.

Device Driver Operation

Refer to the device driver source code in Appendix C. Note the Device Header and the name assigned to the driver. For this example, the driver name has been assigned DIGIO$. The name must be eight characters in length, and must be space-padded for up to eight character positions. The '$' character was used in case a file or directory had the same name as the driver, for instance \drivers\digio.

INIT

In the INIT section in Figure 7-2, the DevHlp routine SetTimer is called to register the timer handler we will use to periodically check a bit from the parallel port. If the SetTimer call fails, the driver returns a failure to the kernel and gives up the memory it had occupied during initialization. If the call was successful, the driver displays a sign-on message and returns the DONE status to the kernel. The INIT section also initializes the 8255 parallel chip to setup port address base+0 as the read-port address, and base+1 as the write-port address.

As soon as the timer handler is registered, the timer handler begins receiving timer interrupts every 31.25 milliseconds. The ReadID variable is used to ignore timer interrupts when no driver requests are pending.

```
int Init(PREQPACKET rp)
{
    // store DevHlp entry point

    DevHlp = rp->s.Init.DevHlp;

    // install timer handler

    if(SetTimer((PFUNCTION)TIMER_HANDLER)) {

        // if we failed, effectively deinstall driver with cs+ds=0

        DosPutMessage(1, 8, devhdr.DHname);
        DosPutMessage(1,strlen(FailMessage),FailMessage);
        rp->s.InitExit.finalCS = (OFF) 0;
        rp->s.InitExit.finalDS = (OFF) 0;
        return (RPDONE | RPERR | ERROR_BAD_COMMAND);
```

Figure 7-2. INIT section. (Continued)

```
    }

   // configure 8255 parallel chip

   outp (DIGIO_CONFIG,0x91);

   // output initialization message

   DosPutMessage(1, 2, CrLf);
   DosPutMessage(1, 8, devhdr.DHname);
   DosPutMessage(1, strlen(InitMessage1), InitMessage1);
   DosPutMessage(1, strlen(InitMessage2), InitMessage2);

   // send back our code and data end values to os/2

   if (SegLimit(HIUSHORT((void far *) Init),
      &rp->s.InitExit.finalCS) || SegLimit(HIUSHORT((void far *) InitMessage2),
      &rp->s.InitExit.finalDS))
         Abort();
   return(RPDONE);
}
```

Figure 7-2. INIT section.

OPEN

When the application program is started, it issues a DosOpen call to the kernel, which routes it to the driver via an OPEN Request Packet. If the DosOpen is successful, the kernel returns a handle to the application for subsequent driver access. When the driver receives the OPEN Request Packet (see Figure 7-3), it checks to see whether the driver had been opened prior to this call. This might happen if more than one thread of an application opened the driver. If the driver had not been opened, it gets the PID of the opening program and saves it for later use. It then bumps the open counter and returns DONE to the kernel. The DONE status with no errors is mapped to the standard "no error" return to the DosOpen call, and returned to the application. If the open count was greater than zero, the PID of the opening program is compared to the previously saved PID to see if they are the same. If the new PID is not the same as the old PID, the request is rejected by sending the BUSY status back to the kernel. The kernel maps the return to a standard return code and sends that code to the application as a failure. In all cases, whether errors occurred or not, the driver must return with the DONE status.

```
case RPOPEN:                                    // 0x0d open driver

  // get current processes' id

  if (GetDOSVar(2,&ptr))
        return (RPDONE | RPERR | ERROR_BAD_COMMAND);

  // get process info

  liptr = *((PLINFOSEG far *) ptr);

  // if this device never opened, can be opened by anyone

  if (opencount == 0)                    // first time this dev opened
  {
      opencount=1;                       // bump open counter
      savepid = liptr->pidCurrent;       // save current PID
  }
  else
  {
      if (savepid != liptr->pidCurrent)  // another proc
          return (RPDONE | RPERR | ERROR_NOT_READY);//err
      ++opencount;                       // bump counter, same pid
  }
  return (RPDONE);
```

Figure 7-3. OPEN section.

CLOSE

The driver will receive a close Request Packet as a result of a DosClose API call from the application, or from the kernel in the event that the application was terminated by a <cntl-c>, <cntl-break> or other fault. In the CLOSE section (see Figure 7-4), the driver checks the PID of the closing application to make sure that it has the same PID as the program that opened it. If not, the request is rejected by returning an error to the kernel. If it is the same, it was a valid close request, so the driver decrements the open counter and returns the DONE status to the kernel.

```
case RPCLOSE:                    // 0x0e DosClose,ctl-C, kill

    // get process info of caller

    if (GetDOSVar(2,&ptr))
        return (RPDONE | RPERR | ERROR_BAD_COMMAND);

    // get process info from os/2

    liptr= *((PLINFOSEG far *) ptr); // ptr to linfoseg

    // make sure that the process attempting to close this device
    // is the one that originally opened it and the device was
    //  open in the first place.


    if (savepid != liptr->pidCurrent || opencount == 0)
        return (RPDONE | RPERR | ERROR_BAD_COMMAND);

    —opencount;            // close counts down open cntr
    return (RPDONE);       // return 'done' status
```

Figure 7-4. CLOSE section.

IOCtls

The IOCtl Request Packets are received as a result of a DosDevIOCtl API call from the application. In this example, the driver supports three IOCtls. They are read a byte from a port, write a byte to a port, and read a port with wait.

The IOCtl section first checks to make sure that the category is correct for this driver. Each device driver should have its own category, assigned by the driver writer. Categories from 0 to 127 are reserved for OS/2, and categories 128-255 are available for use by special drivers. You should avoid using category 128, however, as this category is sometimes used by OS/2 for drivers such as VDISK.SYS or OEMHLP. There are some cases where the category of a device driver might be the same as the category for an existing OS/2 device driver. An example would be a driver that replaced the COM01.SYS or COM02.SYS serial driver, or one that augmented an existing device driver. An example of this might be a device driver that adds support for COM5-COM12. Since certain IOCtls of a particular category are used to perform operations such as setting parity, changing the baud rate or the character length, the replacement driver should support the same number and type of IOCtl requests.

If the category is not valid, the driver returns the DONE status to the kernel without performing any operations. It is generally acceptable to ignore unrecognized IOCtl requests, because the kernel will, from time to time, issue IOCtls to your driver which your driver does not support.

If the category is valid, the driver checks the IOCtl function code.

CASE 0x01

If the IOCtl request is a 1, the write-port function has been requested (see Figure 7-5). The driver calls the DevHlp routine VerifyAccess with the virtual address of the IOCtl parameter buffer to verify that the caller owns the memory that it points to. It also checks to see that the application has the correct read and write privileges. If the address is valid, the driver copies the byte to be output from the application, using a simple virtual-to-virtual copy. Using the standard run-time library routine outp, the driver writes the byte to the particular port. The driver then sends the DONE status back to the kernel and exits.

```
    case 0x01:                              // write byte to digio port

    // verify caller owns this buffer area

    if(VerifyAccess(
    SELECTOROF(rp->s.IOCtl.parameters),    // selector
    OFFSETOF(rp->s.IOCtl.parameters),      // offset
    1,                                      // 1 byte
    0) )                                    // read only
        return (RPDONE | RPERR | ERROR_GEN_FAILURE);

    if(MoveBytes(rp->s.IOCtl.parameters,(FARPOINTER)&output_char,1))
        return (RPDONE | RPERR | ERROR_GEN_FAILURE);

    outp(DIGIO_OUTPUT,output_char);         //send to digio

    return (RPDONE);
```

Figure 7-5. IOCtl 0x01, write port.

CASE 0x02

If the IOCtl code was 2, read with wait, the driver performs the identical operations to the previous IOCtl (see Figure 7-6). In this IOCtl, the application sends the driver a bit to wait for, and the driver will not return until that particular bit becomes set.

First, the driver verifies the IOCtl virtual buffer pointer to make sure that the application owns the memory. Note that in this particular IOCtl, the data buffer pointer was used and not the parameter buffer pointer. The data buffer contains not only the port address to read from, but the space for the data read by the driver. Either buffer area can be used for reading or writing data. In this case, the data buffer was used for read IOCtls and the parameter buffer was used for write IOCtls. Which buffers are used and how they are interpreted is entirely up to the driver writer.

Since the driver will Block until completion, it must lock down the applications buffer to ensure it is still there when the driver is UnBlocked. Otherwise, the buffer addresses previously UnBlocked might not be valid due to swapping. Once the memory has been verified and locked, the data is transferred from the application to the driver. In this driver, the data is only one byte in size, which contains the bit to wait for. Next, the variable ReadID is cast to a ULONG of the Request Packet pointer to be used as an ID for the DevHlp Block call. The driver then Blocks with a -1L for a time-out, which indicates that the driver will wait forever (no timeout). When the Block returns, it was either the result of a signal, such as <cntl-c>, or a call to the DevHlp Run routine with the same 32-bit ID used for the Block. The driver checks the return code form the Block. If the error code is a 2, which means a <cntl-c> caused the return from the Block, the driver returns ERROR_CHAR_CALL_INTERRUPTED to the kernel. If the error code was not a 2, the driver assumes that it was a valid Run call that caused the driver to become UnBlocked. The driver copies the result of the port read to the application, UnBlocked the caller's memory and returns the DONE status to the kernel. How the data is actually read from the I/O port is detailed in the Timer Handler section in Figure 7-9. The driver copies the result of the port read to the application.

Note that, in this IOCtl, the device driver locked the application's buffer to prevent it from being swapped out. This is necessary when the device driver issues a DevHlp Block request, but is not necessary in the other two IOCtls, where no Blocking occurs.

```
case 0x02:                              // read w/wait from port

   // verify caller owns this buffer area

   if(VerifyAccess(
   SELECTOROF(rp->s.IOCtl.buffer), // selector
   OFFSETOF(rp->s.IOCtl.buffer),   // offset
   1,                              // 1 bytes)
   0))                             // read only
       return (RPDONE | RPERR | ERROR_GEN_FAILURE);

   // lock the segment down temp

   if(LockSeg(
   SELECTOROF(rp->s.IOCtl.buffer), // selector
   1,                              // lock forever
   0,                              // wait for seg loc
   (PLHANDLE) &lock_seg_han))      // handle returned
       return (RPDONE | RPERR | ERROR_GEN_FAILURE);

   if(MoveBytes(rp->s.IOCtl.parameters,(FARPOINTER)&input_mask,1))
       return (RPDONE | RPERR | ERROR_GEN_FAILURE);
```

Figure 7-6. IOCtl 0x02. (Continued)

```
    // wait for bit to be set

    ReadID = (ULONG)rp;
    if (Block(ReadID,-1L,0,&err))
       if (err == 2)
          return(RPDONE | RPERR | ERROR_CHAR_CALL_INTERRUPTED);

    // move result to users buffer

    if(MoveBytes((FARPOINTER)&input_char,rp->s.IOCtl.buffer,1))
         return(RPDONE | RPERR | ERROR_GEN_FAILURE);

    // unlock segment

    if(UnLockSeg(lock_seg_han))
         return(RPDONE | RPERR | ERROR_GEN_FAILURE);

    return (RPDONE);
```

Figure 7-6. IOCtl 0x02.

CASE 0x03

The purpose of this case is to provide a read without wait (see Figure 7-7). Instead of waiting for a bit to be set as in IOCtl 0x02, this IOCtl returns immediately with the value of a port. Instead of Blocking, the driver calls the run-time library routine inp to get the contents of the port and sends the data back to the application.

```
case 0x03:                              // read byte immed digio port

   // verify caller owns this buffer area

   if(VerifyAccess(
   SELECTOROF(rp->s.IOCtl.buffer),   // selector
   OFFSETOF(rp->s.IOCtl.buffer),     // offset
   1,                                 // 1 byte
```

Figure 7-7. IOCtl 0x03. (Continued)

```
    0))                             // read only
        return (RPDONE | RPERR | ERROR_GEN_FAILURE);

    input_char = inp(DIGIO_INPUT);  // get data

    if(MoveBytes((FARPOINTER)&input_char,rp->s.IOCtl.buffer,1))
        return(RPDONE | RPERR | ERROR_GEN_FAILURE);

    return (RPDONE);
```

Figure 7-7. IOCtl 0x03.

READ And WRITE

The READ and WRITE sections are entered as the result of a DosRead or DosWrite standard driver request from the application. The use of the standard read and write requests in Figure 7-8 is shown as an example to contrast the differences of the standard READ and WRITE functions with the IOCtl read and write functions. The READ section performs the exact same operation as the IOCtl function 0x03, read without wait, and the WRITE section does the same for IOCtl function 0x01, write a byte. Either call will perform the same operation. Instead of issuing an IOCtl request to write a byte to a port, the application can issue a DosWrite with the byte to be written. Instead of issuing an IOCtl function 0x03, the application can issue a DosRead.

The standard READ and WRITE sections are slightly different than their IOCtl counterparts. First, the application's buffer address in the Request Packet is the *physical address*, not the virtual address, and second, OS/2 verifies and locks the buffer segment prior to calling the device driver. Since our data transfer routine requires virtual pointers, the device driver calls the PhysToVirt DevHlp to convert the physical address to a virtual address and the data is transferred.

```c
case RPREAD:                            // 0x04

    rp->s.ReadWrite.count = 0;          // in case we fail

    input_char = inp(DIGIO_INPUT);      // get data

    if (PhysToVirt( (ULONG) rp->s.ReadWrite.buffer,
        1,0,&appl_ptr))
            return (RPDONE | RPERR | ERROR_GEN_FAILURE);

    if (MoveBytes((FARPOINTER)&input_char,appl_ptr,1))
            return (RPDONE | RPERR | ERROR_GEN_FAILURE);

    rp->s.ReadWrite.count = 1;          // one byte read
    return (RPDONE);

case RPWRITE:                           // 0x08

    rp->s.ReadWrite.count = 0;

    if (PhysToVirt( (ULONG) rp->s.ReadWrite.buffer,
        1,0,&appl_ptr))
            return (RPDONE | RPERR | ERROR_GEN_FAILURE);

    if (MoveBytes(appl_ptr,(FARPOINTER)&output_char,1))
            return (RPDONE | RPERR | ERROR_GEN_FAILURE);

    outp (DIGIO_OUTPUT,output_char); // send byte

    rp->s.ReadWrite.count = 1;          // one byte written
    return (RPDONE);
```

Figure 7-8. READ and WRITE section.

Timer Handler

In CASE 0x02, the driver blocks waiting for a particular bit to be set before returning to the caller. Other threads in the system will run only when the driver completes its job and returns DONE to the kernel, or when the driver becomes Blocked. Recall earlier that SetTimer was called to hook the OS/2 timer interrupt, and that access to the timer handler was controlled by the variable ReadID. In CASE 0x02, the ReadID was set to a ULONG cast of the Request Packet pointer. Since the ReadID is no longer zero, each time that the timer handler (see Figure 7-9) is entered, the driver can do an *inp* of the parallel port, "and" it to the bit mask, and if non-zero, run the Blocked driver thread. The input port value is checked every tick of the OS/2 system clock, or every 31.25 milliseconds. If the bit is not set, the driver will block forever until a <cntl-c> or <cntl-break> is detected, or the bit finally becomes set. If set, the driver clears the timer handler entry flag, ReadID. It then calls the Run DevHlp to UnBlock the driver Strategy thread, which set the DONE status in the Request Packet and returns to the OS/2 kernel.

```
timr_handler()
{

    if (ReadID != 0) {

        // read data from port

        input_char = inp(DIGIO_INPUT );// get data

        if ((input_char && input_mask) !=0) {
           Run (ReadID);
           ReadID=0L;
           }
      }
}
```

Figure 7-9. Timer handler.

CHAPTER 8

The Micro Channel Bus

The Micro Channel bus is found on most IBM PS/2 machines and on Micro Channel machines supplied by other manufacturers such as Reply and NCR. The Micro Channel bus provides increased speeds, interrupt sharing, full 32-bit data path and increased noise immunity. Current specifications for Micro Channel II provide for transfers at speeds of 160MB per second.

Micro Channel Adapter Cards

Micro Channel adapters have no interrupt or address jumpers. Information about the adapter, such as interrupt level and memory-mapped address, is stored on the board in a set of nonvolatile registers called the *Programmable Option Select*, or *POS,* registers. The information stored in the POS registers is either factory-set or configured by a setup disk supplied by the manufacturer. On an IBM PS/2, this is usually done with the IBM PS/2 Reference Diskette.

The POS registers are not directly accessible to a program, so the driver can't get at them by doing simple "IN" and "OUT" instructions. A special programmable switch must be set to allow direct register access to the configuration program. The driver must, however, get the contents of the POS registers in order to configure itself properly. Once the POS registers are "visible", they can be accessed starting at I/O port address 0x100.

Normally, the driver accesses the POS registers using the PS/2 *Advanced BIOS*, or *ABIOS*, routines. ABIOS is a set of BIOS routines that are executable in the protect mode. ABIOS routines provide a device-independent access to supported devices through a *logical ID*, or *LID*. The driver obtains a LID from the ABIOS by a call to the GetLIDEntry DevHlp routine. Once the driver has the LID, it can use the LID to access the board registers.

The Micro Channel bus is unique in that the position of each adapter in the motherboard or *planar* is important. Unlike the ISA bus where boards can be placed in any slot, each slot in the Micro Channel machine is addressable. For this reason, calls to the ABIOS routines to read the POS registers of a particular adapter must contain an argument specifying the slot number of that adapter. Slot 0 is the planar, and the remaining slots are numbered starting at 1. Some of the largest PS/2 models, such as the IBM PS/2 Model 80, contain 8 slots.

Micro Channel Adapter ID

Each I/O card has a unique ID number, assigned by the manufacturer. IBM reserves IDs 8000-FFFF for its own use. These device ID numbers can be found in the first two POS registers, 0 and 1. The low byte is in POS register 0, the high byte in POS register 1. The rest of the POS register data is in POS registers 2-5. Thus POS register 0 can be read with an input from port address 0x100, and POS register 1 can be read from address 0x101.

Beware of conflicting definitions. Since the card ID can't be changed, the first available POS register, which is actually POS register 2, is sometimes referred to as POS register 0.

During driver INIT, it is a good idea to search the planar for a card with the correct ID for the device driver before trying to initialize the driver. Once an adapter is found, the POS registers of the adapter can be accessed. ABIOS requests must be formatted into a special structure called an ABIOS Request Block. Refer to the *IBM Personal System/2 BIOS Interface Technical Reference* for more detailed information on ABIOS Request Blocks and the various types of ABIOS requests.

Since device drivers for the Micro Channel bus differ slightly from their ISA bus counterparts, it is sometimes advantageous to write one device driver that will handle both a Micro Channel and ISA version of a particular adapter. The driver can check to see if the machine has a Micro Channel bus, and if so, read the required driver configuration information from the POS registers. If the machine has an ISA bus, the driver can set hard-coded values for the driver configuration parameters, or can read them from the DEVICE= statement in the CONFIG.SYS entry for the driver. Recall from Chapter 6 that one of pointers sent in the INIT request packet is the address of the parameters from the DEVICE= line in CONFIG.SYS. This allows the user with an ISA bus system to enter a line such as "DEVICE=DRIVER.SYS 3E8 D8000" in the CONFIG.SYS file, where 3E8 is the base port address and D8000 is the memory-mapped adapter address. The driver can parse the parameters, convert them to numeric values, and use them in the driver as actual configuration parameters.

The code shown in Figure 8-1 shows how to determine whether the system has a Micro Channel or ISA bus, and if Micro Channel, how to search the bus for a particular device ID and read its POS registers. If the system has an ISA bus, the parameters are read from the DEVICE= line in CONFIG.SYS.

Note that the ABIOS command used to read the POS registers from the card is READ_POS_REGS_CARD. This command specifies that the POS register contents be read directly from the adapter. PS/2 computers keep a copy of the current adapter configuration in NVRAM. When the system is powered up, the Power On Self Test routine, or *POST,* checks the installed adapter IDs against the current NVRAM configuration. If a difference is found, the POST issues an error message on the screen directing the user to run the setup program.

Occasionally, a device driver may reprogram a Micro Channel adapter "on the fly". For example, assume the device driver had to perform Binary Synchronous (BiSync) communications using a modem that could only dial using the High level Data Link Control (HDLC) protocol. The IBM Multiprotocol Adapter, or *MPA* is an example of an adapter that supports several modes of operation. It supports asynchronous, BiSync and HDLC protocols, but its POS registers can only be configured for one type of protocol at one time. The MPA adapter's mode of operation is determined by the POS register settings, which are normally be changed only with the PS/2 Reference Diskette.

The device driver for this application rewrites the POS registers on the fly. The device driver configures the adapter for normal BiSync operation and waits for a command to dial a number. When a dial command is received, the driver saves the contents of the MPA's POS registers and writes the HDLC configuration data to the POS registers. It initializes the HDLC controller, sends the dial information to the modem using the HDLC protocol and waits for a connection. When the modem is connected, the device driver rewrites the POS registers with the previously saved POS register data, initializing it back to BiSync operation. The result? Two adapters for the price of one.

```
// Ex.INIT section, combination ISA and MicroChannel bus driver

// This driver is loaded in the config.sys file with the DEVICE=
// statement. For ISA configuration, the first parameter to the
// "DEVICE=" is the base port address. The next parameter is the
// board base address. All numbers are in hex. For Micro Channel
// configuration, the board address and port address are read
// from the board POS regs.
//

PHYSADDR   board_address;              // base board address
USHORT     port_address;               // base port address
USHORT     bus = 0;                    // default ISA bus
REQBLK     ABIOS_r_blk;                // ABIOS request block
LIDBLK     ABIOS_l_blk;                // ABIOS LID block
USHORT     lid_blk_size;               // size of LID block
CARD       card[MAX_NUM_SLOTS+1];      // array for IDs and POS reg
CARD       *pcard;                     // pointer to card array
USHORT     matches = 0;                // match flag for card ID
USHORT     port1,port2;                // temp variables for addr calc

char    NoMatchMsg[]  = " no match for DESIRED card ID found.\r\n";
char    MainMsgMCA[]  = "\r\nOS/2 Micro Channel (tm) Device
Driver installed.\r\n";
char    MainMsg[] = "\r\nOS/2 ISA Device Driver installed.\r\n";

// prototypes

int     hex2bin(char);
USHORT  get_POS();
UCHAR   get_pos_data();
.
.
* Device Driver Strategy Section Here *
.
.
int   hex2bin(char c)
{
        if(c < 0x3a)
```

Figure 8-1. ISA and Micro Channel INIT section. (Continued)

```
                    return (c - 48);
        else
                    return (( c & 0xdf) - 55);
}

USHORT get_POS(USHORT slot_num,USHORT far *card_ID,
        UCHAR far *pos_regs)
{
USHORT rc, i, lid;

    // get a POS LID

    if (GetLIDEntry(0x10, 0, 1, &lid))
        return (1);

    // Get the size of the LID request block

    ABIOS_l_blk.f_parms.req_blk_len = sizeof(struct lid_block_def);
    ABIOS_l_blk.f_parms.LID = lid;
    ABIOS_l_blk.f_parms.unit = 0;;
    ABIOS_l_blk.f_parms.function = GET_LID_BLOCK_SIZE;
    ABIOS_l_blk.f_parms.ret_code = 0x5a5a;
    ABIOS_l_blk.f_parms.time_out = 0;

    // make the actual ABIOS call

    if (ABIOSCall(lid,0,(void far *)&ABIOS_l_blk))
        return (1);

    lid_blk_size = ABIOS_l_blk.s_parms.blk_size;

    // Fill POS regs with 0 and card ID with FF

    *card_ID = 0xFFFF;
    for (i=0; i<NUM_POS_BYTES; i++) { pos_regs[i] = 0x00; };

    // Get the POS registers and card ID for the commanded slot

    ABIOS_r_blk.f_parms.req_blk_len = lid_blk_size;
    ABIOS_r_blk.f_parms.LID = lid;
```

Figure 8-1. ISA and Micro Channel INIT section. (Continued)

```c
      ABIOS_r_blk.f_parms.unit = 0;;
      ABIOS_r_blk.f_parms.function = READ_POS_REGS_CARD;
      ABIOS_r_blk.f_parms.ret_code = 0x5a5a;
      ABIOS_r_blk.f_parms.time_out = 0;

      ABIOS_r_blk.s_parms.slot_num = (UCHAR)slot_num & 0x0F;
      ABIOS_r_blk.s_parms.pos_buf = (void far *)pos_regs;
      ABIOS_r_blk.s_parms.card_ID = 0xFFFF;

      if (ABIOSCall(lid,0,(void far *)&ABIOS_r_blk))
         rc = 1;
       else {
         *card_ID = ABIOS_r_blk.s_parms.card_ID;// fill in ID
         rc = 0;
         }

      // give back the LID

      FreeLIDEntry(lid);
      return(rc);

}

UCHAR get_pos_data (int slot, int reg)
{
   UCHAR pos;
   CARD *cptr;

   cptr = &card[slot-1];            // set ptr to beg of array
   if (reg == 0)                    // card ID
      pos = LOUSHORT(cptr->card_ID);
   else
     if ( reg == 1)
        pos = HIUSHORT(cptr->card_ID);
     else
        pos = cptr->pos_regs[reg-2];  // POS data register
   return (pos);
}
```

Figure 8-1. ISA and Micro Channel INIT section. (Continued)

```c
// Device Initialization Routine

int Init(PREQPACKET rp)
{
    USHORT lid;

    register char far *p;

    // store DevHlp entry point

    DevHlp = rp->s.Init.DevHlp;              // save DevHlp entry point

    if (!(GetLIDEntry(0x10, 0, 1, &lid))){   // get LID for POS
       FreeLIDEntry(lid);

       // Micro Channel (tm) setup section

       bus = 1;                              // Micro Channel bus

       // Get the POS data and card ID for each of 8 slots

       for (i=0;i <= MAX_NUM_SLOTS; i++)
          get_POS(i+1,(FARPOINTER)&card[i].card_ID,
             (FARPOINTER)card[i].pos_regs);

       matches = 0;
       for (i=0, pcard = card; i <= MAX_NUM_SLOTS; i++, pcard++){
          if (pcard->card_ID == DESIRED_ID) {
             matches = 1;
             break;
             }
          }

       if (matches == 0) {                   // no matches found
          DosPutMessage(1, 8, devhdr.DHname);
          DosPutMessage(1,strlen(NoMatchMsg),NoMatchMsg);
          rp->s.InitExit.finalCS = (OFF) 0;
          rp->s.InitExit.finalDS = (OFF) 0;
          return (RPDONE | RPERR | ERROR_BAD_COMMAND);
```

Figure 8-1. ISA and Micro Channel INIT section. (Continued)

```c
        }

    // calculate the board address from the POS regs

    board_address = ((unsigned long) get_pos_data(i+1, 4)
        << 16) | ((unsigned long)(get_pos_data(i+1, 3) & 1) << 15);

    // calculate the port address from the POS regs data

    port1 = (get_pos_data(i+1, 3) << 8) & 0xf800;
    port2 = (get_pos_data(i+1, 2) << 3) & 0x07e0;
    port_address = (port1 | port2);

    }
  else
    {
    // ISA bus setup
    bus = 0;                        // ISA bus

   // get parameters, port addr and base mem addr

    for (p = rp->s.Init.args; *p && *p != ' ';++p);
    for (; *p == ' '; ++p);        // skip blanks after name
    if (*p)
      {
      port_address = 0;
      board_address=0;              // i/o port address
      for (; *p != ' '; ++p)        // get port address
      port_address = (port_address << 4) + (hex2bin(*p));
      for (; *p == ' '; ++p);       // skip blanks after address
      for (; *p != '\0'; ++p)       // get board address
      board_address = (board_address << 4) + (hex2bin(*p));
      }
    }

    if (bus)
       DosPutMessage(1,strlen(MainMsgMCA),MainMsgMCA);
    else
       DosPutMessage(1,strlen(MainMsg),MainMsg);
```

Figure 8-1. ISA and Micro Channel INIT section. (Continued)

```
    // send back our end values to os/2

if (SegLimit(HIUSHORT((void far *) Init),
    &rp->s.InitExit.finalCS) ||
    SegLimit(HIUSHORT((void far *) MainMsg),
    &rp->s.InitExit.finalDS))
        Abort();

return (RPDONE);
}
```

Figure 8-1. ISA and Micro Channel INIT section.

Accessing the POS Register During Debug

While debugging an OS/2 Micro Channel device driver, it is sometimes necessary to access the POS registers directly without using the ABIOS routines. Under OS/2, the driver should always use the ABIOS routines to access the POS registers, as they serialize access to the adapter. During debug, however, the POS register contents can be checked by using simple IN and OUT instruction from the kernel debugger.

The -CD SETUP line, which enables the POS registers, is controlled by a register at I/O port address 96h. The POS registers for a particular card are enabled by performing an "OUT 96h,slot+7", where the slot is 0 for the motherboard and 1-8 for one of up to eight slots. Once a particular slot is enabled, the POS registers are visible with simple IN instructions. The POS registers are at the base address of 100h. POS register 0, which is the least significant bit of the adapter ID, can be read by an IN 100 command issued by the kernel debugger (see Chapter 13). POS register 1, the most significant byte of the adapter ID, can be found at address 101h. Other POS register data, which might contain such things as the adapter interrupt level, DMA arbitration level, or memory map, begins at address 102h. Only one slot can be enabled at a time. The -CD SETUP line is disabled by performing an OUT 96h,0.

Micro Channel Interrupts

Interrupts on ISA bus machines are edge-triggered and cannot be shared. Once an ISA bus adapter registers for a particular interrupt level, another driver cannot gain access to the same interrupt level. Device drivers that run on ISA bus machines must own their interrupt or interrupts exclusively, which severely limits the extendibility of ISA bus systems. With over half of the interrupts already assigned to system components such as the timer, hard disk, and floppy disk, not many interrupts are left over for other adapters.

Under OS/2, the Micro Channel bus supports interrupt sharing of up to four adapters on the same interrupt level. Micro Channel device drivers can register for an interrupt level even if another device driver had previously signed up for it. This requires some minor changes in device driver design for the two different bus architectures. In a Micro Channel device driver, when registering the interrupt level with the SetIRQ call, the nonexclusive option is used so the interrupt may be shared. In an ISA bus device driver, the exclusive option is used because interrupts cannot be shared. In addition, the interrupt handler needs to be modified slightly to claim or "pass on" the interrupt to the next interrupt handler. A flowchart showing the differences between an ISA bus interrupt handler and a Micro Channel interrupt handler is shown in Figure 8-2.

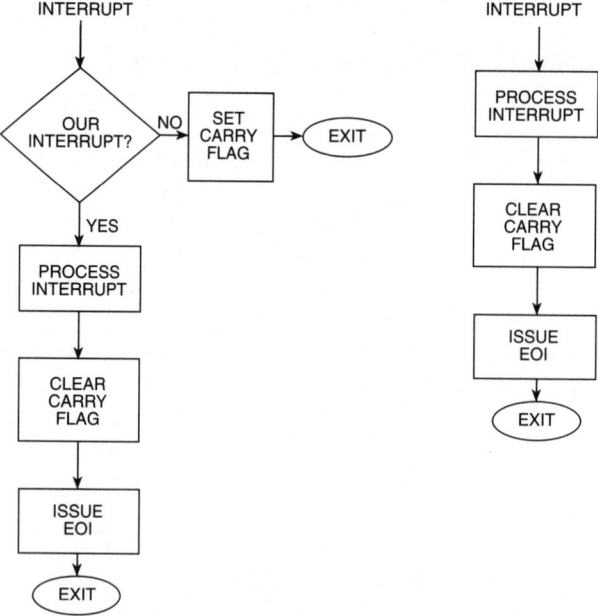

Figure 8-2. Micro Channel vs. ISA bus interrupt handler.

Since any one the four adapters on a single interrupt level can cause an interrupt, the device driver's interrupt handler must have a way to tell the kernel that it accepts or denies responsibility for the interrupt. If the interrupt does not belong to this particular interrupt handler's device, the interrupt handler must set the carry flag (STC), and return to the kernel. If the interrupt belongs to the particular device, the interrupt handler must claim the interrupt by clearing the carry flag before returning to the kernel. If the kernel finds the carry flag set, it will call each of the interrupt handlers that have registered for that particular interrupt until one of the handlers claims the interrupt by clearing the carry flag. If the interrupt is not claimed, OS/2 will continue to call the registered interrupt handlers until one of them claims the interrupt by clearing the carry flag.

CHAPTER 9

OS/2 2.1 Virtual Device Drivers

One of the shortcomings of OS/2 1.x was its inability to run DOS applications. Many of these DOS applications were written for the IBM PC and IBM XT computers, which were, by today's standards, fairly slow machines. To provide acceptable performance, these programs frequently accessed the system hardware and peripherals directly without using the BIOS or DOS system services. For example, instead of writing to the display with a DOS int system call, most programs wrote directly to video memory. Game programs frequently used processor-speed-dependent timing loops for making sounds or pausing between messages and screens. Other DOS programs reprogrammed the system timer circuit to generate voice-like sounds from the computer's speaker.

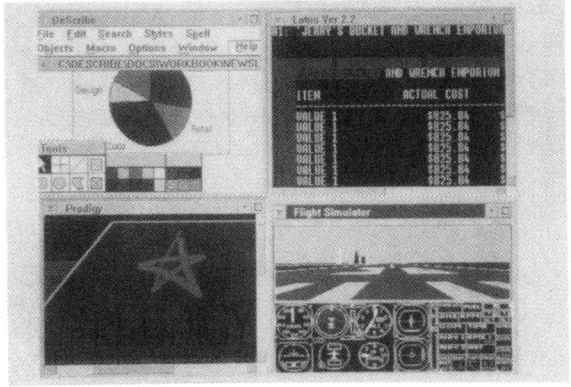

Figure 9-1. OS/2 2.1 VDMs. (Courtesy of International Business Machines Corporation.)

DOS programs can write to any memory location without checking to see if that location is valid or being used by another program. A programming error under DOS will, at the worst, cause the system to crash and have to be rebooted. This is not generally a problem, as only one program can be running at one time. With OS/2, however, a system crash could represent a major problem, as many programs could be running at the time of the crash. The result could be a loss of data, corrupt files, and a host of other problems.

To accommodate DOS applications, OS/2 1.x used a real mode session, referred to as the compatibility box, to run well-behaved DOS applications. Well-behaved DOS applications are those that do not directly manipulate the system hardware or devices, but use DOS system calls to perform their required operations. OS/2 1.x allowed only one real mode session to be active at one time. When the DOS program was running, the processor was in real mode, so a defective DOS application could still bring down the entire system. When the DOS session was switched to the background, it was frozen in its current state to prevent it from bringing down the system while an OS/2 application was running.

The Virtual DOS Machine

The Intel 80386 and 80486 processors have a built-in feature that allows real mode programs to run in their own one megabyte address space, isolated from the rest of the programs running on the system. This special mode is called the Virtual 8086 or V86 mode, and is used by OS/2 2.1 to run DOS applications in their own *DOS Session*. In OS/2 jargon, a DOS session in the V86 mode of the processor is called a *Virtual DOS Machine*, or *VDM*. OS/2 can support a large number of DOS VDMs, and the capability to do that is referred to as *Multiple Virtual DOS Machines*, or *MVDMs*.

DOS programs run in their own VDM without knowledge of other programs running in the system. The V86 mode is a protected mode of operation, and it will terminate the DOS session if it attempts a memory reference outside of its own one megabyte space. In the V86 mode, an errant DOS application can trash its own DOS session, but cannot bring down the rest of the system.

DOS programs that write directly to system hardware or devices are permitted to run in a DOS session. The DOS application does not have to be modified, but can run "out of the box." When the DOS program attempts to write directly to the system hardware or a system device, the operation is trapped by the kernel and routed to a *Virtual Device Driver*, or *VDD*. The VDD is a special driver that emulates the functions of a particular hardware device, such as the system timer, interrupt controller or communications port. The DOS application sees the VDD as the actual device, but direct access to the device is actually performed through a *Physical Device Driver* (PDD).

The PDD performs the actual I/O and passes the results to the VDD, which in turn sends the results back to the DOS application. OS/2 2.1 is supplied with a set of VDDs that virtualize the standard system device services such a DMA, timer, COM ports, video, and PIC.

When VDDs are loaded at boot time, the VDD claims ownership of the system resources it is responsible for while running in a VDM. The VDD can hook all I/O associated with a particular port or the interrupts associated with a particular IRQ. For example, the virtual COM driver, VCOM.SYS, claims ownership of I/O address 0x3f8, which is the address of COM1. A DOS program that attempts to perform direct I/O to 0x3f8 will be trapped by the COM VDD. The VDD must emulate the actual hardware device, and make the DOS application believe its talking directly to the device.

If a DOS program attempts to access an I/O port which has not been claimed by a VDD, it is allowed to perform that I/O directly without going through a VDD. The DOS application can turn interrupts off, although OS/2 will turn the interrupts back on if the DOS program leaves them off too long.

If an adapter can be shared by a protect mode application and a DOS application, a VDD should always be used to perform DOS I/O. Before performing I/O to the adapter, the VDD should first ask the PDD for permission to do so. The PDD and VDD should serialize access to the common adapter.

Although VDMs can run DOS applications that access hardware directly, there are some limitations. Existing DOS block device drivers for disk and tape cannot be used in the standard VDM. For character drivers, only those that perform I/O by polling can be used. Standard DOS drivers for the clock and mouse are not permitted to be used. DOS INT 21 requests are formatted into a standard OS/2 Request Packets and sent to the PDD for disposition.

VDMs, in which a specific version of DOS has been booted, can utilize existing DOS block device drivers. The block device should not be accessible to protect mode applications, so it must be dedicated to DOS operation.

Since versions of DOS differ in functionality, a DOS Setting is provided to specify which version of DOS should be booted instead of the built-in DOS emulator.

VDDs are loaded at system boot time, after any PDDs have been loaded and before the PM shell is started. The system first loads the base VDDs which are shared by multiple DOS sessions, such as the video virtual device driver, and then loads the installable VDDs from the DEVICE= line in CONFIG.SYS. Global code and data objects are loaded into low system memory to allow the PDD to call the VDD at interrupt time, regardless of the current process context. After the VDD is loaded, the VDD entry point is called to see if the load was performed without error. If so, the VDD returns TRUE, and if not, FALSE.

Virtual Device Drivers use a set of C callable helper routines, called the *Virtual Device Helper* (*VDH*) to perform their operations. Unlike the PDD DevHlps, which are register-based, the VDH routines are C callable, and exist in a DLL. They use the 32-bit C calling convention.

VDD Architecture

The VDD is nothing more than a 32-bit DLL, which may contain the following:

- initialization code
- initialization data
- swappable global code

The VDD must have at least one object of the following types:

- swappable global data
- swappable instance data
- resident global code
- resident global data
- resident instance data

A VDD that does not communicate with a PDD does not need a resident object section. Run-time memory can be private or shared. The typical VDD has a global code object, global data object, and a private instance data object.

VDDs are loaded by the DOS emulation component after all of the PDDs have been loaded. When the VDD is loaded, the VDD entry point is called by OS/2 to initialize the VDD. The entry point of the DLL is defined by writing a small assembly language program, which calls the DLL initialization entry point. The last statement in the assembly language program should be an END statement, with the parameter to the END statement being the name of the entry point. If the name of the VDD initialization entry point is, for example, VDDInit, the last statement in the assembly language routine should be END VDDInit. The IBM C Set/2 Compiler now supports the *pragma entry* keyword which is used to specify the initialization entry point for VDDs written in C.

After the VDD is loaded, the VDD entry point is called to see if the load was performed without error. If it was, the VDD returns TRUE, if not, the VDD returns FALSE.

VDD Initialization

The VDD performs initialization in a manner similar to the PDD. It verifies the presence of the hardware device, establishes contact with the corresponding PDD, reserves regions of linear memory containing device ROM and/or RAM, saves the current state of the device, and finally, sets hooks for DOS session events, such as session create, session destroy, and foreground/background switch requests. VDDs cannot make Ring 3 calls during initialization, and must use the Virtual Device Helper routines.

When a DOS session is started, the DOS Session Manager calls the VDD, allowing it to perform a per-DOS session initialization. The VDD allocates memory regions and passes control to the DOS emulation kernel, which loads the DOS shell, usually COMMAND.COM. The DOS emulation kernel then calls the VDD session creation entry points, allowing the VDD to set up aliases to physical memory, and optionally to allocate a block of memory between 256K and RMSIZE for a LIM 4.0 alias window.

When a DOS session is started, the DOS Session Manager calls each VDD that has registered a DOS session create hook. This allows VDDs to perform a per-DOS-session initialization. Control is then passed to the DOS emulation kernel, which loads the DOS shell, usually COMMAND.COM. At DOS session creation, the VDD may also:

- initialize the virtual device state.
- initialize the ROM BIOS state.
- map memory.
- hook I/O ports.
- enable/disable I/O port trapping.
- hook the software interrupts.
- allocate per-DOS session memory.

The OS/2 Session Manager notifies the DOS Session Manager if the session is being switched. The DOS Session Manager notifies any VDD that has registered to get this event via the VDHInstallUserHook VDH call. Depending on the VDD type, different actions will be taken. In the case of the virtual video device driver, VVIDEO, the driver will appropriately disable or enable I/O port trapping for the video board and remap the physical video memory to logical memory. The video will continue to be updated, but in logical video memory. When the session is switched back to the foreground, the logical memory is written to the physical video memory to update the display.

When the DOS session is exited, the VDD must perform any clean-up that is necessary. This usually includes releasing any allocated memory and restoring the state of the device. The VDD termination entry points are called by the DOS Session Manager at DOS program termination time.

OS/2 2.1 Virtual Device Drivers may only call OS/2 2.1 Physical Device Drivers that contain the "new level" bits. Older PDDs will return an error if called by a VDD. When a new level PDD receives an IOCtl, it must check the InfoSeg to determine whether it was called by a DOS session. If it was, it assumes that any pointers passed in IOCtl packets are in segment:offset format, computes the linear address directly (segment << 4 + offset) and then uses the LinToGDTSelector to make a virtual address.

DOS Settings

OS/2 2.1 allows users to customize the configuration of a DOS session. Using the DOS Settings, the user can adjust certain DOS session parameters via the Desktop Manager's Settings menu for the DOS session. Device drivers must call the VDHRegisterProperty routine to register their settings. A VDD can call VDHQueryProperty at DOS session creation to get the value of the current DOS settings. The user can also change some of the settings while the DOS session is running, via a settings dialog box. The standard DOS settings are shown in Table 9-1.

Table 9-1. DOS Settings

Property	Type	Operation
BREAK	BOOLEAN	Controls <cntl-c> checking in the INT 21 path
FCBS	INTEGER	Controls use of FCBs by errant DOS applications
DEVICE	STRING	Specifies a DOS character driver
SHELL	STRING	Specifies the command interpreter
RMSIZE	INTEGER	Specifies size of DOS memory arena

DOS Settings Registration

At initialization time, the Virtual Device Driver must register any settings that it will need. This information is stored in the kernel, and used to support all property-related operations (see Table 9-2).

\multicolumn{2}{c}{*Table 9-2. DOS Settings Information*}	
Name	The property name presented to the user. The settings should have common prefixes so that they appear sorted together.
Ordinal	The ordinal of the function independent of the name string.
Type	The property type. Boolean, integer, enumeration, and single and multiple line strings are supported.
Flags	Flags control aspects of the property, i.e., whether or not they can be changed while the DOS session is running.
Default Value	The value used if the user does not supply one.
Validation Information	This information allows the user interface to validate property values before sending them to the device driver.
Function	This function is used for validating string settings, and for notifying the VDD when the user has changed a property for a running DOS session.

VDD to PDD Communications

Since many VDDs virtualize or "mimic" hardware that generates interrupts, these drivers will generally have to interact with a PDD. The VDD uses the VDHOpenPDD VDH call to establish communication between the Virtual Device Driver and the Physical Device Driver. The two drivers exchange entry points, and are subsequently free to call each other using any type of protocol, including register-based entry points. Both drivers should also be aware of the shutdown protocol, in case the VDD has to shut down.

VDDs can call PDDs via the OS/2 file system by using the VDHOpen, VDHWrite, VDHIOCtl, and VDHClose function calls. Using this method, a VDD can communicate with an existing PDD without requiring modification of the PDD.

VDDs support Dynamic Linking, and thus can pass data back and forth to other VDDs via dynamic links. VDDs can also communicate with each other via the VDHOpenVDD, VDHRequestVDD, and VDHCloseVDD Virtual Device Helper routines.

The Virtual COM Device Driver

The Virtual COM Device Driver for OS/2 2.1, VCOM.SYS, allows for the emulation and virtualization of the 8250/16450 UART. It provides support for two virtual serial ports on ISA bus machines, and four ports on PS/2 and PS/2-compatible systems. VCOM.SYS does not support the 16550 UART. Due to the added overhead of context switching and system operation, the Virtual COM Device Driver only guarantees error-free operation at 240 characters per second, or about 2400 bits per second. DOS applications that access the I/O hardware directly or through BIOS calls are supported.

The Virtual COM Device Driver "looks" like the 8250 UART, including registers, modem lines, and interrupts. The DOS application sees the Virtual COM Device Driver as the actual device. The Virtual COM Device Driver contains the standard set of 8250/16450 port registers for access by the DOS application. They are:

- Receive/Transmit Buffer and Divisor Latch
- Interrupt Enable and Divisor Latch
- Interrupt Identification
- Line Control
- Modem Control
- Line Status
- Modem Status
- Scratch

Interrupts supported by the Virtual COM Device Driver are:

- Line Status Interrupt
- Receive Data Available Interrupt
- Transmitter Empty Interrupt
- Modem Status Interrupt

Refer to Table 9-3 for a list of 8250/16450 registers supported by the Virtual COM Device Driver.

Table 9-3. Virtualized 8250/16450 Registers

Name	R/W	Address	Purpose
RBR	R	03F8h	Receive Buffer Register
THR	W	03F8h	Transmitter Holding Register
DLL	R/W	03F8h	Low Divisor Latch
DLM	R/W	03F9h	High Divisor Latch
IER	R/W	03F9h	Interrupt Enable Register
IIR	R	03FAh	Interrupt Identification Register
LCR	R/W	03FBh	Line Control Register
MCR	R/W	03FCh	Modem Control Register
LSR	R	03FDh	Line Status Register
MSR	R	03FEh	Modem Status Register
SCR	R/W	03FFh	Scratchpad Register

Adapters with serial ports must conform to this register configuration. For UARTs with additional registers, I/O to those registers will be ignored by the Virtual COM Device Driver. All register bits are compatible with the standard bit assignments of the 8250/16450 UART.

Since interrupts are simulated, there is no physical PIC addressed by the Virtual COM Device Driver. Rather, a simulated PIC, VPIC, is installed to arbitrate interrupt priorities and to provide an End-Of-Interrupt port for those applications that may issue an EOI directly to the PIC.

The Virtual COM Device Driver also supports access to the serial device via INT 14h calls. The Virtual COM Device driver emulates the BIOS call, returning the same information as though the BIOS routine was actually called.

When a character is received at the actual hardware, an interrupt is generated and the PDD gets the character from the UART receive register. The PDD then sends the character to the VDD for the waiting DOS application. When the DOS application sends a character to a port, the Virtual 8086 Emulator traps the operation and calls the VDD. The VDD, in turn, calls the PDD to output the character to the actual device. Simulated interrupts, like their physical counterparts, are not recognized if the interrupt system is disabled, and are only emulated if the interrupt system is on. To maximize performance, the PDD does not call the VDD at the receipt of every interrupt. Rather, it receives the information that PDD device driver events have taken place, and determines whether to continue simulating interrupts or take other action. For more information on the Virtual COM Device Driver, please refer to the *OS/2 2.1 Virtual Device Driver Reference*.

The Virtual Timer Device Driver

The Virtual Timer Device driver provides support for DOS applications by providing the following services:

- Virtualization of timer ports to allow reprogramming of the interrupt rate and speaker tone.
- Distribution of timer ticks to all DOS sessions.
- Maintenance of the timer tick count in the ROM BIOS data area.
- Serialization of timer 0 and timer 2 across multiple DOS sessions.
- Arbitration of the ownership of timer 0 and timer 2 between the VDD and the Clock PDD.

In DOS, timer 0 is used as the system timer, and set to interrupt every 18.2 milliseconds. This timer is used to update the time of day clock and time-out the floppy disk drive motor on-off functions. DOS programs that need a higher tick resolution frequently program timer 0 to a higher frequency. The DOS tick handler intercepts the timer ticks and, at specified intervals, calls the system clock routine so that the time-of-day clock value is not affected. Timer 1 is the memory refresh timer and cannot be modified. Timer 2 is the speaker tone generator, and can be programmed to generate different sounds and tones. Timer 2 has two control bits, one to enable/disable the timer, and one to route the output to the speaker.

Timer 0 ticks can be lost due to system loading, so the Virtual Timer Device Driver continually compares the actual elapsed time with the per-session DOS timer and updates it if necessary to make up for lost ticks. Every second, all of the currently running DOS sessions have their times re-synchronized.

The hardware of timer 2 is virtualized, allowing it to be reprogrammed. The registers appear to the DOS applications exactly the same as the 8254 CTC (see Table 9-4).

Table 9-4. Virtualized Timer Registers

Description	Port
Count word 0	40h
Count word 1	41h
Count word 2	42h
Count word 3	43h

See Table 9-5 for a list of timer registers supported by the Virtual Timer Device Driver.

Table 9-5. Supported Virtualized Timer Registers

Count word 0	read	virtualized
Count word 0	write	virtualized
Count word 1	read	virtualized
Count word 1	write	ignored
Count word 2	read	virtualized
Count word 2	write	virtualized
Control word	read	virtualized
Control word	write	virtualized

The Virtual Disk Device Driver

The VDM supplies DOS applications with a DOS-compatible disk interface via, the INT 13h DOS interrupt. The Virtual Disk Device Driver, VDSK, simulates ROM BIOS for disk access. A list of supported INT 13h functions can be found in Table 9-6.

Table 9-6. Virtualized INT 13 Functions

AH	Function
00h	Reset Diskette System
01h	Status of Disk System
02h	Read Sectors Into Memory (floppy and fixed disk)
03h	Write Sectors From Memory (floppy disk)
04h	Verify Sectors (floppy and fixed disk)
05h	Format Track (floppy)
08h	Get Current Drive Parameters (floppy and fixed disk)
15h	Get Disk Type (floppy and fixed disk)
16h	Change of Disk Status (floppy)
17h	Set Disk Type (floppy)
18h	Set Media Type for Format (floppy)

When a DOS application issues an INT 13h request, the request is trapped by the Virtual Disk Device Driver, transformed into a Request Packet, and sent to the disk PDD for processing. If the disk is currently busy, the PDD queues up the request until it can process it. When the request can be completed, the PDD notifies the Virtual Disk Device Driver, which unblocks the DOS session.

The disk VDD does not support direct register access to and from the disk controller. Any attempts to perform direct I/O are trapped and ignored. Some types of copy protection algorithms that are dependent on disk timing may fail.

Floppy disk access is allowed directly to the floppy disk controller hardware, but only after the application gains exclusive access to the floppy disk drive. When a DOS application gains access to the floppy disk, it disables all port trapping and allows direct port access to the floppy controller (see Table 9-7).

Table 9-7. Virtualized Floppy Disk Ports

Port	Function
3f0h	Status Register A (PS/2 only)
3f1h	Status Register B (PS/2 only)
3f2h	Digital Output Register
3f7h	Digital Input Register
3f7h	Configuration Register
3f4h	Controller Status Register
3f5h	Controller Data Register

While the DOS session has access to the floppy disk, all interrupts from the floppy disk controller are reflected to the owning DOS application. Even when the DOS application has finished with the floppy disk, the ownership of the floppy disk will remain with the original DOS application until another application requests ownership.

The Virtual Keyboard Device Driver

The Virtual Keyboard Device Driver allows DOS applications that access to keyboard to run without a change in the VDM. The Virtual Keyboard Device Driver allows access to the keyboard, using the following methods:

- INT 21h. DOS applications can access the keyboard using the CON device name, or get input from the stdin device.
- BIOS access via the INT 16h function.
- I/O port access, by reading and writing I/O ports 60h and 64h.

The Virtual Keyboard Device Driver must also handle the aspects of translation and code page tables, performance, and idle detection for those applications that poll the keyboard. When the physical keyboard driver receives an interrupt, it sends that interrupt to the Virtual Keyboard Device Driver, which in turn notifies the *Virtual Programmable Interrupt Controller,* or *VPIC*. The Virtual Keyboard Device Driver must supply the key scan codes for those applications that decipher the scan codes themselves. Setting the repeat rate is not supported.

DOS applications frequently wait for a keyboard key to be pressed in a polling loop. The Virtual Keyboard Device Driver detects an idle loop, and adjusts the actual polling time as necessary. The driver increases the sleep between each poll, allowing other programs in the system to run. When a key is hit, the time between polls is reset to a short period, then increased as the inactivity increases. The Virtual Keyboard Device Driver uses the VDHWaitVRR VDH function to sleep in-between polls, and the DOS session is immediately woken up if a key is pressed.

Normally, IRQ1 interrupts are channeled to the INT 09h interrupt service routine, which is usually a BIOS routine that performs key translation. The Virtual Keyboard Device Driver emulates the INT 09h BIOS routine, calling the INT 15h handler for scan code monitoring, handling <cntl-break> (INT 18h), and Print Screen (INT 05h) processing.

The Virtual Mouse Device Driver

DOS applications that require a mouse are supported via the INT 33h interface, which performs the following functions:

- position and button tracking
- position and button event notification
- selectable pixel and mickey mappings
- video mode tracking
- pointer location and shape
- emulation of a light pen

Operation of the virtual mouse driver is similar to other virtual drivers. The mouse physical device driver is always aware of which session owns the mouse. When a full-screen DOS session owns the mouse, the mouse PDD notifies the virtual device driver of mouse events. If the DOS session is a windowed DOS session, the mouse PDD routes the mouse events to the Presentation Manager, which routes them to the virtual mouse device driver. The user may optionally set the exclusive mouse access on in the DOS Settings for the DOS windowed session. If so, events from the mouse PDD are sent directly to the mouse VDD, bypassing the Presentation Manager. This property is used for applications that track and draw their own mouse pointer.

The Virtual Line Printer Device Driver

The *Virtual Line Printer Device Driver, VLPT*, allows DOS applications access to the parallel printer port via INT 17h BIOS calls. It also supports the BIOS INT 05h print screen call. The VLPT supports up to three parallel controllers, and virtualizes the data, status, control, and reserved ports of the printer controller. The VLPT also provides a direct access mode for DOS programs that control the parallel port hardware directly. When the VLPT recognizes that a DOS application wishes to perform direct I/O to the parallel port, it requests exclusive rights to the port from the parallel port PDD.

If another application tries to use the printer after the DOS application has gained exclusive access to it, the access will fail. Print jobs from the spooler will continue to be queued up until the requested parallel port becomes free.

The VLPT continues to handle the traps from the DOS application. The VLPT also traps the IRQ enable bit from a DOS application attempting to enable the parallel port IRQ. Interrupt transfers are not supported for the parallel port, so the VLPT contains no interrupt simulation routines. The VLPT also detects when a DOS application tries to change the direction bit, which is illegal on non-PS/2 systems.

The Virtual Video Device Driver

The Virtual Video Device Driver, or VVIDEO, provides display adapter support for DOS sessions. The VVIDEO driver communicates with the DOS Session Window Manager, ensuring that the DOS window stays relatively synchronized with the DOS application. Some parts of the DOS session environment have been designed especially for the VVIDEO driver. They are:

- foreground/background notification hooks.
- freeze/thaw services.
- code page and title change notification hooks.

The VVIDEO driver is a base driver, loaded at boot time from CONFIG.SYS. If the VVIDEO driver cannot be loaded at boot time, no DOS sessions will be able to be started. The standard VVIDEO drivers support CGA, EGA, VGA, XGA, and 8514/A adapters, and monochrome adapters as secondary display adapters. All adapter memory sizes are supported up to 256KB, and more than one VVIDEO driver can be loaded for the same adapter.

The DOS Window Manager starts a thread for communication to the VVIDEO driver, which calls the VVIDEO driver and waits for a video event. The VVIDEO driver supports both full screen and windowed operation, and can switch back and forth between full screen and windowed, and back. The VVIDEO drivers install hooks to trap all port accesses, maps physical screen memory to logical screen memory, and reports video events to the DOS Session Window Manager. Changes that are trapped by the DOS Session Window Manager, whether the DOS application is in focus or not, are:

- mode changes.
- palette changes.
- a change in the cursor position.

- changing the session title.
- screen switch video memory allocation errors.
- scrolling and other positioning events.

The DOS Session Window Manager can query the state of its DOS session video for the following:

- the current display mode.
- the current palette.
- the cursor position.
- the contents of video memory.

The DOS Session Window Manager can also issue the following directives:

- wait for video events.
- cancel wait for video events.

The VVIDEO driver opens the Virtual Mouse Device Driver, and provides it with the following entry points:

- show mouse pointer.
- hide mouse pointer.
- define text mouse pointer.
- define graphics mouse pointer.
- set video page.
- set for light pen emulation.

The VVIDEO driver calls the Virtual Mouse Device Driver whenever the DOS session changes video modes.

VVIDEO drivers can share the same video adapter by accepting to be temporarily shut down while another VVIDEO driver uses the adapter, and restarted when control of the adapter is released back to the original owner.

The VVIDEO driver supports the DOS INT 10h to support drawing operations and the simultaneous use of the mouse pointer. The VVIDEO also supports INT 2Fh services, which notify an application that it is about to be switched. The 8514/A and XGA adapters can run only in the full screen mode of the DOS session, and will immediately be frozen if it attempts to write directly to the 8514/A or XGA adapter.

Virtual DevHlp Services By Category

Virtual DevHlp functions provide virtual device drivers with access to various services provided by the operating system and by other virtual device drivers. The Virtual DevHlp services are listed alphabetically, with a short explanation of their purpose. A complete reference to the Virtual Device Helper routines, including details on parameter use, can be found in the *IBM OS/2 2.1 Virtual Device Driver Reference*. Virtual DevHlp services can be divided into categories based on the type of service that the virtual DevHlp provides. These categories are:

DOS Settings

VDHRegisterProperty	Register virtual device driver property
VDHQueryProperty	Query virtual device driver property value
VDHDecodeProperty	Decode property string

File (or device) I/O Services

VDHOpen	Open a file or device
VDHClose	Close a file handle
VDHRead	Read bytes from a file or device
VDHWrite	Write bytes to a file or device
VDHIOCtl	Perform IOCtl to a device
VDHPhysicalDisk	Get information about partitionable disks
VDHSeek	Move read/write file pointer for a handle

DMA Services

VDHRegisterDMAChannel	Register a DMA channel with the virtual DMA device driver
VDHCallOutDMA	Let DMA do its work
VDHAllocDMABuffer	Allocate DMA buffer
VDHFreeDMABuffer	Free DMA buffer previously allocated

DOS Session Control Services

VDHKillVDM	Terminate a DOS session
VDHHaltSystem	Halt the system
VDHFreezeVDM	Freeze a DOS session; prevent the DOS session from executing any V86 code
VDHThawVDM	Allow a frozen DOS session to resume executing V86 code
VDHIsVDMFrozen	Determine if a DOS session is frozen
VDHSetPriority	Adjust a DOS session's scheduler priority
VDHYield	Yield the processor

DPMI Services

VDHGetSelBase	Get a flat base address for an LDT selector
VDHGetVPMExcept	Get the current DOS session's protect mode exception vector
VDHSetVPMExcept	Set the current DOS session's protect mode exception vector to a specified value
VDHChangeVMPIF	Change the virtual interrupt flag (IF), enabling or disabling protect mode interrupts
VDHRaiseException	Raise an exception to a DOS session, as if the exception had been caused by the hardware
VDHReadUBuf	Read from protect mode address space
VDHWriteUBuf	Write to a protect mode address space
VDHCheckPagePerm	Check Ring 3 page permissions
VDHSwitchToVPM	Switch a DOS session to protect mode
VDHSwitchToV86	Switch a DOS session to V86 mode
VDHCheckVPMIntVector	Determine if a DOS session protect mode handler exists
VDHGetVPMIntVector	Return the DOS session's protect mode interrupt vector
VDHSetVPMIntVector	Set the DOS session's protect mode interrupt vector
VDHArmVPMBPHook	Obtain the address of a DOS session's protect mode breakpoint
VDHBeginUseVPMStack	Begin using the DOS session's protect mode stack
VDHEndUseVPMStack	End the use of the DOS session's protect mode stack

(The "VPM" in many of the function names in this section stands for "Virtual Protect Mode").

GDT Selector Services

VDHCreateSel	Create a GDT selector to map a linear range
VDHDestroySel	Destroy a GDT selector previously created by VDHCreateSel
VDHQuerySel	Get the selector for an address in the virtual device driver's data or on its stack

Hook Management Services

VDHAllocHook	Allocate the hooks needed for interrupt simulation
VDHArmBPHook	Obtain the address of a V86 breakpoint
VDHArmContextHook	Set a local or a global context hook
VDHArmReturnHook	Set a handler to receive control when an IRET or RETF is executed in V86 mode
VDHArmSTIHook	Sets a handler to receive control when interrupts are enabled in the current DOS session
VDHArmTimerHook	Set a timer handler
VDHFreeHook	Disarm and free a hook
VDHInstallIntHook	Set a handler for a V86 interrupt
VDHInstallIOHook	Install PIC I/O port hooks
VDHInstallUserHook	Install a handler for a DOS session event
VDHQueryHookData	Returns a pointer to a hook's reference data (created during the VDHAllocHook call)

VDHRemoveIOHook	Remove hooks for PIC I/O ports
VDHSelIOHookState	Enable/Disable I/O port trapping
VDHRegisterAPI	Set V86 or protect mode API handler

DOS Application Management

VDHReportPeek	Report DOS session polling activity for the purpose of idle detection
VDHWakeIdle	Wake up a DOS session that is doing VDHSelIOHookState sleep

These services allow virtual device drivers to tell OS/2 when a DOS application appears to be idle, and when there is some activity that could make the DOS application busy.

Inter-Device Communication Services

VDHRegisterVDD	Register a virtual device driver's entry points
VDHOpenVDD	Open a virtual device driver previously registered with VDHRegisterVDD
VDHOpenPDD	Open a physical device driver for VDD - PDD communications
VDHRequestVDD	Issue a request for an operation of a virtual device driver
VDHCloseVDD	Close a virtual device driver opened with VDHOpenVDD

Keyboard Services

| VDHQueryKeyShift | Query the keyboard shift state |

Memory Management Services

There are three subcategories of memory management virtual DevHlp services. The first two are based on the granularity of the memory allocation unit, the third category is for memory locking services.

Byte Granular Memory Management Services

VDHAllocMem	Allocate a small amount of memory
VDHFreeMem	Free memory allocated with VDHAllocMem
VDHAllocDOSMem	Allocate a block of memory from the DOS area
VDHCreateBlockPool	Create a memory block pool
VDHAllocBlock	Allocate a block from a memory block pool
VDHFreeBlock	Free a previously allocated block of memory (return the block to a memory block pool)
VDHDestroyBlockPool	Destroy a memory block pool
VDHCopyMem	Copy from one linear memory address to another
VDHExchangeMem	Exchange the contents of two linear memory regions

Page Granular Memory Management Services

VDHAllocPages	Allocate a page-aligned memory object
VDHReallocPages	Reallocates (re-sizes) a memory object
VDHFreePages	Free a memory object
VDHFindFreePages	Find the largest available linear memory region
VDHGetDirtyPageInfo	Returns the status of the dirty bits for a range of memory pages (resets the bits)
VDHQueryFreePages	Returns the total amount of free virtual memory in bytes
VDHReservePages	Reserve a range of linear addresses
VDHUnreservePages	Unreserve a range of linear addresses
VDHMapPages	Map a specified linear address
VDHInstallFaultHook	Install your own page fault handler
VDHRemoveFaultHook	Remove your page fault handler

Memory Locking Memory Management Services

VDHLockMem	Verify access to a region of memory, then lock that memory
VDHUnlockMem	Release a memory lock

These services allow virtual device drivers to allocate, free, reallocate, and lock memory for global and per-DOS session objects, page or byte granular objects, and with different options, such as fixed or swappable allocations.

Virtual device drivers can also request smaller memory allocations from the kernel heap, which is global and fixed. Small, fixed-size block services are available to speed up frequent allocations and the freeing of memory. For a particular block size, a pool of blocks are maintained, and the requirements are met by taking off a block from the block pool.

Miscellaneous Virtual DevHlp Services

VDHSetFlags	Set the DOS session's FLAGS register to a specified value
VDHSetA20	Enable or disable the A20 line for the current DOS session
VDHQueryA20	Query the current state of the A20 line
VDHDevBeep	Device beep Virtual DevHlp service
VDHGetError	Get the error code from the last Virtual DevHlp service called
VDHSetError	Set the error code for VDHGetError to query
VDHHandleFromSGID	Get the DOS session handle from the screen group ID
VDHHandleFromPID	Get the handle for a given process ID
VDHEnumerateVDMs	For each DOS session in the system, run a worker function
VDHQueryLin	Get the linear address for a FAR16 (16:16) address

VDHGetCodePageFont	Return information about the DOS session's code page font
VDHReleaseCodePageFont	Release code page font returned by VDHGetCodePageFont
VDHQuerySysValue	Query a system value
VDHPutSysValue	Set a system value
VDHPopup	Display a message
VDHSetDosDevice	Register/Install a DOS device driver

NPX (Numeric Coprocessor) Services

VDHReleaseNPX	Give up ownership of NPX
VDHNPXReset	Reset port F1
VDHNPXClearBusy	Clear busy latch
VDHNPXRegisterVDD	Register virtual device driver entry points

Parallel Port and Printer Services

VDHPrintClose	Flush and close all open printers for a DOS session

Semaphore Services

VDHCreateSem	Create an event or mutex semaphore
VDHDestroySem	Destroy a semaphore
VDHResetEventSem	Reset an event semaphore
VDHPostEventSem	Post an event semaphore
VDHWaitEventSem	Wait on an event semaphore
VDHRequestMutexSem	Request a mutex semaphore
VDHReleaseMutexSem	Release a mutex semaphore
VDHQuerySem	Query a semaphore's state

These services are used for synchronizing with an OS/2 process. Virtual device drivers must be careful not to block (VDHRequestSem/VDHWaitSem) in the context of a DOS session task, or that task will receive no more simulated hardware interrupts until it becomes unblocked.

Timer Services

VDHArmTimerHook	Set a timer service handler
VDHDisarmTimerHook	Cancel a timer service before the handler has been called

Virtual Interrupt Services

VDHOpenVIRQ	Register an IRQ handler for a virtual device driver
VDHCloseVIRQ	Deregister an IRQ handler for a virtual device driver
VDHSetVIRR	Set the virtual Interrupt Request Register (IRR), causing an interrupt to be simulated to the DOS session
VDHClearVIRR	Clear the virtual IRR, stopping the simulation of interrupts to the DOS session)
VDHQueryVIRQ	Query the IRQ status in a DOS session
VDHWaitVIRRs	Wait until an interrupt is simulated
VDHWakeVIRRs	Wake up a DOS session that is waiting with VDHWaitVIRRs
VDHSendVEOI	Send a virtual EOI (End-Of-Interrupt) to the VPIC

V8086 Stack Manipulation

VDHPushRegs	Push a client DOS session's registers onto the client's stack
VDHPopRegs	Pop a client DOS session's registers from the client's stack
VDHPushFarCall	Simulate a far call to V86 code
VDHPopStack	Pop data off client stack
VDHPushStack	Push data onto a client's stack
VDHPushInt	Transfer control to a V86 interrupt handler when an interrupt is simulated
VDHPopInt	Remove IRET frame from a client DOS session's stack

Many of the virtual DevHlp functions that are called with invalid parameters or other error conditions often cause a system halt. This is because virtual device drivers run at Ring 0; they have free access to everything in the system. If an invalid parameter is detected, it has probably done enough damage that the system has become unstable. The only thing to do at that point is to halt the system.

DOS Session Interrupts

Table 9-8 describes the DOS hardware interrupts virtualization supplied by the Virtual Device Drivers and the DOS emulation component of the VDM.

Table 9-8. Virtualized DOS Interrupts

Interrupt	Description	Notes
IRQ 0	Timer (INT 08h)	DOS programs can hook this interrupt with the INT 08h call. The INT 08h handler is called for each tick of the channel 0 system clock.
IRQ 1	Keyboard (INT 09h)	The INT 09h handler is invoked for every press and release of a keystroke.
IRQ 2	Cascade Interrupt Controller	Use for the support of interrupts 8-15 to emulate the second PIC
IRQ 3	Serial Port (COM2, COM3)	Supported when VCOM.SYS and COM.SYS are loaded.
IRQ 4	Serial Port (COM1)	Supported when VCOM.SYS and COM.SYS are loaded.
IRQ 5	Parallel Port (LPT2)	Not supported
IRQ 6	Diskette	Not supported
IRQ 7	Parallel Port (LPT1)	Not supported
IRQ 8	Real Time Clock	Not supported
IRQ 9	Redirect cascade	Not supported
IRQ 10		Not supported
IRQ 11		Not supported
IRQ 12	Aux. device	Not supported
IRQ 13	Math Coprocessor	Supported
IRQ 14	Fixed disk	Not supported
IRQ 15		Not supported

Table 9-9 describes the DOS BIOS software interrupts supported in a VDM.

Table 9-9. Virtualized BIOS Interrupts (Continued)

Interrupt	Description	Notes
02h	NMI	Not supported
05h	Print screen	Supported by the Virtual Line Printer driver
08h	System timer	Supported by the Virtual Timer device driver. Due to system overhead, interrupts may come in short bursts
0eh	Diskette	Not supported
10h	Video	Fully supported
13h	Disk/diskette	Supported by a subset of the DOS INT 13h functions. The supported functions are: • 00h - Reset diskette • 01h - Read status • 02h - Read sectors • 03h - Write sectors (diskette only) • 04h - Verify sectors • 05h - Format track (diskette only) • 08h - Get driver parameters • 0ah - Read long (fixed disk only) • 15h - Read DASD type • 16h - Change status (diskette only) • 17h - Set disk type (diskette only) • 18h - Set media type (diskette only)

Table 9-9. Virtualized BIOS Interrupts (continued)

Table 9-9. Virtualized BIOS Interrupts

Interrupt	Description	Notes
14h	Serial Port (Async)	Supported by the Virtual COM driver
15h	System services	Supports the following system services: • 00h - Cassette motor on • 01h - Cassette motor off • 02h - Cassette read • 03h - Cassette write • 0fh - Format periodic int • 4fh - Keyboard intercept • 80h - Open device • 81h - Close device • 82h - program terminate • 83h - Event wait • 84h - Joystick • 85h - SysReq key • 86h - Wait • 87h - Move block • 88h - Get extended memory size • 89h - Switch to protect mode • 90h - Device wait • 91h - Device post • c0h - Get system config parameters • c1h - Get ABIOS data area • c2h - PS/2 mouse functions • c3h - Watchdog timer • c4h - Programmable Option Select
16h	Keyboard	Fully supported
17h	Printer	Fully supported by the VLPT
19h	Reboot	if DOS_STARTUP_DRIVE is set, the session is rebooted; if not, the session is terminated.
1ah	Time of Day	Read only access to Real Time Clock is supported.
1eh	Diskette parameters	Fully supported
70h	Real Time Clock	Not supported

Table 9-10 describes the DOS software interrupts which are supported by the DOS emulation component.

Table 9-10. Virtualized DOS Software Interrupts

Interrupt	Description	Notes
20h	Program terminate	Fully supported
21h	Function request	Fully supported, plus some undocumented functions. The following calls are supported with restrictions: • 38h - Return country information • 44h - Generic IOCtl • 66h - Get/set code page • 67h - Set handle count
22h	Terminate address	Fully supported
23h	Cntl-break exit address	Fully supported
24h	Critical error handler	Fully supported
25h	Absolute disk read	Fully supported
26h	Absolute disk write	Fully supported, but error generated for attempt on fixed disk
27h	Terminate/stay resident	Fully supported
28h	Idle loop	Fully supported
2fh	Multiplex	When a DOS application issues an INT 2fh with AX=1680h, it yields its time slice.
33h	Mouse	Fully support, providing VMOUSE.SYS driver is loaded
67h	LIM expanded memory manager	Supported when Expanded Memory Manager VDD is installed. Supports LIM EMS V4.0 functions.

Sample Virtual Device Driver

The following code represents a sample VDD designed to work with the simple parallel PDD outlined in Chapter 7. It is written using the IBM C Set/2 compiler. This VDD traps I/O to the 8-bit ports from a DOS application running in a VDM. This VDD performs simple input and output to the dedicated parallel port adapter described in Chapter 7.

Note that input and output for OS/2 printer ports is handled much differently than in the sample driver. For OS/2 printer I/O, the OS/2 virtual printer driver VLPT calls the OS/2 kernel, which formats the request into a standard OS/2 Request Packet. The kernel then sends the Request Packet to the PDD for disposition.

The VDD can perform input and output in one of two ways. The VDD can ask the PDD to use the specific ports and, if permission is granted, can do the inputs and outputs directly from within the VDD. The VDD can also call the PDD and have the PDD perform the required I/O, and pass the results back to the VDD. If the adapter is dedicated to the VDM application, and no other programs will access it, the VDD need not call a PDD to perform the operation. If the adapter can be accessed by protect mode programs, the VDD must get permission to use the adapter by calling the PDD. The PDD will queue up any subsequent requests from other threads until the VDD is finished with the adapter.

In most cases, writing a VDD will be unnecessary, as most of the required DOS virtualization is handled by the VDDs that come with OS/2 2.1. Writing a VDD is only necessary if the DOS application needs to support a custom adapter in a VDM which cannot be serviced by the existing VDD supplied with OS/2. This should be rare, as most new applications should be written for protect mode operation.

In this sample VDD, the VDD traps I/O on a per-DOS-session basis, to ports 0x210, 0x211 and 0x212. When the hook is entered, the VDD checks to see that the current requester is the also the current owner of the port. If not, the VDM application attempting the access is terminated. If the requester is valid, port trapping is disabled, allowing subsequent I/O to go directly to the hardware for increased performance. When the DOS session is exited, the I/O hooks are removed and port trapping is reenabled. This VDD shows you how to call some basic VDH functions, such as VDHInstallIOHook, VDHRemoveIOHook, and VDHInstallUserHook.

When a VDM is created, the PIOCreate routine is called, and when the VDM is closed, the PIOTerminate routine is called. PIOCreate is called with a handle to the VDM, which is actually the base linear address of the VDM. You may verify the operation of any of these funtions if you have the kernel debugger installed. Simply place a call to VdhInt3 in the source code, recompile and relink, then reboot. The VdhInt3 call will cause a break at the debugging terminal, and if you used the MAPSYM after the link, you can examine VDD variables. Do not insert the call to VdhInt3 if you do not have the kernel debugger installed, or have the debugging terminal connected.

```c
//    file pioinit.c
//*****************************************************************
//  sample parallel port VDD init section
//*****************************************************************

#include "mvdm.h"            // VDH services, etc.
#include "pio.h"             // PIO  data defines

#pragma entry (_PIOInit)

#pragma data_seg(CSWAP_DATA)

extern   SZ szProplpt1timeout;

#pragma alloc_text(CINIT_TEXT,_PIOInit,PIO_PDDProc)

// init entry point called by system at load time

BOOL EXPENTRY _PIOInit(psz) // PIO VDDInit
{
    // Register a VDM termination handler entry point

    if ((VDHInstallUserHook((ULONG)VDM_TERMINATE,
                    (PUSERHOOK)PIOTerminate)) == 0)
       return 0;             // return FALSE if VDH call failed //

    // Register a VDM creation handler entry point

    if ((VDHInstallUserHook((ULONG)VDM_CREATE,
                    (PUSERHOOK)PIOCreate)) == 0)
       return 0 ;            // return FALSE if VDH call failed

    // Get the entry point to the PDD
```

Figure 9-2. VDD initialization section. (Continued)

```
        PPIOPDDProc = VDHOpenPDD(PDD_NAME, PIO_PDDProc);

    return CTRUE;
}

// entry point registered by VDHOpenPDD, called by the PDD

SBOOL VDDENTRY PIO_PDDProc(ulFunc,f16p1,f16p2)
ULONG ulFunc;
F16PVOID f16p1;
F16PVOID f16p2;
{
    return 0;
}
```

Figure 9-2. VDD initialization section.

```
// piodata.c

#include "mvdm.h"               // VDH services, etc.
#include "pio.h"                // PIO specific

#pragma data_seg(SWAPINSTDATA)

HVDM owner_VDM = 0;             //   actual VDM handle
HVDM current_VDM;
ULONG Resp = 0;

#pragma data_seg(CSWAP_DATA)

FPFNPDD PPIOPDDProc = (FPFNPDD)0;   // addr of PDD entry pt
```

Figure 9-3. VDD data segment.

```c
//  pioin.c

#include "mvdm.h"                          // VDH services, etc.
#include "pio.h"
#include "basemid.h"

// PIO specific

#pragma alloc_text(CSWAP_TEXT,PIODataIn,RequestDirect)

extern IOH Ioh;

// entry from data input trap in VDM

BYTE HOOKENTRY PIODataIn(ULONG portaddr, PCRF pcrf)
{
    BYTE dataread;                         // set up byte to return

    RequestDirect();

    // disable I/O trap

    VDHSetIOHookState(current_VDM,DIGIO_BASE,3,&Ioh,0);

    dataread = inp(portaddr);
    return(dataread);                      // return data read
}
BOOL HOOKENTRY RequestDirect(void)
{
   if (owner_VDM != current_VDM)
   {
      if (owner_VDM !=0)
      {
         VDHPopup(0,0,MSG_DEVICE_IN_USE,&Resp,ABORT,0);
         if (Resp != ABORT)
         {
```

Figure 9-4. VDD input handler. (Continued)

```
            VDHKillVDM(current_VDM);
            owner_VDM = current_VDM;
          }
        }
      else
        owner_VDM = current_VDM;
    }
}
```

Figure 9-4. VDD input handler.

```
// pioout.c

#include "mvdm.h"                    // VDH services, etc.
#include "pio.h"                     // PIO specific

#pragma data_seg(CSWAP_DATA)

extern IOH Ioh;

#pragma alloc_text(CSWAP_TEXT,PIODataOut)

// this routine is the data out trap entry point

VOID HOOKENTRY PIODataOut(BYTE chartowrite,ULONG portaddr,PCRF pcrf)
{
    RequestDirect();

    // disable port trapping

    VDHSetIOHookState(current_VDM,DIGIO_BASE,3,&Ioh,0);

    outp(portaddr,chartowrite);      // write the char
    return;
}
```

Figure 9-5. VDD data port output handler.

```c
//   file piouser.c

#include "mvdm.h"                    // VDH services, etc.
#include "pio.h"                     // PIO specific
#include "basemid.h"

#pragma data_seg(CSWAP_DATA)

// our routines are for 8-bit ports

IOH Ioh = {PIODataIn,PIODataOut,0,0,0};

#pragma alloc_text(CSWAP_TEXT,PIOCreate,PIOTerminate)

//------------------------------------------

// PIOCreate, entered when the VDM is created

//------------------------------------------

BOOL HOOKENTRY PIOCreate(hvdm)
HVDM hvdm;
{
    current_VDM = hvdm;              // save our vdm handle

    // install I/O hooks for our three 8-bit ports

    if ((VDHInstallIOHook(hvdm,
                          DIGIO_BASE,
                          3,
                          (PIOH)&Ioh,
                          !VDH_ASM_HOOK)) == 0)
    {
        PIOTerminate(hvdm);
        return 0;                    // return FALSE
    }

    return CTRUE;
}
```

Figure 9-6. VDD user routines. (Continued)

```
//-----------------------------------------------------------------
// PIOTerminate, called when the VDM terminates. This code is
// optional, as the User and IO hooks are removed automatically by
// the system when the VDM terminates. It is shown for example.
//-----------------------------------------------------------------

BOOL HOOKENTRY PIOTerminate(hvdm)
HVDM hvdm;
{

   owner_VDM = 0;

   VDHRemoveIOHook(hvdm,                  // remove the IO hooks
                   DIGIO_BASE,
                   3,
                   (PIOH)&Ioh);

   return CTRUE;
}
```

Figure 9-6. VDD user routines.

```
//
// digio memory map for os/2 virtual device driver
//

#define  DIGIO_BASE    0x210            // board address
#define  DIGIO_OUTPUT  DIGIO_BASE       // output port
#define  DIGIO_INPUT   DIGIO_BASE+1     // input port
#define  DIGIO_CONFIG  DIGIO_BASE+2     // initialization port

#define  ABORT 0x02

// name of the PDD
```

Figure 9-7. VDD include file. (Continued)

```
#define PDD_NAME        "DIGIO$ \0"      // string

// pioinit.c

BOOL  EXPENTRY  PIOInit(PSZ);
SBOOL VDDENTRY  PIO_PDDProc(ULONG,F16PVOID,F16PVOID);

// piouser.c

BOOL HOOKENTRY PIOCreate(HVDM);
BOOL HOOKENTRY PIOTerminate(HVDM);

// pioin.c

BYTE HOOKENTRY PIODataIn(ULONG, PCRF);
BOOL HOOKENTRY RequestDirect(void);

// pioout.c

VOID HOOKENTRY PIODataOut(BYTE, ULONG, PCRF);
VOID HOOKENTRY PIOConfigOut(BYTE, ULONG, PCRF);

extern ULONG    MachineType;              // Machine Type
extern FPFNPDD  PPIOPDDProc;              // addr of PDD entry point
extern HVDM     owner_VDM;
extern HVDM     current_VDM;
extern ULONG    Resp;

// ioseg

USHORT _Far32 _Pascal inp(ULONG);
VOID   _Far32 _Pascal outp(ULONG,USHORT);
```

Figure 9-7. VDD include file.

```
vpio.sys: pioinit.obj piouser.obj pioin.obj pioout.obj piodata.obj \
ioseg.obj
        link386 /A:16 /M:FULL /NOL pioinit+piouser+pioin+pioout+\
piodata+ioseg,vpio.sys,vpio.map,vdh,pio.def
        mapsym vpio

pioinit.obj: pioinit.c mvdm.h pio.h
        icc /Sm /Ss /O /Q /W2 /Rn /Gr /C pioinit.c

pioin.obj: pioin.c pio.h mvdm.h
        icc /Sm /Ss /Q /O /W2 /Rn /Gr /C pioin.c

pioout.obj: pioout.c pio.h mvdm.h
        icc /Sm /Ss /Q /O /W2 /Rn /Gr /C pioout.c

piouser.obj: piouser.c pio.h mvdm.h
        icc /Sm /Ss /Q /O /W2 /Rn /Gr /C piouser.c

piodata.obj: piodata.c pio.h mvdm.h
        icc /Sm /Ss /Q /O /W2 /Rn /Gr /C piodata.c

ioseg.obj: ioseg.asm
         masm /Mx /x ioseg.asm;

VIRTUAL DEVICE VPIO
PROTMODE

STUB              'OS2STUB.EXE'
SEGMENTS
    CODE32       CLASS 'CODE'       SHARED    NONDISCARDABLE  RESIDENT
    _TEXT        CLASS 'CODE'       SHARED    NONDISCARDABLE  RESIDENT
    CINIT_TEXT   CLASS 'CODE'       SHARED    DISCARDABLE     RESIDENT
    CSWAP_TEXT   CLASS 'CODE'       SHARED    NONDISCARDABLE
    CINIT_DATA   CLASS 'CINITDATA'  SHARED    DISCARDABLE     RESIDENT
    CSWAP_DATA   CLASS 'CSWAPDATA'  SHARED    NONDISCARDABLE
    MVDMINSTDATA CLASS 'MIDATA'     NONSHARED NONDISCARDABLE  RESIDENT
    SWAPINSTDATA CLASS 'SIDATA'     NONSHARED NONDISCARDABLE
    DATA32       CLASS 'DATA'       SHARED    NONDISCARDABLE  RESIDENT
    _DATA        CLASS 'DATA'       SHARED    NONDISCARDABLE  RESIDENT
```

Figure 9-8. VDD Make And DEF Files

Establishing a VDD-PDD Link

Note that, in this VDD, the actual I/O was performed by the VDD routines PIODataIn and PIODataOut. The VDD could have called the PDD to perform the actual I/O. This would be necessary if the I/O involved interrupts, as device interrupts must be handled by a PDD.

The PDD requires slight modifications to support VDD-PDD communications. The PDD must register its ability to provide VDD support by issuing a RegisterPDD DevHlp call in the Init section of the PDD. The RegisterPDD informs OS/2 of the name of the PDD and the 16:16 address of the PDD's communication function. Note that this is not the same entry point as defined by the IDC entry point in the PDD Device Header. The VDD can then establish communications with the PDD by calling the VDHOpenPDD Virtual Device Helper function. This is one of the reasons that OS/2 loads all of the PDDs before the VDDs during system boot. Note that this DevHlp function has no error return. A failure when registering the PDD will cause a system crash during boot.

If the PDD fails initialization for another reason, such as a failed SetIRQ or SetTimer, the PDD must release the PDD-VDD registration by calling RegisterPDD, with the function pointer equal to 0:0. The PDD described in Chapter 7 would be modified as outlined in Figure 9-9.

```
Init code
.
.
RegisterPDD((FPUCHAR)devhdr.DHname,(FARPOINTER)DigioComm);
.
.
more Init code



main Strategy code section
.
.
DigioComm(ULONG Func, ULONG Parm1, ULONG Parm2)
{

    VDD-PDD comm code here
}
.
.
```

Figure 9-9. Registering PDD for VDD-PDD communications.

During initialization, the VDD calls VDHOpenPDD, passing it the ASCII-Z name of the PDD and the 16:32 entry point of the VDD's communication routine. Note the call to VDHOpenPDD in the pioinit.c routine above. If VDHOpenPDD (or any other VDH call) fails, it will return FALSE and the driver must call VDHGetError to retrieve the exact error. If the call succeeds, VDHOpenPDD returns a pointer to the PDD's communication routine, previously registered by the RegisterPDD call in the PDD Init section.

The two drivers communicate by sending a structure back and forth. This structure is described in Figure 9-10. The first parameter is a private function code, which the drivers pass back and forth to identify the operation to be performed. The two parameters can be data or 16:16 pointers to input and output packets. The VDD-PDD communication functions should return nonzero for success, and zero for failure.

If the PDD allocates any resources on behalf of the VDD, the VDD must call the PDD to release those resources when the VDM is destroyed.

```
typedef _DRVCOMM {
    ULONG    FunctionCode;
    ULONG    Parm1;
    ULONG    Parm2;
    } DRVCOMM;
```

Figure 9-10. VDD-PDD communications structure.

CHAPTER 10

Memory-Mapped Adapters and IOPL

A large number of adapters provide on-board memory for communication between the adapter and the program or drivers. Generally, a program or driver maps the on-board memory to a physical memory address, and reads or writes board memory as if it were normal system RAM. These adapters are referred to as memory-mapped adapters. Memory-mapped adapters, when placed in a special hardware mode, appear to a device driver or application as normal RAM memory. An application that is allowed direct access to the adapter memory can transfer data much faster than if it were to call a device driver to perform the transfer. This type of operation, called memory-mapped I/O, can result in increased performance and is the preferred method for transferring large amounts of memory quickly. Memory-mapped adapters may also utilize interrupts or DMA. An example of a memory-mapped adapter would be a video adapter, such as a VGA card.

Programs that perform transfers with memory-mapped adapters usually write data in a special format to an area of memory between the 640K and one megabyte, although some adapters can be mapped in the region above one megabyte.

The most common example of a memory-mapped adapter is, of course, the standard VGA graphics adapter found in most IBM clones. Data to be displayed on the screen is written to the adapter's RAM memory. The video controller constantly reads this memory, converts it to electrical signals and presents these voltage levels to the actual display device. If you power down your display terminal and power it back up, the contents of the display is not lost because the display is actually kept in video memory, not in the display itself.

High and Low Memory Maps

Memory-mapped adapters come in two basic flavors. The first has a memory-mapped address that is selectable in the area between 640K and one megabyte. Some of the memory space between 640K and one megabyte is reserved for such things as BIOS shadow RAM and video memory. There is room, however, to map an adapter board in that space, providing no address conflicts exist. Most memory-mapped adapters were designed for personal computers running DOS, so there was no need to provide memory-mapped addresses greater than one megabyte. Recall that DOS runs in the real mode of the Intel microprocessor, which provides for only a 20-bit address. This limits the addressing capability of the CPU to one megabyte, so an adapter designed for the DOS environment that could be mapped to addresses greater than one megabyte would not be of much use.

The second type has a memory-mapped address of greater than one megabyte. The 32-bit addressing mode of OS/2 2.1 allows adapters to be mapped above the one megabyte boundary and accessed directly.

ISA bus memory-mapped adapters use small jumpers or switches to set their memory-mapped address, while Micro Channel adapters usually contain their memory-mapped address in the POS registers (see Chapter 3). Some recently-introduced adapters designed to run in 32-bit systems like OS/2 have been designed for memory-mapped addresses of greater than one megabyte.

Application Program Access To Adapter Memory

One of the most important features of OS/2 is its ability to protect programs from one another. With the aid of the protect mode circuitry in the CPU, the operating system can determine beforehand if a program is about to read from or write to another program's memory space. If the processor detects this kind of error, the system's error handler is called to display the error and the offending program is immediately terminated. How then does an application operating at Ring 3 gain access to the memory-mapped adapter address that is not within its own address space?

Recall the discussion of the processor architecture in Chapter 3. As was outlined, a program's access to memory is controlled by selectors, which are indexes into the program's Local Descriptor Table. The descriptor contains a physical address and *Requested Privilege Level*, or *RPL*, of the memory object. When a program is executed, it get's its own list of selectors, or LDT, which defines its valid addressable memory areas and their access restrictions. When the program attempts to read or write memory, the CPU compares the target address and type of operation to a corresponding entry in the LDT. If the program does not have access to the target memory, a *General Protect*, or *GP fault* is generated, and the program is immediately terminated. If the address is valid, the CPU verifies that the memory has the correct permissions, such as read and write, and generates a fault if the permissions do not agree with the attempted operation.

If the adapter's memory-mapped address could be placed in the application's LDT, the program would be free to access the adapter's memory. The application's LDT, however, is created at load time, and is not modifiable by the application. If that were permitted, applications would be free to select the memory addresses they wished to read and write, and crash OS/2. The only program that can grant an application access to memory is a device driver. The device driver, operating at Ring 0, is free to manipulate the application's environment, with some limitations.

To allow the application to access the foreign memory, the application program opens up the device driver and passes it the physical address and size of the memory it wishes to access. For most adapter, the memory size is generally 4K, 8K, 16K, or 32K bytes. The driver should first verify that the memory address is within the valid range for the adapter. The driver can be hard-coded with the valid physical addresses, it can be sent the address via an IOCtl, or the valid address could be entered at driver load time in the "DEVICE=XXX.SYS" line in the CONFIG.SYS file (see Chapter 8). The driver then allocates an LDT selector for the new adapter address. Even though the LDT belongs to the application, the driver can access it freely. This is due to the fact that when the driver is called by the application, the driver and application share the same context.

Next, the driver calls the OS/2 system DevHlp function PhysToUVirt (see Figure 10-1), which maps the physical address to an LDT selector in the application's LDT. The result is referred to as a fabricated address. Using an IOCtl, the driver then passes back the new LDT selector:offset value to the application. The application makes a pointer from the selector using the MAKEP macro, and uses this pointer for direct access to adapter memory. The LDT entry remains valid until the program is terminated.

```
if ( PhysToUVirt(0xd8000, 0x8000, 1, &mem))
    return (RPDONE | RPERR | ERROR_GEN_FAILURE);
```

Figure 10-1. PhysToVirt call.

The 0xd8000 is the physical adapter memory address. The 0x8000 is the requested size, the parameter 1 means get a virtual pointer and make the memory read-write, and &mem is the address of DS-relative storage for the returned virtual address.

Access to Adapter Memory In the Interrupt Handler

In some cases, such as upon receipt of an interrupt, the device driver may be required to access memory-mapped adapter inside the interrupt handler. If a driver is required to perform interrupt-time memory transfers, it should set up the references to the memory in the INIT section. Since the interrupt handler can be entered in any context, the LDT of the application may not be in the current context. The driver cannot use an LDT to address memory, but must use a GDT entry for memory access. The GDT entry will be valid in any context.

If the device driver will be performing memory-mapped transfers inside an interrupt handler, it must allocate the required selector(s) by issuing the AllocGDTSelector DevHlp, then map the new selector(s) to the physical address with the PhysToGDTSelector DevHlp call (see Figure 10-2). The driver now has direct addressability to the adapter memory regardless of context, and can freely transfer data to and from the adapter memory at interrupt time. The device driver must allocate and map the GDT selector(s) during INIT. However, remember that the INIT code is run as a Ring 3 thread of the system, so the driver cannot access the memory mapped to the GDT selector at INIT time.

A complete memory-mapped device driver and sample 16-bit and 32-bit application code is shown in the Listings section.

```
FARPOINTER fabricated_ptr = 0;

// allocate space for a GDT selector during INIT

 if (AllocGDTSelector (1,sel_array))
        {                                        // allocate a GDT sel
      DosPutMessage(1, 8, devhdr.DHname);
      DosPutMessage(1,strlen(GDTFailMsg),GDTFailMsg);
      break;
      }

// now map the board memory address to the GDT selector

 if (PhysToGDTSelector (board_address,
                   (USHORT) MEMSIZE,
                   sel_array[0],
                   &err))
      {
      DosPutMessage(1, 8, devhdr.DHname);
      DosPutMessage(1,strlen(SELFailMsg),SELFailMsg);
      break;
      }

 fabricated_ptr = MAKEP(sel_array[0],0);
```

Figure 10-2. Mapping a GDT selector during INIT.

Input/Output Privilege Level (IOPL)

OS/2 allows programs with I/O Privilege (IOPL) enabled to do direct register I/O to a device. If the device your application will be using is a parallel card or digital switch, an actual device driver may not be necessary. With IOPL, the application program can perform direct register I/O using IN and OUT instructions. If the device does not require interrupt or timer support, IOPL may be the ticket.

Note, however, that IOPL is a processor-specific function, and thus is not portable across hardware platforms such as *RISC*. For instance, the port mapping of a MIPS processor is not the same as an Intel processor, so code written for one processor will not necessarily run on another processor. The current trend is to migrate operating systems onto other platforms such as RISC and *SMP*. For these reasons, you can only perform IOPL from a 16-bit segment, and cannot enable a 32-bit C Set/2 segment to perform IOPL. 16-bit segments are allowed to perform IOPL since the 16-bit segments themselves are processor-dependent, and can't be migrated to other processor platforms anyway.

There are circumstances when it makes sense, for performance reasons, to allow the application to perform simple I/O. This could mean something as simple as controlling an external switch, or testing for a single bit from an I/O port. Calling a device driver to accomplish this is the preferred method, since its more likely to be portable. Under some circumstances, however, IOPL may be the best solution.

The IOPL Segment

To enable IOPL, the segment descriptors of the segment that contains the I/O code must be marked *Descriptor Privilege Level*, or *DPL 2*. OS/2 allows segments with properly marked descriptors to perform direct register I/O. There are two ways you can structure your IOPL routines. If you're using Microsoft C 6.0, the inp and outp functions are located in a separate segment called _IOSEG. You can indicate with your DEF file to mark _IOSEG as IOPL, and call the standard run-time library routines inp and outp. You can also write a simple function (See Figure 10-3) to perform the input and output.

```
; Sample IOPL segment

        PUBLIC  IN_PORT
        PUBLIC  OUT_PORT

        .model  large
        .286P

DGROUP  GROUP   _DATA
_DATA   SEGMENT WORD PUBLIC  'DATA'
_DATA   ENDS

_IOSEG  segment word use16 public 'CODE'

        assume  CS:_IOSEG,DS:DGROUP,SS:DGROUP
        .286P
;
IN_PORT proc far
;
  push  bp                ;set up stack frame
  mov   bp,sp             ;save bp
  push  dx                ;save dx
  mov   dx,[bp+6]         ;get port address
  in    ax,dx             ;do input
  pop   dx                ;restore regs
  pop   bp                ;return in ax
  ret   2                 ;remove from IOPL stack
;
IN_PORT endp

OUT_PORT proc far
;
  push  bp                ;set up stack frame
  mov   bp,sp             ;save it
  push  ax                ;save ax
  push  dx                ;and dx
  mov   ax,[bp+6]         ;get data
  mov   dx,[bp+8]         ;get port
```

Figure 10-3. IOPL Segment. (Continued)

```
        out     dx,al           ;do output
        pop     dx              ;restore regs
        pop     ax
        pop     bp
        ret     4               ;remove off local stack
;
OUT_PORT endp

_IOSEG  ends
        end
```

Figure 10-3. IOPL Segment.

During the link operation, the linker is told to mark the special segment as IOPL. The linker must also know the names of the exported routines and the size of the parameters that will be passed to the routines by the Ring 3 application. The number of words that the parameters will occupy on the stack is extremely important. Since the Ring 3 code (application) and the Ring 2 code (the IOPL code) do not share the same physical stack area, OS/2 must copy the contents of the Ring 3 stack to the Ring 2 stack. The linker informs OS/2 of the number of bytes to copy by the size parameter in the EXPORTS statement in the linker module definition file (see Figure 10-4).

```
NAME SAMPLE
STACKSIZE 8192
SEGMENTS
    _IOSEG   IOPL
EXPORTS
    PORTIN 1
    PORTOUT 2
PROTMODE
```

Figure 10-4. IOPL DEF file.

When the application calls either the IN_PORT or OUT_PORT routine, OS/2 will perform a ring transition from Ring 3 to Ring 2, copy the caller's stack to the separate Ring 2 stack, call the I/O routine, and perform another ring transition back to the Ring 3 application. Because of the extra overhead in ring transitions and copying stacks, this method will not be as fast as the DOS equivalent, but will be much faster than calling the device driver for every port input or output.

Remember that devices that generate interrupts, require asynchronous service, or operate in a time-critical environment must utilize a device driver. You may be able to get by using memory-mapping and IOPL, and I suggest using it if possible. Just keep in mind that eventually, OS/2 PDDs will eventually become 32-bit PDDs, and the handy shortcuts like memory-mapping and IOPL will most likely disappear.

IOPL From 32-bit Applications

IOPL is not permitted from 32-bit segments. To use IOPL from a 32-bit application, the application must call I/O routines located in a 16-bit segment. The easiest way to do this is to create a simple 16-bit DLL, then link it to the application with the IMPLIB utility. The same IOPL code can be used for 16-bit and 32-bit applications. A complete set of code for performing IOPL from 16-bit and 32-bit applications can be found in the Listings section.

CHAPTER 11

Direct Memory Access (DMA)

DMA is the ability of a device to access the computer system's memory without going through the CPU. Since DMA reads and writes bypass the CPU, data can be transferred very quickly without affecting system performance. This feature is useful for devices that generate large amounts of data frequently, such as video frame grabbers or an *Analog to Digital* (*A/D*) converter. The measure of a device's ability to transfer large amounts of data at a time is called its bandwidth. The larger the amount of data in a given time period, the higher the bandwidth. Devices that transfer large amounts of data frequently are therefore called high bandwidth devices. An example of a high bandwidth device would be a hard disk drive. The hard disk drive is capable of reading or writing large amounts of data very quickly. So quickly, in fact, that the CPU and device driver software cannot keep up with the disk drive's data transfer rate. If a read was requested from the disk driver using the CPU, the data from the disk would appear faster than the CPU could dispose of it, leading to overruns and data corruption.

The DMA Controller

Since memory is connected to the computer system's bus, the DMA controller must request that the CPU "give up" the bus for a short period of time. The DMA controller is a special set of circuitry responsible for performing the DMA transactions. Since memory is connected to the computer system's bus, the DMA controller must request that the CPU "give up" the bus for a short period of time. When the DMA controller needs to transfer data, it asks the CPU for control of the bus by issuing a HOLD request. When the CPU can release the bus, it grants the DMA controller use of the bus by raising a HOLD ACKNOWLEDGE or HLDA signal. When the DMA controller sees the HLDA signal, it begins transferring data to or from the adapter to the computer's memory. Memory transfers are very fast, much faster than if the CPU was involved. When the DMA controller finishes transferring the data, it drops the HOLD line, allowing the CPU to again use the system bus.

DMA is also a time-saving feature, in that it "steals" machine cycles from the CPU. The net effect is that of no noticeable loss in system performance, even when transferring large amounts of data. During DMA operation, the CPU remains free to execute program threads without knowledge of any DMA activity, other than the occasional giving up of the system bus.

Most IBM-compatibles and clones use a configuration of two 8237A-5 4-channel DMA controllers. Like the 8259 PIC, the 8237A-5 controllers are cascaded to provide additional functionality. One channel of the upper four DMA channels is used for the cascade to the lower DMA controller, so a total of seven DMA channels are available (see Table 11-1). The first DMA controller, called DMA controller 1, contains channels 0-3. Channels 0-3 support 8-bit transfers between adapters and memory. The largest block of memory that can be transferred is 64K bytes. Channels 5-7 support 16-bit transfers between adapters and memory, and the largest block that can be transferred is 128K bytes.

Table 11-1. DMA Channel Assignments

Controller 1	Description	Controller 2	Description
Channel 0	8-bit DMA channel	Channel 4	Cascade for controller1
Channel 1	Reserved for SDLC	Channel 5	16-bit DMA channel
Channel 2	Diskette (IBM PC)	Channel 6	16-bit DMA channel
Channel 3	8-bit DMA channel	Channel 7	16-bit DMA channel

Since the 8237 is a 24-bit DMA controller, all DMA transfers must occur from an address between 0 and 16 MB. The DMA controller contains a 24-bit address register, which limits the memory addressing. The DMA controller also has a count register, which is 16 bits long, limiting the transfers to 64KB (65536*8) with an 8-bit DMA channel and 128KB (65536*16) with a 16-bit channel. When using the 16-bit mode, bytes must be transferred on even-word boundaries.

Table 11-2 lists the DMA controller port assignments.

Table 11-2. DMA Controller Port Assignments (Continued)

Port address	Description
0000h	channel 0 base/current address
0001h	channel 0 base/current word count
0002h	channel 1 base/current address
0003h	channel 1 base/current word count
0004h	channel 2 base/current address
0005h	channel 2 base/current word count
0006h	channel 3 base/current address
0007h	channel 3 base/current word count
0008h	channel 0-3 status register
000Ah	channel 0-3 mask register (set/reset)
000Bh	channel 0-3 mode register (write)
000Ch	clear byte pointer (write)
000Dh	DMA controller reset (write)
000Eh	channel 0-3 clear mask register (write)
000Fh	channel 0-3 write mask register
0018h	extended function register (write)
001Ah	extended function execute
0081h	channel 2 page table register
0082h	channel 3 page table register
0083h	channel 1 page table register

Table 11-2. DMA Controller Port Assignments

Port address	Description
0087h	channel 0 page table register
0089h	channel 6 page table register
008Ah	channel 7 page table register
008Bh	channel 5 page table register
008F	channel 4 page table register
0C0h	channel 4 base/current address
0C2h	channel 4 base/current word count
0C4h	channel 5 base/current address
0C6h	channel 5 base/current word count
0C8h	channel 6 base/current address
0CAh	channel 6 base/current count
0CCh	channel 7 base/current address
0CEh	channel 7 base/current count
0D0h	channel 4-7 read status/write command
0D2h	channel 4-7 write request register
0D4h	channel 4-7 write single mask register bit
0D6h	channel 4-7 write mode register
0D8h	clear byte pointer flip-flop
0DAh	read temporary register/write Master Clear
0DCh	channel 4-7 clear mask register (write)
0DEh	channel 4-7 write mask register bits

Addressing for the DMA controller is accomplished by loading the address and page registers defined in Table 11-3.

Table 11-3. DMA Channel Addressing

For DMA Channels 0-3		
Source	DMA Page Register	Address Register
Address	A23 <-> A16	A15 <-> A0
For DMA Channels 5-7		
Source	DMA Page Register	Address Register
Address	A23 <-> A17	A16 <-> A1

More detailed information on the 8237A DMA controller and support circuitry can be found in the *Intel iAPX 86/88 User's Manual Hardware Reference*.

Using DMA

To utilize DMA, the device adapter must support DMA transfers. When data has to be written, the appropriate DMA channel registers are loaded with the address of the data to be written, the length of the data, and the proper mode (read/write) by the device driver. The adapter circuitry, usually a UART or some type of controller, issues a write request based on a programmed operation initiated by the device driver. An on-board arbiter issues a DMA request, which causes the system bus HOLD line to be raised. When the bus becomes available, the DMA controller raises the hold acknowledge line, HLDA, to signal the adapter that access to the bus has been granted. The adapter controller then begins a read operation on the system bus until the number of requested bytes have been read from memory, and then outputs the data to the device. The adapter normally generates an interrupt when the transfer is complete, so that the device driver can check the status of the transfer.

When data has to be read, the DMA channel registers are loaded with the address of the receive buffer, and the adapter controller programmed to start a read operation. The on-board arbiter requests a DMA operation, and the input data is transferred from the adapter controller directly to the memory buffer without using the CPU. When the required data has been read, or the adapter controller decides that the input should be terminated, it generates an interrupt so that the device driver can examine the received data. The DMA controller will give up the bus by releasing the HOLD line when the DMA channel transfer count goes to zero or the DMA channel is reset. In addition to the adapter initiating the DMA operation, the DMA controller can be programmed to start a DMA transfer using the 8237's request register.

To start the DMA, the particular channel is first masked to prevent it from running. Normally, device drivers are free to utilize DMA channels 5, 6, and 7. The mask register for DMA channels 4-7 is at I/O address 0xD4. The driver masks the DMA channel by setting the proper bits in the DMA mask register (see Table 11-4).

Table 11-4. DMA Mask Register

Bit	Meaning
0-1	00 = select channel 4 mask bit
	01 = select channel 5 mask bit
	10 = select channel 6 mask bit
	11 = select channel 7 mask bit
2	0 = clear mask bit
	1 = set mask bit
3-7	don't care

Next, the mode register for the selected channel is configured by setting the channel bit and the read/write bits (see Table 11-5).

Table 11-5 DMA Mode Register

Bit	Meaning
0-1	00 = channel 4 select
	01 = channel 5 select
	10 = channel 6 select
	11 = channel 7 select
2-3	00 = verify transfer
	01 = write transfer
	10 = read transfer
	11 = illegal
	xx = don't care if bits 6-7 = 11
4	0 = auto-initialize disable
	1 = auto-initialize enable
5	0 = address increment
	1 = address decrement
6-7	00 = demand mode select
	01 = single mode select
	10 = block mode select
	11 = cascade mode select

The DMA Command Registers are defined in Table 11-6.

Table 11-6. DMA Command Register

Bit	Meaning
0	0 = memory to memory disable
	1 = memory to memory enable
1	0 = channel 4 address hold disable
	1 = channel 4 address hold enable
	x = don't care if bit 0 = 0
2	0 = controller enable
	1 = controller disable
3	0 = normal timing
	1 = compressed timing
	x = don't care if bit 0 = 1
4	0 = fixed priority
	1 = rotating priority
5	0 = late write selection
	1 = extended write selection
	x = don't care if bit 3 = 1
6	0 = DREQ sense active high
	1 = DREQ sense active low
7	0 = DACK sense active low
	1 = DACK sense active high

The channel is then programmed to transfer words or bytes by the loading of the page select, base address and count registers. To start the DMA operation, the channel is unmasked by writing the proper mask bits to the mask register.

The code to initiate a DMA transfer is shown in Figure 11-1. A complete listing of the code can be found in Appendix C. The DMACh structure is assumed to be initialized before the call to SetupDMA. The DMA channel might be active at the time that it is needed, so the device driver should examine the status of the DMA channel to verify that it is available. This is done by examining the status word of the controller and checking the DMA channel busy bits.

```
USHORT   SetupDMA(USHORT channel)
    {
    if(DMAChannelBusy(channel))
       return (DMA_CHANNEL_BUSY);
    MaskDMA(channel);
    SetDMAMode(channel,DMA_SINGLE | DMA_READ);
    InitDMA(channel,(UCHAR) DMACh.PageSelect,
               (USHORT) DMACh.BaseAddress,
               (USHORT) DMACh.WordCount);
    UnmaskDMA(channel);
    return (DMA_COMPLETE);
    }
```

Figure 11-1. DMA setup routine.

DMA and Micro Channel

The Micro Channel bus permits adapters to be masters or slaves. During a memory or I/O transfer under DMA, the master owns the bus and transfers data to and from a slave. Adapters that need the bus compete for it using a centralized arbiter, called the *Central Arbitration Control Point*, or *CACP*. The CACP arbitrates DMA channel utilization based on a 4-bit arbitration bus, known as the ARBUS. The ARBUS and CACP work together to ensure that the highest priority master gets control of the bus when it needs it, and that other masters which are competing for the bus get a fair share of the available time.

In a Micro Channel system, the DMA controller is a master, which assists in transfers between slaves during a DMA operation. The DMA controller cannot arbitrate the bus. Rather, a slave initiates the arbitration which is monitored by the DMA controller. The DMA controller then transfers the data between the slave and memory. In this capacity, the DMA controller acts as a "middle man", responsible for helping out with the transfer. Thus this arrangement is sometimes referred to as "third-party DMA".

Micro Channel slave adapters capable of DMA operation are fitted with a second DMA controller, called a DMA arbiter. To perform DMA transfers, the device driver initializes the adapter with the source, destination, and count of the transfer. The on-board hardware DMA arbiter arbitrates for the use of the bus using its preassigned arbitration level, which is usually stored in the adapter's POS registers. Data transfers can also be performed to and from Micro Channel Bus Masters without using the system DMA controller.

CHAPTER 12

Extended Device Driver Interface

The *Extended Device Driver Interface*, *EDDI*, is a new interface developed to take advantage of a new generation of intelligent disk controllers. These new disk controllers are capable of handling transfers to and from discontiguous memory areas. Although EDDI is intended for disk drivers, other types of device drivers can also utilize EDDI.

EDDI improves performance by allowing multiple, prioritized requests to be submitted to the device driver at the same time. Instead of the standard synchronous Request Packet, the EDDI driver is sent a Request List of commands, which it can reorder to provide maximum performance. The Read and Write operations use *scatter/gather descriptors* (*SGDs*), which allow for data transfer to and from discontiguous data buffers. The driver does not need to block waiting for the request to complete, but returns immediately. The actual transfer is usually completed by the disk adapter hardware.

The ability to handle transfers to and from discontiguous memory is more efficient in a system such as OS/2 2.1, which utilizes the 4KB paging functionality of the 80386 and 80486 processors. Data buffers to be written to or from the device driver are normally partitioned into 4K pages, and are not necessarily contiguous. EDDI requires that the device driver contain a second Strategy routine in addition to the normal Strategy routine in an OS/2 device driver. The new extended Strategy routine is also called the Strategy 2 or scatter/gather entry point.

Device Driver Capabilities

The OS/2 kernel issues a Get Driver Capabilities request to the device driver. If the device driver supports the scatter/gather interface, it returns to the kernel a structure containing two 16:16 pointers to special structures that are supported and maintained by the device driver. Contained in one of the structures is a 16:16 pointer to the second Strategy routine to handle synchronous I/O, along with several other parameters. See the Get Driver Capabilities command in Chapter 6.

The first structure returned is the *Driver Capabilities Structure*, or *DCS* (see Figure 12-1). The DCS can be changed only by the device driver.

```
typedef struct _DRIVCAPSTRUCT {
    USHORT     reserved;
    UCHAR      VerMajor;     // major version, should be 01
    UCHAR      VerMinor;     // minor version, should be 01
    ULONG      Capabilities;// capabilities bits
    PFUNCTION  Strategy2;    // 16:16 pointer to STRAT2
    PFUNCTION  SetFSDInfo;   // 16:16 pointer to SetFSDInfo
    PFUNCTION  ChgPriority;  // 16:16 pointer to ChgPriority
    PFUNCTION  SetRestPos;   // 16:16 pointer to RestPos
    PFUNCTION  GetBoundary;  // 16:16 pointer to GetBoundary
} DRIVCAPSTRUCT;
```

Figure 12-1. Driver Capabilities structure.

The major and minor version number specifies the version of the EDDI interface that the driver supports. For OS/2 2.1, these should both be 1.

The capabilities bits are described in Table 12-1.

Table 12-1. Capabilities Bits

Bit(s)	Description
0-2	reserved, must be zero
3	if set, supports disk mirroring
4	if set, supports disk multiplexing
5	if set, driver does not block in STRAT2 requests. LAN Server and LAN Manager require this.
6-31	reserved, should be 0

If the driver does not provide a particular service such as ChgPriority, it must return 0:0 as the pointer to the nonexistent function.

The second pointer returned from the Get Driver Capabilities function is a pointer to the *Volume Characteristics Structure*, or *VCS*. The VCS structure appears in Figure 12-2.

```
typedef struct _VOLCHARSTRUCT {
  USHORT VolDescriptor;
  USHORT AvgSeekTime;
  USHORT AvgLatency;
  USHORT TrackMinBlocks;
  USHORT TrackMaxBlocks;
  USHORT HeadsPerCylinder
  ULONG  VolCylinderCount;
  ULONG  VolMedianBlock;
  USHORT MaxSGList;
  } VOLCHARSTRUCT;
```

Figure 12-2. Volume Characteristics Structure.

The VolDescriptor is defined in Table 12-2.

Table 12-2. Volume Descriptor Word

Bit(s)	Description
0	if set, volume resides on removable media
1	if set, volume is read only
2	if set, average seek time is independent of position, such as a RAM disk
3	if set, outboard cache is supported
4	if set, scatter/gather is supported by the adapter
5	if set, Read Prefetch is supported
6-15	reserved, should be zero

The AvgSeekTime is the disk seek time specified in milliseconds. If unknown, the time should be set to FFFF. If the device is a RAM disk, the time should be 0.

The AvgLatency is the average rotational latency in milliseconds. Like the average seek time, the latency should be set to FFFF when it is unknown, and 0 when the device is a RAM disk.

The TrackMinBlocks specifies the number of blocks available on the smallest capacity track. If this value is not known, it should be set to 1.

The TrackMaxBlocks is the number of blocks available on the largest capacity track. If this value is not known, it should be set to 0.

The Heads Per Cylinder is the number of heads per disk cylinder. If not known or applicable, this value should be set to 1.

The VolCylinderCount is the number of cylinders in the volume. If not known, it should contain the number of sectors in the volume.

The MaxSGList is the maximum number of scatter/gather list entries that can be submitted with one command. If the adapter does not directly support scatter/gather, this field should be set to 0.

Request Lists and Request Control

To enable the EDDI driver to be called with multiple requests at one time, a new request format was defined, and is referred to as a Request List. The Request List allows an EDDI device driver's Strategy entry point to be called with a list of requests. The device driver can reorder the requests to provide maximum performance. Only four types of requests have been defined. The four requests are *Read*, *Write*, *Write Verify*, and *Read Prefetch*. Other commands may be added in the future. The requests have Request Control flags associated with them which can be used to force sequential execution.

The Request list consists of a 20-byte Request List Header shown in Figure 12-3.

```
typedef struct _REQUESTLISTHEADER {
   USHORT     ReqListCount;
   USHORT     Reserved;
   FARPOINTER ListNotifyAddress;
   USHORT     ListRequestControl;
   UCHAR      BlkDevUnit;
   UCHAR      ListStatus;
   ULONG      Reserved1
   ULONG      Reserved2;
   } REQUESTLISTHEADER;
```

Figure 12-3. Request List Header structure.

The ReqListCount is the number of requests in the Request List.

The LstNotifyAddress is a 16:16 pointer to the notification routine to be called when all requests in the Request List have been completed, or when an unrecoverable error has occurred. The LstNotifyAddress is called with ES:BX pointing to the Request List Header, and the carry flag set (STC) if an error has occurred. The device driver must save all registers before making the call to the NotifyAddress, and restore them when the call is complete. This call should not be made if both bit 4 and bit 5 of the LstRequestControl word are clear (0).

The LstRequestControl word is defined in Table 12-3.

Table 12-3. LstRequestControl Word Bits

Bit(s)	Description
0	reserved
1	if set, only one request is in the list
2	if set, execute the requests sequentially (do not reorder)
3	if set, abort on error, set all status, error code and count (BlocksXferred) fields
4	if set, notify immediately (by calling the LstNotifyAddress) if an error is detected
5	if set, call the LstNotifyAddress upon completion regardless of any errors
6-15	reserved, must be set to 0

The BlockDevUnit is the logical unit number of the volume.

The LstStatus contains the current status of the request list as it is being processed. The device driver should update the list as requests are being processed. The LstStatus byte is divided into two 4-byte nibbles. The lower 4 bits indicate the completion status of the requests in the list and the upper 4 bits indicate the error status of the requests in the list. The bits are defined in Tables 12-4 and 12-5.

Table 12-4. LstStatus Byte, Lower Nibble

Value	Meaning
00h	no requests are queued
01h	queueing is in process
02h	all requests queued
04h	all requests completed
08h	reserved

Table 12-5. LstStatus Byte, Upper Nibble

Value	Meaning
00h	no error
01h	recoverable error occurred
02h	unrecoverable error occurred
03h	unrecoverable error with retry
04h	reserved
08h	reserved

Request Format

The valid requests are *Read (1Eh)*, *Write(1Fh)*, *Write Verify(20h)* and *Read Prefetch(21h)*. Each extended request has a Request Header which is different from the Request List Header. The Request Header is 32 bytes long and is described in Figure 12-4.

```
typedef struct _REQUESTHEADER {
    USHORT      ReqLength;
    UCHAR       CmdPrefix;
    UCHAR       CmdCode;
    ULONG       HeaderOffset;
    UCHAR       RequestCtl;
    UCHAR       Priority;
    UCHAR       Status;
    UCHAR       ErrorCode;
    FARPOINTER  NotifyAddress;
    FARPOINTER  HintPointer;
    ULONG       Reserved1;
    ULONG       Reserved2;
    ULONG       Reserved3;
    } REQUESTHEADER;
```

Figure 12-4. Request Header structure.

The ReqLength is the offset to the next request. FFFF terminates the list.

The CmdPrefix is always set to 0x1C to differentiate the request from a standard Request Packet.

The CmdCode is one of the valid command codes, 1Eh, 1Fh, 20h, or 21h.

The HeaderOffset is the offset from the beginning of the Request List Header to the header of this request, and is used as a quick access to the Request List Header.

The RequestCtl field is defined in Table 12-6.

The notify routines should not be called if bits 4 and 5 are both clear (0).

Table 12-6. RequestCtl Byte

Bit(s)	Description
0-3	reserved, must be 0
4	if set, notify on error only by calling the NotifyAddress immediately
5	if set, notify on completion by calling the NotifyAddress
6-7	reserved, must be 0

The Request Priority defines the priority of the request, and is defined in Table 12-7.

Table 12-7. Request Priority

Value	Meaning
00h	prefetch requests
01h	low-priority request
02h	read ahead, low-priority pager I/O
04h	background synchronous user I/O
08h	foreground synchronous user I/O
10h	high-priority pager I/O
80h	urgent request, should be handled immediately

The Status field contains the status of the current request and is defined in Tables 12-8 and 12-9.

Table 12-8. Request Status, Lower Nibble (Completion Status)

Value	Meaning
00h	not queued yet
01h	queued and waiting
02h	in process
04h	done
08h	reserved

Table 12-9. Request Status, Upper Nibble (Error Status)

Value	Meaning
00h	no error
01h	recoverable error occurred
02h	unrecoverable error occurred
03h	unrecoverable error occurred
04h	the request was aborted
08h	reserved

ErrorCode contains one of the errors described in Tables 12-10 and 12-11 if the corresponding error bits are set in the Status field.

Table 12-10. Request Unrecoverable Error Codes

Value	Meaning
00h	write protect violation
01h	unknown unit
02h	device not ready
03h	unknown command
04h	CRC error
06h	seek error
07h	unknown media
08h	block not found
0Ah	write fault
0Bh	read fault
0Ch	general failure
10h	uncertain media
13h	invalid parameter

Table 12-11. Request Recoverable Error Codes

Value	Meaning
1Ah	verify error on write, recovered after 1 try
2Ah	write error, write to duplexed or mirrored driver succeeded
3Ah	write error on mirrored or duplexed drive, write to primary drive succeeded
1Bh	read error, corrected using ECC
2Bh	read succeeded after retry
3Bh	read error, recovered from mirrored or duplexed driver

The NotifyAddress contains a 16:16 pointer to the driver to call when the request has been completed or aborted. If bits 4 and 5 of the RequestCtl field are both clear (0), the Notify Address is not valid and should not be called. The device driver must save all registers before calling the notify routine, and restore them when the call returns.

The HintPointer is a 16:16 pointer to a Request Packet in the Request List. The device driver can use this pointer to determine whether the current request can be grouped with another pending request, providing that the other request has not yet been completed.

Read/Write/Write Verify Request

The format of these requests is described in Figures 12-5 and 12-6.

```
typedef struct _SGD {
   PHYSADDR BufferPtr;
   ULONG    BufferSize;
   } SGD;
```

Figure 12-5. Scatter Gather Descriptor structure.

```
typedef struct _READWRITE {
   REQUESTHEADER ReadWriteHeader;
   ULONG         StartBlock;
   ULONG         BlockCount;
   ULONG         BlocksXferred;
   USHORT        Flags;
   USHORT        SGDescrCount
   ULONG         Reserved;
   SGD           Sgd[SGDescrCount];
} READWRITE;
```

Figure 12-6. Read/Write Request structure.

The StartBlock is the string disk block for the data transfer. A disk block is defined as a 512-byte logical disk sector.

The BlockCount is the number of 512-byte blocks to be transferred.

The BlocksXferred is the number of blocks that have been transferred at the time that the notification routine was called.

The Flags field currently uses only the two least significant bits. All other bits are set to 0. If bit 0 is set, it specifies write-through, defeating any lazy write. If bit 1 is set, the data should be cached on the outboard controller cache.

The SGDescrCount field contains the number of scatter/gather descriptors in the Sgd field.

The Sgd field contains an array of scatter/gather descriptors.

Read Prefetch Request

The format of the Read Prefetch request is described in Figure 12-7.

```
typedef struct _READPREFETCH {
    REQUESTHEADER ReadPreHdr;
    ULONG         StartBlock;
    ULONG         BlockCount;
    ULONG         BlocksXferred;
    USHORT        Flags;
    USHORT        Reserved;
} READPREFETCH;
```

Figure 12-7. Read Prefetch Request structure.

The StartBlock is the string disk block for the data transfer. A disk block is defined as a 512-byte logical disk sector.

The BlockCount is the number of 512-byte blocks to be transferred.

The BlocksXferred is the number of blocks that have been transferred at the time that the notification routine was called.

The Flags field currently uses only the least significant bit. All other bits are set to 0. If bit 0 is set, it specifies that the driver should retain data in the controller prefetch buffers only until it has been read once. This prevents redundant caching in the controller.

Request Control Functions

The EDDI device driver may optionally provide other services to allow OS/2 to manage extended requests. The current implementation is OS/2 2.1 defines four functions that the device driver may support. The device driver exports these functions by placing a 16:16 pointer to the functions in the DCS returned from the Get Driver Capabilities call. If the pointer in the DCS structure is 0:0, the function is not supported by the device driver. Since the request control functions may be called at interrupt time, they must not block. Request control functions are called by the OS/2 File System Driver, or FSD. Request control functions must save and restore the segment registers, as the interrupt context may not be the same as the device driver. The four request control functions are summarized in Table 12-12.

Table 12-12. Request Control Functions

Request Control Function	Description
SetFSDInfo	Send the device driver 16:16 pointers to the FSD's End of Interrupt and Access Validation routines
ChgPriority	Allows the FSD to change the priority of a pending request
SetRestPos	Allows the FSD to inform the device driver where to send the disk drive heads when there are no requests pending
GetBoundary	The device driver returns a block number greater than the block number passed to the device driver

SetFSDInfo

This device driver function is called by the FSD with 16:16 pointers to the FSD's End of Interrupt and Access Validation routines. The driver is called with ES:BX pointing to a FSDInfo structure, described in Figure 12-8.

```
typedef struct _FSDInfo {
    ULONG       Reserved1;   // reserved, must be 0
    FARPOINTER  EndOfInit;   // pointer to FSD's EOI
    ULONG       Reserved2;   // reserved, must be 0
    FARPOINTER  AccValidate; // pointer to FSD's AccValidate
} FSDInfo;
```

Figure 12-8. SetFSDInfo structure.

The device driver should allow this function to be called only once. If the call is the first call, the device driver should return with the carry flag set (STC). Subsequent calls should be ignored, and the device driver should return with the carry flag clear (CLC).

If the EndOfInit pointer is 0, the FSD does not provide an End Of Interrupt routine. All registers are preserved during the call to EndOfInit.

The device driver calls the FSD's AccValidate with the AL register set to 0 for a non-destructive operation, such as READ or VERIFY, and the AL register set to 1 for a destructive operation, such as WRITE or FORMAT TRACK. The FSD's AccValidate function returns with the carry flag clear if access is allowed, or the carry flag set if access is denied. The device driver should return a write-protect violation to the caller if access is denied.

ChgPriority

The device driver's ChgPriority routine is called with ES:BX pointing to the request, and the AL register containing the new priority. The pointer in ES:BX is always a valid pointer. The device driver should return with the carry flag set if the Request Packet was not found or was no longer in the device driver's internal queue. If the priority change was successful, the device driver should return with the carry flag clear.

SetRestPos

The device driver's SetRestPos routine is called with AX:BX containing the block to be used for the resting position. A value of FFFF:FFFF means rest at the block where the heads end up. The device driver should return with the carry flag set if the block number is out of the range for the volume, otherwise it should return with the carry flag clear.

GetBoundary

The device driver's GetBoundary routine is called with AX:BX containing the block number to be used as a reference to calculate the next block number. Using this information, the FSD can store files more optimally. If the next block cannot easily be calculated or is not known, the device driver can return the reference block+1. If the block number is out of the range, the device driver must return with the carry flag set, otherwise it should return with the carry flag clear.

CHAPTER 13

Debugging OS/2 2.1 Device Drivers

The *Kernel Debugger*, or *KDB*, is generally used to debug device drivers as well as the system kernel code. The KDB kernel, OS2KRNLD, is actually a full function replacement OS/2 kernel, which contains the debugger and the debugger support functions. KDB communicates with a standard ASCII terminal through one of the COM ports. If the system contains only one COM port, COM1, KDB uses COM1. If the system has two COM ports, COM1 and COM2, KDB uses the second COM port, COM2. KDB defaults to 9600 baud, no parity, 8 data bits and one stop bit.

The COM port is attached to an ASCII terminal via an RS-232 interface with data leads only in a null modem configuration (pin 2 and 3 switched). Before installing the debugger, the terminal link should first be verified by sending some text out to the terminal using the DIR > COMn command. If the baud rate of the COM port has not been previously initialized to 9600 baud, use the command MODE COM1(or COM2):96,n,8,1 <enter>. The text of the directory list should be displayed on the debugging terminal. You do not have to issue the MODE command when KDB is installed, as KDB will initialize the port on start-up to 9600,n,8,1.

To install the kernel debugger, the system is rebooted using a DOS or OS/2 installation diskette, and the attributes of the OS2KRNL file changed to make it visible. This can be done by using a utility such a chmod or one of the many available OS/2 utilities. The OS2KRNL file is renamed to OS2KRNL.OLD, and the debugging kernel,

OS2KRNLD, copied to OS2KRNL. The OS2KRNL.OLD file is kept to allow reinstallation of the non-debug kernel when reinstalling OS/2. When the system is rebooted, the debugger should sign on at the debug terminal with the message "System Debugger 03/16/89 [80386]".

The IBM OS/2 Toolkit contains an install utility for the kernel debugger which will perform the above steps automatically.

KDB can be entered normally in several ways. Three special keys entered on the debugging terminal cause KDB to be entered prior to the complete boot of OS/2. The "r" key causes the debugger to be entered at the beginning of DOS initialization in real mode. The "p" key causes the debugger to be entered after OS/2 goes into the protect mode for the first time. The "<space-bar>" causes the debugger to be entered after most of DOS has been initialized. Symbols for DOS have been loaded at this time.

After initialization is complete, the debugger can be entered at any time by typing <cntl-c> at the debug terminal. The debugger is entered when and where the next timer tick is taken after the key was pressed.

When KDB is entered, it will execute the current default command, usually the "r" (register contents), and then display the debugger prompt, "##". The system will not run until the debugger is exited, usually by entering the GO command (g). KDB will also be entered when the system detects an "INT 3" instruction. A common debug technique is to insert INT 3 instructions in the driver source code while debugging, which will cause KDB to be entered. Once KDB has been entered, the KDB commands can be used to display the contents of variables, system information, or memory contents, and to run from or single-step from the breakpoint.

After any symbols files are loaded, an initialization file, called KDB.INI, is read and executed. Any debugger command or list of debugger commands can be in the KDB.INI file. A "g" command should usually be at the end of the command list, unless the debugger is to remain stopped.

At any time during the display of data on the debug terminal, the display can be stopped with a <cntl-s>, and restarted with a <cntl-q>. The GO command (g) always resumes execution at the instruction displayed in the CS:IP register.

KDB displays information in machine code, and requires a thorough understanding of machine language and processor architecture to fully utilize its capabilities.

A complete list of the valid KDB commands can be displayed by entering the "?" command at the KDB prompt for internal KDB commands, and ".?" for external commands.

KDB obtains its symbolic debug information from a symbol file with the extension of .SYM. These files can be created with the MAPSYM utility, which creates a symbol file from the .MAP file created during the link operation. When loading a device driver during system boot, the debug kernel looks for a .SYM file with the same file name as the driver .SYS file, and in the same directory as the driver .SYS file. If the device driver "TEST.SYS" were being loaded, the debug kernel would look in the same directory as "TEST.SYS" for the file "TEST.SYM", and load the symbols. The symbol file is not necessary, and the driver will load without it, but variables will not be able to be accessed by name. Several drivers may be loaded, each with their own .SYM file.

If the KDB was supplied with the operating system SYM files, these will also be loaded if they are placed on the root directory with the OS2KRNL file. The system symbol files will allow access to system variables and structures by name. Symbols are displayed using a KDB command such as *display word* (*dw*), *display byte* (*db*), or *display double* word (*dd*). They are referenced by the symbolic name preceded by the underscore ("_"), if the driver is written in C. For example, to display the 16-bit variable "bytecount", the command "dw _bytecount" would be entered.

KDB Keywords

KDB supports the keywords in Table 13-1 which return their value when used in expressions.

Table 13-1. KDB Keywords (Continued)	
[E]AX, [E]BX, [E]CX, [E]DX, [E]SI, [E]DI, [E]BP, DS, ES, SS, CS, [E]SP, [E]IP	register values
FLG	value of flags
GDTB	value of GDT base physical address
GDTL	value of GDT limit
IDTB	value of IDT base physical address
IDTL	value of IDT limit
TR, LDTR, MSW	value of TR, LDTR, MSW registers

Table 13-1. KDB Keywords

BR0, BR1..BR9	value of breakpoint address
FS, GS	segment registers
EFLG	value of extended flags
CR0, CR2, CR3	value of control registers
DR0, DR1, DR2, DR3, DR4, DR5, DR6, DR7	value of debug registers
TR6, TR7	value of test registers

KDB Operators

KDB supports the binary operators described in Table 13-2.

Table 13-2. KDB Binary Operators (Continued)

Operator	Meaning
()	Parentheses
+	Addition
-	Subtraction
*	Multiplication
/	Division
MOD	Modulo
>	Greater than
<	Less than
>=	Greater than or equal to

Table 13-2. KDB Binary Operators

Operator	Meaning
<=	Less than or equal to
!=	Not equal to
==	Equal to
AND	Boolean AND
XOR	Boolean exclusive OR
OR	Boolean inclusive OR
&&	Logical AND
||	Logical OR
:	Address separator

KDB supports the unary operators described in Table 13-3.

Table 13-3. KDB Unary Operators (Continued)

Operator	Meaning
|	Task number/address operator
&addr	Interpret address using segment value
#addr	Interpret address using selector
%addr	Interpret address as 32-bit linear
%%addr	32-bit physical address

Table 13-3. KDB Unary Operators

Operator	Meaning
-	Two's complement
!	Logical NOT
NOT	One's complement
SEG	Segment address
OFF	Address offset
BY	Low byte of address
WO	Low word of address
DW	Doubleword from address
POI	Pointer from address
PORT	One byte from a port
WPORT	Word from a port

The operator precedence is as follows:

( )

| :

& # % %% - ! NOT SEG OFF BY WO DW POI PORT WPORT (unary operators)

* / MOD

+ -

> < >= <=

==

!=

AND

XOR

OR

&&

||

KDB Command Reference

In the following command descriptions, the following rules apply:

- brackets ([]) mean the parameter is optional
- the "or" sign (|) means either of the parameters is valid
- parameters surrounded by carets (<>) are mandatory
- parameters may be separated by a comma (,) or blank
- multiple commands on the same line are separated by a semicolon (;)
- all numeric entry is defaulted to hexidecimal
- (...) means repeats

Table 13-4 lists the KDB parameter types and their meaning.

Table 13-4. KDB Parameter Definitions

Parameter	Definition
<expr>	evaluates to an 8, 16, or 32-bit value
<number>	a number in decimal, octal, hex or binary
<string>	any number of characters between " " or ' '
<range>	<addr> [<word>]	[<addr>] [L <word>]
<addr>	[&	#][<word>:]<word>	%<dword>
<list>	<byte>, <byte>, ...	"string"
<bp commands>	a list of debugger commands, separated by ;
<string>	"char"	'char'
<dword>,<word>,<byte>	expressions that evaluate to the size in <>

Expressions

An expression (expr) is a combination of parameters and operators that evaluate to an 8, 16 or 32-bit value.

Numbers

A number (number) parameter can be any number with hex as the default. Numbers may be evaluated in a different radix by appending a special character to the number. These special characters are y for binary, o for octal, T for decimal and h for hex (default).

Strings

A string (string) parameter is any number of characters within double (" ") or single (' ') quotes. Double quotes within the string should be preceded by another double quote to be correctly evaluated.

Ranges

A range (range) parameter specifies an address followed by either a length or an end address. An additional parameter may also be used to specify the number of times to perform the operation.

Addresses

An address (addr) parameter indicates a memory address in one of four modes. The four modes are: real mode (&segment:offset), protect mode (#selector:offset), linear address (%dword), and physical address (%%dword). The operators preceding the address override the current address type.

Lists

A list is a list of two-character bytes separated by a space, or a string surrounded by double quotes.

Commands

Commands (bp cmds) are one or more debugger commands, separated by semi-colons (;), to be executed when a condition is met, such as a breakpoint encountered.

Strings

A string is a list of characters bounded by single or double quotes.

Dwords, words, bytes

Expressions that evaluate to the specified size.

Breakpoints

There are two kinds of breakpoints in the kernel debugger. Temporary breakpoints are set as an option to the go (g) command, and disappear when the go command is executed again. Sticky breakpoints are set with a KDB set breakpoint command, and remain until cleared with a KDB command or the system is rebooted. Sticky breakpoints are numbered 0-9, inclusive.

On a 386, the debug registers can be used in a sticky breakpoint (see the br command).

When a breakpoint is encountered, the current default command is executed. This command is set to r, or the dump registers command. The default command may be changed by the zs command, and listed with the z command.

Internal Commands

Set Breakpoint

```
bp[bp number] [<addr>] [<passcnt>] [<bp cmds>]
```

Set a new sticky breakpoint, or change an existing old breakpoint. The number parameter is an optional breakpoint number, which selects a new breakpoint by the number or changes an existing breakpoint with the same number.

The passcnt parameter specifies how many times the breakpoint will be passed by before it is executed. If passcnt is omitted or 0, the breakpoint will be executed the first time that it is encountered.

The commands parameter is a list of KDB commands to be executed when the breakpoint is encountered.

Set Register Breakpoint

```
br[<bp number>] e|w|r|1|2|4 [<addr>] [<passcnt>] ["<bp cmds>"]
```

Sets a 386 debug register. Debug registers can be used to break on data reads and writes, and on instruction execution. Up to four debug registers can be set and enabled at one time. Disabled br breakpoints don't occupy a debug register.

The e parameter specifies a one-byte length (default)

The w parameter specifies break on write operation.

The r parameter specifies break on read operation

The 1 parameter specifies a one-byte length.

The 2 parameter specifies a word length. Word-length breakpoints must be on a word boundary.

The 4 parameter specifies a doubleword length.

Set Time Stamping Breakpoint

```
bt[<bp number>] [<addr>]
```

Set a time stamping breakpoint.

Show Timestamp Entries

```
bs
```

Show the time stamp entries.

List Breakpoint(s)

```
bl
```

Lists the currently set breakpoints with current and original passcnt, and breakpoint commands (bp cmds) associated with them.

An "e" after the breakpoint number means that the breakpoint is enabled; a "d" means that it is disabled. After either one, there may be an "i", which indicates that the address was invalid the last time the debugger tried to set or clear the breakpoint.

Clear Breakpoint(s)

```
bc[bp number],[bp number],...
```

Removes (clears) the list of breakpoint numbers from the debugger's breakpoint table.

Enable Breakpoint

```
be [bp number],[bp number],...
```

Enables the list of breakpoint numbers.

Clear Breakpoint(s)

```
bd[bp number],[bp number],...
```

Disables the list of breakpoint numbers. The breakpoint is not removed, but disabled so that it can be re-enabled later.

Compare Bytes

```
c <range> <addr>
```

Compares the bytes in the memory location specified by <range> with the corresponding bytes in the memory locations beginning at <addr>. If all corresponding bytes match, the kernel debugger displays its prompt and waits for the next command. If one or more corresponding bytes do not match, each pair of mismatched bytes is displayed.

Dump Memory

```
d [<range>]
```

Dump memory in the last format selected (byte, word, doubleword).

Dump Bytes

```
db [<range>]
```

Dump memory in byte format and ASCII representation.

Dump Words

```
dw [<range>]
```

Dump memory in word format.

Dump Doublewords

```
dd [<range>]
```

Dump memory in doubleword format.

Dump GDT Entries

```
dg [a] [<range>]
```

Dump global descriptor table entries.

The a parameter specifies a dump of all entries, not just valid entries.

Without the a parameter, the dg command will display only the valid GDT entries. If the range is an LDT selector, KDB will display "LDT" and the associated entry.

Dump IDT Entries

```
di [a] [<range>]
```

Dumps the interrupt descriptor table.

The a parameter specifies a dump of all of the IDT entries.

The default is to display only the valid IDT entries.

Dump LDT Entries

```
dl [a|p|s|h] [<range>]
```

Dump local descriptor table entries.

The a parameter specifies a dump of all of the LDT entries.

The default is to display only the valid LDT entries.

The p parameter specifies the private selectors only.

The s parameter specifies the shared selectors only.

The h parameter specifies the huge segment selectors only.

Dump Page Directory/Page Table Entries

```
dp [a|d] [<range>]
```

Dump the page directory and page tables. Page tables are skipped if the corresponding page directory entry is not present. Page directory entries with an asterisk next to the page frame should be ignored.

The a parameter specifies a dump of all of the page directory and page table entries.

The default is to skip entries that are zero.

The d parameter specifies a dump of page directory entries only.

Table 13-5. Page Bit Definitions (bit set/clear)

Dc	Dirty/clean
Au	Accessed/unaccessed
Us	User/supervisor
Wr	Writable/read-only
Pn	Present/not present

The pteframe field contains the contents of the high 20 bits in the pte. If the page is present, the value is the high 20 bits of the physical address that the page maps to. To find out information about the physical address, use the .mp command. If the page is not present, the pteframe field contains an index into the *Virtual Page (VP)* structure. The .mv command can dump information from the VP structure. A not-present page may still be cross-linked to a page of physical memory via the VP, and if so, that physical address is in the frame column.

Note: uvirt pages in the state column represent a direct mapping of physical memory without any other page manager structures associated with them.

Dump Task State Segment (TSS)

```
dt [<addr>]
```

Dumps the TSS. If no address is given, the dt command will dump the current TSS pointed to by the TR register, extracting the type (16- or 32-bit) from the descriptor access byte. If an address is given, the type is determined by the 386env flag.

Dump Loadall Buffer

```
dx
```

Dump the 80286 loadall buffer.

Enter Data

```
e <addr> [<list>]
```

Enter one or more byte values into memory at the specified addr.

The list parameter specifies a list of bytes to be stored at addr and each subsequent address, until all of the data in the list has been used.

If the list is omitted, KDB prompts the operator for a byte. If an error occurs, the contents of memory are left unchanged. Each time the space bar is hit, the address is incremented by one byte. The minus key (-) decrements the address. The return key with no data terminates the entry and returns to the KDB prompt.

Fill Memory With Pattern

    f <range> <list>

Block fills the addresses in the range with the values in the list.

The list parameter specifies a pattern or list of bytes to be stored.

If the range specifies more bytes than the number of values in the list, the pattern of bytes in the list is repeated until all bytes in the range are filled. If the list has more values than the number of bytes in the range, the extra bytes are ignored.

Go

    g [s] [t] [=<start addr>][<break addr>],[<break addr>...]

Passes execution control to the code at the start addr. Execution continues to the end of the code, or until the break addr or a breakpoint is encountered.

If no start addr is given, the command passes execution to the address specified by the current CS:IP.

The equal sign (=) parameter is used only when a start addr is given.

The s parameter causes the number of timer ticks since the system was started to be displayed.

The t parameter allows trapped exceptions to resume at the original trap handler address without having to unhook the exception.

Up to 10 addresses may be used. Only the first address encountered during execution will cause a break. All others are ignored. If more than 10 breakpoints are entered, an error message will be displayed.

When the breakpoint is encountered, the default command is executed.

Help/Print Expression

```
?[<expr>][|'string']
```

If no arguments are entered, KDB displays the command syntax help for the internal debugger commands.

The expr parameter is an expression to be evaluated. The evaluated expression is displayed in hex, decimal, octal, and binary.

The string parameter prints the ASCII string on the debugger terminal.

Hex Arithmetic

```
h <number 1> <number 2>
```

Perform hex arithmetic in two values. KDB adds number 1 to number 2, subtracts number 1 from number 2, multiplies number 1 by number 2, divides number 1 by number 2, and displays the results.

Input Port

```
i <port>
```

Reads and displays one byte from the specified port.

List Near Symbols

```
ln [<addr>]
```

Lists the nearest symbol both forward and back from addr.

List Groups

```
lg [<mapname>]
```

Lists the selector or segment and the name for each group in the active maps or the specified map mapname.

List Maps

    lm

Lists all of the current symbol files loaded, and which ones are active.

List Absolute Symbols

    la [<mapname>]

Lists all of the absolute symbols in the active maps or the specified map mapname.

List Symbols

    ls <addr>

Lists all of the symbols in the group that the address addr is in.

Add/Remove Active Map

    wa <mapname> | *
    wr <mapname> | *

Adds (wa) or deletes (wr) a map to the active map list. The active maps are listed with the lm command.

The mapname parameter is the name of a map file to make active or an active map to be removed.

The * parameter adds or removes all map files.

Conditional Execution

    j <expr> [<command list>]

Executes the command list if the expression evaluates to TRUE (nonzero). Otherwise, it continues to the next command in the command line, but not including the ones in the command list. The command list is one or more commands surrounded by single or double quotes. If more than one command appears in the command list, the commands must be separated by the semicolon (;) character.

The j command is normally used to set a conditional breakpoint at a particular address.

Stack Trace

```
k [s|b] [<ss:bp addr>] [<cs:ip addr>]
```

Traces the bp chain on the stack and prints the address, 4 words/dwords of parameters, and any symbol found for the address.

The s parameter specifies a 16-bit frame width.

The b parameter specifies a 32-bit frame width.

The ss:bp specifies a stack address other than the current ss:bp.

The cs:ip parameter specifies an execution address other than the current cs:ip values.

Move Memory

```
m <range> <addr>
```

Moves the block of memory specified by a range to the location starting at addr.

Ouput Byte

```
o <port> <byte>
```

Sends the byte to the specified output port.

Ptrace/Program Step

    p [n|t] [=<start-addr>] [<count>]

Executes the instruction at the start address, then executes the current default command.

The n parameter causes the register to be suppressed if the default command is r.

The t parameter allows the original trap handler address to be traced without having to unhook the exception.

The start addr parameter is an optional address to start at, otherwise execution begins at the current cs:ip.

The count parameter specifies the number of instructions to execute before stopping.

The p command is different than the t command, in that the p command will allow a function call to complete before stopping again. A p command executed at a call instruction will stop only after the call has been completed. The t command will trace into the call and stop at every instruction.

Register

    r [t][<register-name> [<value>]]

Displays the contents of CPU register and allows its contents to be changed.

The t parameter toggles the terse register display flag.

The register name is any one of the valid register names listed in Table 13-6.

Table 13-6. KDB Register Definitions

Register name	Meaning
AX, BX, CX, DX, SI, DI, BP, SP, IP	general registers
DS, ES, SS, CS	segment registers
GDTB	GDT base as a linear address
GDTL	GDT limit
IDTB	IDT base as a linear address
IDTL	IDT limit
TR, LDTR	TR, LDTR registers
IOPL	iopl portion of flag registers
F	flag register
MSW	Machine status word
EAX, EBX, ECX, EDX, ESI, EDI, EBP, ESP, EIP	extended general registers
FS, GS	segment registers
EF	extended flag register
CR0, CR2, CR3, CR4	control registers
DR0, DR1, DR2, DR3, DR6, DR7	debug registers
TR6, TR7	test registers
IP, PC	the Instruction Pointer
F	the Flags register

If no register name parameter is supplied, the r command displays all of the registers, flags, and the instruction at the current cs:ip.

If a register name parameter is supplied, the current value of the register is displayed, and KDB prompts for a new value. If both the register name and value are given, the command changes the register name to the value.

To change one of the flag values, supply the register name f when entering the Register command. The f register parameter will display the current value of each flag as a two-letter name. Table 13-7 contains a list of flag values by name.

Table 13-7. KDB Flag Register Definitions

Flag name	Set	Clear
Overflow	OV	NV
Direction	DN (Decrement)	UP (Increment)
Interrupt	EI (Enabled)	DI (Disabled)
Sign	NG (Negative)	PL (Plus)
Zero	ZR	NZ
Aux Carry	AC	NA
Parity	PE (Even)	PO (Odd)
Carry	CY	NC
Nested Task	NT	(toggles)

At the end of the list of values, the command displays a minus sign (-). The new values for the flags can now be entered in any order. To terminate the flags entry, press the return key.

To change the MSW (Machine status word), use names outline in Table 13-8.

Table 13-8. KDB Machine Status Word

Flag	Set	Clear
Protected Mode	PM	(toggles)
Monitor Processor Extension	MP	(toggles)
Emulate Processor Extension	EM	(toggles)
Task Switched	TS	(toggles)

Toggles means that if the flag is set, using the flag name will clear it. If the flag is clear, it will be reset.

Search

    s <range> <list>

Searches the memory range for a pattern matching the list parameter.

Trace

    t [a|c|n|s|t|x][=<start addr>][<count>][<addr>]

Executes the instruction at the start address or current cs:ip.

The a parameter specifies an ending address for the trace.

The c parameter suppresses all output and counts the instructions traced.

The n parameter suppresses the register display. Only the assembly line is displayed. This option works only if the default command is r.

The s parameter is a special trace that which causes the instruction and count for every call and return to be displayed.

The t parameter allows the original trap handler address to be traced without unhooking the exception.

The x parameter forces KDB to trace regions of code known to be untraceable.

Unassemble

    u [<range>]

Display the instructions in a range in a mnemonic format. All of the 286 and 287 opcodes can be displayed.

List Real/Protect Mode Exceptions

`vl[n | p | v | r | f]`

Lists the real and protected mode exceptions that the debugger intercepts.

The n option specifies the traps that beep when hit.

The p option specifies only the protect mode vectors.

The r option specifies only the real mode vectors.

The v option specifies both real and protect mode vectors.

The f option directs the kernel to route fatal faults to the debugger and not to display a pop-up message.

Vectors set with vt (as opposed to vs) will be printed with a star following the vector number.

Add Interrupt/Trap Vector, All Rings

`vt[n | p | v | r | f] n[,n,..]`

Adds a new intercept vector that the debugger intercepts.

The r option will install a debugger handler in the real mode IDT.

The p option will install a debugger handler in the protect mode IDT.

The n option causes the intercepted traps to beep when hit.

The f option directs the kernel to route fatal faults to the debugger and not to display a pop-up message.

Intercept Trap Vector Except Ring 0

vs[n | p | v | r | f] n[,n,..]

Identical to vt except that vs will not intercept ring 0 interrupts.

vsv or vtv intercepts V86 mode exceptions or traps.

For GP faults, vsf d is the same a vsp d. For page faults, vsp e would trap all ring 3/2 page faults, but vsf e would trap only the invalid page faults.

Clear Interrupt/Trap Vectors

vc[n | p | v | r | f] n,[n],..

Clears the vectors indicated, reinstalling whatever address was in the vector before the debugger grabbed the vector.

The n option causes the trap(s) not to beep when hit. The trap remains intact.

To intercept general protection faults before OS/2 does, use vtp d before the fault is hit, examine the information about the fault, and do a vcp d and g, which will let the OS/2 GP handler get control (and kill the process, etc). Another option would be to enter a vcp d after hitting the fault and trace into the exception handler. The tt or gt commands perform this automatically.

Debugger Options

y[?] [386env|dislwr|regterse]

Toggles one of the debugger option flags.

386env   386 environment

dislwr   display lower case

regterse   terse register display flag

The 386env flag controls the size of addresses, registers, and other information when displayed. When 386env is on, the display format is 32 bits. When off, the display format is 16 bits.

The dislwr flag, when enabled, displays assembler code in lower case. When disabled, assembler code is shown in upper case.

The regterse flag determines the number of registers displayed with the r command. If regterse is on, only the first three lines of registers are displayed. If regterse is off, all six lines of registers, plus the unassembled instruction, are displayed.

The ? parameter displays the currently supported options.

The y command without any parameters displays the current state of the option flags.

Execute Default Command

z

Executes the current default command. The default command is a string of debugger commands that are executed any time that the debugger is entered and there is no breakpoint command attached to the entry. The r command is initialized as the default command when the system is rebooted.

List Default Command

    zl

Lists the current default command.

Change Default Command

    zs <string>

Changes the default command to a string. Any errors will cause the default command to be reset to r.

External Commands

Help

    .?

Prints the help menu for the external debugger commands.

Baud Rate

    .b <baud rate> [<port addr>]

This command will set the baud rate of the debugging port.

The legal baud rate values are 150t, 300t, 600t, 1200t, 2400t, 4800t, 9600t, and 19200t.

The port addr parameter is 1 for COM1 and 2 for COM2. The default port addr is 2.

Dump ABIOS Common Data Area

    .c

Dumps the ABIOS common data area.

Display Data Structure

    .d <data struct name> [<addr>]

Displays an OS/2 data structure. The valid data structure names appear in Table 13-9.

Table 13-9. KDB Recognized Structures

Name	Description
BPB	BIOS Parameter Block
BUF	File system buffer
DEV	Device driver header
DPB	Disk Parameter Block
MFT	Master File Table entry
REQ	Request Packet
SFT	System File Table entry
CDS	Current Directory Structure
SEM32	32-Bit Semaphore Structure
OPENQ	32-Bit Semaphore OPENQ chain
MUXQ	32-Bit Semaphore MUXQ chain
KSEM	32-Bit Kernel Semaphore Structure
DT	Task State Segment Structure
VPB	Volume Parameter Block

Swap In TSD or Page

```
.i[d|b] [<addr>]
.it[d|b] [<slot>]
```

Swaps in a TSD or Page.

The i command with an address will cause the page enclosing the address addr to be swapped in. The address may contain an optional task slot number override, such as %2|40000.

The it command swaps in the corresponding task's TSD.

The d option queues up a single swap-in request to be acted upon by the KDB daemon thread.

The slot parameter is the task's slot number.

Trace User Stack

```
.k[s|b] [<ss:bp addr>] [<cs:ip addr>]
```

Traces the bp chain on the user stack and prints the address, 4 words/dwords of parameters, and any symbol found for the address.

The s option specifies a 16-bit frame width.

The b option specifies a 32-bit frame width.

The ss:bp specifies a stack address other than the current ss:bp.

The cs:ip parameter specifies an execution address other than the current cs:ip values.

Display MTE Segment Table

`.lm[o][l|p|v|x] <hobmte|laddr|"module name"]`

Prints module table entries and their associated object and segment table entries.

The o option suppresses the object or segment table display.

The l option displays only library (.DLL) MTEs.

The p option displays only Physical Device Driver (PDD) MTEs.

The v option displays only Virtual Device Driver (VDD) MTEs.

The x option displays only executable (.EXE) MTEs.

If a nonzero hobmte is supplied, only those MTEs with a matching hobmte are printed. If a nonzero linear address is given, only the MTE pointed to by the linear address is printed. If a quoted string is given, only those MTEs with a matching module name are printed.

The module name for a:\bar.dll and c:\foo\bar.exe are both "bar". No drive, path, or extension information should be given.

Dump Memory Arena Records

```
.ma[a|b|c|f|h|l|m|r] [<har|laddr>] | [<har|laddr> L<number of entries>]
```

This command displays the virtual memory manager's arena records. If no handle or linear address is given, the entire table is displayed. If a linear address is given, it is taken to be a pointer to an arena record. One record or a range of records can be displayed.

The a option displays all contexts.

The b option displays only busy entries (default).

The c option finds the corresponding object record, and displays the arena, object, alias, and context record chains.

The h option walks hash links, displaying the entries.

The l option walks forward links, displaying the entries.

The r option walks reverse links, displaying the entries.

The m option specifies the display of all arena records whose linear address encloses the supplied linear address to be displayed. A linear address must also be supplied, and no count is allowed. Context information is ignored, so if the linear address is valid in multiple contexts, multiple arena records will be displayed. A physical address may be supplied instead of a linear address, to allow not-present linear addresses to get past the debugger's expression analyzer. If a selector address type is used, it must be converted to a linear address in the command line.

To find out who owns a selector because of a GP fault in some unknown LDT or GDT segment or memory object, the following command is used:

.m or .mamc cs:eip

This will display the arena record and memory object record (and the owner) of the code segment. It will also walk the context record chains and display them. The cs can be substituted with any selector, and the eip with any offset. This command converts the selector:offset into a linear address automatically, so the resulting address can be used to find and interpret the arena record(s) and memory object record(s).

Dump Memory Context Record

.mc[b|c|f] [<hco|laddr>] | [<hco|laddr> L<number of entries>]

Displays the virtual memory manager's context records. If no parameters are supplied, the entire table is displayed. If a linear address is given, it is taken to be a pointer to a context record. One record or a range of records can be displayed.

The b option specifies only busy files.

The f option displays only free entries.

The c option walks context record chains and displays them.

Dump Memory Alias Record

.ml[b|c|f] [<hal|laddr>] | [<hal|laddr> L<number of entries>]

Displays the virtual memory manager's alias records.

If no parameters are supplied, the entire table is displayed.

If a linear address is supplied, it is taken to be a pointer to an alias record. One record or a range of records can be displayed.

The b option displays only busy entries.

The f option displays only free entries.

The c option finds the corresponding object record, and displays the arena, object, alias, and context record chains.

Dump Memory Object Record

`.mo[b|c|f|m|n|p|s|v] [<hob|laddr>] | [<hob|laddr> L<number of entries>]`

Display the virtual memory manager's memory object records. If no handle or linear address is supplied, the entire table is displayed. If a linear address is given, it is taken to be a pointer to an object record. One record or a range of records can be displayed.

The b option causes busy object records to be displayed.

The f option causes free object records to be displayed.

The c option displays the arena, object, alias, and context record chains.

The m option causes all pseudo-object records with an exactly matching linear address to be displayed. A linear address must also be supplied, and no count is allowed. If a selector address type is used, it must be converted to a linear address on the command line. A physical address may be supplied instead of a linear address, to allow not-present linear addresses to get past the debugger's expression analyzer.

The n option causes non-pseudo object records to be displayed.

The p option causes pseudo-object records to be displayed.

The s option causes object records with the semaphore busy or wanted to be displayed.

The v option causes object record linear addresses to be displayed. It also disables the owner interpretation. This command attempts to display what process, MTE, or PTDA owns the segment. It will display the owner as a short ASCII string, when appropriate. It will display the PID of the process and, if possible, the name of the module that owns this segment. Code segments will normally have only a module name and no process ID. If the segment is an MTE, PTDA, or LDT, KDB will display the object name, process ID (if the segment is a PTDA), and the module name, if possible.

Dump Memory Page Frame

.mp[b|f|h|l|r|s] [<frame|laddr>] | [<frame|laddr> L<number of entries>]

Displays the page manager's page frame structures. If no handle or linear address is supplied, the entire table is displayed. If a linear address is given, it is taken to be a pointer to a page frame structure. One record or a range of records can be displayed.

The b options displays only busy entries.

The f option displays only free entries.

The h option walks hash links, displaying entries.

The l option walks forward links, displaying entries.

The r options walks reverse links, displaying entries.

This data structure contains per-physical page information. To find out the owner of a particular physical page, use .mp FrameNumber where FrameNumber is the physical address shifted right by 12 (take off 3 zeros). If the page isn't free, the pVP field contains a flat pointer to the virtual page structure. Use .mv %pVP where pVP is the value from the .mp dump, to get the contents of the VP. The Hob field of the VP is a handle to the Object Record. Use .mo Hob to dump it. That will display a readable string for the owner on the right of the display. ma of the Har field in the object record will give the base virtual address of the object containing the page (under va). Use the HobPg field of the VP to get the page offset within the object.

Dump Virtual Page Structure

.mv[b|f|l|r] [<vpid|laddr>] | [<swapid|laddr> L<number of entries>]

Displays the swap manager's swap frame structures. If no handle or linear address is supplied, the entire table is displayed. If a linear address is given, it is taken to be a pointer to a swap frame structure. One record or a range of records can be displayed.

The b option displays only busy entries.

The f option displays only free entries.

The l option walks forward links, displaying entries.

The r option walks reverse links, displaying entries.

Process Status

`.p[b|u] [<slot> | # | *]`

Displays the current process and thread status. An asterisk (*) by the slot number indicates the currently running task. A # by the slot number indicates what the debugger thinks the current task is.

The .p command, with no options, displays the following information:

- slot number
- PID of the current process
- PID of the parent process
- command subtree number
- thread number
- current state
- priority
- Block ID
- Per Task Data Area (PTDA)
- Task Control Block (TCB) offset
- dispatch sp register value
- screen group
- name of the process or thread

The pb command directs KDB to display detailed block information including the:

- slot
- Block ID
- name
- address blocked at
- symbol blocked on
- semaphore type.

The pu command directs KDB to display user state information including:

- cs:ip and ss:sp values at the time the kernel was entered
- number of arguments passed and their PTDA offset
- offset of the register stack frame
- thread number
- PTDA address
- name.

Display User Registers

.r [<slot> | # | *]

Displays the contents of the user's CPU registers, flags, and the next instruction to be executed for a specified slot, at time of entry to the kernel.

The slot parameter is the slot number to use.

The # parameter specifies the use of the current slot.

The * parameter specifies to use the currently scheduled slot or the last one blocked.

Reboot

.reboot

Warm-boot the machine.

Change Task Context

.s[s] [<slot> | *]

Changes what the debugger thinks the current task context is. If no slot number is passed, it will print the current task number.

The s option changes the ss and sp to the new task's PTDA selector and dispatch sp value. The original ss and sp is restored when the debugger exits or when the ss command is used to switch back to the current task.

The * parameter changes the current debugger's task number to the real OS/2 task number.

Dump RAS Trace Buffer

.t [<count>] [maj=<xx> [min=<yy>]]

Dumps the RAS trace buffer, optionally dumping only events with the specified major and minor event codes.

CHAPTER 14

An Introduction To Presentation Drivers

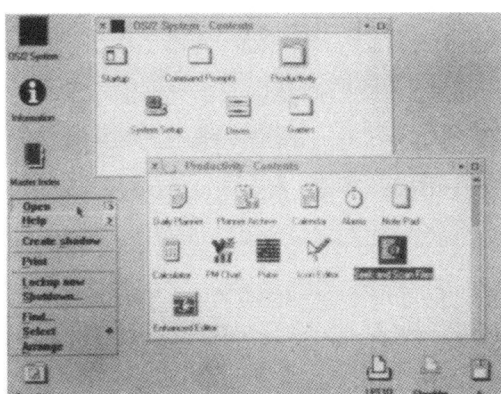

Figure 14-1. OS/2 2.1 Workplace Shell. (Courtesy of International Business Machines Corporation.)

*P*resentation Device Drivers (PMDDs) for OS/2 provide support for graphics devices such as display terminals, printers, plotters, and scanners. Presentation drivers provide hardware independence for application programs that perform I/O to these devices.

The presentation driver in OS/2 2.1 is a DLL, which runs at Ring 3, and has the filename extension DRV. When an application needs to perform I/O to a Presentation driver, it calls a system DLL, which in turn calls the Presentation Manager graphics engine. The Presentation Manager graphics engine is contained in PMGRE.DLL.

When a presentation driver is loaded, the graphics engine allocates a dispatch table containing pointers to routines in the graphics engine. The first time that the presentation driver is called at its OS2_PM_DRV_ENABLE entry point, it replaces pointers in the dispatch table with pointers to functions supported by the presentation driver. Some of the pointer replacements are mandatory, and others are optional. The presentation driver is passed the pointer to the dispatch table by the graphics engine with the FillLogicalDeviceBlock routine function call.

Presentation drivers are called using the C (_cdecl) calling convention. The first parameter passed is the function number and flags word. The function numbers are defined in PMDDIM.H, and represent ordinals for graphics engine (Gre...) calls. The flag bits are defined in Table 14-1.

Table 14-1. Presentation driver flag bits

Bit	#define	Description
0	COM_DRAW	if set, draw the output at the device, if clear, don't draw the data but update the internal data
1	COM_BOUND	if set, the driver calculates the bounding rectangle for the output. When done, the driver calls its own GreAccumulateBounds to accumulate the bounding rectangle (GPI_BOUNDS). All presentation drivers must supply this function.
2	COM_CORR	for display drivers only, if set, the presentation driver must determine if the output intersects a pick window, and returns TRUE or FALSE.
3	COM_ALT_BOUND	directs a display driver to accumulate USER_BOUNDS in screen coordinates
4	COM_AREA	if set, specifies that the function call is part of an area.
5	COM_PATH	if set, the function is part of a path
6	COM_TRANSFORM	if set, the presentation driver must convert the coordinates for the specified function from world to device coordinates using GreConvert.
7	COM_RECORDING	this bit should be ignored.
8	COM_DEVICE	if set, the driver should handle this function and not pass it back to the graphics engine for disposition.
9-15	N/A	ignored.

Device Context

The presentation application usually makes a KDB, MOU, VIO, DEV, AVIO, GPI, or WIN call to perform I/O. These functions exist in Ring 3 DLLs, and they call the graphics engine in PMGRE.DLL. PMGRE.DLL, in turn, calls the display or printer driver. The display driver may then access the adapter hardware directly through memory-mapped I/O, or may call the OS/2 kernel via the standard driver interface mechanism to perform the I/O.

The application program that needs to write to a Presentation Manager device first opens a *Device Context* (*DC*), using the DevOpenDC call. The application associates a presentation space with the DC and writes or draws in that space. Each time DevOpenDC is called, a new instance of a DC is created. This instance is destroyed when the application closes the Device Context with the DevCloseDC function call. Each instance of a DC has:

- a device context type
- data type
- instance data
- stack

When the DC is enabled, the type of device that is being opened is passed to the presentation driver, using one of the context types described in Table 14-2.

Table 14-2. Device Context Types

Type	Description
OD_INFO	The context is for information only. The driver does not generate output. All Gre... functions are processed by the presentation driver.
OD_MEMORY	The driver processes the output for the device, but the output is written to a device-compatible bitmap.
OD_DIRECT	The presentation driver processes the Gre... routines to generate device specific data. The data is passed to the adapter PDD via the kernel (hard-copy drivers only).
OD_QUEUED	The output is spooled using the Spl... interface (hard-copy drivers only).

Data Types

Presentation drivers that write to a spool file (OD_QUEUED) must support the two data types described in Table 14-3.

Table 14-3. Data Types for Queued Date

Data type	Description
PM_Q_STD	the driver uses the spooler to create a device-independent spool file using the SplStd... and SplQm... functions
PM_Q_RAW	the driver processes the Gre... functions to generate device-specific output data, which is written to a spool file using the SplQm... functions.

Instance Data

Each instance of a DC contains a double word pointer to information about the current context. The pointer is returned to the system by the presentation driver when the driver context is enabled. The pointer is passed back to the driver as a parameter in every call through the dispatch table.

Program Stack

Presentation drivers get a 500-byte stack, but should allocate their own stack of about 4K bytes.

DLL Functions

The initialization section of the presentation driver must be compiled and linked to run in Ring 3, and must EXPORT the following functions:

- MoveCursor (display drivers only)
- MoveCursorForInterrupt (display drivers only)
- OS2_PM_DRV_ENABLE (all drivers)
- OS2_PM_DRV_DEVMODE (hard-copy presentation drivers only)
- OS2_PM_DRV_DEVICENAMES (hard-copy presentation drivers only)

Hard-copy presentation drivers should also export entry points for routines that handle user interaction.

The graphics engine exports the entry points listed in Table 14-4.

Table 14-4. Graphics Engine Exports

Entry Point	Description
InnerGreEntry	main entry point for all Gre... ordinals
GETDRIVERINFO	used by the presentation driver to get the instance pointer for a device context or pointer to a bitmap header
SETDRIVERINFO	used by the presentation driver to set a specific value in the instance pointer of a device context

To access the graphics engine, the module definition file would have most of the function references associated with the InnerGreEntry point by ordinal.

Presentation Driver Design Considerations

Presentation drivers must always return a 32-bit value.

Coordinate values are normally passed as 32-bit world coordinates, and can be converted to other coordinate systems by calling the graphics engine function GreConvert. Screen coordinates are device coordinates to which the DC origin has been added.

Transform Matrix values are signed values represented by a 16-bit integer and 16-bit fraction. This resolution is maintained by the graphics engine matrix functions.

Angles are 32-bit signed values, where 0 represents a positive X-axis and FFFFFFFF represents 360 degrees.

Application bounds (COM_BOUND) are accumulated in model space, and user bounds (COM_ALT_BOUND) are accumulated in device-coordinate space.

If the presentation driver hooks all of the Gre... path and area functions, it is responsible for generating closures for figures within areas or paths. Otherwise, the graphics engine will generate the closures.

The presentation driver must provide clipping for drawing and text functions except GreDrawLinesInPath and GrePolyShortLine. Clipping for these two functions is provided by the graphics engine.

Presentation Driver Errors

When an error occurs in a presentation driver, the driver should call the WinSetErrorInfo functions to log the error. The presentation driver must validate all symbol sets, fonts, bitmaps, and regions before calling the graphics engine. The presentation driver must also verify all passed parameters and log any errors detected. Four severity levels are provided for presentation driver errors. The error levels are defined in Table 14-5.

Table 14-5. Presentation Driver Errors

Severity	Description
Warning	A problem was detected but a workaround was found.
Error	A problem was found, but no workaround was available. The system state remains intact.
Severe Error	A problem occurred and the system cannot reestablish its state.
Irrecoverable Error	An error occurred and it is impossible for the system to reestablish its state. It is also impossible for the application to restore the system to a known state.

Presentation Driver Error Codes

The presentation driver must call WinSetErrorInfo with the severity of the error and error code. Some of the general error codes are defined in Table 14-6. Refer to the Gre... function call reference in the *IBM OS/2 Presentation Driver Reference* for error codes specific to each Gre... function.

Table 14-6. Presentation Driver Error Codes

Error	Logged by
PMERR_COORDINATE_OVERFLOW	functions requiring matrix computations
PMERR_INSUFFICIENT_MEMORY	functions that allocate memory
PMERR_INV_BITMAP	functions with hbm as a parameter
PMERR_INV_HRGN	functions with hrgn as a parameter
PMERR_INV_COORDINATE	functions with coordinates as parameters
PMERR_INV_IN_AREA	functions valid inside an open area
PMERR_BASE_ERROR	functions that call DOS routines
PMERR_DEV_FUNC_NOT_INSTALLED	functions not supported by the presentation driver

Additional Presentation Driver Functions

Presentation drivers must also provide correlation to identify whether an object picked with the mouse, for example, lies within the pick aperture, and must consider if the object is visible or invisible. Hard-copy presentation drivers may need to support banding for raster technology hard-copy devices. Banding is technique where the output page is broken up into one or more bands, recorded in memory as a bitmap and sent to the device or the spooler.

Hard-copy presentation drivers must work with back-level and forward-level drivers across a network. Hard-copy presentation drivers can also support output to a file. They must also provide the user with the following push buttons.

- Retry (default position)
- Abort
- Ignore

The hard-copy presentation driver should respond as described in Table 14-7 to each of the returns.

Table 14-7. Job Error Returns

Return	What the hard copy driver should do
MBID_RETRY	continue sending data to the output buffer
MBID_ABORT	issue a PrtAbort to notify the spooler to delete the current job.
MBID_IGNORE	continue sending data to the output buffer

Examples of presentation drivers can be found in the sample code included with the *IBM OS/2 2.1 Toolkit*. Refer to the *OS/2 2.1 Presentation Device Driver Reference* and the toolkit documentation for more information on writing presentation drivers.

CHAPTER 15

Working With Pointers

OS/2 2.1 exploits the flat memory model of the Intel 80x86 processors. This permits applications to be written using a 32-bit compiler and/or a 32-bit assembler. When the 32-bit application references a variable or function by reference, it uses a 32-bit linear or *flat* address. Applications written for OS/2 2.1 can be as large as 512MB, so it is likely that data items such as buffers and structures will cross 64KB tiled boundaries. This represents somewhat of a problem for driver writers, as the PDD is still operating in a 16-bit mode. Fortunately, OS/2 2.1 provides the necessary DevHlp routines to make it easier for the device driver to deal with these 32-bit applications.

C Set/2

The C Set/2 compiler is a 32-bit flat model C compiler from IBM. The C Set/2 compiler utilizes full 32-bit linear addressing and pointer manipulation. If the application that uses your 16-bit device driver is written in a 32-bit compiler such as C Set/2, there are some special considerations you should take into account. You should also know if your driver will be called by a 16-bit C/2 or Microsoft C 5.1/6.0 application. If you're not sure, you should assume the application is a 16-bit application, and design your driver to work with either 16-bit or 32-bit applications. However, if the application will be written in a 32-bit compiler such as C Set/2, the device driver can optimize performance by using 32-bit pointers.

Applications written in MS C5.1/6.0 or IBM C/2 will require no changes when they are run on OS/2 2.1 and access your 16-bit PDD. Application pointers are 16-bit virtual addresses which can be used directly by the device drivers. However, a C Set/2 application is a 32-bit process, and pointers within the application are 32-bit linear addresses in the *process address space*. Linear addresses are special addresses which are decoded by special page decoding hardware to produce a 32-bit physical address. Your PDD, however, is a 16-bit program which must deal with the 32-bit addresses generated by the 32-bit compiler.

When a 32-bit application calls the OS/2 kernel via a standard device driver request, the kernel converts the addresses contained in the request packet to 16:16 addresses. Thus, the PDD sees only 16:16 addresses, and has no direct knowledge if the application is a 16-bit or 32-bit process. The process of converting the pointers and/or addresses from 32-bit to 16-bit is called *thunking*. Conversely, pointers may be also converted from 16-bit to 32-bit by thunking. Thunking is accomplished by invoking the DosSelToFlat and DosFlatToSel macros. There is a performance penalty when you use thunks, however, so it is best to avoid thunking whenever possible.

When your device driver receives a request packet for a DosRead or DosWrite, the caller's buffer address in the request packet is the 32-bit physical address of the caller's buffer. The conversion necessary to convert the caller's 32-bit linear address to a valid physical address has already been performed by the kernel. When your device driver is called via an IOCtl request from a 32-bit process, the caller's data and parameter buffer pointers are also converted from linear addresses to 16:16 virtual addresses. This is done automatically for you by the OS/2 kernel.

If, however, you use the private IOCtl data or parameter buffers to pass the linear address from the process to the driver, the address is not thunked. This is because the data and parameter buffers in an IOCtl packet are private data areas shared by the process and the driver, so the kernel has no way to differentiate the address from a 32-bit data item. Before using linear addresses passed in this fashion, you must convert them to an address which the device driver can use.

A 32-bit linear address, such as the address of a variable in a process, is said to be in the *process address space*, or mapped into the *local descriptor table* (*LDT*) of the process. Addresses within the process address space may be used freely by the application, providing it has the proper access rights. However, the address is not valid for a device driver. Since the device driver is operating in ring 0, it needs an address which is global, or mapped to a *global descriptor table* (*GDT*) entry. Pointers which are valid for the device driver are said to be in the *global address space* because they utilize a GDT selector for access.

Sharing the pointers between the process and the device driver is easy. A linear address in the process address space can be made valid for the device driver by a call to the VMProcessToGlobal DevHlp function. Conversely, a linear address in the global address space can be made valid for the process by calling the VMGlobalToProcess DevHlp function. Thus, processes and device drivers can share each other's common memory areas. An example of this is shown in the Figure 15-1.

```
// convert driver-relative address to a process address

if (VMGlobalToProcess(linaddr,0x1000,0x01,(FARPOINTER) &new_linaddr))
    return(RPDONE | RPERR | ERROR_GEN_FAILURE);


// convert an application address to a global 32-bit address

if (VMProcessToGlobal(linaddr,0x1000,0x01,(FARPOINTER) &new_linaddr))
    return(RPDONE | RPERR | ERROR_GEN_FAILURE);
```

Figure 15-1. VMGlobalToProcess and VMProcessToGlobal

Your driver may also allocate virtual memory with the VMAlloc DevHlp (see Figure 15-2). VMAlloc will return a 32-bit linear address to the allocated memory. Depending on the flags parameter passed the VMAlloc, the 32-bit linear address returned will be in the process address range or the global address range. Thus, a device driver may allocate a buffer and pass a 32-bit pointer to that buffer to the 32-bit process. VMAlloc parameters can also specify that the memory to be allocated is above or below the 16MB line, and whether or not the memory is contiguous. This is especially helpful for DMA buffers which for most clones, must be in the memory area under 16MB.

```
// use VMAlloc to map the adapter address to a linear address in
// the global address space

ULONG    MapAddress   = 0xd8000;
LINADDR  LinAddress   = 0;      // linear address to MapAddress
LINADDR  dev_linaddr  = 0;      // for global linear address

// VMalloc requires a linear address to the physical map address

VirtToLin((FARPOINTER)&MapAddress,(PLINADDR)&LinAddress);

if (VMAlloc(LinAddress,0x1000,0x3,(PLINADDR)&dev_linaddr))
{
  DosPutMessage(1, 2, CrLf);
  DosPutMessage(1, strlen(AllocFailMessage), AllocFailMessage);
}
else
{
  DosPutMessage(1, 2, CrLf);
  DosPutMessage(1, strlen(AllocPassMessage), AllocPassMessage);
}
```

Figure 15-2. Using VMAlloc

Virtual Addresses

A 16:16 virtual address which has be mapped to a 32-bit linear address is called a *tiled* virtual address. It represents a selector/offset of the same physical address as defined by the 32-bit linear address. The normal addresses used in your device driver are 16:16 virtual addresses. Several DevHlp calls, such as VMLock and LinToPageList, require the addresses of parameters to be 32-bit linear addresses. If these data items or parameters exist in the driver's data segment, passing the pointer to these items will cause these DevHlps to fail. You must first convert the 16:16 virtual addresses to linear by calling VirtToLin, and then call the DevHlp function as shown in Figure 15-3.

```
Flags = 0x1a;

// first convert address arguements to linear

if (VirtToLin((FARPOINTER)PageList,(PLINADDR) &lPageList));

if (VirtToLin((FARPOINTER)LockHandle,(PLINADDR)&lLockHandle));

if (VMLock(linaddr,100,lPageList,lLockhandle,
    Flags,(FARPOINTER) &Elements))
{
   DosPutMessage(1, 2, CrLf);
   DosPutMessage(1, strlen(LockFailMessage), LockFailMessage);
}
else
{
  DosPutMessage(1, 2, CrLf);
  DosPutMessage(1, strlen(LockPassMessage), LockPassMessage);
}
```

Figure 15-3. Calling VMLock

Pointers In A VDM

DOS applications running in a VDM utilize real mode addressing. A 20-bit real mode address in the *segment:offset* form can refer to a physical address within the VDM's one megabyte address space. If the VDM makes an IOCtl call to your device driver with pointers in the private data and/or parameter buffers, the driver must take an extra step to ensure the pointers are converted correctly. The driver checks the TypeProcess variable in the local info seg structure to determine of the application is a VDM application (bit 1 = 1).

If it is a DOS application, the driver allocates a GDT selector and convert the segment:offset address to a VDM-relative physical address by shifting the segment left 4 bits and adding in the offset. This is the same way the physical address is calculated in real mode for a real-mode application. The driver then calls LinToGDTSelector with the 20-bit physical address of the VDM application's buffer and/or parameter address. This call maps the 20-bit physical address to the caller's address using a GDT selector which can be accessed at kernel or interrupt time. The selector should be released by a call to FreeGDTSelector when the driver is finished with it. It is important to note that normally, LinToGDTSelector requires a 32-bit linear address and not a 20-bit physical address. This is possible only because LinToGDTSelector can determine that the current process making the call is in a VDM. If LinToGDTSelector determines that the caller is a VDM application, it converts the 20-bit real address to a valid 32-bit linear address before mapping it to the GDT selector.

CHAPTER 16

PCMCIA Device Drivers

The latest technology to affect OS/2 device drivers is called the *Personal Computer Memory Card Interface Association*, or *PCMCIA*, architecture. The PCMCIA is an organization of hardware and software vendors who are developing a set of standards for small, credit-card size adapters, dubbed PCMCIA cards. The PCMCIA has attempted to define both the hardware and software standards for the PCMCIA adapters, and the standards are still emerging. In order to support this new emerging technology, OS/2 2.1 has introduced support for the current PCMCIA standards.

The information supplied here either exists or is planned, and is therefore subject to change. Since the PCMCIA specifications are still evolving, it is possible that some of the information presented in this chapter may not be accurate at the time of publication. In addition, OS/2 2.1 does not support, nor is it planned to support, the full implementation of the PCMCIA 2.00 services. Future versions of OS/2 2.x may provide additonal support for PCMCIA services. Please refer to the latest publications from IBM for the most accurate description of the OS/2 2.1 PCMCIA support.

At the time of this writing, the hardware specification outlines three different size PCMCIA adapters, although more may be added. The different sizes, or form factors, specify the thickness of the adapter. The current sizes defined by the PCMCIA specification are 3.3, 5, and 10 millimeters. The adapters are inserted into a PCMCIA slot (called a *socket*) with the power on. The adapter hardware must therefore accommodate inrush currents associated with power-on insertion. Although the PCMCIA adapter is usually inserted into a slot without latches or hardware restraints, the PCMCIA specification does not preclude such additional hardware. Up to 256 PCMCIA adapters can be installed on a system, and each adapter can have up to 16 sockets. PCMCIA adapters can be such things as RAM, flash RAM, hard disks, modems, LAN adapters, or any other device which can fit within the PCMCIA form factor. Whatever the size or type device, OS/2 regards the PCMCIA device as just another device, and is not aware of the PCMCIA architecture.

The PCMCIA Software Trilogy

The software specification outlines three major software components. The OS/2 PDD that deals with the specific device characteristics is called the *client*. There must be a client for each adapter type, but the driver may handle multiple instances of the same adapter type. This is analogous to a device driver for a multiport serial adapter, which can handle each port with the same driver. The client driver is usually supplied by the PCMCIA card vendor, although its possible that generalized OS/2 PCMCIA drivers will be available from other sources. The client driver may also have a VDD counterpart for operation in a VDM.

The second part of the PCMCIA software architecture is called *card services*. Card services is responsible for providing the client an interface to the operating system In OS/2 2.1, card services is implemented as a ring 0 PDD, called PCMCIA$. The PCMCIA client performs an AttachDD DevHlp to PCMCIA$, which yields a 16:16 pointer to the PCMCIA$ device driver's IDC entry point. Subsequent calls to card services are performed by setting up the proper registers and calling the IDC entry point from the client. Since card services needs hooks into OS/2, card services is supplied by IBM.

Card services, like the DevHlp routines, are register-based, so in order to write your PCMCIA driver in C, you'll need to provide a library of C callable functions similar to the DevHlp library. The optional PDD driver library (see order form at the end of this book) contains the C callable routines for the PCMCIA card services, allowing you to write your PCMCIA drivers in C.

The third component of the PCMCIA software is *socket services*. Socket services is a hardware-specific layer of software which isolates the socket specific architecture from the other the software components. It is expected that the supplier of the system will supply this driver in software form or in the BIOS. The simplified architecture is shown in Figure 16-1. It should be noted, however, that the PCMCIA specifications allows the client to perform direct I/O and memory-mapped operation with the adapter, avoiding the card services or socket services layer.

```
┌─────────────────┐
│   Client PDD    │
├─────────────────┤
│  Card Services  │
│    PCMCIA$      │
├─────────────────┤
│ Socket Services │
│  PDD or BIOS    │
├─────────────────┤
│ PCMCIA Adapter  │
│    Hardware     │
└─────────────────┘
```

Figure 16-1. PCMCIA software architecture.

OS/2 2.1 PCMCIA Initialization

The first component loaded in CONFIG.SYS is the card services PDD. The card services PDD assumes that the following system resources are available:

- Non-system memory from C0000h to DFFFFh
- IRQ 2-15
- I/O ports 0x108-0xffff, except 0x3b4, 0x3b5, 0x3bah, ox3bbh, 3c0-3dfh, and 3f0-3f7h

These are the default resources that card services expects to be available. To determine what is actually available, another PDD, called the *Resource Map Utility* or *RMU*, is loaded from CONFIG.SYS. When the RMU receives the CMDInitComplete strategy command, the RMU pokes around the system and verifies the actual resources available, opens the card services driver PCMCIA$, and calls the card services driver with the AdjustResourceInfo function. The card services PDD then adjusts the information on the available resources so it can more intelligently respond to a subsequent client request for those resources. It is important to note that the RMU driver has the special bit (bit 4) in the capabilities bit strip word set, informing the kernel to call it with the InitComplete strategy command. It is also important to note that if no RMU is loaded, or the RMU fails to call the card services driver, that the card services driver will assume that all the default resources are available.

Next, the socket services driver is loaded, and when processing the InitComplete strategy command, the socket services driver calls DevHlp AttachDD with PCMCIA$, which returns a 16:16 pointer to the PCMCIA$ driver's IDC entry point. It then calls the card services AddSocketServices to establish bidirectional communications with card services. When card services receives the socket services AddSocketServices request, it must:

- identify the socket services resources required by calling socket services GetSetSSAddr, GetSSInfo, InquireAdapter, GetAdapter, InquireSocket and GetSocket. The socket services are provided by the socket service PDD when the card services driver calls the socket service driver's IDC entry point.
- allocate resources, if necessary, from the current resource map.
- install any necessary client interrupt handlers by calling DevHlp SetIRQ.
- program socket service hardware with SetAdapter and SetSocket socket services.

Next, the client PDD is loaded to support the particular adapter. The client establishes communications with card services by calling the AttachDD DevHlp during InitComplete processing. It is possible that the AttachDD call might fail in the case that the card services driver is not yet loaded (out of proper sequence in CONFIG.SYS). In this case, the client driver should enter a dormant state, waiting for the card services driver to be loaded. When the client driver detects that the card services driver is loaded, it issues a RegisterClient request and commences normal operation.

Note that the sequence these drivers appear in CONFIG.SYS will determine if processing occurs normally. Therefore, each driver should be sensitive to that fact and execute accordingly. The card services driver must be loaded first, but the other drivers may appear out of sequence. Note also that the CMDInitComplete strategy command is issued in the reverse order of the way they appear in CONFIG.SYS.

Client Device Driver Architecture

The client driver is a normal OS/2 PDD, but contains additional resource allocation logic not usually found in a PDD. First, since the client driver exports its entry points, those entry points must never move or be relocated. This means all of the exported entry points must exist in the first 64KB code segment. This segment must also contain the strategy, interrupt, timer, and IDC entry points. Second, although a normal PDD allocates resources using the device helper routines, the client PDD allocates its resources by calling the card services driver. Since the client driver is activated only be an inserted card or insertion event, it should not allocate extra memory or resources until the card is actually detected.

When the user inserts a card into a PCMCIA slot, the card services interrupt handler is called to signal the insertion. The card services driver acknowledges the card insertion interrupt by calling the socket services driver with the AcknowledgeInterrupt function, which returns the identification of the socket that caused the interrupt. The card services driver sets up a timer handler to handle the card insertion event.

The timer handler calls the socket services driver's GetStatus, GetSocket, and SetSocket functions to determine the cause of the interrupt. The timer handler then calls each client that has previously registered for a card insertion event for that particular socket.

The client processes the card insertion event by calling the card services function GetConfigurationInfo to determine if the card was previously claimed by another client driver. The client may get more detailed information from the card by calling the card service tuple functions GetFirstTuple, GetNextTuple, and GetTupleData. If the card cannot be supported by the client, the client just returns. If the card can be supported, the client calls the card services functions RequestIO and RequestConfiguration to allocate the resources. The card services driver then calls the socket services SetSocket function to program the card for the proper configuration. The client then calls the SetIRQ DevHlp routine to hook its interrupt handler like a normal PDD.

Under normal operation, the client driver processes requests like any other PDD.

When the PCMCIA card is removed, the card causes a status change interrupt to the card services driver. Card services calls the socket services driver's AcknowledgeInterrupt function to get the socket that generated the interrupt. The card services driver then sets up a timer handler like it did in the card insertion event.

When the timer handler is entered, it processes the interrupt by calling the socket service GetStatus, GetSocket, and SetSocket function to determine the cause of the interrupt. The timer handler then calls all the clients that have registered for the particular socket.

The client drivers process the event by calling the card services ReleaseConfiguration, ReleaseIO, and ReleaseIRQ functions. When the card services driver receives the ReleaseConfiguration command, it calls socket services to reprogram the card to stop generating interrupts or other events.

If the client previously claimed a system interrupt with a SetIRQ call, the must call UnSetIRQ to give back to interrupt to OS/2.

OS/2 2.1 Restrictions

The OS/2 2.1 card services driver contains the following restrictions:

- a maximum of 4 adapters
- a maximum of 8 sockets
- a maximum of 16 clients
- a maximum of 4 socket services drivers
- a maximum of 16 Memory Technology Drivers (MTDs)
- a maximum of 16 memory handles
- a maximum of 16 erase queues
- a maximum of 16 memory regions
- a maximum of 16 disk partitions
- a maximum of 7 memory *windows* (5 memory and 2 I/O)

In addition, card services provides no power management support or write protection. For PCMCIA disk drivers, the following restrictions apply:

- the client must claim all the logical drives it supports, even if the DASD card is not currently inserted
- disks with multiple partitions must have a driver letter assigned to each partition
- PCMCIA disk cards do not support HPFS or disk caching

Card Services Functions

Card services provides for the following client services:

- function
- callbacks
- events
- MTD helpers
- media access routines
- return code information

The OS/2 PCMCIA implementation also has reserved IOCtl category 13 for a PCMCIA application interface. OS/2 2.1 supports or is planned to support the card services functions shown in Table 16-1.

Table 16-1. OS/2 PCMCIA Card Services (Continued)

Function	Code
CloseMemory	0x01
DeregisterClient	0x02
GetClientInfo	0x03
GetConfigurationInfo	0x04
GetFirstPartition	0x05
GetFirstRegion	0x06
GetFirstTuple	0x07
GetNextPartition	0x08
GetNextRegion	0x09
GetNextTuple	0x0a
GetCardServicesInfo	0x0b
GetStatus	0x0c
GetTupleData	0c0d
GetFirstClient	0x0e
RegisterEraseQueue	0x0f
RegisterClient	0x10
ResetCard	0x11

Table 16-1. OS/2 PCMCIA Card Services (Continued)

Function	Code
MapLogSocket	0x12
MapLogWindow	0x13
MapMemPage	0x14
MapPhySocket	0x15
MapPhyWindow	0x16
ModifyWindow	0x17
OpenMemory	0x18
ReadMemory	0x19
RegisterMTD	0x1a
ReleaseIO	0x1b
ReleaseIRQ	0x1c
ReleaseWindow	0x1d
ReleaseConfiguration	0x1e
RequestIO	0x1f
RequestIRQ	0x20
RequestWindow	0x21
RequestSocketMask	0x22
ReturnSSEntry	0x23
WriteMemory	0x24

Table 16-1. OS/2 PCMCIA Card Services

Function	Code
CheckEraseQueue	0x26
ModifyConfiguration	0x27
SetRegion	0x29
GetNextClient	0x2a
ValidateCIS	0x2b
RequestExclusive	0x2c
ReleaseExclusive	0x2d
GetEventMask	0x2e
ReleaseSocketMask	0x2f
RequestConfiguration	0x30
SetEventMask	0x31
AddSocketServices	0x32
ReplaceSocketServices	0x33
AdjustResourceInfo	0x35

Calling Card Services

Card services, like the OS/2 DevHlps, are register-based. The current registers assigned to these functions under OS/2 2.1 are shown in Tables 16-2 and 16-3.

Table 16-2. Card Services Register Interface (input)

Register	Contents
AL	function number
AH	set to AFh
DX	handle
DI:SI	pointer
ES:BX	arg pointer
CX	arg length

Table 16-3. Card Services Register Interface (output)

Register	Contents
AX	status argument
CF	pass/fail carry flag

All addresses must be in 16:16 form, and the caller must set DS to the DS value returned from the AttachDD call before calling card services. Card services are not reentrant, so a function request may be returned BUSY.

Callbacks

Client device drivers can be called by card services when certain events occur. The action of calling the client device driver from card services is called a *callback*. The callbacks that are supported or planned to be supported by OS/2 2.1 are described in Table 16-4.

Table 16-4. OS/2 2.1 Callbacks (Continued)	
Function	**Function Code**
BATTERY_DEAD	0x01
BATTERY_LOW	0x02
CARD_LOCK	0x03
CARD_READY	0x04
CARD_REMOVAL	0x05
CARD_UNLOCK	0x06
EJECTION_COMPLETE	0x07
EJECTION_REQUEST	0x08
INSERTION_COMPLETE	0x09
INSERTION_REQUEST	0x0a
EXCLUSIVE_COMPLETE	0x0d
EXCLUSIVE_REQUEST	0x0e

Table 16-4. OS/2 2.1 Callbacks

Function	Function Code
RESET_PHYSICAL	0x0f
RESET_REQUEST	0x10
CARD_RESET	0x11
MTD_REQUEST	0x12
CLIENT_INFO	0x14
SS_UPDATED	0x16
CARD_INSERTION	0x40
RESET_COMPLETE	0x80
ERASE_COMPLETE	0x81
REGISTRATION_COMPLETE	0x82

The callback interface is described in Tables 16-5 and 16-6. The ClientData structure is shown in Figure 16-2.

Table 16-5. Callback Register Interface (input)

Register	Contents
AL	function argument
CX	socket argument
DL	card status
DH	socket status
DI	ClientVal from ClientData struct
DS	ClientDS from ClientData struct
SI	ClientOff from ClientData struct
ES:BX	buffer argument
BX	misc argument when no buffer argument

Table 16-6. Callback Register Interface (output)

Register	Contents
AX	status argument
CF	pass/fail carry flag

```
#typedef struct _ClientData
{
  USHORT   ClientVal;  // client specific data value
  USHORT   ClientDS;   // clients DS value
  USHORT   ClientOff   // client's callback offset
  USHORT   Reserved    // for future use
} ClientData;
```

Figure 16-2. ClientData structure.

CHAPTER 17

Tips And Techniques

I get a large number of questions from driver writers on how to perform certain driver-related tasks. This chapter outlines some of the things you might want to do in your device driver. Some of these may seem apparent, but to my knowledge, this information does not appear anywhere else.

Q. I have an application that allocates a local buffer which is semaphore protected for access by several threads. I want the driver to send data to this buffer from my interrupt handler, but I don't want to keep calling the device driver. How can I do this?

A. The application sends the device driver, via an IOCtl, the address of the buffer. The device driver calls VMProcessToGlobal to get a pointer to the buffer, and VMLock to lock the buffer. The driver then calls LinToGDTSelector to gain GDT access to the buffer. The device driver calls VMLock to prevent the buffer from being paged. The driver then transfers data freely from the interrupt handler.

Q. How can I get control of the floppy disk controller registers to support an add-on tape drive that uses the floppy disk controller?

A. Call IOCtl Category 8, function 0x5d. This function toggles the floppy disk driver and Sets/UnSets the floppy IRQ.

Q. My company sells ISA bus adapters which can be jumpered to one of several memory-mapped addresses. I only want to supply one device driver. How can I dynamically configure the device driver for the particular system?

A. Place the configuration information on the same line as the DEVICE= statement in the CONFIG.SYS file. During initialization, the kernel sends the driver a 16:16 virtual address of the DEVICE= command buffer. The driver can use this pointer to parse driver-specific information and use it to configure the device driver. For instance, the CONFIG.SYS file entry might contain DEVICE=MYDRIVER.SYS d8000 3e8 5, where d8000 is the memory-mapped address, 3e8 is the base port address, and 5 is the IRQ.

Q. My company supplies an ISA and Micro Channel version of the same adapter. How can I tell if the machine contains an ISA bus or Micro Channel bus, and can I use the same device driver for both systems?

A. Using the same driver for ISA and Micro Channel machines is a common occurrence. The first thing your device driver should do is determine the bus type. You can do this by calling GetLIDEntry, requesting a POS LID. If the call fails, its not a Micro Channel machine. If the call succeeds, the system is Micro Channel-based. You can then take the appropriate action. For Micro Channel, scan the planar for your target adapter ID, and call SetIRQ with the share flag to verify your interrupt level. For ISA bus systems, call SetIRQ with the no-share flag.

Q. How can I reboot my machine from the command line?

A. Write a simple device driver that calls the SendEvent DevHlp with the parameter to reboot for IOCtl function 1. Then write an application that calls the IOCtl.

Q. My driver needs to identify the caller and determine its PID. How can I do this?

A. From your driver, call GetDOSVar, which returns a pointer to the application's local infoseg. Using that pointer, you can extract the necessary information.

Q. My Micro Channel initialization section is setting up the wrong memory-mapped address from the POS registers. How can I check the value of the POS registers while debugging?

A. First, you must know what slot the particular adapter is in. The slots are number 0-7, with 0 being the motherboard, and 1-7 the 8 slots on the motherboard. Slot 1 is the slot closest to the power supply. Once the slot number is known, turn on the -CD SETUP line for that slot using the debugger, by issuing the command *o 96,slot+1*. If the adapter was located in slot 2, the command would be *o 96,3*. Once enabled, the adapter POS register contents can be read by an input of address 0x100, 0x101, 0x102, etc. The adapter ID is located in POS register 0 and 1, located at 0x100 and 0x101, in the low-high format. To make the POS registers invisible again and bring the system back to normal, issue the *o 96,0* command.

Q. I need to change the contents of the adapter POS registers while my driver is running. How can I read or write the Micro Channel POS registers "on the fly" with my device driver?

A. Call GetLIDEntry to get a POS LID. Next, get the size of the LID Request Block by calling ABIOSCall. Initialize the Request Block for the request and call ABIOSCall. The ABIOS routines will fill in the Request Block with the POS register data. Change the data and Request Block command field and call ABIOScall again to write the data. Remember that the POS register information is kept in two places. The first is the adapter itself, and the second is the motherboard's NVRAM. When the POST is run on power-up, the system compares the NVRAM configuration with the actual POS register configuration to determine if an adapter was reconsidered or removed. If you're going to make the POS register change permanent, be sure to write to both places.

Q. My adapter requires a program be downloaded to it during Init. How can I get access to my adapter's memory during Init, and how can I download the program to the adapter?

A. To access the adapter during Init, you'll need to create LDT access, since Init is a ring 3 thread. Call PhysToUVirt to get a selector to the adapter memory. Then call DosOpen and DosRead to read the adapter's program from a binary file, and move it to the adapter using the pointer from the PhysToUVirt call.

Q. I need to delay for 5 seconds during the Init of my driver so my adapter can get set up. I can't call DosSleep, so how can I do this?

A. Call the Beep DevHlp with a duration of 5 seconds, and a frequency out of the audible range.

Q. How can I return specific errors from my driver?

A. If you return an error via one of the standard driver calls, the system adds a hex 13 to the value. If you use an IOCtl, the lower 8 bits are your's to set as you please. The system will not touch the value. The error code returned to your program will have 0xff in the upper 8 bits. Thus, returning a 0x14 from an IOCtl will yield a 0xff14 at the application level.

Q. When my driver times out, I get a coffin on my screen. How can I suppress this?

A. Be sure to set the OPEN_FLAGS_FAIL_ON_ERROR bit in the DosOpen call.

APPENDIX A

Device Helper Reference

Device Helper Functions

Table A-1. Device Helper Functions (Continued)

DevHlp Function	Code	Description
SchedClockAddr	00	Get system clock routine address
DevDone	01	Device I/O complete
Yield	02	Yield the CPU
TCYield	03	Yield the CPU to a time-critical thread
Block	04	Block thread on event
Run	05	UnBlock a previously Blocked thread
SemRequest	06	Claim a semaphore
SemClear	07	Release a semaphore
SemHandle	08	Get a semaphore handle

Table A-1. Device Helper Functions (Continued)

DevHlp Function	Code	Description
PushReqPacket	09	Add a Request Packet to list
PullReqPacket	0a	Remove a Request Packet from list
PullParticular	0b	Remove a specific Request Packet from list
SortReqPacket	0c	Sort Request Packets
AllocReqPacket	0d	Allocate a Request Packet
FreeReqPacket	0e	Free a Request Packet
QueueInit	0f	Initialize a character queue
QueueFlush	10	Clear a character queue
QueueWrite	11	Put a character in the queue
QueueRead	12	Get a character from the queue
Lock	13	Lock segment
Unlock	14	Unlock segment
PhysToVirt	15	Map physical to virtual address
VirtToPhys	16	Map virtual to physical address
PhysToUVirt	17	Map physical address to user virtual address
AllocPhys	18	Allocate physical memory
FreePhys	19	Free physical memory
SetIRQ	1b	Attach a hardware interrupt handler

Table A-1. Device Helper Functions (Continued)

DevHlp Function	Code	Description
UnSetIRQ	1c	Detach a hardware interrupt handler
SetTimer	1d	Attach a timer handler
ResetTimer	1e	Detach a timer handler
MonitorCreate	1f	Create a device monitor
Register	20	Install a device monitor
DeRegister	21	Remove a device monitor
MonWrite	22	Pass data records to a device monitor
MonFlush	23	Remove all data from device monitor stream
GetDOSVar	24	Return a pointer to DOS variable
SendEvent	25	Indicate an event
VerifyAccess	27	Verify Memory Access
ABIOSGetParms	29	Get ABIOS parameters for LID
AttachDD	2a	Establish communications with another Physical Device Driver
InternalError	2a	Signal an internal error
AllocGDTSelector	2d	Allocate GDT Descriptors
PhysToGDTSelector	2e	Map physical address to GDT virtual
EOI	31	Issue an end-of-interrupt to the PIC
UnPhysToVirt	32	Mark physical to virtual complete

Table A-1. Device Helper Functions (Continued)

DevHlp Function	Code	Description
TickCount	33	Modify/Create timer setting
GetLIDEntry	34	Get a Logical ID (PS/2 only)
FreeLIDEntry	35	Release a Logical ID (PS/2 only)
ABIOSCall	36	Invoke an ABIOS function (PS/2 only)
ABIOSCommonEntry	37	Invoke an ABIOS Common Entry Point (PS/2 only)
GetDeviceBlock	38	Get ABIOS Device Block (PS/2 only)
RegisterStackUsage	3a	Indicate Stack Usage
VideoPause	3c	Suspend/resume video active threads
SaveMsg	3d	Display a message (base drivers)
RegisterDeviceClass	43	Register an ADD device class
RegisterPDD	50	Register a 16:16 drv for PDD-VDD comm.
RegisterBeep	51	Register a PDDs Beep Entry Point
Beep	52	Create a Beep
FreeGDTSelector	53	Free allocated GDT selector
PhysToGDTSel	54	Map physical address to GDT selector
VMLock	55	Lock linear address range in segment
VMUnlock	56	Unlock linear address range

Table A-1. Device Helper Functions (Continued)

DevHlp Function	Code	Description
VMAlloc	57	Allocate a block of physical memory
VMFree	58	Free memory or mapping
VMProcessToGlobal	59	Map process address space into global
VMGlobalToProcess	5a	Map global address into process address
VirtToLin	5b	Convert sel:offset to linear address
LinToGDTSelector	5c	Convert linear address to virtual address
GetDescInfo	5d	Get descriptor info
LinToPageList	5e	Get physical pages mapped to the linear address
PageListToLin	5f	Map physical pages to linear address
PageListToGDTSelector	60	Map physical address to a selector
RegisterTmrDD	61	Get kernel address of the Tmr value
AllocateCtxHook	63	Allocate a context hook
FreeCtxHook	64	Free a context hook
ArmCtxHook	65	Arm a context hook
VMSetMem	66	Commit/decommit physical memory
OpenEventSem	67	Open a 32-bit shared event semaphore
CloseEventSem	68	Close a 32-bit shared event semaphore
PostEventSem	69	Post a 32-bit shared event semaphore

Table A-1. Device Helper Functions

DevHlp Function	Code	Description
ResetEventSem	6a	Reset a 32-bit shared event semaphore
RegisterFreq	6b	Register PTD freq service with kernel
DynamicAPI	6c	Create a ring 0 callgate to a worker

DevHlp Services and Device Contexts

OS/2 device drivers may run in one of three modes or contexts. These three contexts are:

1. Kernel mode - the context in which the device driver Strategy section runs. This is sometimes referred to as "Strategy time" or "task time".

2. Interrupt mode - the context in which the driver's interrupt handler runs while servicing hardware interrupts.

3. INIT mode - the context in which the device driver runs when called by the kernel to INIT the driver. This is a special mode at Ring 3 with I/O privileges.

Not all DevHlp services are available in each mode. Table A-2 describes which DevHlp functions are available in the various modes.

Table A-2. Device Helper Contexts (Continued)

DevHlp Function	Code	Kernel	Interrupt	INIT
SchedClockAddr	00h	X		X
DevDone	01h	X	X	
Yield	02h	X		
TCYield	03h	X		
Block	04h	X		
Run	05h	X	X	
SemRequest	06h	X		
SemClear	07h	X	X	
SemHandle	08h	X	X	
PushReqPacket	09h	X		
PullReqPacket	0Ah	X	X	
PullParticular	0Bh	X	X	
SortReqPacket	0Ch	X		
AllocReqPacket	0Dh	X		
FreeReqPacket	0Eh	X		
QueueInit	0Fh	X	X	X
QueueFlush	10h	X	X	
QueueWrite	11h	X	X	
QueueRead	12h	X	X	

Table A-2. Device Helper Contexts (Continued)

DevHlp Function	Code	Kernel	Interrupt	INIT
LockSeg	13h	X		X
UnlockSeg	14h	X		X
PhysToVirt	15h	X	X	X
VirtToPhys	16h	X		X
PhysToUVirt	17h	X		X
AllocPhys	18h	X		X
FreePhys	19h	X		X
SetIRQ	1Bh	X		X
UnSetIRQ	1Ch	X	X	X
SetTimer	1Dh	X		X
ResetTimer	1Eh	X	X	X
MonCreate	1Fh	X		X
DeRegister	21h	X		
MonWrite	22h	X	X	
MonFlush	23h	X		
GetDOSVar	24h	X		X
SendEvent	25h	X	X	
VerifyAccess	27h	X		
ABIOSGetParms	29h	X	X	X

Table A-2. Device Helper Contexts (Continued)

DevHlp Function	Code	Kernel	Interrupt	INIT
AttachDD	2Ah	X		X
InternalError	2Bh	X	X	X
AllocGDTSelector	2Dh			X
PhysToGDTSelector	2Eh	X	X	X
EOI	31h		X	X
UnPhysToVirt	32h	X	X	X
TickCount	33h	X	X	X
GetLIDEntry	34h	X		X
FreeLIDEntry	35h	X		X
ABIOSCall	36h	X	X	X
ABIOSCommonEntry	37h	X	X	X
GetDeviceBlock	38h			X
RegisterStackUsage	3Ah			X
VideoPause	3Ch	X	X	X
SaveMsg	3Dh			X
RegisterDeviceClass	43h	X*		
RegisterPDD	50h	X		X
RegisterBeep	51h	X		X
Beep	52h	X	X	X

Table A-2. Device Helper Contexts (Continued)

DevHlp Function	Code	Kernel	Interrupt	INIT
FreeGDTSelector	53h	X		X
PhysToGDTSel	54h	X	X	X
VMLock	55h	X		X
VMUnlock	56h	X		X
VMAlloc	57h	X		X
VMFree	58h	X		X
VirtToLin	5Bh	X	X	X
LinToGDTSelector	5Ch	X	X	X
GetDescInfo	5Dh	X	X**	X
LinToPageList	5Eh	X	X	X
PageListToLin	5Fh	X	X	X
PageListToGDTSelector	60h	X	X	X
RegisterTmrDD	61h			X
AllocateCtxHook	63h	X		X
FreeCtxHook	64h	X		X
ArmCtxHook	65h	X	X	X
VMSetMem	66h	X		X
OpenEventSem	67h	X		
CloseEventSem	68h	X		

Table A-2. Device Helper Contexts

DevHlp Function	Code	Kernel	Interrupt	INIT
PostEventSem	69h	X		
ResetEventSem	6Ah	X		
DynamicAPI	6Ch	X		X

* ADD initialization is performed at ring 0

** This function can return information on a Global Descriptor only at interrupt time.

Device Helper Categories

The OS/2 DevHlp Functions can also be grouped by functionality into 13 major categories.

Category 1 - System Clock Management
- SchedClockAddr

Category 2 - Process Management
- Block
- DevDone
- Run
- TCYield
- Yield

Category 3 - Semaphore Functions
- CloseEventSem
- OpenEventSem
- PostEventSem
- ResetEventSem
- SemClear
- SemHandle
- SemRequest

Category 4 - Request Queue Functions

- AllocReqPacket
- FreeReqPacket
- PullParticular
- PullReqPacket
- PushReqPacket
- SortReqPacket

Category 5 - Memory Management Functions

- AllocGDTSelector
- AllocPhys
- FreeGDTSelector
- FreePhys
- LinToGDTSelector
- LinToPageList
- Lock
- PageListToGDTSelector
- PageListToLin
- PhysToGDTSel
- PhysToGDTSelector
- PhysToUVirt
- PhysToVirt
- Unlock
- UnPhysToVirt
- VerifyAccess
- VirtToLin
- VirtToPhys
- VMAlloc

- VMFree
- VMGlobalToProcess
- VMLock
- VMProcessToGlobal
- VMSetMem
- VMUnlock

Category 6 - Device Monitor Functions

- DeRegister
- MonFlush
- MonitorCreate
- MonWrite
- Register

Category 7 - Character Queue Functions

- QueueFlush
- QueueInit
- QueueRead
- QueueWrite

Category 8 - Interrupt Management

- EOI
- SetIRQ
- UnSetIRQ

Category 9 - Timer Functions
- RegisterTmrDD
- ResetTimer
- SetTimer
- TickCount

Category 10 - System Functions
- Beep
- SaveMsg
- DynamicAPI
- GetDescInfo
- GetDOSVar
- RegisterBeep
- RegisterDeviceClass
- SendEvent
- VideoPause

Category 11 - Advanced BIOS (ABIOS) Functions (PS/2 Only)
- ABIOSCall
- ABIOSCommonEntry
- ABIOSGetParms
- FreeLIDEntry
- GetDeviceBlock
- GetLIDEntry

Category 12 - PDD - VDD Communications Services

- RegisterPDD

Category 13 - Context Hook Services

- AllocateCtxHook
- ArmCtxHook
- FreeCtxHook

DevHlp Routines

The DevHlp functions are register based calls to the OS/2 kernel to perform functions necessary for OS/2 device driver operation. All parameters are passed and returned in registers. To provide an environment in which to write OS/2 2.1 device drivers in C, you will have to provide a C-language interface to the DevHlp routines. You can write your own, or you can order them using the order form at the back of the book. All C callable routines use the PASCAL calling convention.

ABIOSCall   *Mode: Kernel, Interrupt, Init*

Invoke an ABIOS service for the Operating System Transfer Convention.

C Calling Convention

```
if (ABIOSCall(USHORT Lid,USHORT Subfunction,
              (FARPOINTER) &ABIOSReqBlock)) error

Lid           = The LID obtained by a previous GetLIDEntry call
Subfunction   = ABIOS define subfunction
&ABIOSReqBlk  = far pointer to DS-relative ABIOS request block
```

Comments

The indicated ABIOS function is called according to the Operating System Transfer Convention. ABIOSCall will clean up the stack before returning to the device driver.

Example

```c
// Get the size of the LID request block

ABIOS_l_blk.f_parms.req_blk_len = sizeof(struct lid_block_def);
ABIOS_l_blk.f_parms.LID = lid;
ABIOS_l_blk.f_parms.unit = 0;;
ABIOS_l_blk.f_parms.function = GET_LID_BLOCK_SIZE;
ABIOS_l_blk.f_parms.ret_code = 0x5a5a;
ABIOS_l_blk.f_parms.time_out = 0;

if (ABIOSCall(lid,(FARPOINTER)&ABIOS_l_blk,0))
    return 1;

lid_blk_size = ABIOS_l_blk.s_parms.blk_size; // Get the block size

// Fill POS regs and card ID with FF in case this does not work

*card_ID = 0xFFFF;
for (i=0; i<NUM_POS_BYTES; i++) { pos_regs[i] = 0x00; };

// Get the POS registers and card ID for the commanded slot

ABIOS_r_blk.f_parms.req_blk_len = lid_blk_size;
ABIOS_r_blk.f_parms.LID = lid;
ABIOS_r_blk.f_parms.unit = 0;;
ABIOS_r_blk.f_parms.function = READ_POS_REGS_CARD;
ABIOS_r_blk.f_parms.ret_code = 0x5a5a;
ABIOS_r_blk.f_parms.time_out = 0;

ABIOS_r_blk.s_parms.slot_num = (unsigned char)slot_num & 0x0F;
ABIOS_r_blk.s_parms.pos_buf = (FARPOINTER)pos_regs;
ABIOS_r_blk.s_parms.card_ID = 0xFFFF;

if (ABIOSCall(lid,(FARPOINTER)&ABIOS_r_blk,0))
    rc = FAILURE;
else
{                                              // Else
    *card_ID = ABIOS_r_blk.s_parms.card_ID; // Set the card ID value
    rc = SUCCESS;
}
FreeLIDEntry(lid);
return(rc);
```

ABIOSCommonEntry   *Mode: Kernel, Interrupt, Init*

Invoke an ABIOS Common Entry Point according to the Advanced BIOS Transfer Convention.

C Calling Convention

```
if (ABIOSComm(USHORT Subfunction,(FARPOINTER) &ABIOSReqBlk)) error

Subfunction  = ABIOS defined subfunction
&ABIOSReqBlk = far pointer to DS-relative ABIOS request block
```

Comments

ABIOSCommonEntry invokes the indicated ABIOS common entry point.

Example

```
if (ABIOSCommonEntry(0,(FARPOINTER)&ABIOS_r_blk))
     error;
```

ABIOSGetParms *Mode: Kernel, Interrupt, Init*

Get ABIOS Parameters.

C Calling Convention

```
if (ABIOSGetParms(USHORT Lid,(FARPOINTER) &ABIOSParmBlock)) error

Lid            = The LID obtained by a previous GetLIDEntry call
&ABIOSParmBlk  = far pointer to DS-relative ABIOS parameter block
```

Comments

Refer to the *IBM Personal System/2 and Personal Computer BIOS Interface Technical Reference*, part number S68X-2341-00, for more detailed information on the use of ABIOS and its associated data structures.

AllocateCtxHook   *Mode: Kernel, Init*

Allocate a context hook.

C Calling Convention

```
if (AllocateCtxHook((OFF)&HookHandler,ULONG Val,
                    (PLHANDLE) &NewHandle)) error

&HookHandler = 16 bit offset to context hook handler
Val          = 0xffffffff (reserved value)
NewHandle    = far pointer to returned handle
```

Comments

AllocateCtxHook allocates a context hook for use by a device driver that needs task time processing, but has no task time thread available to complete it.

When the context hook is armed and triggers, the Hook Handler function is called with register EAX equal to the value passed in the HookData parameter of the ArmCtxHook call, and EBX equal to -1L.

The hook handler is responsible for saving and restoring registers on entry and exit. The hook handler address should be zero extended.

Context hooks should never block.

AllocGDTSelector   Mode: Init

Allocate one or more GDT selectors for a device driver to use.

C Calling Convention

```
if (AllocGDTSelector(USHORT Count,(FARPOINTER) &SelArray)) error

Count     = number of selectors to allocate
&SelArray = far pointer to selector array
```

Comments

This allocation is performed at device driver INIT time.

AllocGDTSelector is used to allocate one or more GDT selectors for a device driver to use for kernel and interrupt mode operations.

Allocating a GDT selector and then mapping an address to it using the PhysToGDTSelector DevHlp allows a driver to access the memory defined by the GDT selector in any context.

Even though GDT selectors can be allocated at INIT time, they cannot be used during INIT since INIT is perfomed at ring 3. Ring 3 threads have no access to the GDT.

Example

```
if (!(SetIRQ(5,(PFUNCTION)INTERRUPT_HANDLER,0)))
{
  if (!(AllocGDTSelector(1,(FARPOINTER)&Sel)))
  {
    if (!(PhysToGDTSelector(0xd8000,0x1000,Sel,&err)))
    {

        // output initialization message

        DosPutMessage(1, 2, CrLf);
        DosPutMessage(1, 8, devhdr.DHname);
        DosPutMessage(1, strlen(InitMessage), InitMessage);

        // send back our cs and ds end values to os/2

        if (SegLimit(HIUSHORT((void far *) Init), &rp->s.InitExit.finalCS)
            || SegLimit(HIUSHORT((void far *) InitMessage),
            &rp->s.InitExit.finalDS))
               Abort();
        return(RPDONE);
    }
  }
}
```

AllocPhys   *Mode: Kernel, Init*

Allocate a block of physical memory.

C Calling Convention

```
if (AllocPhys(ULONG Size,USHORT Flag,far (PPHYSADDR) &pPhysAddr)) error

Size      = number of bytes to allocate
Flag      = 0 - Allocate memory above 1MB
          = 1 - Allocate memory below 1MB
&Physaddr = pointer to returned physical address
```

Comments

The memory allocated by this function is fixed memory, and may not be "unfixed" through the Unlock call.

If memory is requested to be allocated high (above 1MB), and no memory above 1MB is available, then an error is returned. The device driver could then attempt to allocate low memory.

Conversely, if memory is requested to be allocated low (below 1MB), and no memory below 1MB is available, then an error is returned and the device driver could try allocating high memory, if appropriate.

Example

```
// allocate a 64KB segment above 1MB

if (AllocPhys(0x10000,1,(PPHYSADDR) &AllocAddress)) error
```

AllocReqPacket   Mode: Kernel

Return a pointer to an empty request packet.

C Calling Convention

```
if(AllocReqPacket(USHORT Flag,(PREQPACKET) &Ptr)) error

Flag = 0 - wait
     = 1 - do not wait
&Ptr = far pointer to Request Packet returned
```

Comments

AllocReqPacket returns a pointer to a maximum-size request packet. Some OS/2 device drivers need to have additional request packets to service requests. Once the Request Packet address is obtained, it can be pushed on the request packet work queue with the PushReqPacket DevHlp.

Request packets allocated by the AllocReqPacket DevHlp should be returned to the kernel as soon as possible by calling the FreeReqPacket DevHlp, as the number of free request packets is limited system wide.

ArmCtxHook   *Mode: Kernel, Interrupt, Init*

Arm a context hook.

C Calling Convention

```
if (ArmCtxHook(ULONG HookData,LHANDLE HookHandle,ULONG Val)) error

HookData   = data to be passed to hook handler
HookHandle = handle returned from AllocCtxHook
Val        = 0xffffffff (reserved value)
```

Comments

ArmCtxHook arms a context hook allocated by the AllocateCtxHook DevHlp function. This function can be called at interrupt time. The next available task time thread will be used to call the function address specified at hook allocation time.

After the context hook is armed, it operates once and automatically disarms itself. It is an error to attempt to arm a context hook that is already armed. Once the context hook starts execution, the hook can be rearmed.

Context hooks should never block.

AttachDD Mode: Kernel, Init

Return the address of the Inter-Device Driver Communication (IDC) Entry Point to a specified device.

C Calling Convention

```
if (AttachDD("DEVICE   ",(PATTACHAREA) &AttachArea)) error

&AttachArea = near pointer to returned structure, type AttachArea

AttachArea struct {
  USHORT RealOffset;   // real mode offset of IDC entry point
  USHORT RealSegment;  // real mode segment of IDC entry point
  USHORT RealDS;       // real mode DS of IDC device driver
  USHORT ProtOffset;   // protect mode offset of IDC entry point
  USHORT ProtCS;       // protect mode CS selector of IDC entry
  USHORT ProtDS;       // protect mode DS of IDC driver
  }
```

Comments

The name field contains the ASCII name of the target device driver which must be eight characters in length. If the target device driver is a character device driver, the device driver name must match the name in the target device driver's Device Header.

Before the device driver calls the entry point, it must verify that the entry point received is nonzero. The IDC entry point of the target device driver must follow the FAR CALL/RET model.

Beep   Mode: Kernel, Interrupt, Init

Generate a beep.

C Calling Convention

```
if (Beep(USHORT Freq,USHORT Duration)) error

Freq     = frequency of beep in hertz
Duration = duration of beep in milliseconds
```

Comments

This function is similar to the DosBeep API. It generates a tone at Freq for Duration milliseconds.

Example

```
Beep (1000,1000);
```

Block   Mode: Kernel

Block the current thread.

C Calling Convention

```
if (Block(ULONG BlockID,ULONG Timeout,USHORT Flag,
          (FARPOINTER) &Error)) error

BlockID  = ID used for Block and subsequent Run
Timeout  = timeout in milliseconds or -1L Block forever
Flag     = 0 - Block is interruptible
         = 1 - Block is noninterruptible
&Error   = far Pointer to error returned
         = 1 - Block timed out
         = 2 - Block interrupted by control-C
```

Comments

The Block DevHlp blocks the current requesting thread and removes it from the run queue until it is released by a call to the Run DevHlp.

The return from the Block call indicates whether the wake-up occurred as the result of a Run DevHlp call or an expiration of the time limit. Block removes the current thread from the run queue, allowing any other waiting threads to run. The thread blocked in the device driver is reactivated and Block returns when Run is called with the same event identifier, when the time limit expires, or when the thread is signalled. The event identifier is an arbitrary 32-bit value, but an acceptable convention is to use the address of the request packet that made the request.

Since the device driver may be Blocked in one mode and Run in the other, using the address of the request packet is the best choice, as this bimodal address is valid in either mode. It is up to the device driver writer to ensure that the Block was woken up by the correct mechanism, and not accidentally. To avoid a deadlock condition by getting a Run before the Block call is completed, the device driver should disable interrupts before issuing the Block. The Block DevHlp re-enables the interrupts.

A timeout value of -1 means that Block waits indefinitely until Run is called. Only the Strategy sections of the device driver can call Block, but Run can be called by the Strategy section, interrupt handler, or timer handler. When using Block to block a thread, the device driver can specify whether or not the Block may be interrupted. If the Block is interruptible, then the kernel can abort the blocked thread and return from the Block without using a corresponding Run. In general, the Block should be marked as interruptible so that a signal such as a control C will UnBlock the thread.

The Block call will return when the thread has been run, when the timeout has expired, or if the thread was UnBlock by a signal, such as a control C. If the Block returns with a 1, the Block has timed out. If the Block returns a 2, the Block was interrupted. If the Block returns a 0, or valid return, then the Block was released by a call to the Run DevHlp, and the device driver should take the appropriate action.

Example

```
if (Block(WriteID,blockcount, 0, &err))
      if (err == 2)         // interrupted
            return(RPDONE|RPERR|ERROR_CHAR_CALL_INTERRUPTED);
      if (err == 1)
            return (RPDONE|RPERR|ERROR_NOT_READY);
```

CloseEventSem *Mode: Kernel*

Close a shared-event semaphore.

C Calling Convention

```
if (CloseEventSem(ULONG SemHandle)) error

SemHandle = handle of shared event semaphore
```

Comments

CloseEventSem closes an event semaphore that was previously opened with OpenEventSem. If this is the last reference to this event, then the event semaphore is destroyed.

CloseEventSem can be called only from a Ring 0 device driver or file system device driver. The handle passed in must be a handle to a shared-event semaphore. If the handle does not exist, or is not a "shared-event" semaphore, or if the semaphore was not previously opened with OpenEventSem, then ERROR INVALID HANDLE will be returned.

The system semaphores reside in a memory buffer. When the last process that has a semaphore open exits or closes that semaphore, the semaphore is destroyed.

Open and close operations may be nested. A maximum of 65,534 opens per process is allowed for each semaphore at any one time. If this limit is exceeded, the OpenEventSem will return ERROR_TOO_MANY_OPENS.

In order for a process to intentionally destroy a semaphore prior to termination, the number of CloseEventSem calls must equal the number of OpenEventSem calls.

DeRegister   Mode: Kernel

Remove a device monitor.

C Calling Convention

```
if (DeRegister(USHORT Handle,USHORT Pid,(PERRCODE) &Error)) error

Handle = the handle of the monitor chain
Pid    = PID of the process that created the monitor chain
&Error = far pointer to error returned
```

Comments

DeRegister removes all of the monitors associated with the specified process from the specified monitor chain.

This function may only be called at Strategy time in protect mode.

To remove a monitor from a monitor chain, the device driver supplies the PID of the process that created the monitor and the handle of the monitor chain. All monitors belonging to the PID are removed from the monitor chain. Since a process may register more than one monitor, all the monitors associated with the PID are removed with one call to DeRegister.

DevDone   Mode: Kernel, Interrupt

Set the done bit in the request packet and run any blocked threads waiting for the request to be completed.

C Calling Convention

```
if (DevDone((PREQPACKET) &RequestPacket)) error

&RequestPacket = far pointer to Request Packet
```

Comments

The DevDone DevHlp sets the DONE bit in the status field of the request packet header and issue RUNs on threads that are blocked in the kernel waiting for the particular request packet to be completed. DevDone will not work with request packets that were allocated from the AllocReqPacket DevHlp call. The device driver does not call DevDone to complete requests in the Strategy routine, rather the device driver returns to the kernel with the done status.

SaveMsg (formerly DispMsg)   Mode: Init

Display a message from a base device driver on the system console.

C Calling Convention

```
DispMsg((FPSTRING) &MsgTbl)

&MsgTbl = far pointer to message table struct
```

Comments

The message is not displayed immediately, but is queued until system initialization retrieves it from the system message file.

The structure of the message table is:

```
MsgTbl struct {
        WORD     Message ID
        WORD     Number of fill-in items
        DWORD    Pointer to first fill-in item of ASCII-Z string
        DWORD    Pointer to second fill-in item of ASCII-Z string
        DWORD    Pointer to last fill-in item of ASCII-Z string
}
```

The messages are obtained, by ordinal, from the system message file OSO001.msg with DosGetMessage. The driver can substitute elements of the message with its own message, but leave country and language-specific data intact. For instance, the word "printer", in English, would be different for each country. The driver can use the data contained in the message file to build a buffer of data to send to the display device. DispMessage then calls DosPutMessage to display the data. Drivers that utilize DispMsg can be used without regard to country or language differences.

If an error message is displayed, the "press any key to continue" message is displayed unless the CONFIG.SYS file contains PAUSEONERROR=NO.

DynamicAPI   Mode: Kernel, Init

Create a Ring 0 call gate to a routine in a device driver.

C Calling Convention

```
if (DynamicAPI((FARPOINTER) &Worker,USHORT ParamCount,USHORT Flag,
          (FPUSHORT) &Sel)) err

&Worker    = 16:16 or 0:32 bit address of driver function
ParamCount = count of the number of parameters
             if 16:16 call gate, the number of words
             if 0:32 call gate, the number of dwords
Flag       = bit 0 = 1 - 16 bit call gate
             bit 0 = 0 - 32 bit call gate
             bit 1 = 1 - 16:16 function address
             bit 1 = 0 - linear function address
Sel        = far pointer to Selector returned
```

Comments

The maximum number of parameters cannot exceed 16. ParamCount cannot be larger than 16 for 16:16 call gates or 8 for 0:32 call gates.

Example

```
// get ring 0 call gate

if(DynamicAPI((FARPOINTER)test_it,0,3,(FARPOINTER)&Newsel))
        return(RPDONE | RPERR | ERROR_GEN_FAILURE);

// send back call gate to application

if (MoveBytes((FARPOINTER) &Newsel,
      rp->s.IOCtl.buffer,
      2))
              return(RPDONE | RPERR | ERROR_GEN_FAILURE);
```

EOI   Mode: Interrupt, Init

Issue an EOI to the 8259 PIC.

C Calling Convention

```
EOI(USHORT IRQnum)

IRQnum = IRQ number to issue EOI against
```

Comments

This routine is used to issue an End-Of-Interrupt to the cascaded 8259 priority interrupt controllers. If the interrupt is located on the second 8259, and EOI is also issued to the lower 8259.

If the specified interrupt level is for the slave 8259 interrupt controller, then this routine will issue the EOI to both the master and slave 8259s.

On ISA bus systems, the interrupt handler is entered with the interrupts off. To prevent the nesting of interrupts, interrupts should not be re-enabled until the EOI has been issued. On PS/2 and EISA systems, the interrupt handler is entered with interrupts enabled. In this case, to prevent nested interrupts, the interrupt routine should disable interrupts, issue the EOI, and return to OS/2, where interrupts will be re-enabled.

Example

```
EOI(10);
```

FreeCtxHook　　　　　　　　　　　　　　　　　　Mode: Kernel, Init

Free a context hook.

C Calling Convention

```
if (FreeCtxHook((LHANDLE) HookHandle)) error

HookHandle  =  handle from AllocateCtxHook
```

Comments

FreeCtxHook frees a context hook allocated by the AllocateCtxHook DevHlp service.

FreeGDTSelector　　　　　　　　　　　　　　　　Mode: Kernel, Init

Free a GDT selector.

C Calling Convention

```
if (FreeGDTSelector(USHORT Sel)) error

Sel  =  selector allocated by AllocGDTSelector call
```

Comments

FreeGDTSelector frees a selector allocated with the AllocGDTSelector DevHlp service.

The selector passed to this function must have been allocated using AllocGDTSelector. This is verified and an error is returned if the selector was not properly allocated.

FreeLIDEntry   Mode: Kernel, Init

Release a Logical ID (LID).

C Calling Convention

```
if (FreeLIDEntry(USHORT Lid)) error

Lid = LID obtained from a previous GetLIDEntry DevHlp call
```

Comments

This routine is used to release a Logical ID. This can be done at either DEINSTALL or when the device driver is closed.

The attempt to free a Logical ID not owned by the device driver, or that does not exist, will fail.

Example

```
if (!(GetLIDEntry(0x10, 0, 1, &lid)))     {     // get LID for POS
     FreeLIDEntry(lid);
```

FreePhys   Mode: Kernel, Init

Release previously allocated memory.

C Calling Convention

```
if (FreePhys((PHYSADDR) &PhysAddress)) error

&PhysAddress = 32 bit physical address of allocated memory
```

Comments

FreePhys is used to release memory previously allocated by the AllocPhys DevHlp call.

Any memory that the device driver allocated by way of the AllocPhys should be released prior to device driver termination.

FreeReqPacket   Mode: Kernel

Release an allocated request packet.

C Calling Convention

```
if (FreeReqPacket((PREQPACKET) &RequestPacket))error

&RequestPacket = far pointer to Request Packet
```

Comments

This function is used to release a request packet previously allocated by a AllocReqPacket DevHlp call.

FreeReqPacket should only be performed on a request packet that was previously allocated by an AllocReqPacket DevHlp call. The DevDone function should not be used to return an allocated request packet. Since the system has a limited number of request packets, it is important that a device driver free up allocated request packets as soon as possible.

GetDescInfo   *Mode: Kernel, Interrupt, Init*

Obtain information about a descriptor's contents.

C Calling Convention

```
if (GetDsecInfo(USHORT Selector,(FPUSHORT) &AX_Reg,(FPULONG) &ECX_Reg,
            (FPULONG) &EDX_Reg)) error

Selector  = any selector
AX_Reg    = AX register (see below)
ECX_Reg   = ecx register (see below)
EDX_Reg   = edx register (see below)

Register Contents Returned

If descriptor was a call gate:
   AL (LOUSHORT AX_Reg)  = descriptors access byte
   AH (HIUSHORT AX_Reg)  = number of parameters
   CX (LOUSHORT ECX_Reg) = selector
   EDX                   = 32-bit offset (0:32 addressing)

If descriptor was not a call gate:
   AL (LOUSHORT AX_Reg)  = descriptors access byte
   AH (HIUSHORT AX_Reg   = BIG and GRANULARITY fields of attribute
                           byte
   ECX                   = the 32 bit linear address in descriptor
   EDX                   = the 32 bit byte-granular size of the
                           decsriptor(0 if 4GB)
```

Comments

When called for an LDT (Local Descriptor Table) descriptor, GetDescInfo may block other threads from executing. Therefore, at interrupt time, this routine is callable only on GDT (Global Descriptor Table) descriptors. The routine can be called with either type of descriptor at initialization or task time.

GetDeviceBlock   Mode: Init

Return an ABIOS Device block pointer.

Calling Sequence

```
if (GetDeviceBlock(USHORT Lid,far (FARPOINTER) &ABIOSDeviceBlock)) error

Lid                  = lid from GetLIDEntry
&ABIOSDeviceBlock    = far pointer to device block data
```

Comments

GetDeviceBlock returns an ABIOS Device block pointer. The function returns a protect mode pointer only. Real mode pointers are not returned, rather the data is initialized to zero.

This function will always fail on non-PS/2 machines.

Refer to the *IBM Personal System/2 and Personal Computer BIOS Interface Technical Reference*, part number S68X-2341-00, for more detailed information on the use of ABIOS and its associated data structures.

GetDOSVar   Mode: Kernel, Init

Return the address of system variables.

C Calling Convention

```
if (GetDOSVar(USHORT ID,(FPFARPOINTER) &Ptr)) error

ID   = identifier number of the variable
&Ptr = far pointer to address of returned pointer
```

Comments

Table A-4 contains a list of read-only variables that can be examined.

Table A-4. Read Only System Variables

ID	Description of Variable
1	SysINFOseg:WORD - segment address of the System Global InfoSeg. Valid at both task time and interrupt time, but not Init time.
2	LocINFOseg:DWORD - Selector/Segment address of the local (LDT) INFO segment. Valid only at task time.
3	Reserved
4	VectorSDF:DWORD - Pointer to the stand-alone dump facility. Valid at both task time and interrupt time.
5	VectorReboot:DWORD - Pointer to restart OS/2. Valid at both task time and interrupt time.
6	Reserved
7	YieldFlag:BYTE - Indicator for performing time-critical yields. Valid only at task time.
8	TCYieldFlag:BYTE - Indicator for performing time-critical yields. Valid only at task time.
9	Reserved
10	Reserved
11	DOS mode Code Page Tag Pointer: DWORD Segment/offset of the current code page tag of DOS mode. Valid only at Strategy time.
14	16:16 pointer to table of registered ADD entry points

Example

```
// get current processes id

if (GetDOSVar(2,&ptr))
        return (RPDONE | RPERR | ERROR_BAD_COMMAND);

// get process info

liptr = *((PLINFOSEG far *) ptr);

// if this device never opened, can be opened by any process

if ( opencount == 0)                    // first time this device opened
        savepid = liptr->pidCurrent; // save current process id
else
{
        if ( savepid != liptr->pidCurrent) // another proc tried to open
                return (RPDONE | RPERR | RPBUSY ); // so return error

        ++opencount[dev];               // bump counter, same pid
}
return (RPDONE);
```

GetLIDEntry   *Mode: Kernel, Init*

Obtain a Logical ID (LID) for an existing device.

C Calling Convention

```
if (GetLIDEntry(USHORT DevType,USHORT Spec,USHORT Type,
    (FPUSHORT) &Lid)) error

DevID  = device type
Spec   = 0 - get first unclaimed LID, 1 - the first LID
Type   = 1 - DMA or POS
       = 0 - all others
&Lid   = far pointer to variable where the LID is returned
```

Comments

GetLIDEntry is used by a device driver to obtain a LID entry. Because OS/2 does not support the Advanced BIOS Sleep/Wake functions, only devices that are "awake" are considered to exist, and thus available to device drivers.

This function may be employed in two ways. One way is for the device driver to specify a relative LID. Because the ordering of LIDs corresponds to the ordering of physical devices, a device driver that desires to support a certain relative device can determine if a LID entry is available. (An example is a character device driver that supports COM4; that is, it wishes to get the LID entry for the fourth COM port.)

The other way to use this function is for the device driver to request the first available LID for its device type. (An example is a block device driver that wishes to get the first available LID for diskettes.)

In either use of this function, GetLIDEntry will search the ABIOS Common Data Area table for an entry corresponding to the specified device ID. If an entry is located that matches the caller's form of request, it is returned to the caller. If a LID entry is found but already owned, an error is returned. If no LID entry is found, an error is also returned.

Example

```
if (!(GetLIDEntry(0x10, 0, 1, &lid)))    {     // get LID for POS
        FreeLIDEntry(lid);
```

InternalError   *Mode: Kernel, Interrupt, Init*

Indicate that an internal error has occurred.

C Calling Convention

```
InternalError((PSTRING) &Msg,USHORT MsgLen)

&Msg    = DS relative offset of message
MsgLen  = length of message
```

Comments

This DevHlp routine should be used only when an major internal problem is detected. Continuing from this point may cause serious problems or possible data loss, so the routine never returns. InternalError should not be used for less than fatal errors.

The maximum message length is 128 characters. Longer messages are truncated to 128 characters. The device driver name should appear as the first item in the message text.

LinToGDTSelector — Mode: Kernel, Interrupt, Init

Convert linear address to virtual address.

C Calling Convention

```
if (LinToGDTSelector(USHORT Selector,LINADDR Address,ULONG Size)) error

Selector  =  selector allocated by AllocGDTSelector
Address   =  32 bit linear address
Size      =  size of memory in bytes
```

Comments

LinToGDTSelector converts a linear address to a virtual (Selector:Offset) address by mapping the given GDT (Global Descriptor Table) selector to the memory region referred to by the given linear address and range. The size of the range mapped must be less than or equal to 64KB.

The memory that is being mapped must be fixed or locked prior to this call. After this call is issued for a particular selector, the addressability will remain valid until the device driver changes its content with a subsequent call to the PageListToGDTSelector, PhysToGDTSel, PhysToGDTSelector, or LinToGDTSelector DevHlp services.

LinToPageList   *Mode: Kernel, Interrupt, Init*

Convert a linear address to PageList array.

C Calling Convention

```
if (LinToPageList(LINADDR LinAddress,ULONG Size,
    (FLATPOINTER) &PageList, FPULONG Elements)) error

LinAddress  = 32 bit linear starting address
Size        = size of the range to translate
&PageList   = flat pointer to PageList structure
Elements    = number of elements in PageList array
```

The linear address range is translated into an array of PageList structures. Each PageList structure describes a single physically contiguous subregion of the physical memory that is mapped by the linear range. The format of the PageList structure is:

```
typedef struct _PAGELIST {
  ULONG pl_PhysAddr;        // physical address of first byte
                            // in this subregion
  ULONG pl_cb;              // Number of contiguous bytes
                            // starting at pl_PhysAddr
  }
```

Comments

LinToPageList translates a linear address range to an array of PageList structures that describes the physical pages to be mapped.

The sum of the pl_cb fields in the PageList array produced by this function will be equal to Size.

The physical pages that are mapped by the linear range must be fixed or locked prior to this call.

It is the device driver's responsibility to ensure that enough entries have been reserved for the range of memory being translated (possibly one entry per page in the range, plus one more if the region does not begin on a page boundary).

LockSeg   *Mode: Kernel, Init*

Lock a segment in memory.

C Calling Convention

```
if (LockSeg(USHORT Sel,USHORT Type,USHORT Wait,(PLHANDLE) &Lhandle)) error

Sel      = selector of user's memory from req packet
Type     = 00 short term, any memory
         = 01 long term, any memory
         = 03 long term, high memory
         = 04 short term, any memory, verify lock
Wait     = 00 block until available
         = 01 return if not immediately available
&Lhandle = far pointer to returned handle
```

Comments

LockSeg is called by device drivers at Strategy time to lock a caller's memory segment.

LockSeg should be called to lock the caller's memory segment before attempting to transfer data from the device driver to the calling application or from the application to the device driver.

LockSeg Type 3:

For type 3, the segment is marked fixed, and the system may move it into the region reserved for fixed segments. If the Lock returns no error, the segment is guaranteed to be in high memory. Type 3 is available only during INIT, and is generally used to reserve extra code or data segments for use by the device driver. A type 3 Lock cannot be undone.

LockSeg Type 4:

The segment remains swappable. It will not be freed or shrunk until the verify lock is removed.

Additional Comments

1. Short term locks are less than 2 seconds. Long-term locks are always greater than 2 seconds. Unless the device driver operation will be completed very quickly, do not use the short-term LockSeg. Using up all swappable memory could cause a system hang if the operating system runs out of swappable memory.

2. Failure to call UnLockSeg to release the locked segment will result in all of the GDT entries being used up and the system will halt.

3. If the device driver is entered with a standard device driver function, such as DosRead or DosWrite, the caller's segment is already locked by the kernel. However, if the device driver is entered as a result of an IOCtl call, the device driver must lock the segment. Although some documentation states that the caller's segment should be locked before verifying that it is valid (with the VerifyAccess call), it is still safe to verify the segment first and then lock it immediately after the VerifyAccess call.

4. OS/2 2.1 device drivers should always call LockSeg with the wait option (wait = 0).

Example

```
// lock the segment down temp

if(LockSeg(
      SELECTOROF(rp->s.IOCtl.buffer),  // selector
      0,                                // lock for < 2 sec
      0,                                // wait for seg lock
      (PLHANDLE) &lock_seg_han))        // handle returned
            return (RPDONE | RPERR | ERROR_GEN_FAILURE);
```

MonFlush   Mode: Kernel

Flush a monitor chain.

C Calling Convention

```
if (MonFlush(SHANDLE Handle,(PERRCODE) &Error))error

Handle = short (16-bit) monitor handle
&Error = far pointer to error code
```

Comments

MonFlush removes all data from the specified monitor chain (such as the data stream).

This function may be called at task time only.

When a device driver calls MonFlush, the OS/2 monitor dispatcher creates and places a flush record into the monitor chain. The general format of monitor records requires that every record contains a flag word as the first entry. One of the flags is used to indicate that this record is a flush record. The flush record consists only of the flag word. This record is used by monitors along the chain to reset internal state information, and to assure that all internal buffers are flushed. The flush record must be passed along to the next monitor, because the monitor dispatcher will not process any more information until the flush record is received at the end of the monitor chain. That is, until it is returned to the device driver's monitor chain buffer at the end of the monitor chain

Subsequent MonWrite requests will fail (or block) until the flush completes, that is, until the flush record is returned to the device driver's monitor chain buffer.

MonCreate   Mode: Kernel, Init

Create or remove a monitor chain.

C Calling Convention

```
if (MonCreate((PSHANDLE) &Handle,(FARPOINTER) &Buf,(FPFUNCTION) &Routine,
     (PERRCODE) &Error)) error

&Handle   = far pointer to handle
&Buf      = far pointer to monitor buffer
&Routine  = far pointer to monitor routine
&Error    = far pointer to returned error
```

Comments

MonCreate creates an initially empty chain of monitors or removes an empty chain of monitors.

This function may be called at task time only.

The monitor chain buffer (final buffer) is a buffer owned by the device driver. On calling MonCreate, the first word of this buffer is the length of the buffer in bytes (including the first word).

When the monitor chain handle specified is 0, a new monitor chain is created. When the monitor chain handle specified is a handle that was previously returned from a call to MonCreate (that is, Handle != 0) the monitor chain referenced by that handle is destroyed.

A monitor chain is a list of monitors, with a device driver monitor chain buffer address and code address as the last element on this list. Data is placed into a monitor chain through the MonWrite function; the monitor dispatcher feeds the data through all registered monitors, putting the resulting data, if any, into the specified device driver monitor chain buffer. When data is placed in this buffer, the device driver's notification routine is called at task time. The device driver should initiate any necessary action in a timely fashion and return from the notification entry point without delay.

The MonCreate function establishes one of these monitor chains. The chains are created empty so that data written into them is placed immediately into the device driver's buffer.

This routine can also destroy a monitor chain if the handle parameter (AX) is nonzero. The nonzero value is the handle of the chain to remove. If the monitor chain to be removed is not empty (that is, all monitors registered with this chain have not been previously deregistered), an invalid parameter error is returned to the device driver.

A MonCreate call must be made before a monitor can be registered with the chain. This can be done at any time, including during the installation of the device driver at system load time.

The device driver's notification routine is called by the monitor dispatcher when a data record has been placed in the device driver's monitor chain buffer. The device driver must process the contents of the monitor chain buffer before returning to the monitor dispatcher.

When the driver's notification routine is called, the first word of the buffer is filled in with the length of the record just sent to the device driver. There is one notification routine call for each record.

MonWrite   Mode: Kernel, Interrupt

Write data to monitor chain.

C Calling Convention

```
if (MonWrite(SHANDLE Handle, (POINTER) &Rec,USHORT Size,USHORT Flag,
    ULONG SyncTime,far &Error))error

Handle   = monitor handle
&Rec     = pointer to data record
Size     = length of data record
Flag     = wait flag, explained below
SyncTime = sync time, see below
&Error   = address of returned error code
```

Comments

This function may be called at task time or interrupt time. The wait flag is set to 0 if the MonWrite request occurs at task or user time and the device driver indicates that the monitor dispatcher is to do the synchronization. If the wait flag is set to 0, the device driver waits until the data can be placed into the monitor chain before the monitor dispatcher returns to the device driver. If the wait flag is set to 1, the device driver does not wait; and if the data cannot be placed into the monitor chain, the monitor dispatcher will return immediately with the appropriate error. The wait flag must be set to 1 if the MonWrite request occurs at interrupt time. Wait flag is set to 2 if the MonWrite request occurs at task or user time, and the device driver indicates that the monitor dispatcher is to do the synchronization for the time in milliseconds, specified in Timeout.

The error, NOT_ENOUGH_MEMORY, will be returned to the device driver when the MonWrite call is made and the monitors are not able to receive the data. If this condition occurs at interrupt time, an overrun occurred. If it occurs at task (or user) time, the process can block.

The error, NOT_ENOUGH_MEMORY, also will be returned to the device driver when a flush record, sent to the monitors by a previous MonFlush call, was not returned to the device driver.

If the thread on which the device driver calls MonWrite blocks (the device driver specified the wait option) and is awakened because the process that owns the thread is terminating, a ERROR_CHAR_CALL_INTERRUPTED is returned to the device driver.

Each call to MonWrite will send a single record. The data sent by this call is considered to be a complete record. A data record must not be longer than two bytes less than the length of the device driver's monitor chain buffer.

OpenEventSem   Mode: Kernel

Open a 32-bit shared-event semaphore.

Calling Sequence

```
if (OpenEventSem(LHANDLE Handle)) error

Handle  =  long handle to shared event semaphore
```

Comments

OpenEventSem can be called only from a Ring 0 device driver or file system device driver. If the handle does not exist, or is not a "shared-event" semaphore, then ERROR_INVALID_HANDLE is returned.

The open and close operations can be nested. A maximum of 65,534 opens per process are allowed for each semaphore at any one time. If this limit is exceeded, OpenEventSem will return ERROR_TOO_MANY_OPENS. In order for a process to intentionally destroy a semaphore prior to termination, the number of CloseEventSem calls must equal the number of OpenEventSem calls.

Event semaphores are used for signaling between threads.

PageListToGDTSelector   *Mode: Kernel, Interrupt, Init*

Map physical pages to a GDT selector.

C Calling Convention

```
if (PageListToGDTSelector(USHORT Selector,ULONG Size,
    (LINADDR) &PageList,USHORT Access,(FPUSHORT) &ModSelector)) error

Selector      = selector to map
Size          = number of bytes to map
&PageList     = flat pointer to an array of PAGELIST structures
Access        = descriptor's type and privilege level
&ModSelector  = far pointer to selector returned with modified RPL bits
```

&PageList is the flat address of an array of PageList structures. Each PageList structure describes a single physically contiguous subregion of the physical memory to be mapped. The format of the PageList structure is:

```
typedef struct _PAGELIST {
  ULONG pl_PhysAddr;          // physical address of first byte
                              // in this subregion
  ULONG pl_cb;                // Number of contiguous bytes
                              // starting at pl_PhysAddr
}
```

Comments

PageListToGDTSelector maps physical addresses described in an array of PageList structures to a *GDT* (*Global Descriptor Table*) selector, setting the access byte of the descriptor to the requested type. The virtual memory needed to map the physical ranges described by the PageList array must not exceed 64KB.

The physical memory that is being mapped must be fixed or locked prior to this call. After this call, offset 0 within the selector will correspond to the first byte in the first entry in the array pointed to by PageList. If the PageList is an unmodified return array from VMLock or LinToPageList, then the mapping returned from this call will be the same as the original linear range. However, if the PageList array was constructed by some other means, or is a concatenation of two or more PageList arrays returned from various other DevHlp services, the selector mapping may be noncontiguous.

The first byte mapped by the selector will correspond to the first byte described in the first entry in the PageList array. The next n bytes, where n is the size parameter of the first PageList entry, will be mapped contiguously from that point.

After this call has been issued for a particular selector, the addressability will remain valid until the device driver changes its content with a subsequent call to the DevHlp PageListToGDTSelector, PhysToGDTSel, PhysToGDTSelector, or LinToGDTSelector.

PageListToLin   **Mode: Kernel, Interrupt, Init**

Map an array of PageList structures.

C Calling Convention

```
if (PageListToLin(ULONG Size,(FLATPOINTER) &PageList,
   (PLINADDR) &LinAddr)) error

Size     = count of bytes of memory to be mapped
&PageList = flat pointer to PageList structs
&LinAddr  = far pointer to variable to receive linear address
```

Each PageList structure describes a single physically contiguous subregion of the physical memory to be mapped. The format of the PageList structure is:

```
typedef struct _PAGELIST {
  ULONG pl_PhysAddr;        // physical address of first byte
                            // in this subregion
  ULONG pl_cb;              // Number of contiguous bytes
                            // starting at pl_PhysAddr
}
```

Comments

PageListToLin maps physical memory pages, described in an array of PageList structures, to a linear address. The size of the linear mapping must not exceed 64KB.

The physical memory that is being mapped must be fixed or locked prior to this call. After this call, the first byte within the returned linear range will correspond to the first byte in the first entry in the array pointed to by PageList. If the PageList is an unmodified return array from VMLock or LinToPageList, then the mapping returned from this call will be the same as the original linear range. However, if the PageList array was constructed by some other means, or is a concatenation of two or more PageList arrays returned from various other DevHlp services, the linear mapping may be noncontiguous.

The first byte in the linear mapping will correspond to the first byte described in the first entry in the PageList array. The next n bytes, where n is the size parameter of the first PageList entry, will be mapped contiguously from that point.

The starting linear address of subsequent PageList entries may be computed by rounding up the linear address of the end of the previous entry to a page boundary, and then adding on the low order 12 bits of the physical address of the target PageList entry.

The linear mapping produced by calling PageListToLin is only valid until the caller yields the CPU, or until it issues another PageListToLin call or a PhysToVirt call. Calling PageListToLin will invalidate any previous PhysToVirt mappings.

PhysToGDTSel Mode: Kernel, Interrupt, Init

Map a GDT selector to a physical address.

C Calling Convention

```
if (PhysToGDTSel(PHYADDR PhysAddr,ULONG Size,SEL Selector,
    USHORT Access, (FPUSHORT) &NewSel)) error

PhysAddr = physical address to be mapped to selector
Size     = size of segment, must be less than or equal to 64KB
Selector = GDT selector, from AllocGDTSelector
Access   = descriptor's type and access level
&NewSel  = address of returned modified selector
```

Comments

PhysToGDTSel maps a given GDT selector to a specified physical address, setting the access byte of the descriptor to the desired privilege value. The specified segment size must be less than or equal to 64KB.

The physical memory that is being mapped must be fixed or locked prior to this call. After this call has been issued the addressability remains valid until the device driver calls PhysToGDTSel, PhysToGDTSelector, PageListToGDTSelector, or LinToGDTSelector.

PhysToGDTSelector   Mode: Kernel, Interrupt, Init

Convert a 32-bit physical address to a GDT selector-offset pair.

C Calling Convention

```
if (PhysGDTSelector(PHYSADDR Physaddr,USHORT Len,SEL Sel,
    (PERRCODE) &Error)) error

Physaddr = physical address to map selector to
Len      = length of segment
Sel      = selector from AllocGDTSelector
&Error   = far pointer to returned error code
```

Comments

PhysToGDTSelector is used to provide addressability through a GDT selector to data. The interrupt handler of a device driver must be able to address data buffers regardless of the context of the current process. The GDT selector will remain valid until another PhysToGDTSelector call is made for the same selector.

The AllocGDTSelector function is used at INIT time to allocate the GDT selectors that the device driver may use with the PhysToGDTSelector.

PhysToGDTSelector creates selector:offset addressability for a 32-bit physical address. The selector created, however, does not represent a normal memory segment, but is a "fabricated segment" for private use by the device driver. Such a segment cannot be passed on system calls, and may only be used by the device driver to fetch data.

Remember that GDT selectors mapped during INIT cannot be used during INIT, as INIT is run as a ring 3 thread.

Example

```c
if (!(SetIRQ(5,(PFUNCTION)INTERRUPT_HANDLER,0)))
{
  if (!(AllocGDTSelector(1,(FARPOINTER)&Sel)))
  {
    if (!(PhysToGDTSelector(0xd8000,0x1000,Sel,&err)))
    {

      // output initialization message

      DosPutMessage(1, 2, CrLf);
      DosPutMessage(1, 8, devhdr.DHname);
      DosPutMessage(1, strlen(InitMessage), InitMessage);

      // send back our cs and ds end values to os/2

      if (SegLimit(HIUSHORT((void far *) Init), &rp->s.InitExit.finalCS)
          || SegLimit(HIUSHORT((void far *) InitMessage),
          &rp->s.InitExit.finalDS))
            Abort();
      return(RPDONE);
    }
  }
}
```

PhysToUVirt   Mode: Kernel, Init

Convert a physical address to a user virtual address.

C Calling Convention

```
if (PhysToUVirt(PHYSADDR Physaddr,USHORT Len,USHORT Type,
    (FPFARPOINTER) &Virt)) error

Physaddr = physical address to map to LDT selector
Len      = length of fabricated segment
Type     = create, release (see comments)
&Virt    = far pointer to returned virtual address
```

Comments

PhysToUVirt converts a 32-bit physical address to a valid selector-offset pair addressable out of the current LDT.

This function is typically used to provide a caller of a device driver with addressability to a fixed memory area, such as a memory-mapped adapter address. The device driver must know the physical address of the memory area to be addressed.

PhysToUVirt creates selector:offset LDT addressability for a 32-bit physical address. This function is provided so that a device driver can give an application process addressability to a fixed memory area, such as in the BIOS-reserved range from 640KB to 1MB. It can also be used to give a ring 3 application addressability to a device driver's data segment.

The selector created, however, does not represent a normal memory segment but is a fabricated segment for private use between a device driver and an application. Data within such a segment cannot be passed on system calls, and may only be used by the receiving application to fetch data variables.

PhysToUVirt mappings are limited to 64KB.

In OS/2 1.x, all LDT selectors returned by the PhysToUVirt Device Helper routine were marked as privilege level 3 selectors. In OS/2 Version 2.1, the device driver can specify whether the selector should be marked with DPL 3 or DPL 2. This allows an LDT selector used by a dynamic link library routine, which is running with IOPL, to be protected from accidental modification by the application program.

Example

```
// map board address to pte

if ( PhysToUVirt(DRIVER_BASE,BASE_LENGTH,1,&mem))
        return (RPDONE | RPERR | ERROR_GEN_FAILURE);
```

PhysToVirt   *Mode: Kernel, Interrupt, Init*

Convert a physical address to a virtual address.

C Calling Convention

```
if (PhysToVirt(PHYSADDR Physaddr,USHORT Len,USHORT Type,
    (FPFARPOINTER) &Virt)) error

Physaddr = physical address to map GDT selector to
Len      = length of fabricated segment
Type     = must be 0 for returned selector in DS:SI
&Virt    = far pointer to returned virtual address
```

Comments

The returned virtual address will not remain valid if the device driver blocks or yields control. The returned virtual address may also destroyed if the device driver routine that issues the PhysToVirt calls another routine.

The device driver must not enable interrupts or change the segment register before the device driver has finished accessing the data. When the device driver has finished accessing the data, it must restore the interrupt state.

While pointers generated by this routine are in use, the device driver may only call another PhysToVirt request. No other DevHlp routines can be called, because they may not preserve the special DS/ES values created by the PhysToVirt.

The converted addresses are valid as long as the device driver does not relinquish control (Block, Yield, or RET). An interrupt handler may use converted addresses prior to its EOI, with interrupts enabled. For performance reasons, a device driver should try to optimize its usage of PhysToVirt and UnPhysToVirt.

Under OS/2 2.1, UnPhysToVirt performs no function.

PhysToVirt mappings are limited to 64KB.

Example

```
// get pointer to screen memory, 16K long

if(PhysToVirt(0xb8000L,0x4000,0,(FARPOINTER) &Address)) error
```

PostEventSem — Mode: Kernel

Post a 32-bit shared-event semaphore.

C Calling Convention

```
if (PostEventSem(LHANDLE Handle)) error

Handle = long handle to shared event semaphore
```

Comments

If the event is already posted, the post count is incremented and the ERROR_ALREADY_POSTED return code is returned. Otherwise, the event is posted, the post count is set to one, and all threads that called DosWaitEventSem are made runnable.

PostEventSem can be called only from a ring 0 device driver or file system driver. The handle passed in must be a handle to a shared-event semaphore. If the handle does not exist, is not a "shared-event" semaphore, or if the semaphore was not previously opened with OpenEventSem, then ERROR_INVALID_HANDLE will be returned.

There is a limit of 65,535 posts allowed per event semaphore. If this limit is exceeded, then ERROR_TOO_MANY_POSTS return code is returned.

Calling ResetEventSem will reset the event, so that any threads that subsequently wait on the event semaphore (with DosWaitEventSem) will be blocked.

PullParticular *Mode: Kernel, Interrupt*

Pull a particular request packet from the request packet linked list.

C Calling Convention

```
if (PullParticular((PQHEAD) &QueueHead,(PREQPACKET) &RequestPacket))error

&QueueHead     = address of queue head
&RequestPacket = far pointer to Request Packet
```

Comments

A device driver uses the PushReqPacket and PullReqPacket DevHlps to maintain a work queue for each of its devices. PullParticular is used to remove a specific request packet from the work queue, typically for the case where a process has terminated before finishing its I/O.

PullParticular may also be used to remove request packets that were allocated by an AllocReqPacket from the request packet linked list.

The pointer to the request packet is used to determine the request packet to be retrieved.

PullReqPacket   *Mode: Kernel, Interrupt*

Pull the next waiting request packet from the selected request packet linked list.

C Calling Convention

```
if (PullReqPacket((PQHEAD) &QueueHead,(PREQPACKET) &RequestPacket)) error
&QueueHead     = address of queue head
&RequestPacket = far pointer to Request Packet
```

Comments

A device driver uses the PushReqPacket and PullReqPacket DevHlps to maintain a work queue for each of its devices/units. The device driver must provide the storage for the work queue head, which defines the start of the request packet linked list. The work queue head must be initialized to 0.

PullReqPacket may also be used to remove request packets that were allocated by an AllocReqPacket from the request packet queue.

PushReqPacket Mode: Kernel

Add the current request packet to the linked list of packets.

C Calling Convention

```
if (PushReqPacket((PQHEAD) &QueueHead,(PREQPACKET) &RequestPacket)) error

&QueueHead     = address of queue head
&RequestPacket = far pointer to of Request Packet
```

Comments

A device driver uses the PushReqPacket and PullReqPacket DevHlps to maintain a work queue for each of its devices. The device driver must provide the storage for the work queue head, which defines the start of the request packet linked list. The work queue head must be initialized to 0.

PushReqPacket may also be used to place request packets that were allocated by an AllocReqPacket in the request packet work queue.

QueueFlush   Mode: Kernel, Interrupt

Clear the specified character queue.

C Calling Convention

```
if (QueueFlush((PCHARQUEUE) &CharQueue)) error

&CharQueue = address of DS relative CHARQUEUE
```

Comments

QueueFlush operates on the simple character queue structure initialized by QueueInit.

```
typedef struct _CHARQUEUE {
  USHORT Qsize;         //  size of queue in bytes
  USHORT QIndex;        //  index of next char out
  USHORT Qcount         //  count of chars in the queue
  UCHAR  buf[Qsize]     //  start of queue buffer
  } CHARQUEUE;
```

QueueInit   *Mode: Kernel, Interrupt, Init*

Initialize the specified character queue.

C Calling Convention

```
if (QueueInit((PCHARQUEUE) &CharQueue)) error

&CharQueue = address of DS relative CHARQUEUE
```

Comments

QueueInit must be called before any other queue manipulation subroutine. The device driver must allocate the character queue buffer and initialize the Qsize field before the queue is used.

```
typedef struct _CHARQUEUE {
   USHORT Qsize;         // size of queue in bytes
   USHORT QIndex;        // index of next char out
   USHORT Qcount         // count of chars in the queue
   UCHAR  buf[Qsize]     // start of queue buffer
   } CHARQUEUE;
```

QueueRead   *Mode: Kernel, Interrupt*

Read a character from the beginning of the specified character queue.

C Calling Convention

```
if (QueueRead((PCHARQUEUE) &CharQueue, (FPUCHAR) &Char)) error

&CharQueue = address of DS relative CHARQUEUE
&Char      = far pointer to returned char
```

Comments

QueueRead reads a single character from the specified queue.

```
typedef struct _CHARQUEUE {
   USHORT Qsize;          // size of queue in bytes
   USHORT QIndex;         // index of next char out
   USHORT Qcount          // count of chars in the queue
   UCHAR  buf[Qsize]      // start of queue buffer
} CHARQUEUE;
```

QueueWrite *Mode: Kernel, Interrupt*

Add a character at the end of the specified character queue.

C Calling Convention

```
if (QueueWrite((PCHARQUEUE) &CharQueue,UCHAR Char)) error

&CharQueue = address of DS relative queue
&Char      = character to write to queue
```

Comments

QueueWrite writes a single character to the specified queue. The queue must have been previously allocated and initialized with QueueInit.

```
typedef struct _CHARQUEUE {
  USHORT Qsize;             //  size of queue in bytes
  USHORT QIndex;            //  index of next char out
  USHORT Qcount             //  count of chars in the queue
  UCHAR  buf[Qsize]         //  start of queue buffer
  } CHARQUEUE;
```

Register   *Mode: Kernel*

Add a device monitor.

C Calling Convention

```
if (Register(SHANDLE Handle,USHORT Position,PID,(FARPOINTER) &Inbuf,
   (OFF) &Outbuf,(PERRCODE) &Error)) error

Handle   = monitor handle
Position = position in chain
PID      = PID of owning program
&Inbuf   = far address of monitor input buffer
&Outbuf  = short offset of output buffer
&Error   = far address of returned error code
```

Comments

Register adds a device monitor to the chain of monitors for a class of device.

This function may be called at task time only. The monitor chain must have previously been created with MonCreate.

A single process may register more than one monitor (with different input and output buffers) with the same monitor chain. The first word of each of the input and output buffers must contain the length in bytes (length-word inclusive) of the buffers. The length of the monitor's input and output buffers must be greater than the length of the device driver's monitor chain buffer plus 20 bytes.

The input buffer, output buffer offset, and placement flag are supplied to the device driver by the monitor application that is requesting monitor registration.

The device driver must identify the monitor chain with the monitor handle returned from a previous MonCreate call. The device driver can determine the PID of the requesting monitor task by calling GetDOSVar, and retrieving it from the local infoseg.

RegisterBeep   *Mode: Kernel, Init*

Register the beep service entry point.

C Calling Convention

```
if (RegisterBeep((FPFUNCTION) &BeepRoutine)) error

&BeepRoutine = 16:16 address of driver's beep routine
```

Comments

RegisterBeep is called by the clock device driver during initialization time to register its beep service entry point.

RegisterDeviceClass Mode: Kernel, Interrupt, Init

Register an ADD Device Class.

C Calling Convention

```
if (RegisterDeviceClass(&DDName,&CmdHandler,Flags,Class,&Handle)) error

&DDName      =     ASCIIZ driver name
&CmdHandler  =     16:16 address of ADD's command handler
Flags        =     0 for ADDs
Class        =     1 for ADDs
&Handle      =     address of returned ADD handle
```

Comments

If this call fails, the driver should fail quietly by returning RPDONE | ERROR_I24_QUIET+INIT_FAIL.

Information about each registered device is kept in a class table. The driver can obtain a 16:16 pointer to the table by calling the GetDosVar DevHlp with the DHGETDOSV_DEVICECLASSTABLE option. The class table format is described in Figure A-1.

A device driver can derive an ADD's entry point using the ADD's handle by calling GetDOSVar, and then using the code stub shown in Figure A-2.

```
//
// Device Class Structure -  returned by dh_GetDOSVar when
// AL=DHGETDOSV_DEVICECLASSTABLE and CX = device_class
//
//

#define   MAXDEVCLASSNAMELEN 16   //   Max len of DevClass Name
#define   MAXDEVCLASSTABLES    2  //   Max num of DevClass tables

#define   MAXDISKDCENTRIES    32  //   Max num of entries in DISK table
#define   MAXMOUSEDCENTRIES    3  //   Max num of entries in Mouse table

// structures for the DeviceClassTable

struct DevClassTableEntry
{
  USHORT    DCOffset;
  USHORT    DCSelector;
  USHORT    DCFlags;
  UCHAR     DCName[MAXDEVCLASSNAMELEN];
};


struct DevClassTableStruc
{
  USHORT                  DCCount;
  USHORT                  DCMaxCount;
  struct DevClassTableEntry DCTableEntries[1];
};
```

Figure A-1. ADD Device Class Table.

```
{
    USHORT Index = AddHandle-1

    AddSel = pClassTable->DCTableEntries[Index].DCSelector;
    AddOff = pClassTable->DCTableEntries[Index].DCOffset;
}
```

Figure A-2. Retreiving an ADD's entry point using GetDOSVar.

RegisterPDD   *Mode: Kernel, Init*

Register a 16:16 PDD to support PDD-VDD communications.

C Calling Convention

```
if (RegisterPDD((FPUCHAR) &DDName,(FPFUNCTION) &DDFunction)) error

&DDName     = address of ASCII-Z driver name
&DDFunction = 16:16 address of PDD function
```

Comments

RegisterPDD registers a 16:16 physical device driver (PDD) for PDD-VDD communication with a virtual device driver (VDD).

The function is used by a physical device driver to register its name and a communication entry point with the DOS Session Manager. Later, a virtual device driver can use VDHOpenPDD to open communication with the physical device driver.

If the function fails, a system halt will occur.

If the address of the PDD function is NULL (0;0), this call removes the registration of this physical device driver's name.

The physical device driver name supplied to this service does not need to match the string in the physical device driver's header.

If a physical device driver ever deactivates itself, it must close down any interaction with virtual device drivers.

If a physical device driver registers an entry point during initialization, but fails later during initialization, it must call this function with a NULL function pointer in order to remove the registration.

RegisterStackUsage   Mode: Init

Register interrupt stack requirements.

C Calling Convention

```
if(RegisterStackUsage((PREGSTACK) &RSUstruct)) error

&RSUstruct = DS-reative address of STACKUSAGE structure
```

Comments

RegisterStackUsage indicates the expected stack usage of the device driver to the interrupt manager.

The StackUsage data structure has the following format:

```
typedef struct _STACKUSAGE { // StackUsage struct
  USHORT  cbStruct;    // set to 14 before using
  USHORT  flags;       // Bit 0x0001 indicates that the interrupt
                       // procedure enables interrupts. All other
                       // bits are reserved.
  USHORT  iIRQ;        // IRQ of interrupt handler that is being
                       // described by the following data.
  USHORT  cbStackCLI;// Number of bytes of stack used in the
                       // interrupt proc when rupts are disabled.
  USHORT  cbStackSTI;// Num of bytes of stack after interrupt
                       // procedure enables interrupts.
  USHORT  cbStackEOI;// Number of bytes of stack used after
                       // interrupt procedure issues EOI.
  USHORT  cNest;       // Maximum number of levels that the device
                       // driver expects to nest.
} STACKUSAGE;
```

A device must issue RegisterStackUsage once for each IRQ that it expects to receive. OS/2 2.1 supports a total of 8KB of interrupt stack.

RegisterTmrDD   Mode: Init

Get pointers to Tmr variables.

C Calling Convention

```
if (RegisterTmrDD((FPFUNCTION) &TimerEntry,FPFARPOINTER &TmrRollover,
    (FPFARPOINTER) &TmrValue)) error

&TimerEntry = 16:16 address of Timer entry point
```

Comments

RegisterTmrDD sends the device driver pointers to the Tmr value and Tmr rollover count in kernel address space.

RegisterTmrDD is callable only at Timer device driver initialization time. It returns the Tmr value and rollover count.

ResetEventSem *Mode: Kernel*

Reset a 32-bit shared-event semaphore.

C Calling Convention

```
if (ResetEventSem(LHANDLE Handle,(PLINADDR) &Posts)) error

Handle = semaphore handle
&Posts = address of variable to receive # of posts before reset
```

Comments

ResetEventSem resets an event semaphore that has previously been opened with OpenEventSem.

The number of posts performed on the event before it was reset is returned to the caller in the pulPostCt parameter. If the event was already reset, the ERROR ALREADY RESET return code is returned, and zero is returned in the pulPostCt parameter. It is not reset a second time.

ResetEventSem can only be called from a Ring 0 device driver or file system driver. The handle passed in must be a handle to a shared-event semaphore. If the handle does not exist or is not a "shared-event" semaphore, or if the semaphore was not previously opened with OpenEventSem, then ERROR_INVALID_HANDLE will be returned.

To reverse this operation, call PostEventSem. This will post the event, so that any threads that were waiting for the event semaphore to be posted (with DosWaitEventSem) will be allowed to run.

ResetTimer   Mode: Kernel, Interrupt, Init

Remove a timer handler.

C Calling Convention

```
if (ResetTimer((PFUNCTION) &TimerRoutine)) error

&TimerRoutine = address of DS relative timer
```

Comments

This function removes a timer handler from the list of timer handlers. Timer handlers are analogous to the user timer interrupt (INT 1Ch) of DOS.

DS should be set to the device driver's data segment. If the device driver had done a PhysToVirt referencing the DS register, it should restore DS to the original value.

Run   Mode: Kernel, Interrupt

Run a blocked thread.

C Calling Convention

```
if (Run((ULONG) ID)) error

ID = ID of previously Blocked thread
```

Comments

This is the companion routine to Block. When Run is called, it awakens the threads that were blocked for this particular event identifier.

Run returns immediately to its caller; the awakened threads will be run at the next available opportunity. Run is often called at interrupt time.

SchedClockAddr   Mode: Kernel, Init

Get system clock tick handler address.

C Calling Convention

```
if (SchedClockAddr((PFARPOINTER) &Ptr)) error

&Ptr = DS-relative far pointer to returned address
```

Comments

This service is provided to the clock device driver to allow it to obtain a pointer to the address of the system's clock tick handler, SchedClock. SchedClock must be called on each occurrence of a periodic clock tick.

The clock device driver calls this DevHlp service during the clock device driver's initialization. SchedClock must be called at interrupt time for each periodic clock tick to indicate the passage of system time. The "tick" is then dispersed to the appropriate components of the system.

The clock device driver's interrupt handler must run with interrupts enabled as the convention, prior to issuing the EOI for the timer interrupt. Any critical processing, such as updating the fraction-of-seconds count, must be done prior to calling SchedClock. SchedClock must then be called to allow system processing prior to the dismissal of the interrupt. When SchedClock returns, the clock device driver must issue the EOI and call SchedClock again. Note that once the EOI has been issued, the device driver's interrupt handler may be reentered. The DevHlp SchedClock is also reentrant.

The device driver must not get the actual address of the SchedClock routine, but instead use the pointer returned by the DevHlp call.

SemClear   Mode: Kernel, Interrupt

Clear a 16-bit semaphore.

C Calling Convention

```
if (SemClear(LHANDLE Handle)) error

Handle = handle to semaphore
```

Comments

This function releases a semaphore and restarts any blocked threads waiting on the semaphore.

A device driver may clear either a RAM semaphore or a system semaphore. The device driver may obtain (own) a semaphore through SemRequest.

The semaphore handle for a RAM semaphore is the virtual address of the doubleword of storage allocated for the semaphore. To access a RAM semaphore at interrupt time, the device driver must locate the semaphore in the device driver's data segment.

For a system semaphore, the handle must be passed to the device driver by the caller by way of a generic IOCtl. The device driver must convert the caller's handle to a system handle with SemHandle.

A RAM semaphore can be cleared at interrupt time only if it is in storage that is directly addressable by the device driver, that is, in the device driver's data segment.

SemClear cannot be used to clear a 32-bit application semaphore.

SemHandle   Mode: Kernel, Interrupt

Get handle to a 16-bit semaphore.

C Calling Convention

```
if (SemHandle(LHANDLE Handle,USHORT Flag,(PLHANDLE) &NewHandle)) error

Handle     = handle of user's semaphore
Flag       = see comments
&NewHandle = pointer to new DD-specific handle
```

Comments

This function provides a semaphore handle to the device driver.

This function is used to convert the semaphore handle provided by the caller of the device driver to a system handle that the device driver may use. This new handle becomes the handle that the device driver uses to reference the system semaphore. This allows the system semaphore to be referenced at interrupt time by the device driver.

SemHandle is called at task time to indicate that the system semaphore is IN-USE, and is called at either task time or interrupt time to indicate that the system semaphore is NOT-IN-USE. IN-USE means that the device driver may be referencing the system semaphore. NOT-IN-USE means that the device driver has finished using the system semaphore and will not be referencing it again.

The handle of a RAM semaphore is its virtual address. SemHandle may be used for RAM semaphores. Because RAM semaphores have no system handles, SemHandle will simply return the RAM semaphore handle back to the caller.

SemHandle cannot be used to obtain the handle of a 32-bit application semaphore.

It is necessary to call SemHandle at task time to indicate that a system semaphore is IN-USE because:

1. The caller-supplied semaphore handle refers to task-specific system semaphore structures. These structures are not available at interrupt time, so SemHandle converts the task-specific handle to a system-specific handle.

2. An application could delete a system semaphore while the device driver is using it. If a second application were to create a system semaphore soon after, the system structure used by the original semaphore could be reassigned. A device driver that tried to manipulate the original process's semaphore would inadvertently manipulate the new process's semaphore. Therefore, the SemHandle IN-USE indicator increases a counter so that, although the calling thread may still delete its task-specific reference to the semaphore, the semaphore remains in the system.

SemRequest   Mode: Kernel

Request a 16-bit semaphore.

C Calling Convention

```
if (SemRequest(LHANDLE Handle,ULONG Timeout,(PERRCODE) &Error)) error

Handle    = handle of DD semaphore
Timeout   = how long to wait in ms
&Error    = far address of variable to receive error code
```

Comments

If the semaphore is already owned, the thread in the device driver is blocked until the semaphore is released or until a time-out occurs.

SemRequest checks the state of the semaphore. If it is unowned, SemRequest marks it "owned" and returns immediately to the caller. If the semaphore is owned, SemRequest will optionally block the device driver thread until the semaphore is unowned, then try again. The time-out parameter is used to place an upper limit on the amount of time to block before returning to the requesting device driver thread.

SemClear is used at either task time or interrupt time to release the semaphore.

The semaphore handle for a RAM semaphore is the virtual address of the doubleword of storage allocated for the semaphore. To access a RAM semaphore at interrupt time, the device driver must locate the semaphore in the device driver's data segment.

For a system semaphore, the handle must be passed to the device driver by the caller through a generic IOCtl. The device driver must convert the caller's handle to a system handle with SemHandle.

SemRequest may not be used to request a 32-bit application semaphore.

SendEvent   *Mode: Kernel, Interrupt*

Simulate the occurrence.

C Calling Convention

```
if (SendEvent(USHORT EventNumber,USHORT Parameter)) error

EventNumber = number of event (see comments)
Parameter   = (see comments)
```

The device driver events are described in Table A-5.

Table A-5. Device Driver Events

Event	Event number	Parameter	Comments
Session manager hot key from the mouse	0	2-byte time stamp	Where the high-order byte is in seconds and the low-order byte is in hundredths of seconds.
Ctrl + Break	1	0	
Ctrl + C	2	0	
Ctrl + NumLock	3	Foreground session number	
Ctrl + PrtSc	4	0	
Shift + PrtSc	5	0	
Session Manager hot key from the keyboard	6	Hot Key ID	The keyboard device driver uses the hot key ID, which was set by way of keyboard IOCtl 56H (SET SESSION MANAGER HOT KEY).
Reboot key sequence from the keyboard	7	0	

SetIRQ   Mode: Kernel, Init

Register for a particular interrupt.

C Calling Convention

```
if (SetIRQ(USHORT IRQNumber,(PFUNCTION) &Handler,USHORT SharedFlag)) error

IRQNumber  = IRQ level
&Handler   = offset to interrupt handler in 1st code segment
SharedFlag = shared or unshared interrupt
```

Comments

This service is used to set a hardware interrupt vector to the device driver interrupt handler.

The attempt to register an interrupt handler for an IRQ to be Shared will fail if the IRQ is already owned by another device driver as Not Shared, or is the IRQ used to cascade the slave 8259 interrupt controller (IRQ 2).

Hardware interrupt sharing is not supported on all systems. A SetIRQ request to share an interrupt level on a system where sharing is not supported (ISA bus) will return an error.

Example

```
if(SetIRQ(10,(PFUNCTION)INT_HNDLR,0))
{
      // if we failed, deinstall driver with cs+ds=0

      DosPutMessage(1, 8, devhdr[dev].DHname);
      DosPutMessage(1,strlen(IntFailMsg),IntFailMsg);
      rp->s.InitExit.finalCS = (OFF) 0;
      rp->s.InitExit.finalDS = (OFF) 0;
            return (RPDONE | RPERR | ERROR_BAD_COMMAND);
}
```

SetTimer   *Mode: Kernel, Init*

Add a timer handler.

C Calling Convention

```
if (SetTimer((PFUNCTION) &TimerHandler)) error

&TimerHandler = offset of timer handler routine in first code segment
```

Comments

SetTimer adds a timer handler to the list of timer handlers to be called on a timer tick.

The DevHlp SetTimer is a subset of the DevHlp TickCount.

This function allows a device driver to add a timer handler to a list of timer handlers called on every timer tick. A device driver may use a timer handler to drive a non-interrupt device instead of using time-outs with the Block and Run services. Timer handlers are required to save and restore registers.

A maximum of 32 timer handlers are available in the system.

SortReqPacket *Mode: Kernel*

Sort request packet queue by sector.

C Calling Convention

```
if (SortReqPacket((PQHEAD) &QueueHead,(PREQPACKET) &RequestPacket))) error

&QueueHead     = address of queue head
&RequestPacket = far address of Request Packet
```

Comments

This routine is used by block (disk) device drivers to add a new request to their work queue. This routine inserts the request packet in the linked list of request packets in the order of starting sector number.

The sorting by sector number is aimed at reducing the length and number of head seeks. This is a simple algorithm and does not account for multiple heads on the media or for a target drive in the request packet. SortReqPacket inserts the current request packet into the specified linked list of packets, sorted by starting sector number.

SortReqPacket may be used to place request packets that were allocated by an AllocReqPacket in the request packet queue.

TCYield   Mode: Kernel

Allow time-critical threads to run.

C Calling Convention

```
TCYield()
```

Comments

This function is similar to the Yield function, except that the CPU may only be yielded to a time-critical thread, if one is available.

It is not necessary for the device driver to do both a Yield and a TCYield. The TCYield function is a subset of the Yield function.

If your device driver transfers large blocks of data, you should periodically check the TCYield Flag, and call the TCYield function to yield the CPU to a time-critical thread.

The location of the TCYield Flag is obtained from the GetDOSVar call.

For performance reasons, the device driver should check the TCYield Flag once every three milliseconds. If the flag is set, then the device driver should call TCYield.

Because the device driver may relinquish control of the CPU, the device driver should not assume that the state of the interrupt flag will be preserved across a call to TCYield.

TickCount   Mode: Kernel, Interrupt, Init

Set up a timer handler with a specified time interval.

C Calling Convention

```
if (TickCount((PFUNCTION) &TimerRoutine,USHORT Count)) error

&TimerRoutine = offset of timer handler in first code segment
Count         = number of ticks
```

Comments

TickCount will register a new timer handler, or modify a previously registered timer handler, to be called on every n timer ticks instead of every timer tick.

A device driver may use a timer handler to drive a non-interrupt device, instead of using time-outs with the Block and Run services. Block and Run are costly on a character-by-character basis; the cost is one or more task switches for each character I/O. Timer handlers are required to save and restore registers.

For a previously registered timer handler, TickCount changes the number of ticks that must take place before the timer handler gets control. This will allow device drivers to support the time-out function without needing to count ticks.

UnlockSeg Mode: Kernel, Init

Unlock a memory segment.

C Calling Convention

```
if (UnLockSeg(LHANDLE Handle)) error

Handle = handle to memory area from LockSeg call
```

Comments

This DevHlp UnLocks a segment previously locked with the LockSeg DevHelp.

Example

```
if(UnLockSeg(lock_seg_han))
        return(RPDONE | RPERR | ERROR_GEN_FAILURE);
```

UnPhysToVirt — Mode: Kernel, Interrupt, Init

Release selector previously allocated by a call to PhysToVirt or PhysToUVirt.

C Calling Convention

```
if (UnPhysToVirt()) error
```

Comments

UnPhysToVirt is required to mark the completion of address conversion from PhysToVirt.

For OS/2 1.x, UnPhysToVirt must be called by the same procedure that issued the PhysToVirt when the use of converted addresses is completed and before the procedure returns to its caller. The procedure that called PhysToVirt may call other procedures before calling UnPhysToVirt. Multiple PhysToVirt calls may be issued prior to issuing the UnPhysToVirt. Only one call to UnPhysToVirt is needed.

Under OS/2 2.1, UnPhysToVirt performs no function, but is left in for compatibility with OS/2 1.x drivers.

Example

```
if (UnPhysToVirt())
      return(RPDONE | RPERR | ERROR_GEN_FAILURE);
```

UnSetIRQ   Mode: Kernel, Interrupt, Init

Remove the current hardware interrupt handler.

C Calling Convention

```
if (UnSetIRQ(USHORT IRQNum)) error

IRQNum = IRQ level to remove
```

Comments

DS must point to the device driver's data segment upon entry.

VerifyAccess *Mode: Kernel*

Verify access to the callers memory area.

C Calling Convention

```
if (VerifyAccess(SEL Sel,OFF Off,USHORT Memsize,USHORT Code)) error

Sel     = selector of memory area
Off     = offset of memory area
Memsize = number of bytes to verify
Code    = read, read/write. (see comments)
```

Comments

This routine verifies that the user process has the correct access rights for the memory that it passed to the device driver. If the process does not have the needed access rights to the memory, then it will be terminated. If it does have the needed access rights, these rights are guaranteed to remain valid until the device driver exits its Strategy routine.

A device driver can receive addresses to memory as part of a generic IOCtl request from a process. Because the operating system cannot verify addresses imbedded in the IOCtl command, the device driver must request verification in order to prevent itself from accidentally erasing memory on behalf of a user process. If the verification test fails, then VerifyAccess will terminate the process.

Once the device driver has verified that the process has the needed access to addresses of interest, it does not need to repeat the verification until it yields the CPU. When the device driver yields the CPU, all address access verifications that it has done become unreliable, except for segments that have been locked. The device driver could yield the CPU by accessing a not-present-segment, exiting its Strategy routine, or calling a DevHlp service that yields while performing the service.

Example

```
// verify caller owns this buffer area

if(VerifyAccess(
        SELECTOROF(rp->s.IOCtl.buffer), // selector
        OFFSETOF(rp->s.IOCtl.buffer),   // offset
        4,                              // 4 bytes
        0) )                            // read only
        return (RPDONE | RPERR | ERROR_GEN_FAILURE);
```

VideoPause   Mode: Kernel, Interrupt, Init

Start or stop high-priority threads.

C Calling Convention

```
if (VideoPause(USHORT PauseFlag)) error

PauseFlag = 0 - turn off pause
          = 1 - turn on pause
```

Comments

This function is called by device drivers when the controller reports a DMA overrun. VideoPause starts or stops high-priority threads. This halts threads using the CPU for video transfers, which allows the diskette DMA to complete termination properly.

Use this function after a DMA transfer retry has failed. Turn VideoPause on just long enough to accomplish the DMA transfer; otherwise, impairment of the system could occur. If multiple device drivers turn VideoPause on, it is not turned off until all device drivers have turned it off.

VirtToLin   *Mode: Kernel, Interrupt, Init*

Convert a Selector:Offset pair into a linear address.

C Calling Convention

```
if (VirtToLin((FARPOINTER) VirtAddress,(PLINADDR) &LinAddr)) error

VirtAddress = 16:16 virtual address
LinAddr     = variable to receive linear address
```

Example

```
Flags = 0x1a;

if (VirtToLin((FARPOINTER)PageList,(PLINADDR)&lpPageList));

if (VirtToLin((FARPOINTER)LockHandle,(PLINADDR)&lpLockHandle));

if (VMLock(linaddr,100,lpPageList,lpLockHandle,
    Flags,(FARPOINTER) &Elements))
{
   DosPutMessage(1, 2, CrLf);
   DosPutMessage(1, strlen(LockFailMessage), LockFailMessage);
}
else
{
   DosPutMessage(1, 2, CrLf);
   DosPutMessage(1, strlen(LockPassMessage), LockPassMessage);
}
```

VirtToPhys   *Mode: Kernel, Init*

Convert a selector-offset pair to a 32-bit physical address.

C Calling Convention

```
if (VirtToPhys((FARPOINTER) &VirtAddr,(PHYSADDR) &PhysAddr))error

&VirtAddr = virtual pointer to memory
&PhysAddr = pointer to returned physical address
```

Comments

The virtual address should be locked by way of the DevHlp Lock call prior to invoking this function, if the segment is not known to be locked already.

This function is typically used to convert a virtual address supplied by a process, by way of a generic IOCtl, in order that the memory may be accessed at interrupt time.

Example

```
// get physical address of buffer

if (VirtToPhys(
        (FARPOINTER) rp->s.IOCtl.buffer,// the virtual address
        (FARPOINTER) &appl_buffer))     // physical address
            return (RPDONE | RPERR | ERROR_GEN_FAILURE);
```

VMAlloc   Mode: Kernel, Init

Allocate memory or map a physical address.

C Calling Convention

```
if (VMAlloc((PLINADDR) &Physaddr,ULONG Size,ULONG Flags,
   (PLINADDR) &Linaddr)) error

Physaddr = physical address to be mapped
Size     = size of object in bytes
Flags    = flags used for allocation request (see comments)
&Linaddr = pointer to linear address returned
```

Comments

VMAlloc allocates virtual memory and, depending on the value of a flag, either commits physical storage or maps virtual memory to a given physical address.

VMAlloc obtains a global, Ring 0 linear mapping to a block of memory. The physical address of the memory can be specified for non-system memory, or the system will allocate the block from general system memory. A linear address is returned to address the memory. For contiguous fixed allocation requests, the physical address is also returned.

The physical address passed to VMAlloc is actually the *linear address* of a variable containing the physical address to be mapped.

Virtual memory is allocated in global (system) address space, unless private process space is requested.

Memory requested in process space can only be swappable.

If requested, memory allocated in process space can be registered under screen group switch control. In that case, a task will be denied write access to this memory unless it is in the foreground.

Flags

Bit 0, if set, specifies the creation of the object in the region below 16MB. Bit 0 is used by device drivers that cannot support more than 16MB addresses. If the device driver requests memory below 16MB, the memory must also be resident at all times.

Bit 1, if set, specifies that the object remain in memory at all times and not be swapped or moved.

Bit 2, if set, specifies the allocation of swappable memory. Bit 1 must be clear if bit 2 is set.

Bit 3, if set, specifies that the object must be in contiguous memory. Bit 1 must also be set if bit 3 is set.

Bit 4, if set, specifies linear address mapping for the physical address in the parameters. If bit 4 is set, virtual memory is mapped to a given physical address. The physical memory must be fixed or locked. This could be used for non-system memory, like memory-mapped adapters or the video buffer. If it is used for system memory, it is the device driver's responsibility to ensure that the physical pages corresponding to the PhysAddr will never move or become invalid.

Bit 5, if set, specifies that the linear address returned will be in the process address range.

Bit 6, if set, specifies that the allocated memory can be registered under screen group switch control, such as a video shadow buffer. Memory-mapping allocated with bit 6 set will be invalid when the process is not in the foreground.

Bit 7 is reserved, and should be set to 0.

Bit 8, if set, specifies that the memory only be reserved, but not actually mapped. If bit 8 is set, the linear address returned will be page-aligned. The size requested will be rounded up to the nearest page boundary. All other allocations may return byte granular size and addresses.

Bits 9-31 must be 0.

Example

```
// use VMAlloc to map the adapter address to a linear address in the
// global address space

ULONG   MapAddress  = 0xd8000;
LINADDR LinAddress  = 0;           // linear address to MapAddress
LINADDR dev_linaddr = 0;           // for global linear address

// VMalloc requires a linear address to the physical map address

VirtToLin((FARPOINTER)&MapAddress,(PLINADDR)&LinAddress);

if (VMAlloc(LinAddress,0x1000,0x3,(PLINADDR)&dev_linaddr))
{
  DosPutMessage(1, 2, CrLf);
  DosPutMessage(1, strlen(AllocFailMessage), AllocFailMessage);
}
else
{
  DosPutMessage(1, 2, CrLf);
  DosPutMessage(1, strlen(AllocPassMessage), AllocPassMessage);
}
```

VMFree   *Mode: Kernel, Init*

Free a mapping to memory.

C Calling Convention

```
if (VMFree(LINADDR Linaddr)) error

Linaddr = 32 bit linear address of memory to release
```

Comments

VMFree frees memory allocated with VMAlloc, or a mapping created by VMProcessToGlobal, or VMGlobalToProcess.

All memory-mapping allocated by the device driver must be released before device driver termination.

VMGlobalToProcess   Mode: Kernel

Map an address in the system region of the global address space into an address in the current process's address space.

C Calling Convention

```
if VMGlobalToProcess(LINADDR Linaddr,ULONG Len,ULONG Flags,
                (PLINADDR) &Plinaddr)) error

Linaddr   = linear address in global address space
Len       = length of memory to be mapped
Flags     = (see comments)
&Plinaddr = pointer to returned linear address
```

Comments

The mapping created by this call must be released with VMFree.

The address range must not cross object boundaries.

The process's address space used in this call is the current process.

Flags

Bit 0, if set, specifies read/write access, Bit 0 clear specifies read-only access.

Bit 1, if set, specifies a map of the 32-bit memory region, using 16-bit selectors.

Bit 2, if set, the mapping is tracked for the validation and invalidation of screen buffers.

Bit 3, if set, specifies that the memory be allocated on a 4K page boundary.

Bits 4-31 must be 0.

Example

```
if (VMGlobalToProcess(linaddr,0x1000,0x01,(FARPOINTER) &new_linaddr))
    return(RPDONE | RPERR | ERROR_GEN_FAILURE);
```

VMLock   Mode: Kernel, Init

Lock a memory object.

C Calling Convention

```
if (VMLock(LINADDR Linaddr,ULONG Len,(PLINADDR) &PageList,
    (PLINADDR) &LockInfo, ULONG Flags, FPULONG )) error

Linaddr    = 32 bit linear address of region to lock
Len        = 32 bit length in bytes
&PageList  = flat pointer to PAGELIST struct
&LockInfo  = linear address of 12-byte variable to receive the lock
             handle
Flags      = (see comments)
```

Each PageList structure will describe a single physically contiguous subregion of the physical memory that was locked. The format of the PageList structure is:

```
typedef struct _PAGELIST {
  ULONG pl_PhysAddr;          // physical address of first byte
                              // in this sub-region
  ULONG pl_cb;                // Number of contiguous bytes
                              // starting at pl_PhysAddr
  }
```

Comments

VMLock verifies accessibility to a region of memory and locks the memory region into physical memory. If the region is unavailable, the caller must specify whether VMLock should block until the region is available and locked, or return immediately.

The use of short-term locks for greater than two seconds can prevent an adequate number of pages from being available for system use. Under these circumstances, a system halt could occur.

If satisfying the lock request will reduce the amount of free memory in the system to below a predetermined minimum, both short- and long-term locks can fail.

Address verification is done automatically with every VMLock request. Locking down memory in fixed physical addresses is done only if the "verify only" bit is not set.

It is the device driver's responsibility to ensure that enough entries have been reserved for the range of memory being locked (possibly one entry per page in the range, plus one more if the region does not begin on a page boundary). If this pointer contains the value - 1, then no physical addresses are returned. This parameter must be - 1 for verify locks.

Since locking occurs on a per-page basis, the VMLock service routine will round linear address down to the nearest page boundary. If physically contiguous locking is requested, length cannot exceed 64KB; otherwise an error is returned. Because locking occurs on a per-page basis, the combination of linear address + length will be rounded up to the nearest page boundary.

Flags

Bit 0, if set, specifies an immediate return if the pages are not available. If bit 0 is 0, the call will block until the pages become available.

Bit 1, if set, specifies that the pages be contiguous.

Bit 2, if set, specifies that the memory be below the 16MB address line.

Bit 3, if set, specifies that the device driver plans to write to the segment.

Bit 4, if set, specifies a long-term lock.

Bit 5, if set, specifies a verify-only lock.

Bits 6-31 must be 0.

Example

```
Flags = 0x1a;

if (VirtToLin((FARPOINTER)PageList,(PLINADDR)&lpPageList));

if (VirtToLin((FARPOINTER)LockHandle,(PLINADDR)&lpLockHandle));

if (VMLock(linaddr,100,lpPageList,lpLockHandle,
    Flags,(FARPOINTER) &Elements))
{
   DosPutMessage(1, 2, CrLf);
   DosPutMessage(1, strlen(LockFailMessage), LockFailMessage);
}
else
{
   DosPutMessage(1, 2, CrLf);
   DosPutMessage(1, strlen(LockPassMessage), LockPassMessage);
}
```

VMProcessToGlobal *Mode: Kernel*

Map an address in the current process address space to an address in the system region of the global address space.

C Calling Convention

```
if (VMProcessToGlobal(LINADDR Linaddr,ULONG Len,ULONG Flags,
    (PLINADDR) &Address)) error

Linaddr  = linear address within process address space that is to be
           mapped into a global context
Len      = len in bytes
Flags    = (see comments)
&Address = pointer to linear address returned
```

Comments

The address range must be on a page boundary and must not cross object boundaries.

Flags

Bit 0, if set, specifies that the mapping be writable, If clear, the mapping will be read-only.

Bits 1-31 must be 0.

This call copies the linear mapping from the process's address space to the system shared address space, which allows the device driver to access the data independent of the current process's context. The following steps show how you would use the DevHlp services to gain interrupt-time access to a process's buffer.

1. Call VMLock to verify the address and to lock the range of memory needed into physical memory.

2. Call VMProcessToGlobal to map a process's private address into global address space. If the device driver requests it, an array of physical addresses corresponding to the locked region will be returned. You may also map the linear address to a GDT selector by calling LinToGDTSelector.

3. Access the memory using the linear address returned by the call to VMProcessToGlobal.

4. Call VMFree to remove global mapping to process address space.

5. Call VMUnlock to unlock the object.

Example

```
if (VMGlobalToProcess(linaddr,0x1000,0x01,(FARPOINTER) &new_linaddr))
    return(RPDONE | RPERR | ERROR_GEN_FAILURE);
```

VMSetMem   Mode: Kernel, Init

Commit and decommit physical storage.

C Calling Convention

```
if (VMSetMem(LINADDR Linaddr,ULONG Size,ULONG Flags)) error

Linaddr  = linear address, page aligned, of memory
Size     = size in bytes in 4k pages
Flags    = (see comments)
```

Comments

VMSetMem commits and decommits physical storage, or changes the type of committed memory reserved with the VMAlloc DevHlp service. The address range specified must not cross object boundaries. The range must be entirely of uniform type, that is, all decommitted (invalid), all swappable, or all resident. The range to be decommitted must be entirely precommitted.

The entire region (linear address + size) must lie within a memory object previously allocated with a VMAlloc 'Reserved Only' call.

Flags

Bit 0, if set, specifies that the address range is to be decommitted.

Bit 1, if set, specifies that the address range is to be made resident.

Bit 2, if set, specifies that the address range is to be made swappable.

VMUnlock   Mode: Kernel, Init

Unlock a memory object.

C Calling Convention

```
if (VMUnlock(LHANDLE LockHandle)) error

LockHandle = handle from VMLock
```

Comments

VMUnlock unlocks a previously locked memory range.

A successful Unlock may modify the caller's lock handle.

Yield   Mode: Kernel

Yield the CPU to higher priority threads.

C Calling Convention

```
Yield();
```

Comments

OS/2 is designed so that the CPU is never scheduled preemptively while in kernel mode. In general, the kernel either performs its job and exits quickly, or it blocks waiting for (usually) I/O or (occasionally) a resource. It is not necessary for the device driver to do both a Yield and a TCYield; the Yield function is a superset of the TCYield function.

The one part of the kernel that can take a lot of CPU time are device drivers, particularly those that perform program I/O on long strings of data, or that poll the device. These drivers should periodically check the Yield Flag and call the Yield function to yield the CPU if another process needs it. Much of the time the context won't switch; Yield switches context only if an equal or higher priority thread is scheduled to run.

The address of the Yield Flag is obtained from the GetDOSVar call. For performance reasons, the device driver should check the Yield Flag once every 3 milliseconds. If the flag is set, then the device driver should call Yield.

Because the device driver may relinquish control of the CPU to another thread, the device driver should not assume that the state of the interrupt flag will be preserved across a call to Yield.

APPENDIX B

Reference Publications

Bowlds, Pat, *Micro Channel Architecture*, New York: Van Nostrand Reinhold, 1991.

Deitel, H. M.; Kogan, M. S., *The Design of OS/2*, New York: Addison-Wesley, 1992.

IBM Corporation, *IBM Operating System/2 Programming Tools and Information: IBM*, 1992.

IBM Corporation, *IBM OS/2 2.1 Physical Device Driver Reference: IBM*, 1992.

IBM Corporation, *IBM OS/2 2.1 Presentation Driver Reference: IBM*, 1992.

IBM Corporation, *IBM OS/2 2.1 Virtual Device Driver Reference: IBM*, 1992.

IBM Corporation, *IBM OS/2 2.1 Control Program Reference: IBM*, 1992.

Intel Corporation, *iAPX 86/88 User's Manual Hardware Reference: Intel*, 1989.

Letwin, Gordon, *Inside OS/2, Redmond*, Washington: Microsoft Press, 1988.

APPENDIX C

Listings

Device Header, One Device

```
// sample Device Header, 1 device

DEVICEHDR devhdr = {
 (void far *) 0xFFFFFFFF,          // link
 (DAW_CHR | DAW_OPN | DAW_LEVEL1), // attribute
 (OFF) STRAT,                      // &strategy
 (OFF) 0,                          // &IDCroutine
 "DEVICE1 "                        // device name
 };
```

Device Header, Two Devices

```
DEVICEHDR devhdr[2] = {
 { (void far *) &devhdr[1],        // link to next dev
 (DAW_CHR | DAW_OPN | DAW_LEVEL1), // attribute
 (OFF) STRAT1,                     // &strategy
 (OFF) 0,                          // &IDCroutine
 "DEVICE1 "
 },

 {(void far *) 0xFFFFFFFF,         // link(no more devs)
 (DAW_CHR | DAW_OPN | DAW_LEVEL1), // attribute
 (OFF) STRAT2,                     // &strategy
 (OFF) 0,                          // &IDCroutine
 "DEVICE2 "
 }
};
```

C Startup Routine, One Device

```
;
;       C startup routine, one device, w/interrupt and timer
;
        PUBLIC  _STRAT
        PUBLIC  __acrtused
        PUBLIC  _INT_HNDLR
        PUBLIC  _TIM_HNDLR

        EXTRN   _interrupt_handler:near
        EXTRN   _timer_handler:near
        EXTRN   _main:near

_DATA   segment word public 'DATA'
_DATA   ends

CONST   segment word public 'CONST'
CONST   ends

_BSS    segment word public 'BSS'
_BSS    ends

DGROUP          group   CONST, _BSS, _DATA

_TEXT   segment word public 'CODE'

        assume  cs:_TEXT,ds:DGROUP,es:NOTHING, ss:NOTHING
        .286P
;
_STRAT proc     far
__acrtused:                     ; no startup code
;
        push    0
        jmp     start           ;signal device 0
;
start:
        push    es              ;send Request Packet address
        push    bx
        call    _main           ;call driver mainline
        pop     bx              ;restore es:bx
```

```
        pop     es
        add     sp,2                    ;clean up stack
        mov     word ptr es:[bx+3],ax   ;send completion status
        ret
;
_STRAT  endp
;
_INT_HNDLR proc far
;
        call    _interrupt_handler      ;handle rupts
        ret                             ;bail out
;
_INT_HNDLR endp
;
_TIM_HNDLR proc far
;
        pusha
        push    es
        push    ds
        call    _timer_handler
        pop     ds
        pop     es
        popa
        ret
;
_TIM_HNDLR endp
;
_TEXT   ends
        end
```

C Startup Routine, Four Devices

```
;
;     C startup routine, 4 devices
;
        PUBLIC   _STRAT1
        PUBLIC   _STRAT2
        PUBLIC   _STRAT3
        PUBLIC   _STRAT4
        PUBLIC   __acrtused
        PUBLIC   _INT_HNDLR
        PUBLIC   _TIM_HNDLR

        EXTRN    _interrupt_handler:near
        EXTRN    _timer_handler:near
        EXTRN    _main:near

_DATA   segment word public 'DATA'
_DATA   ends

CONST   segment word public 'CONST'
CONST   ends

_BSS    segment word public 'BSS'
_BSS    ends

DGROUP  group   CONST, _BSS, _DATA

_TEXT   segment word public 'CODE'

        assume   cs:_TEXT,ds:DGROUP,es:NOTHING,ss:NOTHING
        .286P
;
_STRAT1 proc    far
__acrtused:              ; satisfy EXTRN modules
;
        push    0
        jmp     start           ;signal device 0

_STRAT1 endp
```

```
_STRAT2 proc far
;
        push    1               ;signal second device
        jmp     start

_STRAT2 endp

_STRAT3 proc far
;
        push    2               ;signal third device
        jmp     start

_STRAT3 endp

_STRAT4 proc far
;
        push    3               ;signal fourth device
        jmp     start

;
start:
        push    es              ;send Request Pkt address
        push    bx
        call    _main           ;call driver mainline
        pop     bx              ;restore es:bx
        pop     es
        add     sp,2            ;clean up stack
        mov     word ptr es:[bx+3],ax ;send completion status
        ret
;
_STRAT4 endp
;
_INT_HNDLR proc far
;
        call    _interrupt_handler ;handle rupts
        ret                     ;bail out
;
_INT_HNDLR endp
;
```

```
_TIM_HNDLR proc far
;
        pusha
        push    es
        push    ds
        call    _timer_handler
        pop     ds
        pop     es
        popa
        ret
;
_TIM_HNDLR endp
;
_TEXT   ends
        end
```

Standard OS/2 Device Driver Include File

```
//   file drvlib.h
//   This header file contains definitions intended to go along
//   with DRVLIB.LIB, a C-callable subroutine library.
//
//   This file is for OS/2 2.1

typedef unsigned char      UCHAR;
typedef unsigned short     USHORT;
typedef unsigned short     BOOLEAN;
typedef unsigned long      ULONG;
typedef UCHAR near         *PUCHAR;
typedef UCHAR far          *FPUCHAR;
typedef USHORT near        *PUSHORT;
typedef USHORT far         *FPUSHORT;
typedef ULONG near         *PULONG;
typedef ULONG far          *FPULONG;
typedef char near          *PCHAR;
typedef short near         *PSHORT;
typedef long near          *PLONG;
typedef void near          *POINTER;
```

```
typedef POINTER near      *PPOINTER;
typedef void far          *FARPOINTER;
typedef FARPOINTER near   *PFARPOINTER;
typedef FARPOINTER far    *FPFARPOINTER;

typedef USHORT            ERRCODE;     // error code returned
typedef ERRCODE far       *PERRCODE;   // pointer to an error code
typedef UCHAR             FLAG;        // 8-bit flag
typedef FLAG far          *PFLAG;      // pointer to 8-bit flag
typedef USHORT            SEL;         // 16-bit selector
typedef SEL near          *PSEL;       // pointer to a selector
typedef SEL far           *FPSEL;      // far pointer to selector
typedef USHORT            SEG;         // 16-bit segment
typedef USHORT            OFF;         // 16-bit offset
typedef ULONG             LOFF;        // 32-bit offset
typedef USHORT            PID;         // Process ID
typedef USHORT            TID;         // Thread ID
typedef ULONG             PHYSADDR;    // 32-bit physical address
typedef ULONG             LINADDR;     // 32-bit linear address
typedef LINADDR  far      *PLINADDR;   // pointer to 32 bit lin addr
typedef PLINADDR far      *PPLINADDR;  // pointer to lin addr pointer
typedef PHYSADDR far      *PPHYSADDR;  // pointer to 32-bit phys addr
typedef char near         *PSTRING;    // pointer to character string
typedef char far          *FPSTRING;   // far pointer to string
typedef USHORT            SHANDLE;     // short (16-bit) handle
typedef SHANDLE far       *PSHANDLE;   // pointer to a short handle
typedef ULONG             LHANDLE;     // long (32-bit) handle
typedef LHANDLE far       *PLHANDLE;   // pointer to a long handle

// pointers to functions

typedef int (pascal near          *PFUNCTION) ();
typedef int (pascal near * near   *PPFUNCTION) ();
typedef int (pascal far           *FPFUNCTION) ();
typedef int (pascal far  * near *PFPFUNCTION) ();

// macros

#define FALSE   0
#define TRUE    1
```

```c
#define NP near pascal

// far pointer from selector-offset

#define MAKEP(sel, off)      ( (void far *) MAKEULONG(off, sel) )

// get selector or offset from far pointer

#define SELECTOROF(p)        ( ((USHORT far *) &(p)) [1])
#define OFFSETOF(p)          ( ((USHORT far *) &(p)) [0])

// Combine l(ow) & h(igh) to form a 32 bit quantity.

#define MAKEULONG(l, h) ((ULONG)(((USHORT)(l))|((ULONG)((USHORT)(h)))<<16))
#define MAKELONG(l, h)   ((LONG)MAKEULONG(l, h))
#define MAKEBIGOFFSETOF(p) ((ULONG) (OFFSETOF (p)))

// Combine l(ow) & h(igh) to form a 16 bit quantity.

#define MAKEUSHORT(l, h) (((USHORT)(l)) | ((USHORT)(h)) << 8)
#define MAKESHORT(l, h)  ((SHORT)MAKEUSHORT(l, h))

// get high and low order parts of a 16 and 32 bit quantity

#define LOBYTE(w)       LOUCHAR(w)
#define HIBYTE(w)       HIUCHAR(w)
#define LOUCHAR(w)      ((UCHAR)(w))
#define HIUCHAR(w)      (((USHORT)(w) >> 8) & 0xff)
#define LOUSHORT(l)     ((USHORT)(l))
#define HIUSHORT(l)     ((USHORT)(((ULONG)(l) >> 16) & 0xffff))

//   the driver device header

typedef struct DeviceHdr {
   struct DeviceHdr far *DHnext;   // pointer to next header,or -1
   USHORT DHattribute;             // device attribute word
   OFF    DHstrategy;              // offset of strategy routine
   OFF    DHidc;                   // offset of IDC routine
   UCHAR  DHname[8];               // dev name (char) or #units
   char   reserved[8];
   ULONG  bit_strip;               // bit 0 DevIOCtl2,bit 1 32 bit
```

```c
    } DEVICEHDR;
typedef DEVICEHDR near *PDEVICEHDR;

//   driver device attributes word

#define DAW_CHR      0x8000           // 1=char, 0=block
#define DAW_IDC      0x4000           // 1=IDC available in this DD
#define DAW_IBM      0x2000           // 1=non-IBM block format
#define DAW_SHR      0x1000           // 1=supports shared dev access
#define DAW_OPN      0x0800           // 1=open/close, or rem. media
#define DAW_LEVEL1   0x0080           // level 1
#define DAW_LEVEL2   0x0100           // level 2 DosDevIOCtl2
#define DAW_LEVEL3   0x0180           // level 3 bit strip
#define DAW_GIO      0x0040           // 1=generic IOCtl supported
#define DAW_CLK      0x0008           // 1=CLOCK device
#define DAW_NUL      0x0004           // 1=NUL device
#define DAW_SCR      0x0002           // 1=STDOUT (screen)
#define DAW_KBD      0x0001           // 1=STDIN  (keyboard)

// capabilities bit strip

#define CBS_SHD      0x0001           // 1=shutdown/DevIOCtl2
#define CBS_HMEM     0x0002           // high memory map for adapters
#define CBS_PP       0x0004           // supports parallel ports
#define CBS_ADD      0x0010           // driver is an ADD driver
#define CBS_INIT     0x0020           // CmdInit call from kernel

// SaveMessage structure

typedef struct MessageTable {
    USHORT       id;
    USHORT       fill_in_item;
    FARPOINTER   item1;
    FARPOINTER   item2;
    FARPOINTER   item_last;
    } MESSAGETABLE;

// OS/2 circular character queues

#define QUEUE_SIZE   512              // size of queues
typedef struct CharQueue {
```

```
    USHORT    qsize;                    // number of bytes in queue
    USHORT    qchrout;                  // index of next char to put out
    USHORT    qcount;                   // number of charactes in queue
    UCHAR     qbuf[QUEUE_SIZE];
    } CHARQUEUE;
typedef CHARQUEUE near *PCHARQUEUE;

// AttachDD inter device driver communication data area

typedef struct AttachArea {
    OFF  realOFF;                       // real-mode off of idc ent pt
    SEG  realCS;                        // real-mode CS of IDC ent pt
    SEG  realDS;                        // real-mode DS of IDC DD
    OFF  protOFF;                       // protect-mode off of ent pt
    SEL  protCS;                        // protect-mode CS of ent pt
    SEL  protDS;                        // protect-mode DS of other DD
    } ATTACHAREA;
typedef ATTACHAREA near *PATTACHAREA;

// driver request packet

typedef struct ReqPacket {
    UCHAR RPlength;                     // request packet length
    UCHAR   RPunit;                     // unit code for block DD only
    UCHAR RPcommand;                    // command code
    USHORT  RPstatus;                   // status word
    UCHAR   RPreserved[4];              // reserved bytes
    ULONG RPqlink;                      // queue linkage
    union {                             // command-specific data
    UCHAR    avail[19];
     struct {                           // init
       UCHAR     units;                 // number of units
       FPFUNCTION DevHlp;               // &DevHlp
       char far  *args;                 // &args
       UCHAR     drive;                 // drive #
      }Init;
     struct {
       UCHAR     units;                 // same as input
       OFF       finalCS;               // final offset, 1st code seg
       OFF       finalDS;               // final offset, 1st data seg
       FARPOINTER BPBarray;             // &BPB
```

```
    } InitExit;

struct {                            // read, write, write w/verify
   UCHAR       media;               // media descriptor
   PHYSADDR    buffer;              // transfer address
   USHORT      count;               // bytes/sectors
   ULONG       startsector;         // starting sector#
   USHORT      reserved;
   } ReadWrite;

struct {                            // cached read, write,write ver
   UCHAR       media;               // media descriptor
   PHYSADDR    buffer;              // transfer address
   USHORT      count;               // bytes/sectors
   ULONG       startsector;         // starting sector#
   USHORT      reserved;
   } CReadWrite;

struct {                            // system shutdown
   UCHAR       subcode;             // sub request code
   ULONG       reserved;
   } Shutdown;

struct {                            // open/close
   USHORT      sysfilenum;          // system file number
   } OpenClose;

struct {                            // IOCtl
   UCHAR       category;            // category code
   UCHAR       function;            // function code
   FARPOINTER  parameters;          // &parameters
   FARPOINTER  buffer;              // &buffer
   } IOCtl;

struct {                            // read, no wait
   UCHAR       char_returned;       // char to return
   } ReadNoWait;

struct {                            // media check
   UCHAR       media;               // media descriptor
   UCHAR       return_code;         // see #defines
```

```
        FARPOINTER prev_volume;        // &previous volume ID
      } MediaCheck;

    struct {                           // build BPB
      UCHAR     media;                 // media descriptor
      FARPOINTER buffer;               // 1-sector buffer FAT
      FARPOINTER BPBarray;             // &BPB array
      UCHAR     drive;                 // drive #
      } BuildBPB;

    struct {                           // query part. fixed disks
      UCHAR     count;                 // # disks
      ULONG     reserved;
      } Partitionable;

    struct {                           // fixed disk LU map
      ULONG     units;                 // units supported
      ULONG     reserved;
      } GetFixedMap;

    struct {                           // get driver capabilities
      UCHAR     reserved[3];
      FARPOINTER capstruct;            // 16:16 pointer to DCS
      FARPOINTER volcharstruct;        // 16:16 pointer to VCS
      } GetDriverCaps;

    } s;                               // command info
} REQPACKET;

typedef REQPACKET far *PREQPACKET;
typedef PREQPACKET far *PPREQPACKET;
typedef PREQPACKET QHEAD;              // Queue Head is &ReqPacket
typedef QHEAD near *PQHEAD;

// Global Info Seg

typedef struct _GINFOSEG {
    ULONG    time;                     // time in seconds
    ULONG    msecs;                    // milliseconds
    UCHAR    hour;                     // hours
    UCHAR    minutes;                  // minutes
```

```c
        UCHAR   seconds;                    // seconds
        UCHAR   hundredths;                 // hundredths
        USHORT  timezone;                   // minutes from UTC
        USHORT  cusecTimerInterval;         // timer interval, .0001 secs
        UCHAR   day;                        // day of month
        UCHAR   month;                      // month, 1-12
        USHORT  year;                       // year
        UCHAR   weekday;                    // day of week,0-Sunday,1=Monday…
        UCHAR   uchMajorVersion;            // major version number
        UCHAR   uchMinorVersion;            // minor version number
        UCHAR   chRevisionLetter;           // rev level
        UCHAR   sgCurrent;                  // current foreground session
        UCHAR   sgMax;                      // max number of sessions
        UCHAR   cHugeShift;                 // shift count for huge elements
        UCHAR   fProtectModeOnly;           // protect mode only
        USHORT  pidForeground;              // pid of last process in foreground
        UCHAR   fDynamicSched;              // dynamic variation flag
        UCHAR   csecMaxWait;                // max wait in seconds
        USHORT  cmsecMinSlice;              // min timeslice in milliseconds
        USHORT  cmsecMaxSlice;              // max timeslice in milliseconds
        USHORT  bootdrive;                  // boot drive (0=a, 1=b…)
        UCHAR   amecRAS[32];                // system trace major code flag bits
        UCHAR   csgWindowableVioMax;        // max number of VIO sessions
        UCHAR   csgPMMax;                   // max number of PM sessions
} GINFOSEG;
typedef GINFOSEG far *PGINFOSEG;

// local info seg

typedef struct _LINFOSEG {
        PID     pidCurrent;                 // current process pid
        PID     pidParent;                  // process id of parent
        USHORT  prtyCurrent;                // priority of current thread
        TID     tidCurrent;                 // thread id of current thread
        USHORT  sgCurrent;                  // current session id
        UCHAR   rfProcStatus;               // process status
        UCHAR   dummy1;                     // reserved
        USHORT  fForeground;                // current process is in foreground
        UCHAR   typeProcess;                // process type
        UCHAR   dummy2;                     // reserved
        SEL     selEnvironment;             // selector of environment
```

```c
    USHORT  offCmdLine;         // command line offset
    USHORT  cbDataSegment;      // length of data segment
    USHORT  cbStack;            // stack size
    USHORT  cbHeap;             // heap size
    USHORT  hmod;               // module handle of application
    SEL     selDS;              // data segment handle of application
} LINFOSEG;

typedef LINFOSEG far *PLINFOSEG;

typedef struct _REGSTACK {      // stack usage structure
        USHORT  usStruct;       // set to 14 before using
        USHORT  usFlags;        // 0x01 means that the interrupt proc
                                // enables interrupts. All others resvd
        USHORT  usIRQ;          // IRQ of interrupt handler
        USHORT  usStackCLI;     // # of stack bytes with interrupts off
        USHORT  usStackSTI;     // # of stack bytes with interrupts on
        USHORT  usStackEOI;     // number of bytes needed after EOI
        USHORT  usNest;         // max number of nested levels
        } REGSTACK;

typedef REGSTACK near *PREGSTACK;

// page list struct

typedef struct _PAGELIST {
    ULONG pl_Physaddr;
        ULONG pl_cb;
        } PAGELIST;
typedef PAGELIST far *PPAGELIST;

// RPstatus bit values

#define RPERR    0x8000         // error occurred, err in RPstatus
#define RPDEV    0x4000         // error code defined by driver
#define RPBUSY   0x0200         // device is busy
#define RPDONE   0x0100         // driver done with request packet

// error codes returned in RPstatus

#define ERROR_WRITE_PROTECT     0x0000
```

```c
#define ERROR_BAD_UNIT              0x0001
#define ERROR_NOT_READY             0x0002
#define ERROR_BAD_COMMAND           0x0003
#define ERROR_CRC                   0x0004
#define ERROR_BAD_LENGTH            0x0005
#define ERROR_SEEK                  0x0006
#define ERROR_NOT_DOS_DISK          0x0007
#define ERROR_SECTOR_NOT_FOUND      0x0008
#define ERROR_OUT_OF_PAPER          0x0009
#define ERROR_WRITE_FAULT           0x000A
#define ERROR_READ_FAULT            0x000B
#define ERROR_GEN_FAILURE           0x000C
#define ERROR_DISK_CHANGE           0x000D
#define ERROR_WRONG_DISK            0x000F
#define ERROR_UNCERTAIN_MEDIA       0x0010
#define ERROR_CHAR_CALL_INTERRUPTED 0x0011
#define ERROR_NO_MONITOR_SUPPORT    0x0012
#define ERROR_INVALID_PARAMETER     0x0013
#define ERROR_DEVICE_IN_USE         0x0014

// driver request codes  B=block, C=character

#define RPINIT          0x00    //  BC
#define RPMEDIA_CHECK   0x01    //  B
#define RPBUILD_BPB     0x02    //  B
#define RPREAD          0x04    //  BC
#define RPREAD_NO_WAIT  0x05    //  C
#define RPINPUT_STATUS  0x06    //  C
#define RPINPUT_FLUSH   0x07    //  C
#define RPWRITE         0x08    //  BC
#define RPWRITE_VERIFY  0x09    //  BC
#define RPOUTPUT_STATUS 0x0a    //  C
#define RPOUTPUT_FLUSH  0x0b    //  C
#define RPOPEN          0x0d    //  BC
#define RPCLOSE         0x0e    //  BC
#define RPREMOVABLE     0x0f    //  B
#define RPIOCTL         0x10    //  BC
#define RPRESET         0x11    //  B
#define RPGET_DRIVE_MAP 0x12    //  B
#define RPSET_DRIVE_MAP 0x13    //  B
#define RPDEINSTALL     0x14    //  C
```

```c
#define RPPARTITIONABLE 0x16        //  B
#define RPGET_FIXED_MAP 0x17        //  B
#define RPSHUTDOWN      0x1c        //  BC
#define RPGET_DRIVER_CAPS 0x1d      //  B
#define RPINIT_DONE     0x1f        //  BC

// check for monitor call in DosOpen/DosClose

#define MON_OPEN_STATUS   0x08      // open from DosMonOpen
#define MON_CLOSE_STATUS  0x08      // close from DosMonClose

// media descriptor byte

#define MDB_REMOVABLE     0x04      //  1=removable
#define MDB_EIGHT_SECTORS 0x02      //  1=8 sectors per track
#define MDB_DOUBLE_SIDED  0x01      //  1=double-sided media

// return codes from MediaCheck

#define MC_MEDIA_UNCHANGED 0x01
#define MC_MEDIA_CHANGED   0xFF
#define MC_MEDIA_UNSURE    0x00

// event numbers for SendEvent

#define EVENT_SM_MOUSE    0x00      // session switch via mouse
#define EVENT_CTRLBRK     0x01      // control break
#define EVENT_CTRLC       0x02      // control C
#define EVENT_CTRLNUMLK   0x03      // control num lock
#define EVENT_CTRLPRTSC   0x04      // control printscreen
#define EVENT_SHFTPRTSC   0x05      // shift printscreen
#define EVENT_SM_KBD      0x06      // session switch hot key

// defines for 1.x movedata function

#define   MOVE_PHYSTOPHYS  0        // move bytes from phys to phys
#define   MOVE_PHYSTOVIRT  1        // move bytes from phys to virt
#define   MOVE_VIRTTOPHYS  2        // move bytes from virt to phys
#define   MOVE_VIRTTOVIRT  3        // move bytes from virt to virt

// Micro Channel specific
```

```
int  NP GetLIDEntry    (USHORT, USHORT, USHORT, FPUSHORT);
int  NP FreeLIDEntry   (USHORT);
int  NP ABIOSCall      (USHORT, USHORT, FARPOINTER);
int  NP ABIOSComm      (USHORT, FARPOINTER);
int  NP GetDeviceBlock(USHORT, FARPOINTER);

// special routines

void NP INT3       (void);
void NP Enable     (void);
void NP Disable    (void);
void NP Abort      (void);
int  NP SegLimit   (SEL,OFF far *);
int  NP MoveBytes  (FARPOINTER,FARPOINTER,FLAG);
int  NP MoveData   (FARPOINTER,FARPOINTER,USHORT,USHORT);

// system services and misc.

int  NP GetDOSVar      (USHORT,FPFARPOINTER);
int  NP SendEvent      (USHORT,USHORT);
void NP SchedClockAddr(PFARPOINTER);
int  NP AttachDD       (PSTRING,PATTACHAREA);
int  NP InternalError (PSTRING,USHORT);
int  NP SaveMessage    (FPSTRING);
int  NP ProtToReal     (void);
int  NP RealToProt     (void);
int  NP SetROMVector   (USHORT,PFUNCTION,PFUNCTION,FARPOINTER);

// process mgmt

void NP Yield      (void);
void NP TCYield    (void);
int  NP Block      (ULONG,ULONG,USHORT,FARPOINTER);
void NP Run        (ULONG);
void NP DevDone    (PREQPACKET);
int  NP VideoPause(USHORT);

// memory management

int  NP AllocPhys     (ULONG,USHORT,PPHYSADDR);
```

```
int  NP FreePhys        (PHYSADDR);
int  NP VerifyAccess    (SEL,OFF,USHORT,USHORT);
int  NP LockSeg         (SEL,USHORT,USHORT,PLHANDLE);
int  NP UnLockSeg       (LHANDLE);

// address conversion

int  NP AllocGDTSelector (USHORT,FARPOINTER);
int  NP PhysToGDTSelector(PHYSADDR,USHORT,SEL,PERRCODE);
int  NP VirtToPhys      (FARPOINTER,PPHYSADDR);
int  NP PhysToUVirt     (PHYSADDR,USHORT,USHORT,FPFARPOINTER);
int  NP PhysToVirt      (PHYSADDR,USHORT,USHORT,FARPOINTER);
int  NP UnPhysToVirt    (void);

// request packet queue stuff

int  NP AllocReqPacket(USHORT,PPREQPACKET);
void NP FreeReqPacket (PREQPACKET);
void NP PushReqPacket (PQHEAD,PREQPACKET);
void NP SortReqPacket (PQHEAD,PREQPACKET);
int  NP PullReqPacket (PQHEAD,PPREQPACKET);
int  NP PullParticular(PQHEAD,PREQPACKET);

// driver semaphores

int  NP SemHandle  (LHANDLE,FLAG,PLHANDLE);
int  NP SemRequest (LHANDLE,ULONG,PERRCODE);
void NP SemClear   (LHANDLE);

// circular character queues

void NP QueueInit  (PCHARQUEUE);
void NP QueueFlush (PCHARQUEUE);
int  NP QueueWrite (PCHARQUEUE,UCHAR);
int  NP QueueRead  (PCHARQUEUE,FPUCHAR);

// interrupt stuff

int  NP SetIRQ          (USHORT,PFUNCTION,USHORT);
int  NP UnSetIRQ        (USHORT);
int  NP EOI             (USHORT);
```

```
void NP ClaimInterrupt    (void);
void NP RefuseInterrupt   (void);
int  NP RegisterStackUsage(PREGSTACK);

// timer stuff

int  NP SetTimer    (PFUNCTION);
int  NP ResetTimer  (PFUNCTION);
int  NP TickCount   (PFUNCTION,USHORT);

// device monitors

int  NP MonCreate  (PSHANDLE,FARPOINTER,FARPOINTER,PERRCODE);
int  NP Register   (SHANDLE,USHORT,PID,FARPOINTER,OFF,PERRCODE);
int  NP MonWrite   (SHANDLE,POINTER,USHORT,USHORT,ULONG,PERRCODE);
int  NP MonFlush   (SHANDLE,PERRCODE);
int  NP DeRegister (SHANDLE,PID,PERRCODE);

// 2.1   specfic

int  NP RegisterPDD         (FPUCHAR,FPFUNCTION);
int  NP RegisterBeep        (FPFUNCTION);
int  NP Beep                (USHORT,USHORT);
int  NP FreeGDTSelector     (USHORT);
int  NP PhysToGDTSel        (PHYSADDR,ULONG,SEL,USHORT,FPUSHORT);
int  NP VMLock              (LINADDR,ULONG,LINADDR,LINADDR,ULONG,FPULONG);
int  NP VMUnlock            (LHANDLE);
int  NP VMAlloc             (PLINADDR,ULONG,ULONG,PLINADDR);
int  NP VMFree              (PHYSADDR);
int  NP VMProcessToGlobal   (LINADDR,ULONG,ULONG,PLINADDR);
int  NP VMGlobalToProcess   (LINADDR,ULONG,ULONG,PLINADDR);
int  NP VirtToLin           (FARPOINTER,PLINADDR);
int  NP LinToGDTSelector    (SEL,LINADDR,ULONG);
int  NP GetDescInfo         (SEL,FPUSHORT,FPULONG,FPULONG);
int  NP LinToPageList       (LINADDR,ULONG,LINADDR,FPULONG);
int  NP PageListToLin       (ULONG,LINADDR,PLINADDR);
int  NP PageListToGDTSelector(SEL,ULONG,LINADDR,USHORT,FPUSHORT);
int  NP RegisterTmrDD       (FPFUNCTION,FPFARPOINTER,FPFARPOINTER);
int  NP AllocateCtxHook     (OFF,ULONG,PLHANDLE);
int  NP FreeCtxHook         (LHANDLE);
int  NP ArmCtxHook          (ULONG,LHANDLE,ULONG);
```

```
int    NP  VMSetMem              (LINADDR,ULONG,ULONG);
int    NP  OpenEventSem          (LHANDLE);
int    NP  CloseEventSem         (LHANDLE);
int    NP  PostEventSem          (LHANDLE);
int    NP  ResetEventSem         (LHANDLE,FPULONG);
int    NP  DynamicAPI            (FARPOINTER,USHORT,USHORT,FPUSHORT);

// these are the only API's available to the driver at Init time

#define APIENTRY far pascal

USHORT APIENTRY DosBeep(USHORT,USHORT);
USHORT APIENTRY DosCaseMap(USHORT,FARPOINTER,FARPOINTER);
USHORT APIENTRY DosChgFilePtr(SHANDLE,long,USHORT,FARPOINTER);
USHORT APIENTRY DosClose(SHANDLE);
USHORT APIENTRY DosDelete(FARPOINTER,ULONG);
USHORT APIENTRY DosDevConfig(FARPOINTER,USHORT,USHORT);
USHORT APIENTRY DosDevIOCtl(FARPOINTER,FARPOINTER,USHORT,USHORT,USHORT);
USHORT APIENTRY DosFindClose(SHANDLE);
USHORT APIENTRY DosFindFirst(FARPOINTER,FARPOINTER,USHORT,FARPOINTER,
        USHORT, FARPOINTER,ULONG);
USHORT APIENTRY DosFindNext(SHANDLE,FARPOINTER,USHORT,FARPOINTER);
USHORT APIENTRY DosGetEnv(FARPOINTER,FARPOINTER);
USHORT APIENTRY DosGetMessage(FARPOINTER,USHORT,FARPOINTER,USHORT,
        USHORT, FARPOINTER,FARPOINTER);
USHORT APIENTRY DosOpen(FARPOINTER,FARPOINTER,FARPOINTER,ULONG,
        USHORT,USHORT,USHORT,ULONG);
USHORT APIENTRY DosPutMessage(SHANDLE,USHORT,FARPOINTER);
USHORT APIENTRY DosQCurDir(USHORT,FARPOINTER,FARPOINTER);
USHORT APIENTRY DosQCurDisk(FARPOINTER,FARPOINTER);
USHORT APIENTRY DosQFileInfo(SHANDLE,USHORT,FARPOINTER,USHORT);
USHORT APIENTRY DosQFileMode(FARPOINTER,FARPOINTER,ULONG);
USHORT APIENTRY DosRead(SHANDLE,FARPOINTER,USHORT,FARPOINTER);
USHORT APIENTRY DosWrite(SHANDLE,FARPOINTER,USHORT,FARPOINTER);

// end of DRVLIB.H
```

Skeleton Strategy Section

```c
int main(PREQPACKET rp, int dev)
{
switch(rp->RPcommand) {

    case RPINIT:                // 0x00

        // init called by kernel

        return Init(rp);

    case RPREAD:                // 0x04

        return (RPDONE);

    case RPWRITE:               //  0x08

        return (RPDONE);

    case RPINPUT_FLUSH:         // 0x07

        return (RPDONE);

    case RPOUTPUT_FLUSH:        // 0x0b

        return (RPDONE);

    case RPOPEN:                // 0x0d

        return (RPDONE);

    case RPCLOSE:               // 0x0e

        return (RPDONE);

    case RPIOCTL:               // 0x10

        switch (rp->s.IOCtl.function) {
            case 0x00:       // our function def 1
```

```
                    return (RPDONE);

            case 0x01:          // our function def 2
                return (RPDONE);
            }

      // deinstall request

      case RPDEINSTALL:      // 0x14
          return(RPDONE | RPERR | ERROR_BAD_COMMAND);

      // all other commands are ignored

   default:

        return(RPDONE);

    }
}
```

Sample IOCtl Call, 16-Bit

```
if (DosDevIOCtl(&data_buf,&parm_buf,cat,func,dhandle))
    error
```

Sample IOCtl Call, 32-Bit

```
if (DosDevIOCtl(dhandle,cat,func,&parm_buf,parm_buf_length,
    &parm_length,&data_buf,data_buf_length,&data_length))error
```

Sample Interrupt Handler

```c
// 82050 interrupt handler

void interrupt_handler ()
{
    int   rupt_dev;
    int   source;
    int   cmd_b;
    int   st_b;
    int   port;
    int   temp;
    int   rxlevel;


    port=UART_PORT_ADDRESS;
    outp((port+2),0x20);            // switch to bank 1
    source = getsrc ();             // get vector
    switch (source)
    {

    // optional timer service routine

    case timer :

        st_b=inp (port+3);          // dec transmit cnt
        if ( ThisReadRP == 0)       // nobody waiting
            break;
        ThisReadRP->RPstatus=(RPDONE | RPERR | ERROR_NOT_READY);
        Run ((ULONG)  ThisWriteRP); // run thread
        ThisWriteRP=0;
        break;

    case txm   :
    case txf   :

        // spurious write interrupt

        if ( ThisWriteRP == 0)
        {
           temp=inp(port+2);
```

```c
          break;
      }

      // keep transmitting until no data left

      if  (!(QueueRead(&tx_queue,&outchar)))
      {
         outp((port), outchar);
         tickcount=MIN_TIMEOUT;
         break;
      }

      // done writing, run blocked thread

      tickcount=MIN_TIMEOUT;
      disable_write();
      ThisWriteRP->RPstatus = (RPDONE);
      Run ((ULONG)  ThisWriteRP);
      ThisWriteRP=0;
      break;

case ccr   :

      // control character, treat as normal

      inchar=inp(port+5);

case rxf   :

      // rx fifo service routine

      if ( ThisReadRP == 0)
         inchar=inp (port); // get character
      else
      {
      temp=inp(port+4);
      rxlevel=(temp & 0x70) / 0x10;

      // empty out chip FIFO

      while (rxlevel !=0) {
```

```
                inchar=inp (port); // get character
                rxlevel--;
                tickcount=MIN_TIMEOUT;

                // write input data to queue

                if(QueueWrite(&rx_queue,inchar))

                // error, queue must be full

                {
                  ThisReadRP->RPstatus = (RPDONE|RPERR|ERROR_GEN_FAILURE);
                  Run ((ULONG) ThisReadRP);
                  ThisReadRP=0;
                  break;
                }
                com_error_word |= inp(port+5);

          } // while rxlevel
      } // else
  } // switch (source)
}
```

Sample Timer Handler

```
void timer_handler()
{
  if (ThisReadRP == 0)
        return;

  tickcount--;
  if(tickcount == 0)  {
    ThisReadRP->RPstatus=(RPDONE);
    Run ((ULONG) ThisReadRP);
    ThisReadRP=0L;
    tickcount=MIN_TIMEOUT;
    }
}
```

Simple OS/2 Parallel Physical Device Driver

```
//
// This driver supports DosOpen, DosClose, DosRead, DosWrite
// and IOCtl 0x91 codes 1, 2 and 3. All other driver calls and
// IOCtls are ignored (returns ERROR_BAD_COMMAND).
//
// The driver also uses these #defs
//
// #define  DIGIO_CAT     0x91              driver category
// #define  DIGIO_BASE    0x2c0             base port address
// #define  DIGIO_OUTPUT  DIGIO_BASE        output port
// #define  DIGIO_INPUT   DIGIO_BASE+1      input port
// #define  DIGIO_CONFIG  DIGIO_BASE+3      initialization port
//
// 1. Open the driver with:
//
//      if ((RetCode=DosOpen("DIGIO$",
//          &digio_handle,
//          &ActionTaken,
//          FileSize,
//          FileAttribute,
//          FILE_OPEN,
//          OPEN_SHARE_DENYNONE | OPEN_FLAGS_FAIL_ON_ERROR
//          | OPEN_ACCESS_READWRITE,Reserved)) !=0)
//              printf("\nopen error = %d",RetCode);
//
// 2. Output byte to the output port (base +0) with this IOCtl:
//
//      DosDevIOCtl(NULL,&char,1,0x91,digio_handle);
//
//      or with this standard request:
//
//       DosWrite(digio_handle,&char,1,&bytes_written;
//
// 3. Read data from the input port (base + 1) with this IOCtl.
//    The driver will block until the bit in specified in the
//    mask is set:
//
//      DosDevIOCtl(&char,NULL,2,0x91,digio_handle);
```

```c
// 4. Read data from the input port (base + 1) with this IOCtl.
//    This IOCtl returns immediately with the status:
//
//        DosDevIOCtl(&char,NULL,3,0x91,digio_handle);
//
//    or with this standard driver request:
//
//        DosRead(digio_handle,&char,1,&bytes_read;
//
//
#include "drvlib.h"
#include "digio.h"

extern void STRATEGY();                    // name of strat rout. in drvstart
extern void TIMER_HANDLER();               // timer handler in drvstart

DEVICEHDR devhdr = {
    (void far *) 0xFFFFFFFF,               // link
    (DAW_CHR | DAW_OPN | DAW_LEVEL1),      // attribute word
    (OFF) STRATEGY,                        // &strategy
    (OFF) 0,                               // &IDC routine
    "DIGIO$   "                            // name/#units
};

FPFUNCTION   DevHlp=0;                     // pointer to DevHlp entry point
UCHAR        opencount = 0;                // keeps track of open's
USHORT       savepid=0;                    // save thread pid
LHANDLE      lock_seg_han;                 // handle for locking appl. seg
PHYSADDR     appl_buffer=0;                // address of caller's buffer
ERRCODE      err=0;                        // error return
ULONG        ReadID=0L;                    // current read pointer
USHORT       num_rupts=0;                  // count of interrupts
USHORT       temp_char;                    // temp character for in-out
void         far *ptr;                     // temp far pointer
FARPOINTER   appl_ptr=0;                   // pointer to application buffer
char         input_char,output_char;       // temp character storage
char         input_mask;                   // mask for input byte

// messages
```

```c
char      CrLf[]= "\r\n";
char      InitMessage1[] = " 8 bit Digital I/O ";
char      InitMessage2[] = " driver installed\r\n";
char      FailMessage[]  = " driver failed to install.\r\n";

// common entry point for calls to Strategy routines

int main(PREQPACKET rp)
{
  void far *ptr;
  PLINFOSEG liptr;                    // pointer to global info seg
  int i;

  switch(rp->RPcommand)
  {
  case RPINIT:                        // 0x00

        // init called by kernel in protected mode

        return Init(rp);

  case RPREAD:                        // 0x04

        rp->s.ReadWrite.count = 0;    // in case we fail

        input_char = inp(DIGIO_INPUT);// get data

        if (PhysToVirt( (ULONG) rp->s.ReadWrite.buffer,
           1,0,&appl_ptr))
             return (RPDONE | RPERR | ERROR_GEN_FAILURE);

        if (MoveBytes((FARPOINTER)&input_char,appl_ptr,1))
             return (RPDONE | RPERR | ERROR_GEN_FAILURE);

        rp->s.ReadWrite.count = 1;    // one byte read
        return (RPDONE);

  case RPWRITE:                       // 0x08

        rp->s.ReadWrite.count = 0;
```

```c
            if (PhysToVirt( (ULONG) rp->s.ReadWrite.buffer,
                1,0,&appl_ptr))
                    return (RPDONE | RPERR | ERROR_GEN_FAILURE);

            if (MoveBytes(appl_ptr,(FARPOINTER)&output_char,1))
                    return (RPDONE | RPERR | ERROR_GEN_FAILURE);

            outp (DIGIO_OUTPUT,output_char); // send byte

            rp->s.ReadWrite.count = 1;       // one byte written
            return (RPDONE);

    case RPOPEN:                             // 0x0d open driver

            // get current process id

            if (GetDOSVar(2,&ptr))
                return (RPDONE | RPERR | ERROR_BAD_COMMAND);

            // get process info

            liptr = *((PLINFOSEG far *) ptr);

            // if this device never opened, can be opened by anyone

            if (opencount == 0)              // first time this dev opened
            {
                opencount=1;                 // bump open counter
                savepid = liptr->pidCurrent; // save current PID
            }
            else
                {
                if (savepid != liptr->pidCurrent)  // another proc
                    return (RPDONE | RPERR | ERROR_NOT_READY);//err
                ++opencount;                 // bump counter, same pid
                }
            return (RPDONE);

    case RPCLOSE:                            // 0x0e DosClose,ctl-C, kill

            // get process info of caller
```

```c
        if (GetDOSVar(2,&ptr))
            return (RPDONE | RPERR | ERROR_BAD_COMMAND);

        // get process info from os/2

        liptr= *((PLINFOSEG far *) ptr); // ptr to linfoseg

        //
        make sure that process attempting to close this device
        is the one that originally opened it and the device was
        open in the first place.


        if (savepid != liptr->pidCurrent || opencount == 0)
            return (RPDONE | RPERR | ERROR_BAD_COMMAND);

        --opencount;                  // close counts down open cntr
         return (RPDONE);             // return 'done' status

    case RPIOCTL:                     // 0x10

        //
        The function code in an IOCtl packet has the high bit set
        for the DIGIO$ board. We return all others with the done
        bit set so we don't have to handle things like the 5-48
        code page IOCtl


        if (rp->s.IOCtl.category != DIGIO_CAT)// other IOCtls
            return (RPDONE | RPERR | ERROR_BAD_COMMAND);

        switch (rp->s.IOCtl.function)
        {

        case 0x01:                    // write byte to digio port

          // verify caller owns this buffer area

          if(VerifyAccess(
```

```
            SELECTOROF(rp->s.IOCtl.parameters), // selector
            OFFSETOF(rp->s.IOCtl.parameters),   // offset
            1,                                  // 1 byte
            0) )                                // read only
                return (RPDONE | RPERR | ERROR_GEN_FAILURE);

        if(MoveBytes(rp->s.IOCtl.parameters,(FARPOINTER)&output_char,1))
                return (RPDONE | RPERR | ERROR_GEN_FAILURE);

        outp(DIGIO_OUTPUT,output_char); //send to digio
        return (RPDONE);

    case 0x02:                  // read byte w/wait from port

        // verify caller owns this buffer area

        if(VerifyAccess(
            SELECTOROF(rp->s.IOCtl.buffer), // selector
            OFFSETOF(rp->s.IOCtl.buffer),   // offset
            1,                              // 1 bytes)
            0))                             // read only
                return (RPDONE | RPERR | ERROR_GEN_FAILURE);

        // lock the segment down temp

        if(LockSeg(
            SELECTOROF(rp->s.IOCtl.buffer), // selector
            1,                              // lock forever
            0,                              // wait for seg loc
            (PLHANDLE) &lock_seg_han))      // handle returned
                return (RPDONE | RPERR | ERROR_GEN_FAILURE);

        if(MoveBytes(rp->s.IOCtl.parameters,(FARPOINTER)&input_mask,1))
                return (RPDONE | RPERR | ERROR_GEN_FAILURE);

        // wait for switch to be pressed

        ReadID = (ULONG)rp;             // block ID
        if (Block(ReadID,-1L,0,&err))
           if (err == 2)
             return(RPDONE | RPERR | ERROR_CHAR_CALL_INTERRUPTED);
```

```c
            // move data to users buffer

            if(MoveBytes((FARPOINTER)&input_char,rp->s.IOCtl.buffer,1))
                return(RPDONE | RPERR | ERROR_GEN_FAILURE);

            // unlock segment

            if(UnLockSeg(lock_seg_han))
                return(RPDONE | RPERR | ERROR_GEN_FAILURE);

            return (RPDONE);

        case 0x03:                          // read byte immed digio port

            // verify caller owns this buffer area

            if(VerifyAccess(
            SELECTOROF(rp->s.IOCtl.buffer), // selector
            OFFSETOF(rp->s.IOCtl.buffer),   // offset
            4,                              // 4 bytes
            0))                             // read only
                return (RPDONE | RPERR | ERROR_GEN_FAILURE);

            input_char = inp(DIGIO_INPUT);  // get data

            if(MoveBytes((FARPOINTER)&input_char,rp->s.IOCtl.buffer,1))
                return(RPDONE | RPERR | ERROR_GEN_FAILURE);

            return (RPDONE);

        default:
            return(RPDONE | RPERR | ERROR_GEN_FAILURE);
        }

        // don't allow deinstall

    case RPDEINSTALL:                       // 0x14
        return(RPDONE | RPERR | ERROR_BAD_COMMAND);
```

```c
        // all other commands are flagged as bad

   default:
       return(RPDONE | RPERR | ERROR_BAD_COMMAND);


   }
}
timr_handler()
{

   if (ReadID != 0)
   {
     // read data from port

     input_char = inp(DIGIO_INPUT );// get data

     if ((input_char && input_mask) !=0)
     {
       Run (ReadID);
       ReadID=0L;
     }
   }
}

// Device Initialization Routine

int Init(PREQPACKET rp)
{
    // store DevHlp entry point

    DevHlp = rp->s.Init.DevHlp;

    // install timer handler

    if(SetTimer((PFUNCTION)TIMER_HANDLER)) {

    // if we failed, effectively deinstall driver with cs+ds=0

       DosPutMessage(1, 8, devhdr.DHname);
```

```c
        DosPutMessage(1,strlen(FailMessage),FailMessage);
        rp->s.InitExit.finalCS = (OFF) 0;
        rp->s.InitExit.finalDS = (OFF) 0;
        return (RPDONE | RPERR | ERROR_GEN_FAILURE);
        }


    // configure 8255 parallel chip

    outp (DIGIO_CONFIG,0x91);

    // output initialization message

    DosPutMessage(1, 2, CrLf);
    DosPutMessage(1, 8, devhdr.DHname);
    DosPutMessage(1, strlen(InitMessage1), InitMessage1);
    DosPutMessage(1, strlen(InitMessage2), InitMessage2);

    // send back our code and data end values to os/2

    if (SegLimit(HIUSHORT((void far *) Init),
      &rp->s.InitExit.finalCS) || SegLimit(HIUSHORT((void far *)
      InitMessage2), &rp->s.InitExit.finalDS))
        Abort();
    return(RPDONE);
}
```

C Startup Routine for Parallel Device Driver

```
;
;       C Startup routine for parallel device driver
;
        EXTRN   _main:near
        EXTRN   _timr_handler:near
        PUBLIC  _STRATEGY
        PUBLIC  __acrtused
        PUBLIC  _TIMER_HANDLER

_DATA   segment word public 'DATA'
_DATA   ends

CONST   segment word public 'CONST'
CONST   ends

_BSS    segment word public 'BSS'
_BSS    ends

DGROUP  group  CONST, _BSS, _DATA

_TEXT   segment word public 'CODE'

        assume cs:_TEXT, ds:DGROUP, es:NOTHING, ss:NOTHING
        .286

_STRATEGY proc far
__acrtused:                             ;to satisfy C

start:
        push    es                      ; &reqpacket high part
        push    bx                      ; &reqpacket low part
        call    _main
        pop     bx
        pop     es
        mov     word ptr es:[bx+3],ax   ; plug in status word
        ret
_STRATEGY endp
;
_TIMER_HANDLER proc  far
```

```
;
        pusha                   ;save flags, regs
        push    ds
        push    es              ;make up for the 'almost all' push
        call    _timr_handler   ;handle interrupts
        pop     es
        pop     ds
        popa                    ;restore everything and
        ret                     ;bail out
;
_TIMER_HANDLER endp


_TEXT   ends
        end
```

Parallel Device Driver Include File

```
//
// digio.h memory map for os/2 device driver
//
#define DIGIO_CAT    0x91           // category for DosDevIOCtl
#define DIGIO_BASE   0x2c0          // board address
#define DIGIO_OUTPUT DIGIO_BASE     // output port
#define DIGIO_INPUT  DIGIO_BASE+1   // input port
#define DIGIO_CONFIG DIGIO_BASE+3   // initialization port
```

Parallel Device Driver Make File

```
digio.sys: drvstart.obj digio.obj
     link /nod /noi /map drvstart+digio,digio.sys,digio,\
c:\c6\lib\os2+c:\c6\lib\slibcep+c:\drvlib\drvlib\drvlib,digio.def
     mapsym digio

drvstart.obj: drvstart.asm
       masm -Mx -e -t -L -N drvstart;

digio.obj: digio.c drvlib.h digio.h
       cl -c -Asnw -Gs -G2 -Fc -Zl -Zp -Ox digio.c
```

Parallel Device Driver DEF File

```
LIBRARY DIGIO$
PROTMODE
```

Sample OS/2 Serial Device Driver

```c
// file sample.c
// sample OS/2 serial device driver


#include "drvlib.h"
#include "uart.h"
#include "sample.h"

extern void near STRAT();        // name of strat rout.
extern void near TIMER();        // timer handler
extern int  near INT_HNDLR();    // interrupt hand

DEVICEHDR devhdr = {
 (void far *) 0xFFFFFFFF,                // link
 (DAW_CHR | DAW_OPN | DAW_LEVEL1),       // attribute
 (OFF) STRAT,                            // &strategy
 (OFF) 0,                                // &IDCroutine
```

Sample OS/2 Serial Device Driver (Continued)

```c
    "SAMPLES"
   };

CHARQUEUE    rx_queue;              // receiver queue
CHARQUEUE    tx_queue;              // transmitter queue
FPFUNCTION   Device_Help=0;         // for DevHlp calls
LHANDLE      lock_seg_han;          // handle for locking
PHYSADDR     appl_buffer=0;         // address of caller
PREQPACKET   p=0L;                  // Request Packet ptr
ERRCODE      err=0;                 // error return
void         far *ptr;              // temp far pointer
DEVICEHDR    *hptr;                 // pointer to Device
USHORT       i;                     // general counter
UARTREGS     uart_regs;             // uart registers
ULONG        WriteID=0L;            // ID for write Block
ULONG        ReadID=0L;             // ID for read Block
PREQPACKET   ThisReadRP=0L;         // for read Request
PREQPACKET   ThisWriteRP=0L;        // for write Request
char         inchar,outchar;        // temp chars
USHORT       baud_rate;             // current baud rate
unsigned     int savepid;           // PID of driver own
UCHAR        opencount;             // number of times
ULONG        tickcount;             // for timeouts
unsigned     int com_error_word;    // UART status
USHORT       port;                  // port variable
USHORT       temp_bank;             // holds UART bank
QUEUE        rqueue;                // receive queue info

void near init();
void near enable_write();
void near disable_write();
void near set_dlab();
void near reset_dlab();
void near config_82050();

char    IntFailMsg[] = " interrupt handler failed to install.\r\n";
char    MainMsg[] = " OS/2 Serial Device Driver V1.0 installed.\r\n";

// common entry point to strat routines

int main(PREQPACKET rp, int dev )
```

Sample OS/2 Serial Device Driver (Continued)

```c
{
    void far *ptr;
    int far *pptr;
    PLINFOSEG liptr;                        // pointer to local info
    int i;
    ULONG addr;

    switch(rp->RPcommand)
      {
       case RPINIT:                         // 0x00

           // init called by kernel in prot mode

           return Init(rp,dev);

       case RPOPEN:                         // 0x0d

           // get current processes id

           if (GetDOSVar(2,&ptr))
               return (RPDONE|RPERR|ERROR_BAD_COMMAND);

           // get process info

           liptr = *((PLINFOSEG far *) ptr);

           // if this device never opened

           if (opencount == 0)              // 1st time dev op'd
           {
               ThisReadRP=0L;
               ThisWriteRP=0L;
               opencount=1;                 // set open counter
               savepid = liptr->pidCurrent; // PID
               QueueInit(&rx_queue);        // init driver
               QueueInit(&tx_queue);
           }
           else
               {
               if (savepid != liptr->pidCurrent)
                   return (RPDONE | RPERR | RPBUSY );
```

Sample OS/2 Serial Device Driver (Continued)

```
            ++opencount;                        // bump counter
        }
        return (RPDONE);

    case RPCLOSE:                               // 0x0e

        // get process info of caller

        if (GetDOSVar(2,&ptr))
            return (RPDONE|RPERR|ERROR_BAD_COMMAND); // no info

        // get process info from os/2

        liptr= *((PLINFOSEG far *) ptr);        // PID
        if (savepid != liptr->pidCurrent ||
            opencount == 0)
        return (RPDONE|RPERR|ERROR_BAD_COMMAND);
        —opencount;                             // close counts down open

        if (ThisReadRP !=0 && opencount == 0) {
            Run((ULONG) ThisReadRP);            // dangling
            ThisReadRP=0L;
        }
        return (RPDONE);                        // return 'done'

    case RPREAD:                                // 0x04

        //  Try to read a character

        ThisReadRP = rp;
        if (opencount == 0)                     // drvr was closed
        {
            rp->s.ReadWrite.count = 0;          // EOF
            return(RPDONE);
        }
        com_error_word=0;                       // start off no errors
        ReadID = (ULONG) rp;
        if (Block(ReadID, -1L, 0, &err))
            if (err == 2)                       // interrupted
                return(RPDONE|RPERR|ERROR_CHAR_CALL_INTERRUPTED);
```

```
        if (rx_queue.qcount == 0) {
           rp->s.ReadWrite.count=0;
           return (RPDONE|RPERR|ERROR_NOT_READY);
           }

      i=0;
      do {
         if (Movedata(&inchar,
         (FARPOINTER) (rp->s.ReadWrite.buffer+i),
         1,2))
            return(RPDONE|RPERR|ERROR_GEN_FAILURE);
         }
      while (++i < rp->s.ReadWrite.count
         && !QueueRead(&rx_queue,&inchar));
      rp->s.ReadWrite.count = i;
      QueueInit(&rx_queue);
      return(rp->RPstatus);

   case RPWRITE:                         // 0x08

      ThisWriteRP = rp;

      // transfer characters from user buffer

      addr=rp->s.ReadWrite.buffer;   // get addr
      for (i = rp->s.ReadWrite.count; i; —i,++addr)
      {
         if (Movedata((FARPOINTER)addr,
            &outchar,1,1))
               return (RPDONE|RPERR|ERROR_GEN_FAILURE);

         if (QueueWrite(&tx_queue,outchar))
            return (RPDONE|RPERR|ERROR_GEN_FAILURE);
      }
      WriteID = (ULONG) rp;
      enable_write();

      if (Block(WriteID, -1L, 0, &err))
         if (err == 2)                  // interrupted
            return(RPDONE|RPERR|ERROR_CHAR_CALL_INTERRUPTED);
```

```
            tickcount=MIN_TIMEOUT;        // reset timeout
        QueueInit(&tx_queue);
        return (rp->RPstatus);

case RPINPUT_FLUSH:                        // 0x07

        QueueFlush(&rx_queue);
        return (RPDONE);

case RPOUTPUT_FLUSH:                       // 0x0b

        QueueFlush(&tx_queue);
        return (RPDONE);

case RPIOCTL:                              // 0x10

        if (!((rp->s.IOCtl.category == SAMPLE_CAT)
           || (rp->s.IOCtl.category == 0x01)))
                return (RPDONE);

        switch (rp->s.IOCtl.function)
        {
        case 0x41:                         // set baud rate
        // set baud rate to 1.2, 2.4, 9.6, 19.2
        // verify caller owns the buffer area

        if(VerifyAccess(
         SELECTOROF(rp->s.IOCtl.parameters),
         OFFSETOF(rp->s.IOCtl.parameters),
         2,                                // two bytes
         1) )                              // read/write
                return (RPDONE|RPERR|ERROR_GEN_FAILURE);

        // lock the segment down temp

         if(LockSeg(
         SELECTOROF(rp->s.IOCtl.parameters),
         0,                                // lock for < 2 sec
         0,                                // wait for seg lock
         (PLHANDLE) &lock_seg_han))        // handle
                return (RPDONE|RPERR|ERROR_GEN_FAILURE);
```

```c
        // get physical address of buffer
        if (VirtToPhys(
        (FARPOINTER) rp->s.IOCtl.parameters,
        (FARPOINTER) &appl_buffer))
            return (RPDONE|RPERR|ERROR_GEN_FAILURE);

        // move data to local driver buffer

        if(MoveData(
        (FARPOINTER) appl_buffer,   // source
        &baud_rate,                 // destination
        2,                          // 2 bytes
        1))                         // phys to virt
            return (RPDONE|RPERR|ERROR_GEN_FAILURE);

        if (UnPhysToVirt())         // release selector
            return(RPDONE|RPERR|ERROR_GEN_FAILURE);

        // unlock segment

        if(UnLockSeg(lock_seg_han))
            return(RPDONE|RPERR|ERROR_GEN_FAILURE);

        switch (baud_rate)
           {
           case 1200:

                uart_regs.Bal=0xe0;
                uart_regs.Bah=0x01;
                break;

           case 2400:

                uart_regs.Bal=0xf0;
                uart_regs.Bah=0x00;
                break;

           case 9600:

                uart_regs.Bal=0x3c;
                uart_regs.Bah=0x00;
```

```
                    break;

            case 19200:

                uart_regs.Bal=0x1e;
                uart_regs.Bah=0x00;
                break;

            case 38400:

                uart_regs.Bal=0x0f;
                uart_regs.Bah=0x00;
                break;

error:
            return (RPDONE|RPERR|ERROR_BAD_COMMAND);

            }
            init();                     // reconfigure uart
            return (RPDONE);

        case 0x68:                      // get number of chars

            // verify caller owns the buffer

            if(VerifyAccess(
            SELECTOROF(rp->s.IOCtl.buffer),
            OFFSETOF(rp->s.IOCtl.buffer),
            4,                          // 4 bytes
            1) )                        // read/write
                return (RPDONE|RPERR|ERROR_GEN_FAILURE);

            // lock the segment down temp

            if(LockSeg(
            SELECTOROF(rp->s.IOCtl.buffer),
            0,                          // lock for < 2 sec
            0,                          // wait for seg lock
            (PLHANDLE) &lock_seg_han))  // handle
                return (RPDONE|RPERR|ERROR_GEN_FAILURE);
```

```c
            // get physical address of buffer

            if (VirtToPhys(
            (FARPOINTER) rp->s.IOCtl.buffer,
            (FARPOINTER) &appl_buffer))
                return (RPDONE|RPERR|ERROR_GEN_FAILURE);

            rqueue.cch=rx_queue.qcount;
            rqueue.cb=rx_queue.qsize;

            // move data to local driver buffer

            if(Movedata(
            &rx_queue,                    // source
            (FARPOINTER) appl_buffer,  // dest
            4,                            // 4 bytes
            2))                           // virt to phys
                return (RPDONE|RPERR|ERROR_GEN_FAILURE);

            if (UnPhysToVirt())
                return(RPDONE|RPERR|ERROR_GEN_FAILURE);

            // unlock segment

            if(UnLockSeg(lock_seg_han))
                return(RPDONE|RPERR|ERROR_GEN_FAILURE);

            return (RPDONE);

        case 0x6d:                        // get COM error info

            // verify caller owns the buffer

            if(VerifyAccess(
            SELECTOROF(rp->s.IOCtl.buffer),
            OFFSETOF(rp->s.IOCtl.buffer),
            2,                            // two bytes
            1) )                          // read/write
                return (RPDONE|RPERR|ERROR_GEN_FAILURE);

            // lock the segment down temp
```

```c
            if(LockSeg(
            SELECTOROF(rp->s.IOCtl.buffer),
            0,                          // lock for < 2 sec
            0,                          // wait for seg lock
            (PLHANDLE) &lock_seg_han))  // handle
                return (RPDONE|RPERR|ERROR_GEN_FAILURE);

            // get physical address of buffer

            if (VirtToPhys(
            (FARPOINTER) rp->s.IOCtl.buffer,
            (FARPOINTER) &appl_buffer))
                return (RPDONE|RPERR|ERROR_GEN_FAILURE);

            // move data to application buffer

            if(Movedata(
            &com_error_word,            // source
            (FARPOINTER) appl_buffer,   // dest
            2,                          // 2 bytes
            2))                         // virt to phys
                return (RPDONE|RPERR|ERROR_GEN_FAILURE);

            if (UnPhysToVirt())
                return(RPDONE|RPERR|ERROR_GEN_FAILURE);

            // unlock segment

            if(UnLockSeg(lock_seg_han))
                return(RPDONE|RPERR|ERROR_GEN_FAILURE);

            return (RPDONE);

        default:
            return(RPDONE|RPERR|ERROR_GEN_FAILURE);
        }

        // don't allow deinstall

    case RPDEINSTALL:                   // 0x14
```

```
                return(RPDONE|RPERR|ERROR_BAD_COMMAND);

        // all other commands are ignored

        default:
            return(RPDONE);

        }
}

void enable_write()

// enable write interrupts on uart

{
    int   port;
    int   reg_val;

    port=UART_PORT_ADDRESS;
    reg_val=inp(port+2) & 0x60;
    set_bank(00);
    outp((port+1),inp(port+1) | 0x12);
    outp((port+2),reg_val);

}
void disable_write()

// turn off write interrupts on uart

{
    int   port;
    int   reg_val;

    port=UART_PORT_ADDRESS;
    reg_val=inp(port+2) & 0x60;
    set_bank(00);
    outp((port+1),inp(port+1) & 0xed);
    outp((port+2),reg_val);

}
```

```c
void init ()

// intializes software and configures 82050

{
    config_82050 ();                        // Configure 82050
    set_bank(01);
}

void config_82050()

//   Configure the 82050

{
    int  port;
    int inval;

    Disable();                              // disable interrupts
    port=UART_PORT_ADDRESS;

    // set stick bit

    set_bank(01);                           // stick bit
    outp((port+7),0x10);                    // reset port
    outp ((port+1), uart_regs.Txf);         // stick bit

    set_bank (02);                          // general config
    outp ((port + 4), uart_regs.Imd);       //auto rupt
    outp ((port + 7), uart_regs.Rmd);
    outp ((port + 5), uart_regs.Acr1);      // cntl-z
    outp ((port + 3), uart_regs.Tmd);       // no 9 bit
    outp ((port + 1), uart_regs.Fmd);       // rx fifo
    outp ((port + 6), uart_regs.Rie);       // enable

    set_bank (03);                          // modemconfiguration

    outp ((port + 0), uart_regs.Clcf);      // clock
    set_dlab (03);                          //
    outp ((port + 0), uart_regs.Bbl);       // BRGB lsb
    outp ((port + 1), uart_regs.Bbh);       // BRGB msb
    reset_dlab (03);                        //
```

```
    outp ((port + 3), uart_regs.Bbcf); // BRGB
    outp ((port + 6), uart_regs.Tmie); // timer b

    set_bank (00);                     // general cfg
    outp ((port + 1), uart_regs.Ger);  // enable
    outp ((port + 3), uart_regs.Lcr);  // 8 bit
    outp ((port + 7), uart_regs.Acr0); // CR
    outp ((port + 4), uart_regs.Mcr_0);// no DTR
    set_dlab (00);                     //
    outp ((port + 0), uart_regs.Bal);  // BRGA lsb
    outp ((port + 1), uart_regs.Bah);  // BRGA msb
    reset_dlab (00);
    set_bank(01);

    Enable();                          // turn on
}

void set_dlab (bank)

//  Set DLAB bit to allow access to divisior registers

int bank;
{
    int  inval;
    int  port;

    port=UART_PORT_ADDRESS;
    set_bank (00);
    inval=inp(port +3);
    inval =inval | 0x80;               // set dlab in LCR
    outp ((port+3),inval);
    set_bank (bank);
}

getsrc()

{
    int  v,src;
    int  port;

    port=UART_PORT_ADDRESS;            // get base address
```

```c
    v=inp(port+2);              // get data
    src=v & 0x0e;               // mask bits
    src=src/2;                  // divide by 2
    return(src);                // and pass it back
}

set_bank(bank_num)

// set bank of 82050 uart

int   bank_num;

{
    int reg_val;
    int   port;

    reg_val=bank_num*0x20;      // select bank numb
    port=UART_PORT_ADDRESS;     // get real port
    outp(port+gir_addr,reg_val); // output
}

void reset_dlab (bank)

//   Reset DLAB bit of LCR

int bank;

{
    int   inval;
    int   port;

    port=UART_PORT_ADDRESS;
    set_bank (00);
    inval=inp (port +3);
    inval = (inval & 0x7f);     // dlab = 0 in LCR
    outp ((port+3),inval);
    set_bank (bank);
}

// 82050 interrupt handler
```

```c
void interrupt_handler ()
{
    int  rupt_dev;
    int  source;
    int  cmd_b;
    int  st_b;
    int  port;
    int  temp;
    int  rxlevel;


    port=UART_PORT_ADDRESS;
    outp((port+2),0x20);            // switch to bank 1
    source = getsrc ();             // get vector
    switch (source)
    {

    // optional timer service routine

    case timer :

        st_b=inp (port+3);          // dec transmit count
        if ( ThisReadRP == 0)       // nobody waiting
            break;
        ThisReadRP->RPstatus=(RPDONE|RPERR|ERROR_NOT_READY);
        Run ((ULONG) ThisWriteRP);// run thread
        ThisWriteRP=0;
        break;

    case txm  :
    case txf  :

        // spurious write interrupt

        if ( ThisWriteRP == 0) {
            temp=inp(port+2);
            break;
        }

        // keep transmitting until no data left
```

```
        if  (!(QueueRead(&tx_queue,&outchar)))
        {
            outp((port), outchar);
            tickcount=MIN_TIMEOUT;
            break;
        }

        // done writing, run blocked thread

        tickcount=MIN_TIMEOUT;
        disable_write();
        ThisWriteRP->RPstatus = (RPDONE);
        Run ((ULONG)  ThisWriteRP);
        ThisWriteRP=0;
        break;

case ccr   :

        // control character, treat as normal

        inchar=inp(port+5);

case rxf   :

        // rx fifo service routine

        if ( ThisReadRP == 0)
            inchar=inp (port); // get character
        else
        {
        temp=inp(port+4);
        rxlevel=(temp & 0x70) / 0x10;

        // empty out chip FIFO

         while (rxlevel !=0) {

            inchar=inp (port);   // get character
            rxlevel—;
            tickcount=MIN_TIMEOUT;
```

```c
                // write input data to queue

                if(QueueWrite(&rx_queue,inchar))

                // error, queue must be full

                  {
                  ThisReadRP->RPstatus=(RPDONE|RPERR|ERROR_GEN_FAILURE);
                  Run ((ULONG) ThisReadRP);
                  ThisReadRP=0;
                  break;
                  }
                com_error_word |= inp(port+5);

          } // while rxlevel
       } // else
   } // switch (source)
}
void timer_handler()
{
   if (ThisReadRP == 0)
        return;

   tickcount--;
   if(tickcount == 0)  {
     ThisReadRP->RPstatus=(RPDONE);
     Run ((ULONG) ThisReadRP);
     ThisReadRP=0L;
     tickcount=MIN_TIMEOUT;
     }
}

// Device Initialization Routine

int Init(PREQPACKET rp, int dev)
{
    register char far *p;

// store DevHlp entry point

    Device_Help = rp->s.Init.DevHlp;
```

```c
    // install interrupt hook in vector

    if (SetTimer((PFUNCTION)TIMER))
            goto fail;

    rx_queue.qsize=QUEUE_SIZE;
    tx_queue.qsize=QUEUE_SIZE; // init queue
    init();                    // init the port
    tickcount=MIN_TIMEOUT;     // set timeout

    if(SetIRQ(5,(PFUNCTION)INT_HNDLR,0)) {

    // if we failed, deinstall driver cs+ds=0
fail:
    DosPutMessage(1, 8, devhdr.DHname);
    DosPutMessage (1,strlen(IntFailMsg),IntFailMsg);
    rp->s.InitExit.finalCS = (OFF) 0;
    rp->s.InitExit.finalDS = (OFF) 0;
    return (RPDONE | RPERR | ERROR_BAD_COMMAND);
        }

// output initialization message

DosPutMessage(1, 8, devhdr.DHname);
DosPutMessage(1, strlen(MainMsg), MainMsg);

// send back our cs and ds values to os/2

if (SegLimit(HIUSHORT((void far *) Init),&rp->s.InitExit.finalCS)
    || SegLimit(HIUSHORT((void far *) MainMsg),
    &rp->s.InitExit.finalDS))
      Abort();
    return(RPDONE);
}
```

Serial Device Driver Make File

```
sample.sys: drvstart.obj sample.obj drvlib.lib
        link /nod /noi /map drvstart+sample,sample.sys,sample,\
c:\c6\lib\os2+c:\c6\lib\slibcep+c:\drvlib\drvlib\drvlib,sample.def
        mapsym sample

drvstart.obj: drvstart.asm
        masm -Mx -t -L -N drvstart;

sample.obj: sample.c drvlib.h sample.h uart.h
        cl -c -Asnw -Gs -G2 -Fc -Zl -Zp -Ox sample.c
```

Serial Device Driver DEF File

```
LIBRARY SAMPLE$
PROTMODE
```

Sample C Callable DevHlp Interface

```
;       DevHlp 0x35
;       this routine releases the logical ID (LID)
;
;       C Calling Sequence:
;       if (FreeLIDEntry (USHORT id) ) err
;
        include drvlib.inc
;
        public  FREELIDENTRY

        extrn   _DevHlp:dword
        assume  CS: _TEXT
_TEXT   segment word public 'CODE'

FREELIDENTRY    proc near

        push    bp
        mov     bp,sp
        mov     ax,[bp+4]   ; logical ID
        mov     dl,DevHlp_FreeLIDEntry
        call    [_DevHlp]
        jc      error               ; error from device help
        xor     ax,ax               ; no errors
        pop     bp
        ret     2                   ; fix up the stack
error:
        mov     ax,1                ; return error for C
        pop     bp
        ret     2                   ; fix up stack and return

FREELIDENTRY    endp
_TEXT   ends
        end
```

C Callable Debugger Breakpoint

```
;   int3.asm
;
;   this is NOT a DevHlp, but merely a simple way to break the
;   KDB at a specified point
;
;   C calling sequence:
;   INT3();
;
        .286
        public  INT3
        assume  CS: _TEXT
_TEXT   segment word public 'CODE'
INT3    proc near

        int     3
        ret

INT3    endp
_TEXT   ends
        end
```

Data Transfer Routine

```
;       movebyte.asm    OS/2 Version 2.1
;
;       this routine transfers data to and from the device driver
;
;       C Calling Sequence:
;       if (MoveBytes(far &From,far &To,USHORT Lenth))  err
;
        .286
        include drvlib.inc
        public  MOVEBYTES
        extrn   _DevHlp:dword
        assume  CS:_TEXT
_TEXT   segment word public 'CODE'

MOVEBYTES proc near

        push    bp
        mov     bp,sp
        pushf                   ; save flags
        push    di              ; save segment regs
        push    si              ; and others we use
        push    es
        push    ds
        mov     cx,[bp+4]       ; length
        or      cx,cx           ; exit if zero
        mov     ax,1            ; set for bad parameter
        jz      get_out
        lds     si,[bp+10]      ; from
        les     di,[bp+6]       ; to
        cld
        test    cx,3            ; can we optimize?
        jz      double_move     ; yep
        test    cx,1            ; if even number of bytes, save a
        jz      wordmove        ; little time by doing a word move
        rep     movsb
        jmp     short finish    ; done

double_move:
        shr     cx,2
```

```
        rep     movsd           ; blast it
        jmp     short finish    ; done

wordmove:

        shr     cx,1            ; half the number of bytes
        rep     movsw

finish:
        xor     ax,ax

get_out:
        pop     ds
        pop     es
        pop     si              ; restore regs
        pop     di
        popf                    ;restore flags
        pop     bp
        ret     10              ; fix up stack

MOVEBYTES endp
_TEXT   ends
        end
```

Sample DMA Routines

```
// mmap.h DMA Channel data structure

typedef struct _DMACh {
    UCHAR  Filler;              // force all fields aligned
                                // boundaries
    UCHAR  PageSelect;          // page select
    USHORT BaseAddress;         // base address
    USHORT WordCount;           // word count
    } DMACh;

// DMA Channel 5

#define DMA_PAGE_SELECT_5       0x8B
#define DMA_BASE_ADDRESS_5      0xC4
#define DMA_WORD_COUNT_5        0xC6

// DMA Channel 6

#define DMA_PAGE_SELECT_6       0x89
#define DMA_BASE_ADDRESS_6      0xC8
#define DMA_WORD_COUNT_6        0xCA

// DMA Channel 7
#define DMA_PAGE_SELECT_7       0x8A
#define DMA_BASE_ADDRESS_7      0xCC
#define DMA_WORD_COUNT_7        0xCE

// Other DMA Registers

#define DMA_REFRESH_CHANNEL        0x8F
#define DMA_MASK_REGISTER          0xD4
#define DMA_MODE_REGISTER          0xD6
#define DMA_BYTE_POINTER_FLIPFLOP  0xD8
#define DMA_MASTER_RESET           0xDA
#define DMA_RESET_MASK_REGISTER    0xDC

// DMA Mode Flag Bit Definitions

#define DMA_WRITE      0x04     // write transfer
#define DMA_READ       0x08     // read transfer
#define DMA_AUTOINIT   0x10     // autoinit enabled
```

```
#define DMA_DECREMENT    0x20    // address dec selected
#define DMA_SINGLE       0x40    // SINGLE mode selected
#define DMA_BLOCK        0x80    // BLOCK mode selected
#define DMA_CASCADE      0xC0    // CASCADE mode selected
```

```
USHORT   SetupDMA(USHORT channel)
    {
    if(DMAChannelBusy(channel))
        return (DMA_CHANNEL_BUSY);
    MaskDMA(channel);
    SetDMAMode(channel,DMA_SINGLE | DMA_READ);
    InitDMA(channel,(UCHAR) DMACh.PageSelect,
            (USHORT) DMACh.BaseAddress,
            (USHORT) DMACh.WordCount);
    UnmaskDMA(channel);
    return (DMA_COMPLETE);
    }
```

```
void MaskDMA(USHORT channel)
{
UCHAR channel_mask;

// output a channel specific value to mask a DMA channel

switch (channel) {

    case 5:
      channel_mask = 5;
      break;

    case 6:
      channel_mask = 6;
      break;

    case 7:
      channel_mask = 7;
      break;
      }
   out8reg(DMA_MASK_REGISTER,channel_mask);
}
```

```c
void SetDMAMode(USHORT channel,UCHAR mode)
{
unsigned char mode_byte;

// output a channel specific value to unmask a DMA channel

switch (channel) {

    case 5:
        mode_byte = mode | 0x01;
        break;

    case 6:
        mode_byte = mode | 0x02;
        break;

    case 7:
        mode_byte = mode | 0x03;
        break;
        }
    out8reg(DMA_MODE_REGISTER,mode_byte);
}
```

```c
void InitDMA(USHORT channel,UCHAR page,USHORT address,
             USHORT count)
{
// set up page select, addr, and cnt for specified channel

switch (channel) {

    case 5:
        out8reg(DMA_PAGE_SELECT_5,page);
        out16reg(DMA_BASE_ADDRESS_5,address);
        out16reg(DMA_WORD_COUNT_5,count);
        break;

    case 6:
        out8reg(DMA_PAGE_SELECT_6,page);
        out16reg(DMA_BASE_ADDRESS_6,address);
        out16reg(DMA_WORD_COUNT_6,count);
        break;
```

```c
    case 7:
          out8reg(DMA_PAGE_SELECT_7,page);
          out16reg(DMA_BASE_ADDRESS_7,address);
          out16reg(DMA_WORD_COUNT_7,count);
          break;
          }
}
```

```c
void UnmaskDMA(USHORT channel)
{
unsigned char unmask_byte;

// output a channel specific value to unmask a DMA channel

switch (channel) {

case 5:
    unmask_byte = 1;
    break;

case 6:
    unmask_byte = 2;
    break;

case 7:
    unmask_byte = 3;
    break;
    }
 out8reg(DMA_MASK_REGISTER,unmask_byte);
}
```

```c
USHORT DMAChannelBusy(USHORT ch)
{

  UCHAR ch_status;
  USHORT rc;

// returns 0 if not busy, 1 if busy

   ch_status = inp (DMA_STATUS_REG47)
   rc = 0;
   switch(ch) {

      case 5:
         if (ch_status & 0x20)
         rc = 1;
         break;

      case 6:
         if (ch_status & 0x40)
         rc = 1;
         break;

      case 7:
         if (ch_status & 0x80)
         rc = 1;
         break
      }
   return (rc);
}
```

```
; out16reg(port,word);
;
; write a 16-bit value to a DMA register by issuing two
; consecutive writes to an 8-bit register
;
        .286

include mmap.inc

_TEXT   SEGMENT BYTE PUBLIC 'CODE'
_TEXT   ENDS

        assume CS: _TEXT

_TEXT   SEGMENT

_out16reg proc near

public _out16reg

        cli
        push    bp
        mov     bp,sp               ;set up base pointer
        pusha                       ;save regs
        pushf                       ;and flags
        push    es
        push    ds

;make sure that first write goes to low byte of register

        mov     dx,DMA_BYTE_POINTER_FLIPFLOP
        mov     al,0                ;reset byte pointer
        out     dx,al
        jmp     $+2                 ;register delay
        jmp     $+2
        mov     dx,word ptr [bp+4]  ;output port address
        mov     al,byte ptr [bp+6]  ;byte to be output
        out     dx,al               ;output low byte
        jmp     $+2
        jmp     $+2
        mov     al,byte ptr [bp+7]  ;byte to be output
```

```
        out     dx,al           ;output high byte
        jmp     $+2
        jmp     $+2
        pop     ds              ;restore registers
        pop     es
        popf
        popa
        pop     bp
        sti
        ret

_out16reg endp

_text   ends
        end
```

```
; out8reg(port,byte)
;
; write a simple 8 bit register with interrupts off

        .286

        include mmap.inc

_TEXT   SEGMENT BYTE PUBLIC 'CODE'
_TEXT   ENDS

        assume CS: _TEXT

_TEXT   SEGMENT

_out8reg proc near

public _out8reg

        cli
        push    bp
        mov     bp,sp               ;set up base pointer
        pusha                       ;save regs
        pushf                       ;and flags
        push    es
        push    ds
        mov     dx,word ptr [bp+4]  ;output register address
        mov     al,byte ptr [bp+6]  ;byte to be output
        out     dx,al               ;output low byte
        jmp     $+2
        jmp     $+2
        pop     ds                  ;restore registers
        pop     es
        popf
        popa
        pop     bp
        sti
        ret

_out8reg endp

_text   ends
        end
```

```
title _word_dma
        .286P
        .model   small
        include  bsedos.inc
;
; dma set up and execute routine
;
; calling sequence:
;
; word_dma(USHORT operation,    1=write, 2=read              [bp+4]
;          USHORT channel,      5, 6 or 7                    [bp+6]
;          USHORT count,        0-65535 (0=1 word)           [bp+8]
;          ULONG  address,      far to/from address          [bp+10,12]
;          USHORT auto,         0 for single, 1 for auto     [bp+14]
;          USHORT init)         0 no auto init, 1 auto init  [bp+16]
;
_text   segment  public 'CODE'
        assume   cs:_text,ds:NOTHING
        public   _word_dma

_word_dma proc near
        push    bp              ;
        mov     bp,sp           ;current frame pointer
        cli                     ;disable rupts during dma setup
        push    bx
        push    dx
        mov     ax,[bp+6]       ;get channel number
        sub     ax,4            ;minus 4 for second controller
        mov     bx,[bp+4]       ;get mode byte and make command
        shl     bx,2            ;make valid mode bits
        or      ax,bx
        mov     bx,[bp+14]      ;or in initialize bit
        cmp     bx,0            ;autoinitialize selected?
        jz      output          ;no
        or      ax,010h         ;yes, add in autoinitialize bit
output:
        mov     bx,[bp+16]      ;block or single mode?
        or      ax,40h          ;default single
        cmp     bx,0
        jz      single          ;single mode
        and     ax,0bfh         ;make block mode
        or      ax,080h
```

```
single:
        out     0d8h,al         ;set the first/last flip flop
        jmp     short $+2       ;small delay
        out     0d6h,al         ;output the mode byte
        mov     dx,[bp+6]       ;get channel number
        sub     dx,4            ;minus 4 for second controller
        mov     ax,08ah         ;set page register
        add     ax,dx           ;
        push    dx              ;save port temp
        mov     dx,ax           ;put page register address in dx
        mov     ax,ds           ;high page address
        out     dx,al           ;do it
        pop     dx
        rol     dx,2            ;times 4 for proper address
        add     dx,0c0h         ;this is port address
        mov     ax,[bp+10]      ;low offset address
        out     dx,al
        jmp     short $+2
        mov     al,ah           ;now high part
        out     dx,al           ;do it
        jmp     short $+2
        add     dx,2            ;formulate count address
        mov     ax,[bp+8]       ;put low and
        out     dx,al           ;high count to controller
        jmp     short $+2
        mov     al,ah
        out     dx,al
        jmp     short $+2
        sti                     ;re-enable interrupts
        mov     ax,4            ;request dma transfer
        or      ax,[bp+6]       ;add in channel number
        out     0d2h,al         ;request dma transfer
        jmp     short $+2
        pop     dx
        pop     bx
        pop     bp
        ret
;
_word_dma endp

_text   ends
        end
```

Obtaining POS Register Contents

```c
USHORT get_POS(USHORT slot_num,USHORT far *card_ID,UCHAR far *pos_regs)
{
USHORT rc, i, lid;

if (GetLIDEntry(0x10, 0, 1, &lid))   // POS LID
    return (1);

// Get the size of the LID request block

ABIOS_l_blk.f_parms.req_blk_len=sizeof(struct lid_block_def);
ABIOS_l_blk.f_parms.LID = lid;
ABIOS_l_blk.f_parms.unit = 0;;
ABIOS_l_blk.f_parms.function = GET_LID_BLOCK_SIZE;
ABIOS_l_blk.f_parms.ret_code = 0x5a5a;
ABIOS_l_blk.f_parms.time_out = 0;

if (ABIOSCall(lid,0,(void far *)&ABIOS_l_blk))
    return (1);

lid_blk_size = ABIOS_l_blk.s_parms.blk_size;

// Fill POS regs with 0 and card ID with -1

*card_ID = 0xFFFF;
for (i=0; i<NUM_POS_BYTES; i++) { pos_regs[i] =
    0x00; };

// Get the POS registers and card ID for slot

ABIOS_r_blk.f_parms.req_blk_len = lid_blk_size;
ABIOS_r_blk.f_parms.LID = lid;
ABIOS_r_blk.f_parms.unit = 0;;
ABIOS_r_blk.f_parms.function = READ_POS_REGS_CARD;
ABIOS_r_blk.f_parms.ret_code = 0x5a5a;
ABIOS_r_blk.f_parms.time_out = 0;

ABIOS_r_blk.s_parms.slot_num = (UCHAR)slot_num & 0x0F;
ABIOS_r_blk.s_parms.pos_buf = (void far * ) pos_regs;
ABIOS_r_blk.s_parms.card_ID = 0xFFFF;
```

```
if (ABIOSCall(lid,0,(void far *)&ABIOS_r_blk))
     rc = 1;
else {
     *card_ID = ABIOS_r_blk.s_parms.card_ID;
     rc = 0;
     }
FreeLIDEntry(lid);
return(rc);
}
```

ABIOS Specific Include File

```c
// ABIOS specific includes


#define POS_BASE            0x100    // MCA adapter base
#define NUM_POS_BYTES          64    // maximum num POS bytes
#define MAX_NUM_SLOTS           8    // model 80 8 slots
#define POS_PORT           0x96     // use this to enable POS
#define POS_BASE           0x100    // all POS regs start here

// Constants used by ABIOS calls

#define GET_LID_BLOCK_SIZE  0x01    // ABIOS command
#define POS_LID             0x10    // get POS LID from ABIOS
#define READ_POS_REGS_RAM   0x0B    // read POS from NVRAM
#define WRITE_POS_REGS_RAM  0x0C    // write NVRAM POS data
#define READ_POS_REGS_CARD  0x0D    // read POS data from card
#define WRITE_POS_REGS_CARD 0x0E    // write POS data to card

// ABIOS request function parameters

typedef struct function_parms_def {
   USHORT    req_blk_len;           // length, must be init.
   USHORT    LID;                   // the LID
   USHORT    unit;                  // unit within a LID
   USHORT    function;              // category of request
   USHORT    resvd1;                // reserved
   USHORT    resvd2;                // reserved
   USHORT    ret_code;              // return code
   USHORT    time_out;              // timeout in seconds
   } function_parms_type;

typedef struct service_parms_def {
   UCHAR     slot_num;              // 10h slot number
   UCHAR     resvd3;                // 11h reserved
   USHORT    card_ID;               // 12h card ID
   USHORT    resvd4;                // 14h reserved
   UCHAR     far *pos_buf;          // 16h address of buffer
   USHORT    resvd5;                // 1Ah reserved
   USHORT    resvd6;                // 1Ch reserved
```

```
        UCHAR       resvd7[40];             // 1Eh work area
        } service_parms_type;

// LID request parameters

typedef struct lid_service_parms_def {
        UCHAR       irpt_level;             // 10h interrupt level
        UCHAR       arb_level;              // 11h arbitration level
        USHORT      device_id;              // 12h device ID
        USHORT      unit_count;             // 14h count of units
        USHORT      flags;                  // 16h LID flags
        USHORT      blk_size;               // 18h req blk length
        USHORT      secnd_id;               // 1Ah secondary dev ID
        USHORT      resvd6;                 // 1Ch reserved
        USHORT      resvd7;                 // 1Eh reserved
        } lid_service_parms_type;

// complete request block

typedef struct req_block_def {
    function_parms_type f_parms;
    service_parms_type  s_parms;
    } REQBLK;

// complete LID block

typedef struct lid_block_def {
    function_parms_type     f_parms;
    lid_service_parms_type  s_parms;
    } LIDBLK;

// card struct, contains ID and POS reg data

typedef struct card_def {
    USHORT      card_ID;                    // ID of the card slot
    UCHAR       pos_regs[NUM_POS_BYTES];
    } CARD;
```

IOPL Routine For 16-Bit and 32-Bit Applications

```
;
; Sample IOPL segment
;
        PUBLIC  IN_PORT
        PUBLIC  OUT_PORT

        .model large
        .286P

_IOSEG  segment         word public USE16 'CODE'

        assume          CS: _IOSEG, DS: DGROUP, SS: DGROUP
        .286P
;
IN_PORT proc    far
;
        push    bp              ;set up stack frame
        mov     bp,sp           ;save bp
        push    dx              ;save dx
        mov     dx,[bp+6]       ;get port address
        in      ax,dx           ;do input
        pop     dx              ;restore regs
        pop     bp              ;return in ax
        ret     2               ;remove from IOPL stack
;
IN_PORT endp

OUT_PORT proc   far
;
        push    bp              ;set up stack frame
        mov     bp,sp           ;save it
        push    ax              ;save ax
        push    dx              ;and dx
        mov     ax,[bp+6]       ;get data
        mov     dx,[bp+8]       ;get port
        out     dx,al           ;do output
        pop     dx              ;restore regs
        pop     ax
        pop     bp
```

```
            ret     4               ;remove off local stack
;
OUT_PORT endp
_IOSEG   ends
         end
```

IOPL Routine Make File

```
ioseg.dll: ioseg.obj
      link /MAP /NOI /NOD ioseg,ioseg.dll,ioseg,d:\lib\llibcdll+\
os2286,ioseg.def

ioseg.obj: ioseg.asm
      masm ioseg.asm;
```

IOPL Routine DEF File

```
LIBRARY
PROTMODE
STACKSIZE 8192
SEGMENTS
_IOSEG IOPL
EXPORTS
IN_PORT    1
OUT_PORT   2
```

IOPL Test Program, 16-Bit

```
//
//   testio.c - test IOPL functions
//

#define INCL_DOS
#include <os2.h>

#define INPUT_PORT  0x2f8
```

```
#define OUTPUT_PORT 0x2f8
#define TEST_DATA   0x41

extern far pascal in_port();
extern far pascal out_port();

int main()
{
        USHORT in_stuff;

        in_stuff = in_port (INPUT_PORT);
        out_port (OUTPUT_PORT,TEST_DATA);

}
```

IOPL Test Program Make File, 16-Bit

```
testio.exe: testio.obj ioseg.obj
        link /CO /nod /noe /noi /map testio+ioseg,testio.exe,testio,\
c:\c6\lib\os2+c:\c6\lib\llibcep,testio.def

testio.obj: testio.c
        cl -c -AL -G2 testio.c

ioseg.obj: ioseg.asm
        masm /MX /T ioseg.asm;
```

IOPL Test Program DEF File, 16-Bit

```
NAME TESTIO
STACKSIZE 8192
SEGMENTS
  _IOSEG   IOPL
EXPORTS
  IN_PORT 1
  OUT_PORT 2
PROTMODE
```

IOPL Test Program, 32-Bit

```c
// testio.c - test IOPL functions

#define INCL_DOS
#include <os2.h>

#define INPUT_PORT   0x2f8
#define OUTPUT_PORT  0x2f8
#define TEST_DATA    0x41

extern USHORT _Far16 _Pascal in_port(USHORT);
extern void _Far16 _Pascal out_port(USHORT,USHORT);

int main(vide)
{
        USHORT in_stuff;

        in_stuff = in_port (INPUT_PORT);
        out_port (OUTPUT_PORT,TEST_DATA);

}
```

IOPL Test Program Make File, 32-Bit

```
all: ioseg.lib testio32.exe

ioseg.lib: ioseg.def
   implib /nologo ioseg.lib ioseg.def

testio32.exe: testio32.obj ioseg.obj
        link386 /noi /map /pm:vio testio32,,testio32,ioseg,testio32

testio32.obj: testio32.c
        icc -c -Q -Gd testio32.c
```

IOPL Test Program DEF File, 32-Bit

```
NAME TESTIO32
PROTMODE
```

Device Driver For Memory-Mapped Adapters

```
//    OS/2 Device Driver for memory mapped I/O
//
//              © Steve Mastrianni
//
//    This driver is loaded in the config.sys file with the DEVICE=
//    statement. For ISA configuration, the first parameter to the "DEVICE="
//    is the board base memory address in hex.
//
//    This driver also returns a boolean to the calling application to
//    inform it of the bus type (Micro Channel or ISA).
//
//    All numbers are in hex. For MCA configuration, the board address
//    is read from the board POS regs. The POS regs data is specific for
//    each adapter, so the address calculations here may not work with
//    your specific adapter. Refer to the hardware tech reference for the
//    particular adapter to determine where and how the address appears
//    in the POS registers.
//
//
//    This driver allows the application I/O to run in Ring 2 with IOPL.
//    The CONFIG.SYS files *must* contain the IOPL=YES statement.
//
//    This driver supports 4 IOCtls, Category 0x90.
//
//    IOCtl 0x01 test for MCA or ISA bus
//    IOCtl 0x02 gets and returns a selector to fabricated board memory
//    IOCtl 0x03 gets the value of a selected POS register
//    IOCtl 0x04 gets the board address that the driver found
//
//    The driver is made by using the make file mmap.mak.

#include "drvlib.h"
```

```c
#include "mmap.h"

extern void near STRATEGY();        // name of strat rout. in DDSTART

DEVICEHDR devhdr = {
        (void far *) 0xFFFFFFFF,    // link
        (DAW_CHR | DAW_OPN | DAW_LEVEL1),// attribute
        (OFF) STRATEGY,             // &strategy
        (OFF) 0,                    // &IDCroutine
        "MMAP$  "
};

FPFUNCTION  DevHlp=0;               // storage area for DevHlp calls
LHANDLE     lock_seg_han;           // handle for locking appl. segment
PHYSADDR    appl_buffer=0;          // address of caller's buffer
PREQPACKET  p=0L;                   // pointer to request packet
ERRCODE     err=0;                  // error return
void        far *ptr;               // temp far pointer
USHORT      i,j;                    // general counters
PHYSADDR    board_address;          // base board address
USHORT      opencount;              // count of DosOpens
USHORT      savepid;                // save the caller's PID
USHORT      cntr = 0;               // misc counter
USHORT      bus = 0;                // default ISA bus
REQBLK      ABIOS_r_blk;            // ABIOS request block
LIDBLK      ABIOS_l_blk;            // ABIOS LID block
USHORT      lid_blk_size;           // size of LID block
CARD        card[MAX_NUM_SLOTS+1];  // array for IDs and POS reg values
CARD        *pcard;                 // pointer to card array
USHORT      matches = 0;            // match flag for card ID
POS_STRUCT  pos_struct;             // struct to get POS reg
ADDR_STRUCT addr_struct;            // struct for passing addresses
USHORT      chunk1,chunk2;          // temp variables for address calc

char    arguments[64]={0};          // save command line args in dgroup
char    NoMatchMsg[]  = " no match for selected Micro Channel card ID found.\r\n";
char    MainMsgMCA[]  = "\r\nOS/2 Micro Channel memory-mapped driver installed.\r\n";
char    MainMsgISA[]  = "\r\nOS/2 ISA bus memory-mapped driver installed.\r\n";

// prototypes
```

```c
int        hex2bin(char c);
USHORT     get_POS();
UCHAR      get_pos_data();
UCHAR      nget_pos_data();

// common entry point for calls to Strategy routines

int main(PREQPACKET rp )
{
    void far *ptr;
    int far *pptr;
    PLINFOSEG liptr;                    // pointer to local info seg
    int i;
    ULONG addr;
    USHORT in_data;

    switch(rp->RPcommand)
    {
    case RPINIT:                        // 0x00

        // init called by kernel in protected mode ring 3 with IOPL

        return Init(rp);

    case RPOPEN:                        // 0x0d

        // get current processes id

        if (GetDOSVar(2,&ptr))
            return (RPDONE | RPERR | ERROR_BAD_COMMAND);

        // get process info

        liptr = *((PLINFOSEG far *) ptr);

        // if this device never opened, can be opened by any process

        if (opencount == 0)             // first time this device opened
        {
            opencount=1;                // set open counter
            savepid = liptr->pidCurrent; // save current process id
```

```c
            }
        else
            {
            if (savepid != liptr->pidCurrent) // another proc tried to open
                return (RPDONE | RPERR | RPBUSY ); // so return error
            ++opencount;                    // bump counter, same pid
            }
        return (RPDONE);

case RPCLOSE:                               // 0x0e

        // get process info of caller

        if (GetDOSVar(2,&ptr))
            return (RPDONE | RPERR | ERROR_BAD_COMMAND); // no info

        // get process info from os/2

        liptr= *((PLINFOSEG far *) ptr);    // ptr to process info seg

        //
        // make sure that process attempting to close this device
        // one that originally opened it and the device was open in
        // first place.
        //

        if (savepid != liptr->pidCurrent || opencount == 0)
            return (RPDONE | RPERR | ERROR_BAD_COMMAND);

        // if an LDT selector was allocated, free it

        PhysToUVirt(board_address,0x8000,2,&addr_struct.mapped_addr);

        --opencount;                        // close counts down open counter
        return (RPDONE);                    // return 'done' status to caller

case RPREAD:                                // 0x04

        return(RPDONE);

case RPWRITE:                               // 0x08
```

```
        return (RPDONE);

    case RPIOCTL:                              // 0x10

        if (rp->s.IOCtl.category != OUR_CAT) // only our category
            return (RPDONE);

        switch (rp->s.IOCtl.function)
        {

        // this IOCtl returns the bus type. If the type is Micro Channel
        // the return is 0xff01. If ISA, the return is ff00

        case 0x01:                             // check if MCA or ISA
            return (RPDONE | RPERR | bus);

        // this IOCtl maps an adapter memory to an LDT selector:offset,
        // and sends it to the application for direct application reads
        // and writes

        case 0x02:                             // send memory-mapped addr to app

        // verify caller owns this buffer area

            if(VerifyAccess(
            SELECTOROF(rp->s.IOCtl.buffer), // selector
            OFFSETOF(rp->s.IOCtl.buffer),   // offset
            8,                              // 8 bytes
            1) )                            // read write
                return (RPDONE | RPERR | ERROR_GEN_FAILURE);

        // lock the segment down temp

            if(LockSeg(
            SELECTOROF(rp->s.IOCtl.buffer), // selector
            0,                              // lock < 2 sec
            0,                              // wait for seg lock
            (PLHANDLE) &lock_seg_han))      // handle returned
                return (RPDONE | RPERR | ERROR_GEN_FAILURE);
```

```c
            // map the board address to an LDT entry

        if ( PhysToUVirt(board_address,0x8000,1,&addr_struct.mapped_addr))
            return (RPDONE | RPERR | ERROR_GEN_FAILURE);

        // move data to users buffer

        if(MoveBytes(
        &addr_struct,                   // source
        rp->s.IOCtl.buffer,             // dest
        8))                             // 8 bytes
            return (RPDONE | RPERR | ERROR_GEN_FAILURE);

        // unlock segment

        if(UnLockSeg(lock_seg_han))
            return(RPDONE | RPERR | ERROR_GEN_FAILURE);

        return (RPDONE);

    // this IOCtl demonstrates how an application program can get the
    // contents of a Micro Channel Adapter's POS registers

    case 0x03:                          // get pos reg data

    // verify caller owns this buffer area

        if(VerifyAccess(
        SELECTOROF(rp->s.IOCtl.buffer), // selector
        OFFSETOF(rp->s.IOCtl.buffer),   // offset
        6,                              // 6 bytes
        1) )                            // read write
            return (RPDONE | RPERR | ERROR_GEN_FAILURE);

    // lock the segment down temp

        if(LockSeg(
        SELECTOROF(rp->s.IOCtl.buffer), // selector
        0,                              // lock < 2 sec
        0,                              // wait for seg lock
        (PLHANDLE) &lock_seg_han))      // handle returned
```

```c
            return (RPDONE | RPERR | ERROR_GEN_FAILURE);

    // move slot data to driver buffer

    if(MoveBytes(
    (FARPOINTER) appl_buffer,       // source
    &pos_struct,                    // for pos data
    6))                             // 6 bytes
        return (RPDONE | RPERR | ERROR_GEN_FAILURE);

    pos_struct.data = get_pos_data(pos_struct.slot,pos_struct.reg);

    // move POS reg data to users buffer

    if(MoveBytes(
    &pos_struct,                    // for pos data
    (FARPOINTER) appl_buffer,       // source
    6))                             // 6 bytes
        return (RPDONE | RPERR | ERROR_GEN_FAILURE);

    // unlock segment

    if(UnLockSeg(lock_seg_han))

        return(RPDONE | RPERR | ERROR_GEN_FAILURE);

    return (RPDONE);

// this IOCtl is essentially the same as 0x02, except the
// user virtual address is mapped to a linear address in the
// process address range and then sent to the application. This
// saves the SelToFlat and FlatToSel each time the pointer is
// referenced.

case 0x04:                          // 32-bit memory-mapped addr to app

    // verify caller owns this buffer area

    if(VerifyAccess(
    SELECTOROF(rp->s.IOCtl.buffer), // selector
    OFFSETOF(rp->s.IOCtl.buffer),   // offset
```

```c
                    8,                              // 8 bytes
                    1) )                            // read write
            return (RPDONE | RPERR | ERROR_GEN_FAILURE);

        // lock the segment down temp

        if(LockSeg(
        SELECTOROF(rp->s.IOCtl.buffer), // selector
        0,                              // lock < 2 sec
        0,                              // wait for seg lock
        (PLHANDLE) &lock_seg_han))      // handle returned
            return (RPDONE | RPERR | ERROR_GEN_FAILURE);

        // map the board address to an LDT entry
        // we could have used VMAlloc

        if ( PhysToUVirt(board_address,0x8000,1,&addr_struct.mapped_addr))
            return (RPDONE | RPERR | ERROR_GEN_FAILURE);

        // now convert it to a linear address

        if (VirtToLin((FARPOINTER)addr_struct.mapped_addr,
                      (PLINADDR)&addr_struct.mapped_addr))
            return (RPDONE | RPERR | ERROR_GEN_FAILURE);

        // move data to users buffer

        if(MoveBytes(
        &addr_struct,                   // source
        rp->s.IOCtl.buffer,             // dest
        8))                             // 8 bytes
            return (RPDONE | RPERR | ERROR_GEN_FAILURE);

        // unlock segment

        if(UnLockSeg(lock_seg_han))
            return(RPDONE | RPERR | ERROR_GEN_FAILURE);

        return (RPDONE);

    } // switch (rp->s.IOCtl.function
```

```
        case RPDEINSTALL:                      // 0x14

            return(RPDONE | RPERR | ERROR_BAD_COMMAND);

            // all other commands are ignored

        default:
            return(RPDONE);

        }
}
int   hex2bin(char c)
{
 if(c < 0x3a)
    return (c - 48);
 else
    return (( c & 0xdf) - 55);
}

// read all the POS register data into a structure

USHORT get_POS(USHORT slot_num,USHORT far *card_ID,UCHAR far *pos_regs)
{
USHORT rc, i, lid;

   if (GetLIDEntry(0x10, 0, 1, &lid)) // get LID for POS
       return (1);

// Get the size of the LID request block

   ABIOS_l_blk.f_parms.req_blk_len = sizeof(struct lid_block_def);
   ABIOS_l_blk.f_parms.LID = lid;
   ABIOS_l_blk.f_parms.unit = 0;;
   ABIOS_l_blk.f_parms.function = GET_LID_BLOCK_SIZE;
   ABIOS_l_blk.f_parms.ret_code = 0x5a5a;
   ABIOS_l_blk.f_parms.time_out = 0;

   if (ABIOSCall(lid,0,(void far *)&ABIOS_l_blk))
       return (1);
```

```c
   lid_blk_size = ABIOS_l_blk.s_parms.blk_size; // Get the block size

// Fill POS regs and card ID with FF in case this does not work

  *card_ID = 0xFFFF;
  for (i=0; i<NUM_POS_BYTES; i++) { pos_regs[i] = 0x00; };

// Get the POS registers and card ID for the commanded slot

  ABIOS_r_blk.f_parms.req_blk_len = lid_blk_size;
  ABIOS_r_blk.f_parms.LID = lid;
  ABIOS_r_blk.f_parms.unit = 0;;
  ABIOS_r_blk.f_parms.function = READ_POS_REGS_CARD;
  ABIOS_r_blk.f_parms.ret_code = 0x5a5a;
  ABIOS_r_blk.f_parms.time_out = 0;

  ABIOS_r_blk.s_parms.slot_num = (UCHAR)slot_num & 0x0F;
  ABIOS_r_blk.s_parms.pos_buf = (void far *)pos_regs;
  ABIOS_r_blk.s_parms.card_ID = 0xFFFF;

  if (ABIOSCall(lid,0,(void far *)&ABIOS_r_blk))
      rc = 1;
   else {                                          // Else
     *card_ID = ABIOS_r_blk.s_parms.card_ID; //  Set the card ID value
      rc = 0;
       }
  FreeLIDEntry(lid);
  return(rc);

}
UCHAR get_pos_data (int slot, int reg)
{
   UCHAR pos;
   CARD *cptr;

   cptr = &card[slot-1];            // set pointer to beg of card array
   if (reg == 0)                    // card ID
      pos = LOUSHORT(cptr->card_ID);
   else
```

```c
      if ( reg == 1)
        pos = HIUSHORT(cptr->card_ID);
      else
        pos = cptr->pos_regs[reg-2];        // POS data register
      return (pos);
}

// Device Initialization Routine

int Init(PREQPACKET rp)
{
  USHORT lid;

  register char far *p;

// store DevHlp entry point

  DevHlp = rp->s.Init.DevHlp;              // save DevHlp entry point

  if (!(GetLIDEntry(0x10, 0, 1, &lid)))    // get LID for POS regs
  {
     FreeLIDEntry(lid);

// Micro Channel (tm) setup section

     bus = 1;                              // MCA bus

// Get the POS data and card ID for each of 8 possible slots

     for (i=0;i <= MAX_NUM_SLOTS; i++)
      get_POS(i+1,(FARPOINTER)&card[i].card_ID,(FARPOINTER)card[i].pos_regs);

     matches = 0;
     for (i=0, pcard = card; i <= MAX_NUM_SLOTS; i++, pcard++)
     {
        if (pcard->card_ID == TARGET_ID)
        {
          matches = 1;
          break;
        }
     }
```

```c
    if (matches == 0)                       // at least one board found
    {
      DosPutMessage(1, 8, devhdr.DHname);
      DosPutMessage(1,strlen(NoMatchMsg),NoMatchMsg);
      rp->s.InitExit.finalCS = (OFF) 0;
      rp->s.InitExit.finalDS = (OFF) 0;
      return (RPDONE | RPERR | ERROR_BAD_COMMAND);
    }

    // calculate the board address from the POS regs

    board_address = ((unsigned long) get_pos_data(i+1, 4) << 16) |
      ((unsigned long)(get_pos_data(i+1, 3) & 1) << 15);
}
else

{

    // ISA bus setup

    bus = 0;                                // ISA bus

    // get parameters, IRQ (not used yet), port addr and base mem addr

    for (p = rp->s.Init.args; *p && *p != ' ';++p);// skip driver name
    for (; *p == ' '; ++p);         // skip blanks following driver name
    if (*p)
    {
      board_address=0;                      // i/o port address
      for (; *p != '\0'; ++p)               // get board address
      board_address = (board_address << 4) + (hex2bin(*p));
      addr_struct.board_addr = board_address;
    }
}
if (bus)
   DosPutMessage(1,strlen(MainMsgMCA),MainMsgMCA);
else
   DosPutMessage(1,strlen(MainMsgISA),MainMsgISA);
```

```
    // send back our cs and ds end values to os/2

    if (SegLimit(HIUSHORT((void far *) Init), &rp->s.InitExit.finalCS) ||
       SegLimit(HIUSHORT((void far *) MainMsgISA), &rp->s.InitExit.finalDS))
        Abort();

    Beep(200,3000);
       return (RPDONE);

}
```

Memory-Mapped Device Driver DEF File

```
LIBRARY MMAP$
PROTMODE
```

Memory-Mapped Device Driver Make File

```
#  makefile for memory mapped driver

mmap.sys: ddstart.obj mmap.obj
        link /nod /noi /map ddstart+mmap,mmap.sys,mmap,c:\c6\lib\os2+\
c:\lib\slibcep+c:\drvlib\drvlib\drvlib,mmap.def
          mapsym mmap

ddstart.obj: ddstart.asm
        masm -Mx -t -L -N ddstart;

mmap.obj: mmap.c drvlib.h mmap.h
        cl -Fa -c -Asnw -Gs -G2 -Zl -Zp -Ox mmap.c
```

Memory-Mapped Device Driver Header File

```
// include file for memory-mapped driver MMAP$

#define   OUR_CAT     0x91          // category for DosDevIOCtl
#define   MEMSIZE     32800         // 32 K bytes per adapter
#define   POS_BASE 0x100            // MCA adapter base
#define   TARGET_ID 0x6CFD          // adapter ID
#define   NUM_POS_BYTES 64
#define   MAX_NUM_SLOTS 8
#define   MAX_DEV_NUMS 8
#define   POS_PORT 0x96
#define   POS_BASE 0x100

// Constants used by ABIOS calls

#define GET_LID_BLOCK_SIZE 0x01
#define POS_LID            0x10
#define READ_POS_REGS      0x0B
#define READ_POS_REGS_RAM  0x0B
#define READ_POS_REGS_CARD 0x0D

typedef struct _POS_STRUCT {
     USHORT slot;
     USHORT reg;
```

```
        USHORT    data;
            } POS_STRUCT;
typedef POS_STRUCT far *PPOS_STRUCT;

typedef struct _ADDR_STRUCT {
        void     far *mapped_addr;
        ULONG    board_addr;
            } ADDR_STRUCT;
typedef ADDR_STRUCT far *PADDR_STRUCT;

typedef struct function_parms_def {
    USHORT    req_blk_len;
    USHORT    LID;
    USHORT    unit;
    USHORT    function;
    USHORT    resvd1;
    USHORT    resvd2;
    USHORT    ret_code;
    USHORT    time_out;
    } function_parms_type;

typedef struct service_parms_def {
    UCHAR     slot_num;           // 10h
    UCHAR     resvd3;             // 11h
    USHORT    card_ID;            // 12h
    USHORT    resvd4;             // 14h
    UCHAR     far *pos_buf;       // 16h
    USHORT    resvd5;             // 1Ah
    USHORT    resvd6;             // 1Ch
    UCHAR     resvd7[40];         // 1Eh
    } service_parms_type;

typedef struct lid_service_parms_def {
    UCHAR     irpt_level;         // 10h
    UCHAR     arb_level;          // 11h
    USHORT    device_id;          // 12h
    USHORT    unit_count;         // 14h
    USHORT    flags;              // 16h
    USHORT    blk_size;           // 18h
    USHORT    secnd_id;           // 1Ah
    USHORT    resvd6;             // 1Ch
```

```
    USHORT     resvd7;            // 1Eh
    } lid_service_parms_type;

typedef struct req_block_def {
    function_parms_type f_parms;
    service_parms_type  s_parms;
    } REQBLK;

typedef struct lid_block_def {
    function_parms_type     f_parms;
    lid_service_parms_type  s_parms;
    } LIDBLK;

typedef struct card_def {
    USHORT     card_ID;           // ID of the card in this slot
    UCHAR      pos_regs[NUM_POS_BYTES];
    } CARD;
```

Memory-Mapped Device Driver Test Program - 16-Bit

```
#define    INCL_DOSFILEMGR
#define    INCL_DOS
#define    INCL_DOSDEVICES
#define    INCL_DOSDEVIOCTL
#include   <os2.h>
#include   <stdio.h>
#include   "test.h"
HFILE      driver_handle=0;
USHORT     err;
UCHAR      far *myptr=0;
USHORT     ActionTaken;
USHORT     rc;
ULONG      FileSize=0;
USHORT     FileAttribute;
ULONG      Reserved=0L;
```

```c
UCHAR          Data1[8]={0};
UCHAR          Data2=0;
PADDR_STRUCT paddr_ptr;

void main()
{

  // open the driver

  if ((rc = DosOpen("MMAP$    ",
       &driver_handle,
       &ActionTaken,
       FileSize,
       FileAttribute,
       FILE_OPEN,
       OPEN_SHARE_DENYNONE | OPEN_FLAGS_FAIL_ON_ERROR | OPEN_ACCESS_READWRITE,
       Reserved)) !=0)
       {
          printf("\nDosOpen failed, error = %d",rc);
          DosExit(EXIT_PROCESS,0);
       }

  printf ("Bus Type              = ");

  rc = DosDevIOCtl(&Data1,&Data2,0x01,OUR_CAT,driver_handle);

  if (rc & 0x01)
     printf ("Micro Channel (tm)\n");
  else
     printf ("ISA\n");

  if (rc = DosDevIOCtl(&Data1,&Data2,0x02,OUR_CAT,driver_handle))
  {
     printf ("DevIOCtl failed, error code = %d\n",rc);
         DosExit(EXIT_PROCESS,0);
  }

  // pointer to data buffer

  paddr_ptr = (PADDR_STRUCT) Data1;
```

```
    printf ("Memory Mapped Address = %p\nPhysical Address    = %lx\n",
    paddr_ptr->mapped_addr,paddr_ptr->board_addr);

    myptr = (void far *) paddr_ptr->mapped_addr;

    printf ("First Byte Of Adapter = %x\n",*myptr);

    // close driver

    DosClose(driver_handle);
}
```

Memory-Mapped Test Program Header File - 16-Bit

```
//   include file for test.c

#define   OUR_CAT     0x91              // category for DosDevIOCtl
#define   DRIVER_BASE 0xD8000           // board address
#define   BASE_LENGTH 0x1000            // length of memory map

typedef struct _ADDR_STRUCT {
        void     far *mapped_addr;
        ULONG    board_addr;
        } ADDR_STRUCT;
typedef ADDR_STRUCT far *PADDR_STRUCT;
```

Memory-Mapped Test Program Def File - 16-Bit

```
protmode
```

Memory-Mapped Test Program Make File - 16-Bit

```
test.exe: test.obj
    link test,test,test,+c:\c6\lib\os2+c:\c6\lib\llibcep,,test.def

test.obj: test.c
    cl -AL -G2 -c test.c
```

Memory-Mapped Test Program - 32-Bit, 16-Bit Pointers

```c
#define INCL_DOS
#include <os2.h>

#define   EABUF       0L
#define   OUR_CAT     0x91L
#define   BUS_TYPE    0x01L
#define   GET_PTR     0x02L
#define   GET_POS     0x03L

typedef struct _ADDR_STRUCT
{
   void     * _Seg16 mapped_addr; // 16:16 pointer to adapter
   ULONG    board_addr;
} ADDR_STRUCT;

typedef ADDR_STRUCT *PADDR_STRUCT;

char     buf[100] = {0};
USHORT   BytesRead;
ULONG    ActionTaken;             // for file opens
APIRET   rc;                      // return code for driver open
ULONG    FileSize=0;              // NULL file size
ULONG    FileAttribute;           // attribute bits
HFILE    handle=0;
UCHAR    parmbuf [20];
UCHAR    databuf[20];
ULONG    plength,dlength;
PADDR_STRUCT paddr_ptr;
UCHAR    * _Seg16 myptr;

main()
{
    rc = DosOpen("MMAP$   ",
    &handle,
    &ActionTaken,
    FileSize,
    FileAttribute,
    OPEN_ACTION_OPEN_IF_EXISTS,
    OPEN_ACCESS_READWRITE | OPEN_SHARE_DENYNONE | OPEN_FLAGS_NOINHERIT,
```

```c
        EABUF);
          if (rc)
          {
            printf("\nDosOpen failed, error = %ld",rc);
            DosExit(EXIT_PROCESS,0);     // exit gracefully
          }

        printf ("Bus Type              = ");

        rc = DosDevIOCtl(handle,OUR_CAT,BUS_TYPE,0,0L,&plength,databuf,8L,&dlength);

        if (rc & 0x01)
            printf ("Micro Channel (tm)\n");
        else
            printf ("ISA\n");

        rc = DosDevIOCtl(handle,OUR_CAT,GET_PTR,0,0L,&plength,databuf,8L,&dlength);

        if (rc)
        {
          printf ("DevIOCtl failed, error code = %ld\n",rc);
          DosExit(EXIT_PROCESS,0);
        }

        paddr_ptr = (PADDR_STRUCT) databuf;

        printf ("Memory Mapped Address = %p\nPhysical Address      = %lx\n",
                paddr_ptr->mapped_addr,paddr_ptr->board_addr);

        myptr = paddr_ptr->mapped_addr;

        printf ("First Byte Of Adapter = %x\n",*myptr);

        DosClose(handle);
}
```

Memory-Mapped Test Program DEF File - 32-Bit

```
name test32
protmode
```

Memory-Mapped Test Program Make File - 32-Bit

```
test32.exe: test32.obj
     link386 /MAP /NOI /PM:vio test32,test32,test32,,,test32.def

test32.obj: test32.c
     icc /c /Gt+ test32.c
```

Memory-Mapped Test Program - 32-Bit, 32-Bit Pointers

```c
#define INCL_DOS
#include <os2.h>

#define  EABUF      0L
#define  OUR_CAT    0x91L
#define  BUS_TYPE   0x01L
#define  GET_PTR    0x02L
#define  GET_POS    0x03L
#define  GET_LIN    0x04L

typedef struct _ADDR_STRUCT {
        void    *mapped_addr;  // pointer to adapter memory
        ULONG   board_addr;
     } ADDR_STRUCT;
typedef ADDR_STRUCT *PADDR_STRUCT;


char     buf[100] = {0};
USHORT   BytesRead;
ULONG    ActionTaken;          // for file opens
APIRET   rc;                   // return code for driver open
ULONG    FileSize=0;           // NULL file size
ULONG    FileAttribute;        // attribute bits
```

```
HFILE      handle=0;
UCHAR      parmbuf [20];
UCHAR      databuf[20];
ULONG      plength,dlength;
PADDR_STRUCT paddr_ptr;
UCHAR      *myptr;

main()
{
    rc = DosOpen("MMAP$   ",
    &handle,
    &ActionTaken,
    FileSize,
    FileAttribute,
    OPEN_ACTION_OPEN_IF_EXISTS,
    OPEN_ACCESS_READWRITE | OPEN_SHARE_DENYNONE | OPEN_FLAGS_NOINHERIT,
    EABUF);
      if (rc)
       {
         printf("\nDosOpen failed, error = %ld",rc);
         DosExit(EXIT_PROCESS,0);       // exit gracefully
       }

    printf ("Bus Type              = ");

    rc = DosDevIOCtl(handle,OUR_CAT,BUS_TYPE,0,0L,&plength,databuf,8L,&dlength);

    if (rc & 0x01)
        printf ("Micro Channel (tm)\n");
    else
        printf ("ISA\n");

    rc = DosDevIOCtl(handle,OUR_CAT,GET_LIN,0,0L,&plength,databuf,8L,&dlength);

    if (rc)
    {
      printf ("DevIOCtl failed, error code = %ld\n",rc);
      DosExit(EXIT_PROCESS,0);
    }

    paddr_ptr = (PADDR_STRUCT) databuf;
```

```
    printf ("Memory Mapped Address = %p\nPhysical Address    = %lx\n",
    paddr_ptr->mapped_addr,paddr_ptr->board_addr);

    myptr = paddr_ptr->mapped_addr;

    printf ("First Byte Of Adapter = %x\n",*myptr);

    DosClose(handle);
}
```

Memory-Mapped Test Program DEF File - 32-Bit

```
protmode
name test32a
```

Memory-Mapped Test Program Make File - 32-Bit

```
test32a.exe: test32a.obj
     link386 /MAP /NOI /PM:vio test32a,test32a,test32a,,,test32a.def

test32a.obj: test32a.c
     icc /c /Gt+ test32a.c
```

Macros

```
SelToFlat MACRO
;;
;; where AX = selector
;;       BX = offset
;;
;; exit with EAX = linear address
;;
    shl eax,0dh
    and eax,01fff0000h
    mov ax,bx
;;
ENDM

FlatToSel MACRO
;;
;; where EAX = linear address
;;
;; exit with AX = selector, BX = offset
;;
    mov bx,ax
    shr eax,0dh
    or  ax,0x7h
;;
ENDM
```

APPENDIX D

OEMHLP And TESTCFG

OEMHLP

The OEMHLP interface was originally designed to assist *Original Equipment Manufacturers* (*OEM's*) in adapting the OS/2 operating system to their hardware. Prior to OS/2 2.0, OS/2 1.x was built specifically for a particular OEM machine. If an OEM wanted the OS/2 operating system to run on their machine, they would have to build a modified version of the OS/2 operating system to sell under their logo. Having a pre-existing interface helped speed the adaptation of OS/2 to their hardware. However, IBM realized that in order to sell OS/2 2.0 to the largest possible number of users, that OS/2 2.0 had to work on the majority of OEM hardware without any modifications. OS/2 2.0 was designed to meet this goal, and IBM currently tests the OS/2 operating system on a wide variety of OEM hardware and configurations to ensure continued compatibility.

The OEMHLP interface began as a simple interface for obtaining information in real mode and passing it on to protect-mode applications and PDDs, and evolved into a dedicated PDD. Protect-mode applications and PDDs cannot access BIOS through the INT interface, yet they sometimes need information from the BIOS. The OEMHLP interface was extended to allow access to necessary BIOS information. The OEMHLP device support supports several IOCtls for aiding device driver writers. These IOCtls can be found in Table D-1.

Using the OEMHLP device driver, a device driver can use INT 15h calls from the initialization code to determine if a particular EISA adapter is present and to set up that particular adapter. The following example code in Figure D-1 illustrates how you would use the OEMHLP device driver to determine if a particular EISA adapter is present.

```
USHORT FindMyEISACard(void)
{
  HFILE filehandle;
  USHORT action;
  EISAFunctionInfo.efi_SubFunc = OEM_GET_SLOT_INFO;  // Get Slot
  EISAFunctionInfo.efi_Slot    = 0;                  // Slot 0
  if (rc = DosOpen("OEMHLP$",
                   &filehandle,
                   &action,
                   0L,
                   0,
                   1,
                   0x40,
                   0L))
      return 1;

  for(index=1;index<CFG_MAX_EISA_SLOTS;index++)      // For each slot
  {
    EISAFunctionInfo.efi_Slot   = (UCHAR) index;     // Slot Number
    EISASlotInfo.esi_CardID = 0;                     // Reset Card ID
    if (rc = DosDevIOCtl((PVOID)&EISASlotInfo,       // Data Packet
                         (PVOID)&EISAFunctionInfo,   // Parm Packet
                         (USHORT)OEMHLP_QUERYEISACONFIG,
                         (USHORT)OEMHLP_CATEGORY,
                         (HFILE)filehandle))
       return 1;
    // If IOCtl successful and slot has adapter, then store away
       the adapter ID, otherwise mark as empty with a zero.

    if(EISASlotInfo.esi_Error==0)
    {
      if (EISASlotInfo.esi_CardID == MYCARDID)
      DosClose(filehandle);
```

Figure D-1. Locating An EISA Bus Adapter Using OEMHLP (Continued)

```
      return 0;
    }
  }
  DosClose(filehandle);
  return(NOTFOUND);
}
```

Figure D-1. Locating An EISA Bus Adapter Using OEMHLP

Table D-1. OEMHLP Supported IOCtl Calls

Function	Description
00h	Query OEM Adaptation Information
01h	Query Machine Information
02h	Query Display Combination Code
03h	Return Video Fonts
04h	Query EISA Configuration Information
05h	Query ROM BIOS Information
06h	Query Miscellaneous Video Information
07h	Query Video Adapter
08h	Query SVGA Information
09h	Query Memory Information
0ah	Query DMQS Information

FUNCTION 00h - Query OEM Adaptation Information

This function returns information about a specific OEM adaptation of the OS/2 operating system.

Data Packet Format

```
typedef struct _DataPacket
{
  UCHAR OEMName[20];
  UCHAR OS2Revision[10];
} DataPacket;
```

OEMName – If this is a non-IBM-logo'ed version of the OS/2 operating system and additional OEMHLP functions have been added, the OEM Name field contains the ASCIIZ name of the OEM.

OS2Revision – The OS/2 version number, stored as an ASCIIZ string.

Comments

OEM's may add nonstandard OEMHLP IOCtls to the OS/2 operating system if they sell the OS/2 operating system under their logo. Programs that use these IOCtls will only work with that OEM's adaptation of the OS/2 operating system and, as such, should issue the Query OEM Adaptation Information IOCtl routine and verify the OEM Name.

FUNCTION 01h - Query OEM Machine Information

Data Packet Format

```
typedef struct _DataPacket
{
  UCHAR Manufacturer[20];
  UCHAR ModelNumber[10];
  UCHAR RomRevisionNumber[10];
} DataPacket;
```

    Manufacturer   – ASCIIZ name of manufacturer

    ModelNumber   – ASCIIZ machine model number from ROM (if available)

    RomRevisionNumber – ASCIIZ ROM revision number

Comments

This function will attempt to find the name of the manufacturer, the machine model number, and the ROM revision number. If the machine cannot be identified, the fields returned in the Data Packet are set to NULLs.

FUNCTION 02h - Query Display Combination Code

Data Packet Format

```
typedef struct _DataPacket
{
  BYTE DisplayCode;
} DataPacket;
```

This function returns the display combination code.

DisplayCode – binary display combination code returned from INT 10h (AH = 1Ah)

Comments

This function returns the display combination code, as returned from INT 10h (AH=1Ah). If this INT 10h function is not supported by the BIOS, then 0 will be returned.

Pointers returned by this IOCtl are real-mode addresses and must be converted to protect-mode addresses before being used by protect-mode applications and device drivers.

See the *IBM Personal System/2 and Personal Computer BIOS Interface Technical Reference* or the technical reference manual for your personal computer for more information on the display combination codes returned from INT 10h (AH=1Ah).

FUNCTION 03h - Return Pointers To Video Fonts

Data Packet Format

```
typedef struct _DataPacket
{
  FARPOINTER P8X14;
  FARPOINTER P8X8;
  FARPOINTER PT8X8;
  FARPOINTER P9X14;
  FARPOINTER P8X16;
  FARPOINTER P9X16;
} DataPacket;
```

This function returns an array of 16:16 pointers to the ROM video fonts, as returned by the INT 10h, AX=1130h.

P8X14 – 16:16 pointer to 8 x 14 ROM font

P8X8 – 16:16 pointer to 8 x 8 ROM font

PT8X8 – 16:16 pointer to 8 x 8 ROM font (top)

P9X14 – 16:16 pointer to 9 x 14 ROM font

P8X16 – 16:16 pointer to 8 x 16 ROM font

P9X16 – 16:16 pointer to 9 x 16 ROM font

Comments

See the *IBM Personal System/2 and Personal Computer BIOS Interface Technical Reference* or the technical reference manual for your personal computer for more information on the video font pointers returned from INT 10h (AX=1130h).

FUNCTION 04h - Query EISA Configuration Information

Data Packet Format (subfunction 0)

```
typedef struct _DataPacket
{
  BYTE ReturnByte;
  BYTE Flags;
  BYTE MajorRevision;
  BYTE MinorRevision;
  USHORT Checksum;
  BYTE DeviceFunc;
  BYTE FuncInfo;
  ULONG CardID;
} DataPacket;
```

ReturnByte	– return code from BIOS
Flags	– binary value returned from BIOS
MajorRevision	– binary value returned from BIOS
MinorRevision	– binary value returned from BIOS
Checksum	– binary value returned from BIOS
DevFunc	– binary value returned from BIOS
FuncInfo	– binary value returned from BIOS
CardID	– binary EISA card ID returned from BIOS

Data Packet Format (subfunction 1)

```
typedef struct _DataPacket
{
  BYTE  ReturnByte;
  UCHAR ConfigDataBlock[320];
  } DataPacket;
```

ConfigDataBlock - EISA Configuration Data Block

Parameter Packet Format

```
typedef struct _ParmPacket
{
  BYTE SubFuncNum;
  BYTE SlotNum;
  BYTE FuncNum;
} ParmPacket;
```

SubFuncNum – the EISA subfunction to perform (0=Query EISA slot information, 1=Query EISA function information).

SlotNum – binary EISA slot number (planar = 0)

FuncNum – binary EISA function to issue

This function routes selected EISA function calls to the EISA BIOS.

Comments

See the technical reference manual for your personal computer for more information on EISA functions and returned values.

FUNCTION 05h - Query ROM BIOS Information

Parameter Packet Format

```
typedef struct _ParmPacket
{
  USHORT Model;
  USHORT BIOSRevLevel;
  USHORT Flags;
} ParmPacket;
```

Return ROM BIOS Information.

Model — binary machine model byte zero extened

BIOSRevisionLevel — binary machine submodel byte zero extened

Flags — binary value, ABIOS present (bit 0=1), all other bits reserved

Comments

Version 2.0 of the OS/2 operating system does not support RAM-loaded ABIOS machines. Version 2.0 of the OS/2 operating system returns bit 0 set to zero on machines with RAM-loaded ABIOS.

Version 2.1 of the OS/2 operating system supports RAM-loaded ABIOS machines. Version 2.1 of the OS/2 operating system returns bit 0 set to one on machines with RAM-loaded ABIOS.

FUNCTION 06h - Query Miscellaneous Video Information

Data Packet Format

```
typedef struct _DataPacket
{
  BYTE VideoStateInfo;
} DataPacket;
```

Return miscellaneous video state information.

Bit 7 – reserved

Bit 6 – P70 video adapter active

Bit 5 – video attribute bit (0=background intensity, 2=blinking)

Bit 4 – cursor emulation active

Bit 3 – mode set default palette loading disabled

Bit 2 – monochrome display attached

Bit 1 – summing active

Bit 0 – all modes on all displays active

Comments

Bit 0 and bit 4 are always 0 for the IBM PS/2 Model 8530.

See the *IBM Personal System/2 and Personal Computer BIOS Interface Technical Reference* or the technical reference manual for your personal computer for more information on the miscellaneous video state information returned from INT 10h (AX=1B00h).

FUNCTION 07h - Query Video Adapter

Data Packet Format

```
typedef struct _DataPacket
{
  BYTE AdapterType;
} DataPacket;
```

Returns the video adapter type.

Bit 0   – MPA

Bit 1   – CGA

Bit 2   – EGA

Bit 3   – VGA

Bits 4-7 – reserved

FUNCTION 08h - Query SVGA Information

ATA Packet Format

```
typedef struct _DataPacket
{
  USHORT AdapterType;
  USHORT ChipType;
  ULONG  VideoMemory;
} DataPacket;
```

Returns SVGA video information.

AdapterType   – binary video adapter type (see Table D-2)

ChipType   – binary value of video chipset (see Table D-2)

VideoMemory   – number of bytes of video RAM

Table D-2. Video Chip Set Information

Manufacturer	Chip Set	AdapterType	Chip Type
Indeterminate		0	0
Headland	HT205	1	1
	HT206	1	2
	HT209	1	3
Trident	8800	2	1
	8900	2	2
Tseng	ET3000	3	1
	ET4000	3	2
Western Digital	PVGA1A	4	1
	WD90C00	4	2
	WD90C11	4	3
	WD90C30	4	4
ATI	18800	5	1
	28800	5	2
IBM	VGA256C	6	1
Cirrus Logic	GD5422	7	1
	GD5424	7	2
	GD5426	7	3

FUNCTION 09h - Query Memory Information

Data Packet Format

```
typedef struct _DataPacket
{
  USHORT LowMemorySize;
  USHORT HighMemorySize;
} DataPacket;
```

LowMemorySize – the amount of RAM available below the 1MB region.

HighMemorySize – the amount of RAM available above the 1MB region.

This function returns the amount of RAM available on the machine.

Comments

The number of KB in high memory is a DWORD field for Version 2.1 of the OS/2 operating system. Previous versions of the OS/2 operating system used a WORD field. Applications should query the version of the OS/2 operating system to determine the size of the data packet required. This can be done by issuing an OEMHELP category 80 IOCtl function 00H, or issuing a GetDosVar DevHlp with index=1 and looking at the MajorVersion and MinorVersion.

FUNCTION 0ah - Query/Set XGA DMQS Information

Data Packet Format

```
typedef struct _DataPacket
{
  PVOID pDqmsInfo;
} DataPacket;
```

pDqmsInfo – a 16:16 pointer to the XGA DQMS information

This function returns a pointer to the XGA DQMS video information block.

Comments

The pointer returned is a protect-mode address. Protect-mode applications and device drivers do not need to convert this address before using it.

The XGA DMQS information is available only for IBM XGA/2 adapters and compatibles.

Information on XGA Display Mode Query and Set (DMQS) can be found in the *IBM Personal System/2 Hardware Interface Technical Reference* — Video Subsystem.

The following program, which was supplied by IBM, demonstrates how you would call the OEMHLP device driver to obtain the necessary configuration information.

```c
// OEMHLP category

#define    OEMHLP_CATEGORY                      0x80

// OEMHLP functions

#define    OEMHLP_QUERYOEMADAPTATIONINFO        0x00
#define    OEMHLP_QUERYMACHINEINFORMATION       0x01
#define    OEMHLP_QUERYDISPLAYCOMBINIATION      0x02
#define    OEMHLP_GETVIDEOFONTS                 0x03
#define    OEMHLP_QUERYEISACONFIG               0x04
#define    OEMHLP_QUERYBIOSINFO                 0x05
#define    OEMHLP_QUERYMISCVIDEOINFO            0x06
#define    OEMHLP_QUERYVIDEOADAPTER             0x07
#define    OEMHLP_QUERYSVGAINFO                 0x08
#define    OEMHLP_QUERYMEMORYINFO               0x09
#define    OEMHLP_QUERYDMQSINFO                 0x0A

typedef struct _OEMADAPTATIONINFO{
    CHAR       oai_OEMName[20];
    CHAR       oai_InternalRevision[10];
} OEMADAPTATIONINFO;

typedef OEMADAPTATIONINFO far * POEMADAPTATIONINFO;

typedef struct _MACHINEINFO{
    CHAR       mi_Manufacturer[20];
    CHAR       mi_ModelNumber[10];
    CHAR       mi_ROMRevision[10];
} MACHINEINFO;

typedef MACHINEINFO far * PMACHINEINFO;

typedef BYTE DISPLAYCOMBINATIONCODE;

typedef struct _VIDEOFONTS{
    ULONG      vf_8X14Font;
    ULONG      vf_8X8Font;
    ULONG      vf_8X8TFont;
    ULONG      vf_9X14Font;
    ULONG      vf_8X16Font;
```

```c
   ULONG         vf_9X16Font;
} VIDEOFONTS;

typedef VIDEOFONTS far * PVIDEOFONTS;

// OEM EISA Subfunctions

#define OEM_GET_SLOT_INFO      0
#define OEM_GET_FUNCTION_INFO  1

// Adapter Slot

#define CFG_MAX_EISA_SLOTS 16

// OEM HELP typedefs

typedef struct _EISASLOTINFO {
   UCHAR     esi_Error;
   UCHAR     esi_Flags;
   UCHAR     esi_MajorVer;
   UCHAR     esi_MinorVer;
   USHORT    esi_CheckSum;
   UCHAR     esi_DevFunc;
   UCHAR     esi_FuncInfo;
   ULONG     esi_CardID;
} EISASLOTINFO;

typedef EISASLOTINFO far * PEISASLOTINFO;

typedef struct _EISAFUNCTIONINFO {
   UCHAR   efi_SubFunc;
   UCHAR   efi_Slot;
   UCHAR   efi_Func;
} EISAFUNCTIONINFO;

typedef EISAFUNCTIONINFO far * PEISAFUNCTIONINFO;

typedef struct _BIOSINFO {
   USHORT bi_Model;
   USHORT bi_SubModel;
   USHORT bi_RevisionLevel;
```

```
  USHORT bi_ABIOS_Present;
} BIOSINFO;

typedef BIOSINFO far *PBIOSINFO;

typedef BYTE MISCVIDEOINFO;

typedef BYTE VIDEOADAPTER;

typedef struct _SVGAINFO {
  USHORT   si_AdapterType;
  USHORT   si_ChipType;
  ULONG    si_VideoMemory;
} SVGAINFO;

typedef SVGAINFO far *PSVGAINFO;

typedef struct _OLDMEMORYINFO {
  USHORT   omi_LowMemory;
  USHORT   omi_HighMemory;
} OLDMEMORYINFO;

typedef OLDMEMORYINFO far *POLDMEMORYINFO;

typedef struct _NEWMEMORYINFO {
  USHORT   nmi_LowMemory;
  ULONG    nmi_HighMemory;
} NEWMEMORYINFO;

typedef NEWMEMORYINFO far *PNEWMEMORYINFO;

typedef PVOID DMQSINFO;

// mainline oemhelp.c

#define INCL_DOSDEVICES
#define INCL_DOSDEVIOCTL
#define INCL_DOSERRORS
#define INCL_DOS
#define INCL_TYPES
```

```c
#include   <os2.h>
#include   <stdio.h>
#include   <stdlib.h>
#include   "OEMHELP.H"

const PSZ OEMHLPDD = "OEMHLP$";

//*****************************************************************
//                    Data/Parameter Packets
//*****************************************************************

OEMADAPTATIONINFO       OEMAdaptationInfo      = {0};
MACHINEINFO             MachineInfo            = {0};
DISPLAYCOMBINATIONCODE  DisplayCombiniationCode = 0;
VIDEOFONTS              VideoFonts             = {0};
EISASLOTINFO            EISASlotInfo           = {0};
EISAFUNCTIONINFO        EISAFunctionInfo       = {0};
BIOSINFO                BIOSInfo               = {0};
MISCVIDEOINFO           MiscVideoInfo          = 0;
VIDEOADAPTER            VideoAdapter           = 0;
SVGAINFO                SVGAInfo               = {0};
OLDMEMORYINFO           OldMemoryInfo          = {0};
NEWMEMORYINFO           NewMemoryInfo          = {0};
DMQSINFO                DMQSInfo               = 0;

//*****************************************************************
//                    Procedure Prototypes
//*****************************************************************

USHORT main(USHORT argc,char *argv[]);

//*****************************************************************
//                        MAIN Procedure
//*****************************************************************

USHORT main(USHORT argc, char * argv[])

{
  USHORT usAction,index;
  USHORT rc = 0;
  HFILE  filehandle;
```

```c
    long templow,temphigh,tempall;

    if (0 != (rc = DosOpen(OEMHLPDD,
                           &filehandle,
                           &usAction,
                           0L,
                           0,
                           1,
                           0xC2,
                           0L)))
    {
      printf("\n Error opening OEMHLP device driver.\n");
      return(rc);
    }

    //***************************************************************
    //              OEMHLP_QUERYOEMADAPTATIONINFO         0x00
    //***************************************************************

     if (rc = DosDevIOCtl((PVOID)&OEMAdaptationInfo,
                          (PVOID)NULL,
                          (USHORT)OEMHLP_QUERYOEMADAPTATIONINFO,
                          (USHORT)OEMHLP_CATEGORY,
                          (HFILE)filehandle))
     {
        printf("\n Error from function OEMHLP_QUERYOEMADAPTATIONINFO,
               RC=%xH.\n",rc);
     }
     else
     {
     printf("\n OEMName         = %s",OEMAdaptationInfo.oai_OEMName);
     printf("\n InternalRevision = %s",
            OEMAdaptationInfo.oai_InternalRevision);
     printf("\n");
     }

    //***************************************************************
    //              OEMHLP_QUERYMACHINEINFORMATION        0x01
    //***************************************************************

     if (rc = DosDevIOCtl((PVOID)&MachineInfo,
```

```
                        (PVOID)NULL,
                        (USHORT)OEMHLP_QUERYMACHINEINFORMATION,
                        (USHORT)OEMHLP_CATEGORY,
                        (HFILE)filehandle))
{
  printf("\n Error from function OEMHLP_QUERYMACHINEINFORMATION,
          RC=%xH.\n",rc);
}
else
{
  printf("\n Manufacturer     = %s",MachineInfo.mi_Manufacturer);
  printf("\n Model            = %s",MachineInfo.mi_ModelNumber);
  printf("\n ROM Revision     = %s",MachineInfo.mi_ROMRevision);
  printf("\n");
}

//*************************************************************
//              OEMHLP_QUERYDISPLAYCOMBINIATION      0x02
//*************************************************************

if (rc = DosDevIOCtl((PVOID)&DisplayCombiniationCode,
                     (PVOID)NULL,
                     (USHORT)OEMHLP_QUERYDISPLAYCOMBINIATION,
                     (USHORT)OEMHLP_CATEGORY,
                     (HFILE)filehandle))
{
  printf("\n Error from function OEMHLP_QUERYDISPLAYCOMBINIATION,
          RC=%xH.\n",rc);
}
else
{
  printf("\n Display Combination code = %xH",DisplayCombiniationCode);
  printf("\n");
}

//*************************************************************
//              OEMHLP_GETVIDEOFONTS                 0x03
//*************************************************************

if (rc = DosDevIOCtl((PVOID)&VideoFonts,
                     (PVOID)NULL,
```

```
                       (USHORT)OEMHLP_GETVIDEOFONTS,
                       (USHORT)OEMHLP_CATEGORY,
                       (HFILE)filehandle))
{
  printf("\n Error from function OEMHLP_GETVIDEOFONTS, RC=%xH.\n",rc);
}
else
{
  printf("\n 8X14Font  = %p",VideoFonts.vf_8X14Font);
  printf("\n 8X8Font   = %p",VideoFonts.vf_8X8Font);
  printf("\n 8X8TFont  = %p",VideoFonts.vf_8X8TFont);
  printf("\n 9X14Font  = %p",VideoFonts.vf_9X14Font);
  printf("\n 8X16Font  = %p",VideoFonts.vf_8X16Font);
  printf("\n 9X16Font  = %p",VideoFonts.vf_9X16Font);
  printf("\n");
}

//****************************************************************
//              OEMHLP_QUERYEISACONFIG              0x04
//****************************************************************

// initialize EISA parameters

EISAFunctionInfo.efi_SubFunc = OEM_GET_SLOT_INFO;// EISA Get Slot
EISAFunctionInfo.efi_Slot    = 0;                // Slot 0

if (rc = DosDevIOCtl((PVOID)&EISASlotInfo,
                     (PVOID)&EISAFunctionInfo,
                     (USHORT)OEMHLP_QUERYEISACONFIG,
                     (USHORT)OEMHLP_CATEGORY,
                     (HFILE)filehandle))
{
  printf("\n Error issuing QueryEISAConfig assuming non-EISA,
         RC=%u.\n",rc);
}
else
{
  printf("\n Slot 0 (planar) ID = %lxH ",EISASlotInfo.esi_CardID);
  printf("\n           Error    = %xH ",(SHORT)EISASlotInfo.esi_Error);
  printf("\n           Flags    = %xH ",(SHORT)EISASlotInfo.esi_Flags);
  printf("\n           MajorVer = %xH ",
```

```c
                       (SHORT)EISASlotInfo.esi_MajorVer);
      printf("\n            MinorVer = %xH ",
                       (SHORT)EISASlotInfo.esi_MinorVer);
      printf("\n            CheckSum = %xH ",
                       (SHORT)EISASlotInfo.esi_CheckSum);
      printf("\n            DevFunc  = %xH ",
                       (SHORT)EISASlotInfo.esi_DevFunc);
      printf("\n            FuncInfo = %xH ",
                       (SHORT)EISASlotInfo.esi_FuncInfo);
   for(index=1;index<CFG_MAX_EISA_SLOTS;index++)    // For each slot
   {
      EISAFunctionInfo.efi_Slot   = (UCHAR) index; // Slot Number
      EISASlotInfo.esi_CardID = 0;                 // Reset Adapter ID
      rc = DosDevIOCtl((PVOID)&EISASlotInfo,       // Data Packet
                       (PVOID)&EISAFunctionInfo,   // Parm Packet
                       (USHORT)OEMHLP_QUERYEISACONFIG,
                       (USHORT)OEMHLP_CATEGORY,
                       (HFILE)filehandle);

      // If IOCTL successful and EISA has adapter, then store away
      // the adapter ID, otherwise mark as empty with a zero.


      if((rc==0)&&(EISASlotInfo.esi_Error==0))
      {
        printf("\n Slot %d ID = %lxH ",index,EISASlotInfo.esi_CardID);
        printf("\n   Error    = %xH ",(SHORT)EISASlotInfo.esi_Error);
        printf("\n   Flags    = %xH ",(SHORT)EISASlotInfo.esi_Flags);
        printf("\n   MajorVer = %xH ",(SHORT)EISASlotInfo.esi_MajorVer);
        printf("\n   MinorVer = %xH ",(SHORT)EISASlotInfo.esi_MinorVer);
        printf("\n   CheckSum = %xH ",(SHORT)EISASlotInfo.esi_CheckSum);
        printf("\n   DevFunc  = %xH ",(SHORT)EISASlotInfo.esi_DevFunc);
        printf("\n   FuncInfo = %xH ",(SHORT)EISASlotInfo.esi_FuncInfo);
      }
      else
      {
        printf("\n Error reading Slot %d ID, RC=%u, EISA Error=%u ",
               index,rc,(SHORT)EISASlotInfo.esi_Error);
      }
   } // for
   printf("\n");
```

```
}
//*************************************************************
//              OEMHLP_QUERYBIOSINFO                  0x05
//*************************************************************

if (rc = DosDevIOCtl((PVOID)&BIOSInfo,
                     (PVOID)NULL,
                     (USHORT)OEMHLP_QUERYBIOSINFO,
                     (USHORT)OEMHLP_CATEGORY,
                     (HFILE)filehandle))
{
  printf("\n Error from function OEMHLP_QUERYBIOSINFO, RC=%xH.\n",rc);
}
else
{
  printf("\n Model byte       = %xH ",BIOSInfo.bi_Model);
  printf("\n Submodel byte    = %xH ",BIOSInfo.bi_SubModel);
  printf("\n Revision level   = %xH ",BIOSInfo.bi_RevisionLevel);
  printf("\n ABIOS Present    = %xH ",BIOSInfo.bi_ABIOS_Present);
  printf("\n");
}

//*************************************************************
//              OEMHLP_QUERYMISCVIDEOINFO             0x06
//*************************************************************

if (rc = DosDevIOCtl((PVOID)&MiscVideoInfo,
                     (PVOID)NULL,
                     (USHORT)OEMHLP_QUERYMISCVIDEOINFO,
                     (USHORT)OEMHLP_CATEGORY,
                     (HFILE)filehandle))
{
  printf("\n Error from function OEMHLP_QUERYMISCVIDEOINFO,
          RC=%xH.\n",rc);
}
else
{
  printf("\n Misc Video Info  = %xH ",MiscVideoInfo);
  printf("\n");
}
```

```c
//***************************************************************
//                OEMHLP_QUERYVIDEOADAPTER                  0x07
//***************************************************************

if (rc = DosDevIOCtl((PVOID)&VideoAdapter,
                     (PVOID)NULL,
                     (USHORT)OEMHLP_QUERYVIDEOADAPTER,
                     (USHORT)OEMHLP_CATEGORY,
                     (HFILE)filehandle))
{
  printf("\n Error from function OEMHLP_QUERYVIDEOADAPTER,
         RC=%xH.\n",rc);
}
else
{
  printf("\n Video Adapter     = %xH ",VideoAdapter);
  printf("\n");
}


//***************************************************************
//                OEMHLP_QUERYSVGAINFO                      0x08
//***************************************************************

if (rc = DosDevIOCtl((PVOID)&SVGAInfo,
                     (PVOID)NULL,
                     (USHORT)OEMHLP_QUERYSVGAINFO,
                     (USHORT)OEMHLP_CATEGORY,
                     (HFILE)filehandle))
{
  printf("\n Error from function OEMHLP_QUERYSVGAINFO, RC=%xH.\n",rc);
}
else
{
  printf("\n Adapter Type   = %xH " ,SVGAInfo.si_AdapterType);
  printf("\n Chip    Type   = %xH " ,SVGAInfo.si_ChipType);
  printf("\n Video memory   = %lxH ",SVGAInfo.si_VideoMemory);
  printf("\n");
}


//***************************************************************
```

```
//                OEMHLP_QUERYMEMORYINFO                    0x09
//*************************************************************

if (strncmp(OEMAdaptationInfo.oai_InternalRevision,"20.",3))
{

   // String is different, use old memoryinfo

   if (rc = DosDevIOCtl((PVOID)&OldMemoryInfo,
                        (PVOID)NULL,
                        (USHORT)OEMHLP_QUERYMEMORYINFO,
                        (USHORT)OEMHLP_CATEGORY,
                        (HFILE)filehandle))
   {
     printf("\n Error from function OEMHLP_QUERYMEMORYINFO,
            RC=%xH.\n",rc);
   }
   else
   {
    templow=OldMemoryInfo.omi_LowMemory;
    temphigh=OldMemoryInfo.omi_HighMemory;
    tempall=templow+temphigh;
    printf("\n Low Memory    = %d " ,OldMemoryInfo.omi_LowMemory);
    printf("\n High Memory   = %d " ,OldMemoryInfo.omi_HighMemory);
    printf("\n Total Memory  = %ld ",tempall);
    printf("\n");
   }
}
else
{

   // String is same use new memoryinfo

   if (rc = DosDevIOCtl((PVOID)&NewMemoryInfo,
                        (PVOID)NULL,
                        (USHORT)OEMHLP_QUERYMEMORYINFO,
                        (USHORT)OEMHLP_CATEGORY,
                        (HFILE)filehandle))
   {
     printf("\n Error from function OEMHLP_QUERYMEMORYINFO,
            RC=%xH.\n",rc);
```

```
      }
    else
    {
      templow=NewMemoryInfo.nmi_LowMemory;
      temphigh=NewMemoryInfo.nmi_HighMemory;
      tempall=templow+temphigh;
      printf("\n Low Memory    = %d " ,NewMemoryInfo.nmi_LowMemory);
      printf("\n High Memory   = %ld ",NewMemoryInfo.nmi_HighMemory);
      printf("\n Total Memory  = %ld ",tempall);
      printf("\n");
    }
  }

  //****************************************************************
  //                 OEMHLP_QUERYDMQSINFO                      0x0A
  //****************************************************************

  if (rc = DosDevIOCtl((PVOID)&DMQSInfo,
                       (PVOID)NULL,
                       (USHORT)OEMHLP_QUERYDMQSINFO,
                       (USHORT)OEMHLP_CATEGORY,
                       (HFILE)filehandle))
  {
    printf("\n Error from function OEMHLP_QUERYDMQSINFO, RC=%xH.\n",rc);
  }
  else
  {
    printf("\n DMQS Pointer = %p",DMQSInfo);
    printf("\n");
  }

  if (rc=DosClose(filehandle))
  {
    printf("\n Error closing OEMHLP device driver, RC=%xH.\n",rc);
  }

  return(rc);
}
```

TESTCFG

The TESTCFG device driver offers some additonal functionality to aid in determining the machine bus type and hardware configuration. It consists of six IOCtls in category 0x80. The IOCtls are described in Table D-3. TESTCFG is opened with the name TESTCFG$.

Table D-3. TESTCFG IOCtls, Category 0x80.

Function	Description
0x40	Get copy of non-system memory
0x41	"IN" instruction
0x42	"OUT" instruction
0x60	Get bus type
0x61	Get POS registers
0x62	Get EISA IDs

FUNCTION 40h - Get Copy Of Non-system Memory

Parameter Packet Format

```
typedef struct _ParmPacket
{
  ULONG   command;       // must be set to 0
  ULONG   physaddr;      // physical address 0xc0000 to 0xfffff
  USHORT  numbytes;      // number of bytes to get
} DataPacket;
```

Data Packet Format

```
typedef struct _DataPacket
{
  BYTE    bytes[numbytes];
} DataPacket;
```

Comments

This IOCtl returns copies the contents of physical memory below the 1MB region to a local buffer.

FUNCTION 41h - Perform an "IN" Instruction

Parameter Packet Format

```
typedef struct _ParmPacket
{
  USHORT portaddress;   // I/O port
  USHORT width;         // # bytes, 1=byte, 2=word, 3=dword
} DataPacket;
```

Data Packet Format

```
typedef struct _DataPacket
{
  ULONG data;           // data read
} DataPacket;
```

Comments

Ports below 0x100 are not accessible.

FUNCTION 42h - Issue An "OUT" Instruction

Parameter Packet Format

```
typedef struct _ParmPacket
{
  USHORT portaddress;    // I/O port
  USHORT width;          // # bytes, 1=byte, 2=word, 4=dword
} DataPacket;
```

Data Packet Format

None.

Comments

Ports below 0x100 are not accessible.

FUNCTION 60h - Query Bus Architecture

Parameter Packet Format

```
typedef struct _ParmPacket
{
  ULONG command;        // must be set to 0
} DataPacket;
```

Data Packet Format

```
typedef struct _DataPacket
{
  ULONG BusType;        // 0 = ISA, 1= Micro Channel, 2=EISA
} DataPacket;
```

Comments

This IOCtl returns the current bus type.

FUNCTION 61h - Get All Micro Channel Adapter IDs

Parameter Packet Format

```
typedef struct _ParmPacket
{
  ULONG command;         // must be set to 0
} DataPacket;
```

Data Packet Format

```
typedef struct _DataPacket
{
  USHORT AdapterID[16];  // receives IDs
} DataPacket;
```

Comments

This function returns AdapterID[n] = 0 for ISA or EISA adapters.

FUNCTION 62h - Get EISA Adapter IDs

Parameter Packet Format

```
typedef struct _ParmPacket
{
  ULONG command;           // must be set to 0
} ParmPacket;
```

Data Packet Format

```
typedef struct _DataPacket
{
  UCHAR EISAtype[16][4]; // EISA adapter IDs returned
} DataPacket;
```

Comments

This function returns EISAType[n][n] = 0 for ISA or Micro Channel adapters.

INDEX

0:32 addressing, 22
16:16 addressing, 22
32-bit applications, 251
80286, 22
80386, 22
80486, 22

A

ABIOS, 59, 88, 107, 226, 274, 321
adapter, 4, 12, 13, 16, 17, 19, 20, 29, 93, 107, 108, 225, 127, 134, 136, 163, 164, 166, 173, 177, 185
Advanced Properties, 124
AT bus, 16
AttachDD, 277, 283

B

bandwidth, 173
BASIC, 1
binary, 4

BIOS, 5, 7, 73, 123, 127, 128, 132, 164
bit, 4
bus, 4, 6, 13, 15, 16, 18

C

C Set/2 compiler, 251
callback, 262, 267, 269
capabilities bit strip, 48
card services, 262
client driver, 267
Close, 60
compatibility box, 30, 144
CP/M, 5
CPU, 3

D

DEF file, 169
DevHlp
    ABIOSCall, 274, 277

ABIOSCommonEntry, 276
AllocateCtxHook, 280
AllocGDTSelector, 166, 281
AllocPhys, 298
AllocReqPacket, 299
ArmCtxHook, 300
AttachDD, 47, 301
Beep, 302
Block, 100, 303
CloseEventSem, 305
DeRegister, 306
DevDone, 307
DispMsg (SaveMsg), 308
DynamicApi, 309
EOI, 311
FreeCtxHook, 312
FreeGDTSelector, 312
FreeLIDEntry, 313
FreePhys, 314
FreeReqPacket, 315
GetDescInfo, 316
GetDeviceBlock, 317
GetDOSVar, 318
GetLIDEntry, 273, 321
InternalError, 323
LinToGDTSelector, 1423, 256, 324
LinToPageList, 325
LockSeg, 327
MonCreate, 330
MonFlush, 329
MonWrite, 332
OpenEventSem, 334
PageListToGDTSelector, 335
PageListToLin, 337

PhysToGDTSel, 339
PhysToGDTSelector, 166, 340
PhysToUVirt, 166, 273, 342
PhysToVirt, 79, 344
PostEventSem, 346
PullParticular, 347
PullReqPacket, 348
PushReqPacket, 349
QueueFlush, 350
QueueInit, 351
QueueRead, 352
QueueWrite, 353
Register, 354
RegisterBeep, 355
RegisterPDD, 356, 359
RegisterStackUsage, 360
RegisterTmrDD, 362
ResetEventSem, 363
ResetTimer, 364
Run, 65, 106, 365
SaveMsg, 308
SchedClockAddr, 366
SemClear, 367
SemHandle, 368
SemRequest, 370
SendEvent, 371
SetIRQ, 60, 373
SetTimer, 66, 95, 374
SortReqPacket, 375
TCYield, 376
TickCount, 66, 377
UnlockSeg, 378
UnPhysToVirt, 379
UnSetIRQ, 88, 380

VerifyAccess, 99, 381
VideoPause, 383
VirtToLin, 384
VirtToPhys, 385
VMAlloc, 253, 386
VMFree, 389
VMGlobalToProcess, 390
VMLock, 271, 392
VMProcessToGlobal, 253, 395
VMSetMem, 397
VMUnlock, 398
Yield, 399
Device Attribute Word, 47, 48
Device Context, 242
Device Header, 46, 48, 49, 95
device monitors, 41
DevOpenDC, 242
DLL, 25, 28, 122, 239
DMA, 61, 163, 173
    channels, 173
    controller, 173
    page registers, 177
DMA controller, 61
DOS emulation component, 122
DOS Session Window Manager, 135
DosDevIOCtl2, 85
DosFlatToSel, 252
DosOpen, 43, 94, 96
DosRead, 55, 85
DosSelToFlat, 252
DosWrite, 55, 85
DPMI, 36
Driver Capabilities Structure, 184
driver functions
    Build BPB, 77
    Deinstall, 88
    Generic IOCtl, 84
    Get Driver Capabilities, 91, 92, 184
    Get Fixed Disk/LU Map, 90
    Get/Set Logical Drive, 87
    Init, 72
    Input/Ouput Flush, 82
    Media Check, 75
    Nondestructive Read No Wait, 80
    Open/Close, 82
    Partitionable Fixed Disk, 89
    Read/Write, 79
    Removable Media, 84
    Reset Media, 86
    Shutdown, 91
    Status, 81
Dynamic Data Exchange, 36

E

EEPROM, 6, 18
EISA bus, 20, 60
EPROM, 2
exports, 170
Extended Device Driver Interface, 183

F

File Allocation Table, 77
File System Driver, 196
flat memory model, 251
floppy disk, 3, 15, 115, 128, 130, 131
FSDInfo structure, 196

G
GDT, 23, 58
GP fault, 164
graphics engine, 240

H
hardware, 2

I
IBM PC AT, 16
IBM XT, 15
idle loop, 132
initialization, 57, 58
INT 05h, 132
INT 09h, 132
INT 10h, 136
INT 14h, 127
INT 15h, 132
INT 18h, 132
INT 21h, 121, 132
INT 2Fh, 136
INT 3, 42
INT 33h, 133
interrupt, 16, 17, 18, 19, 20, 39, 40, 41, 61
    controller, 16
    device, 59
    drivers, 40
    handler, 15, 40, 41, 60, 63, 64, 65, 66
    level, 17, 18
    levels, 16
    processing, 40
    sharing, 107
    system, 10, 15, 25, 40
    timer, 48, 59, 66
    vectors, 60
IOCtl, 56, 60, 100, 165
IOPL, 25, 167
IRQ1, 132
ISA bus, 16

K
KDB, 41
KDB Commands
    Add Interrupt/ Trap Vector, All Rings, 223
    Add/Remove Active Map, 216
    Baud Rate, 226
    Change Default Command, 225
    Change Task Context, 237
    Clear Breakpoint(s), 210
    Clear Interrupt/Trap Vectors, 224
    Compare Bytes, 210
    Conditional Execution, 216
    Debugger Options, 225
    Display MTE Segment Table, 229
    Display User Registers, 236
    Dump ABIOS Common Data Area, 226
    Dump Bytes, 210
    Dump Data Structure, 227
    Dump Doublewords, 211
    Dump GDT Entries, 211
    Dump IDT Entries, 211
    Dump LDT Entries, 211
    Dump Loadall Buffer, 213
    Dump Memory, 210
    Dump Memory Alias Record, 231

Dump Memory Arena Records, 230
Dump Memory Context Record, 231
Dump Memory Object Record, 232
Dump Memory Page Frame, 233
Dump Page Directory/Page Table Entries, 212
Dump RAS Trace Buffer, 237
Dump Task State Segment (TSS), 213
Dump Virtual Page Structure, 234
Dump Words, 211
Enable Breakpoint(s), 210
Enter Data, 213
Execute Default Command, 225
Fill Memory With Pattern, 213
Go, 214
Help, External Commands, 226
Help/Print Expression, 215
Hex Arithmetic, 215
Input Port, 215
Intercept Trap Vector Except Ring 0, 224
List Absolute Symbols, 216
List Breakpoint(s), 209
List Default Command, 225
List Groups, 215
List Maps, 216
List Near Symbols, 216
List Real/Protect Mode Vectors, 223
List Symbols, 217
Move Memory, 217
Ouput Byte, 217
Process Status, 235
Ptrace/Program Step, 218
Reboot, 236
Register, 218
Search, 221
Set Breakpoint, 208
Set Register Breakpoint, 209
Set Timestamping Breakpoint, 209
Show Timestamp Entries, 209
Swap In TSD or Page, 228
Trace, 222
Trace User Stack, 228
Unassemble, 222
Kernel Debugger, 199

L
LDT, 22, 164, 166
LID, 88, 107
LIM, 123, 151
linear addressing, 251
Local Descriptor Table, 43

M
machine code, 3
MAPSYM utility, 201
memory, 2, 13
    addressing, 21, 22, 25
memory-mapped adapters, 163
Micro Channel, 18, 60, 107, 164
Micro Channel II, 20
mouse, 133
MS-DOS, 28

N
NVRAM, 24

O

offset, 22
Open, 60
OS/2
    1.0, 32
    1.1, 32
    1.2, 33
    2.0, 35
    API, 37
OS/2 1.X, 119

P

PC bus, 15
PCMCIA, 303
Physical Device Driver, 93, 120
PID, 96, 97
pixel, 10
PMGRE.DLL, 240
polling, 7, 9, 94, 132
POS registers, 107, 108, 164, 260
POST, 261
Presentation Device Drivers, 239
Presentation Manager, 27
priorities, 30
protect mode, 21, 22, 29, 41, 107
PS/2, 19, 28, 107, 125

Q

queues, 64

R

Read, 60
real mode, 21
Request Header, 189
Request List, 187
Request List Header, 187
Request Packet, 40, 42, 43, 46, 56, 96, 97, 100, 106, 108, 152
Resource Map Utility, 260
ring architecture, 25
ring transition, 170
ROM, 6, 19
RPL, 164

S

scatter/gather descriptors, 183, 194
selector, 22
socket, 258
socket services, 259
software, 2
stack, 94
Strategy 2, 183
Strategy section, 43, 55, 56
swapping, 29
system file number, 79

T

threads, 30
thunking, 252
time slice, 29
timer handler, 40, 51, 65, 66, 95

U

UART, 45, 61
UNIX, 31

V

VDD, 120
VDM, 255
Virtual 8086 Mode, 23, 120
Virtual Clock Device Driver, 128
Virtual COM Device Driver, 126
Virtual Device Helper, 123
    VDHCloseVDD, 126
    VDHInstallUserHook, 123
    VDHOpenPDD, 126
    VDHRequestVDD, 126
    VDHWaitVRR, 132
    VHDRegisterProperty, 124
Virtual Disk Device Driver, 130
Virtual DOS Machine, 120
Virtual Keyboard Device Driver, 132
Virtual Line Printer Device Driver, 133
Virtual Video Device Driver, 134
virtualization, 29
Volume Characteristics Structure, 185
VVIDEO, 123

W

Work Place Shell, 36

LIBRARY ORDER FORM

A C callable DevHlp library is available for $79.00 without the library source, or for $149.00 with complete source of the 1.3 and 2.1 libraries, supplied on 3.5" 1.4 MB floppy disk. Company P.O.s accepted by mail or Fax. Checks should be made payable to Personal Systems Software, Inc. International orders must include check payable in US dollars drawn on an international bank or wired to our account. Sorry, we do not take credit cards. Use the order blank below to order the DevHlp library. Please allow 1 week for delivery.

_____

Qty ____ C Callable 2.1 DevHlp Library without source @ $79.00

Qty ____ C Callable 2.1 DevHlp Library with source @ $149.00

Mail total plus $5.00 shipping to: Personal Systems Software, Inc.
                                       15 Great Oak Lane
                                       Unionville, CT 06085
                                       Fax   (203) 693-9042

Ship to: _____

_____

_____

_____